D0918721

Poetry of the
Romantic Period

The Routledge History of English Poetry

General Editor

R. A. Foakes
Professor of English
The University of Kent at Canterbury

The Routledge History of English Poetry

Volume 4

Poetry of the
Romantic Period

J. R. de J. Jackson
Victoria College
University of Toronto

Routledge & Kegan Paul
London, Boston and Henley

WILLIAM MADISON RANDALL LIBRARY UNC AT WILMINGTON

First published in 1980
by Routledge & Kegan Paul Ltd
39 Store Street,
London WC1E 7DD,
Broadway House,
Newtown Road,
Henley-on-Thames,
Oxon RG9 1EN and
9 Park Street,
Boston, Mass. 02108, USA
Photosetting by Thomson Press (India) Ltd., New Delhi
and printed in Great Britain by Caledonian Graphics Ltd.

© J. R. de J. Jackson 1980
No part of this book may be reproduced in
any form without permission from the
publisher, except for the quotation of brief
passages in criticism

British Library Cataloguing in Publication Data

Jackson, James Robert de Jager
Poetry of the Romantic period. – (The Routledge
history of English poetry; vol. 4).
1. English poetry – 18th century – History and
criticism 2. English poetry – 19th century
– History and criticism 3. Romanticism
I. Title
821'.6'0914   PR571   79-40914

ISBN 0 7100 0289 0

PR502
.R58
v. 4

For Heather

207905

Contents

General editor's preface

The last major history of English poetry was that published in six volumes by W. J. Courthope between 1895 and 1910. In this century there have been some discoveries, some major shifts of critical opinion, and many revaluations of particular authors or periods. Twentieth-century poets have both added an exciting new chapter to the story and in doing so altered perspectives on the nineteenth and earlier centuries. In addition, there has been a massive growth in the publication of works of criticism and scholarship, many of which have helped to provide a better context for understanding what poets at various periods were trying to do, and for appreciating their achievement. Courthope's principal interest was in poetry as an aspect of intellectual history, as related to ideas, culture and political institutions. It is time for a fresh appraisal, and one of a rather different kind.

This new critical history of English poetry is planned to extend through six volumes, each written by a different author. Each author, a specialist in his period, has been encouraged to develop his own argument about the poetry he deals with, and to select his own historical emphases. The volumes will be uniform in appearance, but each will reflect in style, presentation, critical perspectives, and historical emphases, one person's viewpoint, and, no doubt, his own intellectual background; for, as is appropriate at a time when so much of the best criticism of English literature is being produced outside England, the authors are drawn from the USA and Canada, as well as Britain. The aim of the volumes is not to provide merely another account of the major figures, but to reassess the development of English poetry. The authors have been asked to take into account poetry that seemed important when it was published, and to set what now seems important in the context of the views held at the time it was written. The volumes are not necessarily separated in terms of a strict chronological division, and some poets may figure in different aspects in more than one of them, for a degree of overlapping has been encouraged where it seems appropriate.

Above all, each volume represents its author's personal testimony about a range of poets and poetry in the light of current knowledge, and taking into account, so far as this is helpful, current modes of criticism. In the present volume, the period covered, roughly 1780–1835, is more self-contained than usual, but the author has been especially concerned to place the great poems and poets of the age in the context of the conventions and traditions in which they wrote, providing new perspectives on familiar works. Poems still famous are examined often in relation to works of a similar kind fashionable at the time but now neglected, and these unconventional groupings throw fresh light on Romantic poetry as a whole. The appendix is designed to be read as a supplement to the main text, providing both a chronology and a brief guide to works which do not fall within the scope of the main argument.

R. A. F.

Acknowledgments

The more various one's obligations are, the harder it is to describe them satisfactorily or to be sure of their extent. First as a student and then as a teacher, I have had access to contemporary scholarship and criticism. Adequate acknowledgment of this privilege is obviously impossible. Suffice it to say that I have tried to learn from others whenever I could and that only the blunders in this book can be confidently ascribed to me.

It is easier to record the personal help I have received while writing. Colleagues and friends have put up with my enthusiasms; some have even added grist to the mill—among them Kenneth MacLean, S. P. Rosenbaum, Eric Rothstein, G. E. Bentley, Jr, John Baird, Julian Patrick, and Paul Stevens. My students have often made me aware that my ideas were muddled and have occasionally made me change my mind. To all these I am properly grateful.

R. A. Foakes and H. J. Jackson both read my manuscript and made detailed and generously constructive comments on it. I have tried to profit from their advice.

The John Simon Guggenheim Memorial Foundation, the Killam Program and the Canada Council freed time for me to read as well as to write, and the University of Toronto has provided for some of the secretarial consequences. To the staff of the British Library, and especially of the North Reading Room, I owe thanks for patient and expert assistance.

List of editions

Quotations are based on the following editions:

William Blake, *The Poems*, ed. W. H. Stevenson and David V. Erdman (New York, 1971).

Robert Burns, *The Poems and Songs*, ed. James Kinsley (Oxford, 1968), 3 vols.

Lord Byron, *The Works: Poetry*, ed. Ernest Hartley Coleridge (1918), 7 vols.

Samuel Taylor Coleridge, *The Complete Poetical Works*, ed. Ernest Hartley Coleridge (Oxford, 1912), 2 vols.

William Cowper, *The Poetical Works*, ed. H. S. Milford and Norma Russell (1971).

George Crabbe, *The Borough* (1810).

George Crabbe, *The Poetical Works*, ed. George Crabbe (1834), 8 vols.

John Keats, *The Poetical Works*, ed. H. W. Garrod (Oxford, 1958).

Percy Bysshe Shelley, *The Complete Poetical Works*, ed. Thomas Hutchinson (1960).

Robert Southey, *The Poetical Works* (1837–8), 10 vols.

William Wordsworth, *The Poetical Works*, ed. E. de Selincourt and Helen Darbishire (Oxford, 1965–8), 5 vols.

William Wordsworth, *The Prelude or Growth of a Poet's Mind*, ed. Ernest de Selincourt and Helen Darbishire (Oxford, 1968), the 1805 version.

Place of publication is London unless otherwise stated. Quotations from poems by other authors are taken from first editions in volume form unless a note specifies otherwise. References are given in such a way as to make passages easy to find in other editions, however. Usually line numbers are provided (11. 32–3), but, in some cases, book and line numbers (III, 32–3), in some, canto and stanza numbers (III, xxi–xxxv), and in a few, act, scene and line numbers (III, ii, 14–34). In the case of quotations from Blake, the standard practice of referring to the numbers of the engraved plates that constitute the pages of his works is followed (pl. 2).

Introduction

This volume is concerned with poetry written between 1780 and 1835. The addition of ten or fifteen years to the beginning of what is usually referred to as the Romantic period has made it possible to include Burns and Cowper, but it is not meant to imply that their resemblance to the poets who came after them is greater or more significant than it is generally thought to be. The Romantic period is brief by comparison with the periods considered in other volumes of *The Routledge History of English Poetry*, and it seemed only fair to annex some neighbouring territory; the 1780s offered the commencements of great careers that could be followed to their close. Practical considerations apart, however, the boundaries of literary periods are at best arbitrary conveniences, and there is something to be said for shifting them slightly from time to time.

This is a history of poems rather than of poets. If the poet is given pride of place, his poems have a way of assembling themselves as components of a career, revealing development, consistency or variety, and even providing glimpses of the poet's personal character and experience — all concerns that are worthy enough in themselves but which tend to draw our attention away from the unique qualities of individual poems that interested readers in him in the first place. It is surprisingly difficult to detach poems from poets without at the same time detaching them from the age in which they were written. My solution has been to let them keep company with other poems of roughly the same kind by other poets, major and minor. Our sense of the distance between poet and poetaster is increased artificially by the passage of time, and while we may think it odd to find Byron, whom we do read, borrowing with frank admiration from Bland, whom we do not, such interplay between great writers and the illustrious obscure is the stuff of which the best Romantic poems are made. The chapters that emerge from these juxtapositions do not correspond closely to traditional genres or to formal categories that were much discussed during the Romantic period, but they are related to literary contexts that were then taken for granted by reader and writer alike. The first three chapters are particularly concerned with literary fashions that have largely been forgotten and with the famous poems on which they left their mark. Thereafter, well-known poems assume a more conventional prominence, but I have tried throughout to provide a sense of the background of popular verse.

This history is interpretative. It reflects the values and viewpoints of modern criticism and, no doubt, bears the marks of my own preferences and prejudices, but I have sought to interpret poems in a way that is compatible with the literary sensibilities of their time. These sensibilities differed slightly from modern ones. Plot and characterization, for example, are not much talked about by critics of poetry nowadays; they have become the preserve of conventional critics of the novel. In the Romantic period, however, this division of critical responsibilities had not yet taken place because narrative poems still vied with novels as popular works of fiction. Verse fiction is a lost cause, but to neglect the element of fiction in poems like *Don Juan* that now interest us for other reasons and to separate them artificially from the narrative tradition is to deny ourselves a very real pleasure. I have attempted to restore the balance by providing some account of verse fiction and have even ventured to supply necessary information about unfamiliar plots. At the other end of the scale, short poems such as Keats's odes have been analysed so exhaustively in recent years that it has become difficult for all but the most innocent readers to preserve the freshness and directness that is such an important part of their charm. Interest in the poets' techniques, and, indeed, in their poems as examples of poetic technique, can easily replace enjoyment of effects that are more immediately accessible. In such cases I have concentrated on the broad outlines of readings that I believe the poets themselves would have recognized.

It has seemed more sensible to discuss representative poems at length than to comment briefly on everything. Poems omitted from the text will generally be found in the Chronological Table (Appendix) where they are listed in the order in which they were published. Each poem is dated when it is first mentioned, and the date given, unless a note specifies otherwise, is the date of publication. The notes at the end of the volume identify quotations, or they recommend secondary sources that carry the subject farther or that support a contrary point of view that deserves to be considered. For systematic guidance in secondary literature the reader should consult the following resources: Frank Jordan, ed., *The English Romantic Poets: A Review of Research and Criticism* (New York, 1972); Carolyn Washburn Houtchens and Lawrence Huston Houtchens, eds, *The English Romantic Poets and Essayists: A Review of Research and Criticism* (New York, 1966); Ronald S. Crane *et al.*, eds, *English Literature 1660–1800: A Bibliography of Modern Studies* (Princeton, 1950–72), 6 vols, with annual supplement in the *Philological Quarterly*; A. C. Elkins, Jr and L. J. Forstner, eds, *The Romantic Movement Bibliography 1936–70* (Ann Arbor, 1973), 7 vols, with its annual supplement in *English Language Notes*. For a reliable selective guide, see Richard Harter Fogle, ed., *Romantic Poets and Prose Writers* (New York, 1967).

1 Deliberate simplicities

In 1779, Samuel Johnson said of Pope's poetry:

> New sentiments and new images others may produce, but to attempt any further improvement of versification will be dangerous. Art and diligence have now done their best, and what shall be added will be the effort of tedious toil and needless curiosity.[1]

For Johnson it was Pope's manner that defied improvement, and his opinion was widely shared. His younger contemporaries were of two minds. Edmund Burke, for instance, is to be found in 1796 admonishing a conservative poetical friend that

> After the elaborate things that we have seen at the end of the last Age and nearly to the middle of this, we are become more fastidious than perhaps we ought to be with regard to the last hand that is given to Verses.[2]

Art and diligence could be carried too far. Twelve years earlier, William Cowper had objected in a more positive spirit to having his poetry smoothed by someone else before publication. 'There is', he said, 'a roughness on a plum which nobody that understands fruit would rub off, though the plum would be more polished without it.'[3] Interest in kinds of poetry that were different from Pope's was an acknowledgment of his mastery. Feeble imitations of his style persisted into the 1830s, but the successful poets of the Romantic period sought other models.

The distance that one senses between Pope and the three great emergent spirits of the 1780s, Cowper, Robert Burns and William Blake, was social as well as aesthetic. Their deliberate experiments with a less studied style are obviously alternatives to Pope's sophistication, but they also reflect an outlook that had little in common with the literary world of London. Cowper, to be sure, was bred up for that world at Westminster School, but he had suffered a nervous breakdown, had undergone a religious conversion, and had retired to live simply in the country. Burns was a farmer in south-west Scotland, augmenting his meagre living by

1

working as an exciseman. Blake was a Londoner, but as an engraver by trade he could at best hope for the patronage of the sort of men with whom Johnson had fraternized. Experience made each of them feel that simplicity of language, simplicity of thought and simplicity of life were worthwhile in themselves, and the literary world was in a receptive mood. What came naturally to Cowper, Burns and Blake was inherited as a newly established tradition by the poets who followed them.

Simplicity of manner can be employed in various ways. In Wordsworth's 'We are Seven' (1798), for example, the poet records a conversation he once had with an eight-year-old girl. He asks her how many brothers and sisters she has and she tells him that there are 'Seven in all'. It then transpires that two of them have died, but the child persists in making no distinction:

> 'Seven boys and girls are we;
> Two of us in the church-yard lie,
> Beneath the church-yard tree' . . . .
>
> 'But they are dead; those two are dead!
> Their spirits are in heaven!'
> 'Twas throwing words away; for still
> The little Maid would have her will,
> And said, 'Nay, we are seven!'   (11. 30–2, 65–9)

The artlessness of the conversation is part of its appeal, and the question with which the poem begins—'A simple Child . . ./ What should it know of death?'—prompts us to reflect upon our own notions concerning death.

A similar situation is the basis for Mary Robinson's heavy-handed companion piece 'All Alone' (1800), in which a traveller asks a ragged urchin why he is sighing and weeping beside a churchyard. The child explains that his father has perished abroad, lightning has destroyed their cottage, his mother and their faithful dog have both died, and he has been left an orphan. The traveller tries to reassure him that he himself has been keeping an eye on him, but the boy is not to be consoled:

> My Father never will return,
>   He rests beneath the sea-green wave;
> I have no kindred left to mourn
>   When I am hid in yonder grave:
> *Not one* to dress with flow'rs the stone!
> *Then—surely*, I AM LEFT ALONE!'[4]

The object of this poem is to make us feel sorry for the child; it belongs to a class of poems of pathos in which pity is elicited for its own sake.

Years later, Ebenezer Elliott wrote yet another variant on Wordsworth's poem. His 'Song', in his *Corn Law Rhymes* (1830), combines the little girl's unawareness with the boy's misery:

Child, is thy father dead?
  Father is gone!
Why did they tax his bread?
  God's will be done!
Mother has sold her bed;
Better to die than wed!
Where shall she lay her head?
  Home we have none!...

Doctor said air was best,
  Food we had none;
Father, with panting breast,
  Groan'd to be gone:
Now he is with the blest—
Mother says death is best!
We have no place of rest—
  Yes, ye have one![5]

The object here is not pathos but indignation at a social wrong and the terrible conflict of values that it imposes on the labouring poor.

These poems are representative of three impulses toward experiments with simplicity of style and simplicity of thought in the Romantic period: first, to remind the worldly of feelings and truths that they tend to forget; second, to awaken sympathy for the unfortunate; and third, to feed resentment at social injustice. To these may be added a fourth that arises out of a genuine interest in the daily lives of people in simple circumstances; it begins as part of a reaction against literary sentimentality, and then begins to develop a separate existence on its own account that outlasts the Romantic period.

I

The wisdom of children is proverbial. In the latter part of the eighteenth century, however, the force of Christ's admonition, 'Except ye ... become as little children, ye shall not enter into the kingdom of heaven', began to seem less figurative than before. What had been merely a recommendation of innocence, receptiveness and obedience, came to be taken for a more general recommendation of the childlike. There had always been a streak of literalmindedness in the evangelical movement—it is evident in the hymns of Isaac Watts and of both John and Charles Wesley, to mention only the most distinguished examples—and it must have been reinforced by their habit of addressing themselves to uneducated people. The notion of observing children in order to learn how to share their qualities, however, does not seem to appear until the Sentimental movement was under way. Hugh Downman expresses it in his didactic poem *Infancy* (1774–6):

3

> To my theme again
> Well-pleased I turn, and view the artless race
> Of Infant Innocence, as yet unwarp'd
> By education, blameless nature their's,
> And passions undebauch'd, from envy free,
> From guile, and that assembled crew of Ills
> Produced by commerce with a tainted world.   (III, 11. 11–17)

By the time Wordsworth developed a similar thought in his 'Ode, Intimations of Immortality' (1807) a quarter of a century later, it was possible for him to address a six-year-old as 'Thou, whose exterior semblance doth belie/Thy Soul's immensity;/Thou best Philosopher . . .'.[6]

Blake was one of the first to exploit the more sophisticated possibilities of this attitude. In his *Songs of Innocence* (1789) there are several poems that recall the happinesses of childhood and the different outlook on the world that children have. The 'Nurse's Song', for instance, opens with an idyllic pastoral scene:

> When the voices of children are heard on the green,
> And laughing is heard on the hill,
> My heart is at rest within my breast,
> And everything else is still.   (11. 1–4)

It then records the children's exchange with the nurse who thinks that it is time for them to go home:

> 'No, no, let us play, for it is yet day,
> And we cannot go to sleep;
> Besides, in the sky the little birds fly,
> And the hills are all covered with sheep'.
>
> 'Well, well, go and play till the light fades away,
> And then go home to bed'.
> The little ones leaped and shouted and laughed,
> And all the hills echoed.   (11. 9–16)

We approve of the nurse's sympathetic indulgence, and we are attracted and reassured by seeing that happiness can be so cheaply won. No moral is drawn, but Blake's contemporaries could hardly have missed the echo of Beattie's 'The Hermit' (1776) in the first stanza:

> At the close of the day, when the hamlet is still,
> And mortals the sweets of forgetfulness prove,
> When nought but the torrent is heard on the hill,
> And nought but the nightingale's song in the grove . . . .

The association with this popular poem, with its gloomy contemplation of the prospect of death and conventional comfort of an after-life, heightens our sense of the special value of childish joy. The same theme is taken up in 'The Echoing Green', in which 'the old folk' watch the children playing, and recall the happiness of their own childhoods and are able to 'laugh away care'.

Blake does not concern himself with the details of children's play, and when we read him we flesh out his suggestive abstractions with our own experience. We respond favourably but variously. In Wordsworth's 'The Idiot Boy' (1798), by contrast, we are provided with a circumstantial illustration of the values of innocents. In manner the poem resembles a comic ballad with such antecedents as Goldsmith's 'The Death of a Mad Dog', Cowper's 'John Gilpin', and Burns's 'Tam o'Shanter'. The appreciative but occasionally condescending voice of the narrator, the dialogue of the characters and the frustrated expectations of a story, all lead us to expect a joke. But although the poem does contain humour, and although Wordsworth himself recorded later that he 'never wrote anything with so much glee',[7] it is really an ambitious experiment in the rendering of naive happiness.

The happiness of the idiot boy himself is described at considerable length. When his mother, Betty, sends him on an urgent errand to bring the doctor to look after the suffering Susan Gale, Johnny is wholly engrossed in the novel experience of being allowed to ride off by himself. He pays no attention to his mother's instructions:

> But when the Pony moved his legs,
> Oh! then for the poor Idiot Boy!
> For joy he cannot hold the bridle,
> For joy his head and heels are idle,
> He's idle all for very joy . . . .
>
> His heart it was so full of glee
> That, till full fifty yards were gone,
> He quite forgot his holly whip,
> And all his skill in horsemanship:
> Oh! happy, happy, happy John. (11. 72–6, 82–6)

And even his mother is so carried away by the sight of him that she forgets the seriousness of the occasion: 'And Betty's standing at the door/And Betty's face with joy o'erflows,/Proud of herself, and proud of him . . .'.[8] But as the night wears on and she sits by Susan's bedside without any sign of his return, her confidence fails her and she alternately blames her son and fears for him. In the end she sets out to look for him, so distracted by the accidents that she imagines may have befallen him that when she awakens the doctor she quite forgets about poor Susan and only asks after Johnny. There is humour in her contretemps with the doctor:

'He's not so wise as some folks be':
'The devil take his wisdom!' said
The Doctor, looking somewhat grim,
'What, Woman! should I know of him?'
And, grumbling, he went back to bed!   (11. 257–61)

But Betty's distress is evident and genuine, and it continues until, when she finds
Johnny, she is suddenly beside herself with relief:

She kisses o'er and o'er again
Him whom she loves, her Idiot Boy,
She's happy here, is happy there,
She is uneasy everywhere;
Her limbs are all alive with joy.   (11. 387–91)

As she leads the pony slowly homewards, they meet old Susan hobbling towards
them. Concern for her friends has brought her from her sick bed to look for them,
'As if by magic cured'.

She spies her Friends, she shouts a greeting;
Oh me! it is a merry meeting
As ever was in Christendom.   (11. 429–31)

In the second edition of *Lyrical Ballads* (1800), Wordsworth claimed that 'the
feeling therein developed gives importance to the action and situation, and not the
action and situation to the feeling'. In 'The Idiot Boy', the feelings of affection are
real, even if the action and situation are trivial. And Johnny's account of his night's
ride—'The cocks did crow to-whoo to-whoo,/And the sun did shine so
cold'—reminds us in its inconsequentiality how little maternal affection depends
on rational behaviour.

'The Idiot Boy' has always been a subject of controversy, and was for a while an
occasion for ridicule. Many readers have felt that Wordsworth in exploring the
truths of human simplicity has skirted the borders of silliness. He himself persisted
in the belief that unaffected feelings are interesting and valuable in themselves no
matter how humble or accidental their cause, and he recorded a number of
experiences of them that have given more general satisfaction. Some of these, such
as 'My heart leaps up when I behold/A rainbow in the sky' (1807) merely record
the continuance of a childhood experience. Some, such as 'I wandered lonely as a
cloud' (1807) and 'The Solitary Reaper' (1807), record experiences that were
moving at the time and which he continues to value but which he makes no
attempt to analyse. A few of his so-called 'Lucy poems' describe feelings that spring
from affection, and although they are not concerned with children, their simplicity
of expression and their unguarded quality touch us in somewhat the way 'We are
Seven' does. In 'Strange fits of passion have I known' (1800), the author describes
how while riding to his Lucy's cottage he kept his eye fixed upon the sinking moon,

and when it dipped suddenly behind the cottage roof, ' "O mercy!" to myself I cried,/"If Lucy should be dead".' The oddness of the incident makes us feel that it really happened[9]—and although the thought as he says is a 'fond and wayward' one we recognize in it the fanciful state of mind of the lover who is totally preoccupied with the well-being of his sweetheart. 'She dwelt among the untrodden ways' (1800) calls for a similar act of recognition on our part, as the poet says of Lucy's death only, 'But she is in her grave, and, oh,/The difference to me!' The lines would not be out of place in a popular song, but within the spare frame of this poem they convey the emphasis of strong feelings kept under a powerful restraint.

II

The insights of unfeigned innocence are rare. Objects of pity, on the other hand, are commonplace, and poetry which insists that we should contemplate them runs the risk of exciting shallow sympathies. Mrs Robinson's 'All Alone' is an example of the poem of pathos in which feelings of pity are an end in themselves, and it is a throwback to the sentimentalities of the 1780s when small animals, the weakest of the unfortunate, were a favourite subject. William Gifford singled out one of the lesser lights among the Della Cruscans, for teasing, in his *Baviad* (1791):

> We come now to a character of high respect, the profound
> Mr. T. Vaughan, who, under the alluring signature of Edwin, favours us
> from time to time with a melancholy poem on the death of a bug, the
> flight of an earwig, the miscarriage of a cock-chaffer, or some other event
> of equal importance.[10]

Burns had shown in 'To a Mouse' (1785) that insignificant sufferers could sustain fine poems, but he was very careful to relate the mouse's predicament elaborately to man's. If the warmth of his homely anthropomorphism and the vivacity of his description make us remember the mouse and forget the moral, the moral is nevertheless necessary to the poem. His 'To a Mountain Daisy' (1786) is similarly sustained by its human analogy.

Short poems and songs about people in distress were a familiar feature of periodical literature in the 1790s. Their subjects were chosen for their helplessness and hopelessness—convicts, slaves, discharged veterans, the aged poor, orphans, the mad, beggars and abandoned mothers—and they reappear with monotonous regularity. These poems aimed at realism by imitating the informality and directness of street ballads, even to the point of deliberate repetitiveness and ungainliness of expression. A few, such as Thomas Holcroft's, imply that we ought to do something about the conditions that give rise to the distresses described, but most of them aspire merely to what Coleridge called the genius of an onion, 'the power of drawing tears'. They are no longer read because, like Mrs Robinson's 'All Alone', they deal in crude and unconvincing stereotypes, and because a more interesting kind of poem absorbed and superseded them.

7

Wordsworth's 'The Thorn' (1798) contains the pathetic tale of Martha Ray, who goes mad after being left with child by a fiancé—she is a cut above the typical fallen woman—and who still distractedly visits the grave of her infant. By annexing it to the analogous figure of the thorn and combining it with the narrator's speculating but sympathetic interest in her, Wordsworth creates a lasting impression. In keeping with the simplicity of the genre, Wordsworth builds his poem upon a prosaic description of an unprepossessing and stunted shrub:

> Not higher than a two years' child
> It stands erect, this aged Thorn;
> No leaves it has, no prickly points;
> It is a mass of knotted joints,
> A wretched thing forlorn.   (ll. 5–9)

He describes the thorn as if it were a person, departing significantly from the more usual convention of comparing beautiful flowers or impressive trees to people. He describes its condition in such a way as to make us feel sorry for it:

> Up from the earth these mosses creep,
> And this poor Thorn they clasp it round
> So close, you'd say that they are bent
> With plain and manifest intent
> To drag it to the ground;
> And all have joined in one endeavour
> To bury this poor Thorn for ever.   (ll. 16–22)

He sets it in a desolate place, and punctures any pretensions it might have to the sublimity of wild weather by placing beside it 'a little muddy pond':

> High on a mountain's highest ridge,
> Where oft the stormy winter gale
> Cuts like a scythe, while through the clouds
> It sweeps from vale to vale;
> Not five yards from the mountain path,
> This Thorn you on your left espy;
> And to the left, three yards beyond,
> You see a little muddy pond
> Of water—never dry,
> Though but of compass small, and bare
> To thirsty suns and parching air.   (ll. 23–33)

The decrepitude of the thorn joined to the flat account of its dreary situation provides us with a compelling metaphor for human misery before we have a chance to turn away in indifference from yet another distressed mother.[11]

Wordsworth then throws us further off the scent by introducing the contrasting hill of moss nearby:

> A beauteous heap, a hill of moss,
> Just half a foot in height.
> All lovely colours there you see,
> All colours that were ever seen;
> And mossy network too is there,
> As if by hand of lady fair
> The work had woven been;
> And cups, the darlings of the eye,
> So deep is their vermilion dye.
>
> Ah me! what lovely tints are there
> Of olive green and scarlet bright,
> In spikes, in branches, and in stars,
> Green, red, and pearly white!   (11. 36–48)

The enthusiasm of the narrator is apparent here, and we are taken aback when he chooses to describe the size of the hill of moss as 'like an infant's grave'.

The figure of Martha is introduced in the following stanza:

>   oft there sits between the heap
> So like an infant's grave in size,
> And that same pond of which I spoke,
> A Woman in a scarlet cloak,
> And to herself she cries,
> 'Oh misery! oh misery!
> Oh woe is me! oh misery!'   (11. 60–6)

The narrator quickly satisfies our curiosity in so far as he can, and all that is known of Martha Ray's past is told in about thirty lines (in a poem of 242). What remains has to do with inconclusive superstitious gossip about her—was her child born alive or dead, did she kill it, is it buried beneath the heap of moss?[12]—but more strikingly with the narrator's account of his own first sight of her while he was seeking shelter from a storm:

> 'Twas mist and rain, and storm and rain:
> No screen, no fence could I discover;
> And then the wind! in sooth, it was
> A wind full ten times over.
> I looked around, I thought I saw
> A jutting crag,—and off I ran,
> Head-foremost, through the driving rain,
> The shelter of the crag to gain;

And, as I am a man,
Instead of jutting crag, I found
A Woman seated on the ground.

I did not speak—I saw her face;
Her face!—it was enough for me;
I turned about and heard her cry,
'Oh misery! oh misery!' (ll. 177–91)

The particulars of Martha's story do not really matter; like the narrator and the local people, we may speculate upon them if we wish. It is her total absorption in misery that is impressed upon us; her mind is so consumed by despair that she is oblivious of the mountain storm that rages about her. The poem closes with a reminder of the thorn dragged down by tufts of moss, making the parallel inescapable. Wordsworth does not present us with an unfortunate person and declare that she is wretched, he tries ways of making us aware first of what the experience of wretchedness is like. As a consequence his poem stands clear of the fashionable convention on which he drew.

The misfortunes of the poor are generally less lurid than the cruder attempts to elicit pity allowed. One of the devices used by reform-minded poets like Southey and Wordsworth was to replace the extravagance of madness and despair with the understatement of simple resignation in the face of misfortune. Our sympathies are still called upon. The ordinary circumstantiality of the cases set before us hints disturbingly that they are of common occurrence, and the sufferers have a way of harking back to happier days—rather as Goldsmith had done on their behalf in *The Deserted Village*—that is a standing reproach to the social forces that have deprived them. Southey's 'Botany Bay Eclogues' (1797) are made up of the reminiscences of ordinary people who have been transported to Australia as felons. Some of them remember England with nostalgia, but all have gone through experiences that make Botany Bay seem like a welcome haven. His 'English Eclogues' (1799) steal upon us less obviously and offer glimpses of rural life and rustic dignity. In one of them, 'The Ruined Cottage', a village maiden is seduced, but the point of the poem is the life led by her widowed grandmother who dies of a broken heart:

A widow here
Dwelt with an orphan grandchild: just removed
Above the reach of pinching poverty,
She lived on some small pittance which sufficed,
In better times, the needful calls of life,
Not without comfort. I remember her
Sitting at evening in that open door-way,
And spinning in the sun. Methinks I see her
Raising her eyes and dark-rimm'd spectacles
To see the passer-by, yet ceasing not

> To twirl her lengthening thread: or in the garden,
> On some dry summer evening, walking round
> To view her flowers, and pointing as she lean'd
> Upon the ivory handle of her stick,
> To some carnation whose o'erheavy head
> Needed support . . . .   (Vol. 3, pp. 31–2)

Trivial details of occupation like these, simply told, bring before us pictures of frugal and industrious contentment, and they undermine the self-complacent assumption that misfortune is only visited upon people who deserve it. Wordsworth's 'Old Cumberland Beggar' (1800) too presents a person who is poor, and old, and weak and solitary, and who yet passes uncomplainingly from door to door and by reminding the community of the act of charity does it good. The argument deserves our attention:

> man is dear to man; the poorest poor
> Long for some moments in a weary life
> When they can know and feel that they have been,
> Themselves, the fathers and the dealers-out
> Of some small blessings . . . .   (11. 147–51)

But what arrests us is the unsparing but sympathetic observation of the old man on his round—the crumbs 'scattered from his palsied hand,/That, still attempting to prevent the waste,/Was baffled still . . .' (11. 16–18), his gaze fixed on the roadway on 'some straw,/Some scattered leaf, or marks which, in one track,/The nails of cart or chariot-wheel have left/Impressed on the white road . . .' (11. 54–7)—and the interest in feelings that even so feeble a creature must have.

The increased circumstantiality of such poems could not quite be called realism, but the abstractness of beggar and orphan has been replaced with what purport to be genuine individuals in whom we might be expected to take an interest. These eclogues or idylls are dominated by a sense of the worth and dignity of the lives of the rural poor. They avoid the more obvious tricks of story-telling—coincidence, surprise, demonstrations of strong feeling—and depend instead upon the accumulation of a few simple but telling observations of daily life. We are shown the attractive side of human character, but we are also made to feel that it really exists.

Wordsworth's 'Michael' (1800) is probably the finest poem to emerge from the form, and, like 'The Thorn', it absorbs and transcends its model. It is characteristic of the Southeyan eclogue to describe people in straitened circumstances who, though virtuous, hard-working and harmless, are struck down by misfortune. In 'Michael', Wordsworth builds upon this convention. Old Michael and Isabel, we are told, 'were as a proverb in the vale/For endless industry' (11. 94–5). From an economic point of view they are exemplary. The light by which they work late into the night 'was famous in its neighbourhood,/And was a public symbol of the life/That thrifty Pair had lived' (11. 129–31). Their constancy, as they work with their eighteen-year-old son Luke, 'Making the cottage through the silent

11

hours/Murmur as with the sound of summer flies' (11. 127–8), is the constancy of labour independent of any overseer. The name, 'Evening Star', given to their cottage light by the local people, is a tribute to their regularity, and it carries overtones of a shining example in gathering gloom. If their life leaves them 'neither gay perhaps/Nor cheerful' (11. 120–1), the family is close-knit and affectionate. Their simple but sufficient fare—'Each with a mess of pottage and skimmed milk,/Sat round the basket piled with oaten cakes,/And their plain home-made cheese' (11. 100–2)—is reminiscent of the biblical rather than the classical pastoral.

Mere virtue might aspire so far. Michael, however, is a man of unusual capacities.

> An old man, stout of heart, and strong of limb.
> His bodily frame had been from youth to age
> Of an unusual strength: his mind was keen,
> Intense, and frugal, apt for all affairs,
> And in his shepherd's calling he was prompt
> And watchful more than ordinary men.　　　　　　　　　(11. 42–7)

He is robust and intelligent. As an acute observer of the winds he is alert to the signs of weather in the offing. His most unexpected quality is his love of the place where he has lived:

> 　　　　　　　　　grossly that man errs, who should suppose
> That the green valleys, and the streams and rocks,
> Were things indifferent to the Shepherd's thoughts . . . .
> Those fields, those hills—what could they less? had laid
> Strong hold on his affections, were to him
> A pleasurable feeling of blind love,
> The pleasure which there is in life itself.　　　　　　　(11. 62–4, 74–7)

Michael has few hostages to give to fortune, but fortune makes the most of them.

The financial failure of a nephew costs Michael 'little less/Than half his substance' (11. 216–17). He is in no way to blame for the loss, and in standing surety he had had nothing to gain; his involvement is the result of a family tie and even so had originally seemed to be safe, pledged as it was for 'a man/Of an industrious life, and ample means' (11. 211–12). Michael's substance is his land, and he has worked so long for it that the idea of its independence has an understandable hold upon his mind:

> 　　　　　　　　　　　　　it seemed
> The Shepherd's sole resource to sell at once
> A portion of his patrimonial fields.
> Such was his first resolve; he thought again,
> And his heart failed him. 'Isabel', said he,

12

Two evenings after he had heard the news,
'I have been toiling more than seventy years,
And in the open sunshine of God's love
Have we all lived; yet if these fields of ours
Should pass into a stranger's hand, I think
That I could not lie quiet in my grave'.   (11. 222–32)

To this feeling is added his expectation that it would pass on to his only son.

The relationship between father and son is analysed for us with an insight that would add meaning to the story of Abraham and Isaac:

                    to Michael's heart
This son of his old age was yet more dear—
Less from instinctive tenderness, the same
Fond spirit that blindly works in the blood of all—
Than that a child, more than all other gifts
That earth can offer to declining man,
Brings hope with it, and forward-looking thoughts,
And stirrings of inquietude, when they
By tendency of nature needs must fail.   (11. 142–50)

Besides this aspect of the tie there is the more obvious one of family affection, in which, as in all things, Michael is exceptional. He has assisted Isabel during Luke's infancy 'with patient mind enforced/To acts of tenderness . . .' (11. 156–7); during his boyhood he has kept watch over him while at work, at first near home under the Clipping Tree, and, later, taking him with him into the hills. The relations of the two could hardly be closer, and their grief on parting—'He sobbed aloud. The old Man grasped his hand,/And said, "Nay, do not take it so . . ." ' (11. 358–9)—is intense. Michael's love for his son is an important part of his wish to keep his land unencumbered; his love for his son is also what causes him such uneasiness and such a sense of loss in sending him off to the city to earn the money they need. Isabel shares in these feelings. Her simple hopes and fears add a further dimension to Michael's, and she is the first to realize that Michael will be broken by Luke's departure—'do not go away,/For if thou leave thy Father he will die' (11. 297–8).

Building the sheepfold was to have been the joint work of Luke and Michael. Michael has Luke lay the first stone as a reminder that although they are to be physically separated they will continue to work together in spirit and for a single purpose—'When thou return'st, thou in this place wilt see/A work which is not here: a covenant/'Twill be between us . . .' (11. 413–15). Michael's emotion is too deep for words: 'The old Man's grief broke from him; to his heart/He pressed his Son, he kissèd him and wept;/And to the house together they returned' (11. 431–3). Only gesture and inarticulate sound seem adequate to the occasion. But when the news comes of Luke's disgrace and flight abroad, the supreme simplicity of inaction conveys to us Michael's despair:

> And to that hollow dell from time to time
> Did he repair, to build the Fold of which
> His flock had need. 'Tis not forgotten yet
> The pity which was then in every heart
> For the old Man—and 'tis believed by all
> That many and many a day he thither went,
> And never lifted up a single stone. (11. 460–6)

The poem of pathos has at last been furnished with a subject that deserves our respect as well as our pity. Nothing beyond the heap of stones remains, the mute emblem with which the poem begins. By contrast with 'The Thorn', the emblem has no identity without its story.

III

The poem of pathos has its counterpart in the poem of social indignation. When pathos is exploited as an indictment of society, literary quality tends to develop in an inverse proportion to the intensity of the zeal expressed. Coleridge's 'To a Young Ass' (1794), begins with sentiments that should please anyone who is opposed to cruelty to animals:

> Poor little Foal of an oppresséd race!
> I love the languid patience of thy face:
> And oft with gentle hand I give thee bread,
> And clap thy ragged coat, and pat thy head . . . .
> Do thy prophetic fears anticipate,
> Meek Child of Misery! thy future fate?
> The starving meal, and all the thousand aches
> 'Which patient Merit of the Unworthy takes'? (11. 1–4, 9–12)

But it moves on quickly to speculations about the ass's master—'much I fear me that *He* lives like thee,/Half famish'd in a land of Luxury!' (11. 21–2). The point being made here is that the miserable condition of domestic animals that the sentimental complain of is often only a reflection of the miserable lives led by the classes that employ them. Southey's 'The Widow' (1795) is a more forceful example of this indirect attack. In it a poor woman wanders on the downs in a snowstorm asking for help but being ignored by the passers-by. At last she dies. Sapphic metre is employed for ungainly but emphatic effects:

> Cold was the night wind, drifting fast the snow fell,
> Wide were the downs and shelterless and naked,
> When a poor Wanderer struggled on her journey,
> Weary and way-sore. (Vol. 2, p. 141, 11. 1–4)

Pathos is aimed at, but the uncaring well-to-do are at fault in her failure to find relief:

> 'I had a home once—I had once a husband—
> I am a widow, poor and broken-hearted!'
> Loud blew the wind, unheard was her complaining,
>   On drove the chariot.   (11. 17–20)

Political tempers had risen high in the aftermath of the French revolution and Pitt's gagging bills, and it is not surprising that supporters of the government should have objected to these innuendoes. The *Anti-Jacobin* struck back in 1797 with a sketch of the writers of such poems:

> A human being, in the lowest state of penury and distress, is a treasure to a reasoner of this cast. He contemplates, he examines, he turns him in every possible light, with a view of extracting from the variety of his wretchedness, new topics of invective against the pride of property.[13]

The use of simplicity for ironic effects is most often found during the Romantic period in seditious literature. Its finest and subtlest examples, however, are achieved by William Blake in his *Songs of Innocence and Experience* (1794), a collection that is only partly political. In this book, sub-titled 'Showing the Two Contrary States of the Human Soul', the 'Songs of Innocence' are placed near 'Songs of Experience' on the same or related topics in such a way as to cause the 'Songs of Innocence' to be read from a different and usually unsympathetic point of view. The collection is neither so systematic nor so single-minded as to produce sets of pairs that are opposed in quite the same way. Instead it seems to provide the sort of second thoughts that Blake had already indulged in as a critical and inventive illustrator of the works of other people; these second thoughts in their turn reward reflective reading.

The best-known pair is probably 'The Lamb' and 'The Tiger'. The childish piety of 'Little lamb, who made thee?' with its echoes of Charles Wesley's 'Gentle Jesus meek and mild' from his *Hymns and Sacred Poems* (1742) is juxtaposed with the incantatory similarities to Gray's 'The Bard' of 'Tiger, tiger, burning bright', and the challenging question, 'Did he who made the Lamb make thee?' The extent of the irony is difficult to define, even if we feel confident that the range of God's nature is being indicated. In Mrs Barbauld's discussion of the lion for instance, in her *Hymns in Prose for Children* (1781), the animal's strength is used as an aid to imagining God's: 'The lion is strong, but he that made the lion is stronger than he: his anger is terrible; he could make us die in a moment, and no one could save us out of his hand' (p. 22). Blake seems to be asking a question or pointing out an anomaly rather than impressing the baleful capacities of God upon us, however, and it has often been observed that his accompanying picture of a tiger looks uncommonly like a kindly domestic tabby-cat that would require no special dispensation to lie down with the lamb.

15

Blake's two poems entitled 'Holy Thursday' are less equivocal examples of irony, and though they are not seditious in the sense of supporting a particular campaign to undermine the state, they do raise fundamental doubts about the social order. The 'Holy Thursday' in *Songs of Innocence* describes the sight of a procession of children from the charity schools going to church at St Paul's:

> Oh, what a multitude they seemed, these flowers of London town!
> Seated in companies they sit, with radiance all their own.
> The hum of multitudes was there, but multitudes of lambs,
> Thousands of little boys and girls raising their innocent hands.   (11. 5–8)

Their singing is compared to 'a mighty wind' and to 'harmonious thunderings the seats of Heaven among', and the poem closes with a rather trite moral:

> Beneath them sit the aged men, wise guardians of the poor:
> Then cherish pity, lest you drive an angel from your door.   (11. 11–12)

The convention of hymns for charity children was an old one.[14] John and Charles Wesley's *A Collection of Psalms and Hymns* (1743) contains 'An Hymn for the Georgia Orphans', another 'For their Benefactors', and 'Hymns for Charity-Children', in which gratitude is expressed and the wish that the benefactors may find a welcome in heaven. Blake's poem responds to the angelic beauty and innocence of the children and seems to recommend charity without any reserve. In 'Holy Thursday' from the 'Songs of Experience', however, it is hard to believe that a similar scene is being observed. The condition of the children is one of misery.

> And their sun does never shine,
> And their fields are bleak and bare,
> And their ways are filled with thorns;
> It is eternal winter there!   (11. 9–12)

The 'mighty wind' of their song has become a 'trembling cry', and in place of the wise guardians of the poor we are told that the children are 'Fed with cold and usurous hand'. The wretchedness of children and the fact of poverty are declared to be at odds with nature:

> For where'er the sun does shine,
> And where'er the rain does fall,
> Babe can never hunger there,
> Nor poverty the mind appal.   (11. 13–16)

There must be some doubt as to whether someone who could write the second 'Holy Thursday' could have written the first without irony, but the effectiveness of putting the two together and pulling the rug out from under smug benevolence is considerable.

Blake's 'The Chimney Sweeper' in *Songs of Innocence* has its twin in 'Songs of Experience'. In the innocent version little Tom Dacre dreams that the sweeps are released by an angel from their 'coffins of black' and allowed to 'wash in a river and shine in the sun'. The poem concludes with an innocuous moral:

And so Tom awoke, and we rose in the dark,
And got with our bags and our brushes to work.
Though the morning was cold, Tom was happy and warm;
So if all do their duty, they need not fear harm.   (ll. 21–4)

The version in 'Songs of Experience', like the second version of 'Holy Thursday', makes no bones about the child's misery and blames it squarely on its parents and on established society. There had been agitation throughout the 1780s against using children as sweeps, and it came to a head, fruitlessly, in 1788, when a bill was presented in parliament. Blake's poems reflect his sympathy with the cause but he seems to be more concerned with its emblematic possibilities. The contrast between their blackness and the 'innocent faces clean' of the children in 'Holy Thursday'; the contrast between their blackness and the snow that was often on the ground during the part of the year when they were busiest; their cry, 'Sweep! sweep!', which he renders as ''weep 'weep'—these visible contradictions of childhood are what interest him. The concluding stanza is damning but abstract:

'And because I am happy and dance and sing,
They think they have done me no injury—
And are gone to praise God and his priest and king,
Who make up a Heaven of our misery'.   (ll. 9–12)

By comparison, say, with serious propaganda such as James Montgomery's affecting poem 'The Dream' in his *The Climbing Boy's Soliloquies* (1824)—a series influenced by Blake—it seems to be a very mild form of persuasion. It is this very abstractness, however, which allows it to be applied as an analogy to other abuses and helps it to survive after the abuse it describes has ceased to exist.

'The Little Black Boy' in *Songs of Innocence* does not have a counterpart in 'Songs of Experience', but it too seems to have ironic overtones. There was a great deal of writing about slavery at the end of the 1780s in support of efforts to have the slave trade abolished. In Blake's poem the child declares to an English child:

I am black, but oh, my soul is white;
White as an angel is the English child,
But I am black as if bereaved of light.   (ll. 2–4)

He explains that his mother has told him that his body is like a cloud and that after death the blackness and whiteness of the cloud will vanish:

17

And thus I say to little English boy:
When I from black and he from white cloud free
And round the tent of God like lambs we joy,

I'll shade him from the heat till he can bear
To lean in joy upon our Father's knee;
And then I'll stand and stroke his silver hair,
And be like him and he will then love me.   (11. 22–8)

The parallel to the chimney sweep's dream will be apparent. The ingenuousness of the little black boy's plea is both pathetic and disarming, and it may be intended as that and no more.[15] Nevertheless the topic begs for ironical treatment, and it received it at the hands of William Cowper, who wrote five poems on slavery, of which four have survived. In 1788 he wrote to a friend, 'If you hear ballads sung in the streets on the hardships of the negroes in the islands, they are probably mine'.[16] One of them, 'Sweet Meat has Sour Sauce, or, the Slave-trader in the Dumps' (written in 1788), begins jauntily enough:

A TRADER I am to the African shore,
But since that my trading is like to be o'er,
I'll sing you a song that you ne'er heard before,
        Which nobody can deny, deny,
        Which nobody can deny.   (11. 1–5)

But it continues more darkly:

Here's padlocks and bolts, and screws for the thumbs,
That squeeze them so lovingly till the blood comes,
They sweeten the temper like comfits or plums,
        Which nobody, &c.   (11. 15–18)

In the light of such contemporary writing, Blake's 'Little Black Boy' seems inescapably ironical.

IV

Goldsmith's *The Deserted Village* (1770) is a point of departure for most verse about rural life in the Romantic period. Because he was preaching that the national craving for luxury was depopulating villages, Goldsmith made the vanished life of sweet Auburn seem as attractive as he could. His sentimental sketches of the village preacher and the village master have proved to be lastingly popular; his descriptions of the lives of the poor had a more immediate influence on his successors. Life in the village was picturesquely pastoral:

Sweet was the sound when oft at evening's close,
Up yonder hill the village murmur rose;
There as I past with careless steps and slow,
The mingling notes came softened from below;
The swain responsive as the milk-maid sung,
The sober herd that lowed to meet their young;
The noisy geese that gabbled o'er the pool,
The playful children just let loose from school;
The watch-dog's voice that bayed the whispering wind,
And the loud laugh that spoke the vacant mind,
These all in soft confusion sought the shade,
And filled each pause the nightingale had made. (11. 113–24)

It was also harmlessly sociable. Goldsmith describes the interior of the village inn
with sufficient detail to interest the social historian:[17]

Imagination fondly stoops to trace
The parlour splendours of that festive place;
The white-washed wall, the nicely sanded floor,
The varnished clock that clicked behind the door;
The chest contrived a double debt to pay,
A bed by night, a chest of drawers by day;
The pictures placed for ornament and use,
The twelve good rules, the royal game of goose;
The hearth, except when winter chill'd the day,
With aspen boughs, and flowers, and fennel gay,
While broken tea-cups, wisely kept for shew,
Ranged o'er the chimney, glistened in a row. (11. 225–36)

Goldsmith's nostalgia suited his theme and was in accord with the benevolently
sentimental feelings popularized in novels such as Henry Mackenzie's *The Man of
Feeling* (1771). It was essentially the recollection of a city writer addressing himself
to city readers and it encouraged them to take a kindly interest in the lives of the
rural poor. But Goldsmith, like the rest of his contemporaries, had many readers
who were neither well-to-do nor urban. Country people took *The Deserted Village* to
their hearts as a celebration of their own way of life. There were many harmless
imitations, but the best of the provincial poets reacted in a creatively critical spirit
that was a truer compliment to Goldsmith's success. Complacent readers might
imagine that the social contentment of Auburn was still to be found, but
Goldsmith himself had been unsparing in his account of the lonely survivor:

yon widowed, solitary thing
That feebly bends beside the plashy spring;
She, wretched matron, forced, in age, for bread,
To strip the brook with mantling cresses spread,

19

> To pick her wintry faggot from the thorn,
> To seek her nightly shed, and weep till morn . . . .   (11. 129–34)

But the overall impression of the poem tended to efface one's memory of her.[18] Anyone who, like Goldsmith, was anxious to relieve the distresses of the poor, would naturally wish to reinforce the dark side of his account. George Crabbe's *The Village* (1783) confronts the problem relentlessly, reviewing the misleading distortions of the pastoral tradition, and forcing his readers to 'own the Village Life a life of pain . . .' (Vol. 2, p. 91). One by one he replaces the sentimental figures of innocent lovers, hearty labourers, frolicking children and dignified old age with ugly and despairing substitutes:

> See the stout churl, in drunken fury great,
> Strike the bare bosom of his teeming mate!
> His naked vices, rude and unrefined,
> Exert their open empire o'er the mind;
> But can we less the senseless rage despise,
> Because the savage acts without disguise?   (p. 92)

The labourers 'hoard up aches and anguish for their age' (p. 80), the 'hoary swain' trembles in the cold and longs for death (pp. 81–3), and ragged infants are torn at by thistles (p. 77). The unvarnished precision of Crabbe's descriptions sets them apart from Goldsmith's, and there is a hint of desperation in his appeal that makes it uncomfortable to read. *The Village* is a reproach to a decade of sentimental misreading of *The Deserted Village*. In terms of realistic description Crabbe's account may be regarded as an improvement on Goldsmith's. Such improvements were also possible to authors whose outlook was more fashionably sentimental, or whose experience of country life was less grim.

Both conditions were fulfilled to some degree by Robert Burns, and while his poetry seems far removed from Crabbe's in spirit, he too uses his personal experience of rural life as a means of replacing the polite pastoralism of the preceding generation. The epigraph to Burns's 'The Cotter's Saturday Night' (1786) is taken from Gray's 'Elegy, written in a Country Churchyard'. Burns is taking its sympathy for 'the short and simple annals of the poor' seriously, and by practising what Gray preached he breathes new and different life into Gray's dignified abstractions. Every reader would have remembered the opening stanza of the 'Elegy':

> The curfew tolls the knell of parting day,
>   The lowing herd winds slowly o'er the lea,
> The ploughman homeward plods his weary way,
>   And leaves the world to darkness and to me.[19]

Burns's setting challenges comparison:

> November chill blaws loud wi' angry sugh;
>   The short'ning winter-day is near a close;

The miry beasts retreating frae the pleugh;
  The black'ning trains o' craws to their repose:
The toil-worn COTTER frae his labor goes,
  This night his weekly moil is at an end,
Collects his *spades*, his *mattocks* and his *hoes*,
  Hoping the *morn* in ease and rest to spend,
And weary, o'er the muir, his course does hameward bend.   (11. 10–18)

The lowland Scots vocabulary strikes us at once, and the bleakness of the season, the reminder of dirt and implements, and the implications of daily physical exhaustion for a man who has only the Sabbath to recover from it. Even the choice of the Spenserian stanza in place of Gray's trim quatrains adds an ungainly and uncouth air to Burns's lines.

Though he wishes us to appreciate the contrast, Burns is not repudiating Gray as we have seen Crabbe repudiate Goldsmith. Where Gray was satisfied to notice the ploughman as part of his picturesque scene, Burns follows the cotter home and stays with him until bed-time:

At length his lonely *Cot* appears in view,
  Beneath the shelter of an aged tree;
Th' expectant wee-things, toddlan, stacher thro'
  To meet their *Dad*, wi' flichterin noise and glee.
His wee-bit ingle, blinkan bonilie,
    His clean hearth-stane, his thrifty *Wifie*'s smile,
  The *lisping infant*, prattling on his knee,
    Does a' his weary kiaugh and care beguile,
And makes him quite forget his labor and his toil.   (11. 19–27)

Burns does not abjure Gray's polish in order to mock it; he wishes to present the life of a country labourer as it is seen by a member of the labouring class and to replace Gray's melancholy attitude towards obscure life with a hearty preference for it. Having made this intention plain he falls back on a sentimentally appreciative account of domestic happiness. The children, returning home, gather 'With joy unfeign'd' (1. 37), 'And each for other's weelfare kindly spiers' (1. 38); they talk; the parents give good advice about working hard, obeying their employers and remembering their prayers. 'Their eldest hope, their *Jenny*, woman-grown,/In youthfu' bloom, Love sparkling in her e'e' (11. 32–3), hesitantly brings home a bashful young man who is welcomed into the family circle. A frugal but cheerful supper is followed by hymn-singing, reading from scripture and finally prayers:

Then homeward all take off their sev'ral way;
  The youngling *Cottagers* retire to rest:
The Parent-pair their *secret homage* pay,
  And proffer up to Heaven the warm request,

That 'HE who stills the *raven's* clam'rous nest,
    And decks the *lily* fair in flow'ry pride,
Would, in the way His *Wisdom* sees the best,
    For *them* and for their *little ones* provide;
But chiefly, in their hearts with *Grace divine* preside'.   (11. 154–62)

This rustic idyll is introduced by an address to a friend which suggests that had he lived in a cottage he would have been happier though unknown; it closes with patriotic stanzas that identify rural contentment with national reputation. It is at this point that the subversion of the political assumptions behind Gray's 'Elegy' becomes apparent:

From Scenes like these, old SCOTIA's grandeur springs,
    That makes her lov'd at home, rever'd abroad:
Princes and lords are but the breath of kings,
    'An honest man's the noble work of GOD':
And *certes*, in fair Virtue's heavenly road,
    The *Cottage* leaves the *Palace* far behind:
What is a lordling's pomp? a cumbrous load,
    Disguising oft the *wretch* of human kind,
Studied in arts of Hell, in wickedness refin'd!   (11. 163–71)

The democratic sentiment is masked by its Scottish patriotism but not muted. Wordsworth's declaration, a decade and a half later, in the preface to the 1800 edition of *Lyrical Ballads*, that in 'humble and rustic life', 'the essential passions of the heart find a better soil in which they can attain their maturity . . .', is sometimes understood as an aesthetic statement rather than a political one, but it seems more likely that he was proclaiming his acceptance of Burns's lower-class outlook.[20]

    The best poetry of humble life in the period mingles sensitive observation with sentiments in such a way as to make them support one another, but there is a strain of sheer description that may be traced back to *The Deserted Village*, and, beyond it, to Thomson's *The Seasons* (1726–30), and that, while it seldom rose to distinction, contributed to the development of a poetic vocabulary for poets later in the nineteenth century. Burns himself was an influential contributor with his account of rustic courtship in 'Hallowe'en' (1786)—to which Blake's 'Blindman's Buff' (1783) might be added—and even with such ironical poems as 'Holy Willie's Prayer' and 'The Holy Fair' (1786).

    The existence of this primarily descriptive strain is recognized in W. H. Ireland's preface to *The Fisher Boy: a Poem Comprising His Several Avocations During the Four Seasons of the Year* (1808) with the remark that 'the taste for literary labours, simple in their construction, and founded on facts, has of late years been highly cherished by the public . . .'.[21] His optimistic reference was to the popular success of Robert Bloomfield's *The Farmer's Boy* (1800), upon which his own publishers were capitalizing.[22] Verse of this kind catered to a growing public that enjoyed reading sentimentally about lower-class life. It is generally devoid of irony. Like the genre paintings of David Wilkie that provide a pleasing if watered down rustic version of Hogarth,[23] these industrious poetical imitations translate the city scenes of Gay's *Trivia*, Swift's 'A Description of a City Shower', and even Pope's *Rape of the Lock*, into a country setting. Bloomfield's *Rural Tales* (1802) adds plot to rural description; Crabbe's 'The Parish Register' (1807) more ambitiously incorporates plot and character into the comprehensive description of life in a country community. His *Tales* (1812) and *Tales of the Hall* (1819) relied more on plot and characterization.

The vogue for mere description of country life helped to prepare public interest in the poetry of John Clare. His *The Village Minstrel* (1821)[24] is a modernization of James Beattie's *The Minstrel* (1770–74). Young Lubin, like Beattie's young Edwin, grows up in rustic poverty, and his enthusiasm for the beauties of nature is not merely asserted, as young Edwin's had been. Clare conveys it by allowing us to perceive the landscape with the eye of physical familiarity. The social life is coarse enough to satisfy even Crabbe, and Clare's homely diction has something of the effect of Burns's dialect. Clare's weakness, at least in all the poetry he published before 1836—*Poems Descriptive of Rural Life and Scenery* (1820), *The Village Minstrel* (1821), *The Shepherd's Calendar* (1827) and *The Rural Muse* (1835)—is that he has so little to say, he is so ineffectually reflective. His strength lies in his observation and in the freshness of his choice of expression.

Charles Lamb once advised Clare to be chary of 'rustick Cockneyism'.[25] He may have had in mind the charge of cockneyism recently levelled at Leigh Hunt's circle.[26] In each case objection was being made to easily identifiable peculiarities of diction, but a more than verbal indecorum seems to have been at work. It was typical of Hunt, for instance, to say of bathing naiads, 'one there from her tender instep shakes/The matted sedge . . .'.[27] The observation is very true of a bather, but its direct realism seems to be out of keeping with the literary fiction of such creatures as naiads. Clare also has a way of slipping from one literary level to another that is both incongruous and arresting. His 'The Nightingales Nest' (1835) is an effective example of this habit. Clare takes his reader, whom he addresses as a companion, into the very presence of the famous and elusive literary bird. He himself has seen her before:

> Ive nestled down
> And watched her while she sung—and her renown
> Hath made me marvel that so famed a bird
> Should have no better dress than russet brown
> Her wings would tremble in her extacy
> And feathers stand on end as twere with joy
> And mouth wide open to release her heart
> Of its out sobbing songs . . . .[28]

Clare's dismantling of a legend is irreverent in a sense, but his evident concern for the real bird introduces us to a reverence for a living creature that is rarer and more valuable. The approach is discreet: 'Hush let the wood gate softly clap—for

23

fear/The noise may drive her from her home of love . . .' (p. 73). And a delightful intimacy develops between country poet, companion and bird as the search proceeds:

> —Hark there she is as usual lets be hush
> For in this black thorn clump if rightly guest
> Her curious house is hidden—part aside
> These hazel branches in a gentle way
> And stoop right cautious neath the rustling boughs
> For we will have another search to-day
> And hunt this fern strown thorn clump round and round
> And where this seeded wood grass idly bows
> Well wade right through—it is a likely nook
> In such like spots and often on the ground
> Theyll build where rude boys never think to look
> Aye as I live her secret nest is here
> Upon this white thorn stulp [stump] . . . .   (p. 74)

The surprise of the discovery and the admiration for the nightingale's skill help to prepare us for the poet's receptive and respectful attitude. As the bird sits nearby, 'Mute in her fears', he reassures her. Then the nest is looked at attentively:

> How curious is the nest no other bird
> Uses such loose materials or weaves
> Their dwellings in such spots—dead oaken leaves
> Are placed without and velvet moss within
> And little scraps of grass—and scant and spare
> Of what seems scarce materials down and hair . . .
>
> Snug lie her curious eggs in number five
> Of deadened green or rather olive brown
> And the old prickly thorn bush guards them well . . . .   (p. 75)

There is a confidence of outlook in such poetry that was denied even to Burns, an expectation that the urban reader will be interested in the same things as the rural author if only he is shown them.

2 From terror to wonder

The impulse in the Romantic period to keep one's eye upon the object and to describe things as they really are was complemented by an interest in describing imaginary worlds. The contrast between the subjects treated in each case conceals a similarity in the approach to them. Deliberate simplicities, as we have seen, concentrated upon the present, featured children, the worthy poor and the unfortunate, and placed them generally in rural surroundings. The search for materials for imaginary worlds led poets to look to the distant past. Relying more upon the traditions of romance than upon history, they thought of it as a time of magic and superstition, of aristocracy, wealth and despotism, and they filled it with characters that were better or worse than people really are. The reality they gave to their imaginings was such that most of us think of the past in their terms to this day.

I

In 1796, the second issue of the newly founded *Monthly Magazine* contained a short article by William Taylor on the German poet Gottfried August Bürger. Taylor praised him for his vigorous and lifelike language, and provided translations of three of his poems as samples. One of these, 'Lenora', immediately caught the public fancy. 'Lenora' is the story of a young woman whose fiancé, William, has gone off to war. When peace is restored and the soldiers return, William is not among them. Lenora is so overcome by despair that she blasphemously accuses God of being merciless. At midnight William comes to her and invites her to ride with him to their bridal bed. Together they ride through the night at terrifying speed until they come to a graveyard. There William is transformed into a skeleton, his horse vanishes, and phantoms who moralize on the wickedness of blasphemy dance around the expiring Lenora. Taylor takes some unnecessary liberties with the tale, but his metre is an inspired rendering of the original. The rollicking refrain of the night ride was particularly admired:

> Tramp, tramp, across the land they speed;
> Splash, splash, across the see:

'Hurrah! the dead can ride apace;
 Dost feare to ride with mee?

The moone is bryghte, and blue the nyghte;
 Dost quake the blast to stem?
Dost shudder, mayde, to seeke the dead?'
 —'No, no, but what of them?'   (p. 137)

Before the year was out, six more translations had appeared.

'Lenora' catered to a new literary fashion. The return of unquiet ghosts had
been the theme of a number of the modern ballads in Percy's *Reliques of Ancient
English Poetry* (1765), but English readers had at first been more interested in the
sentimental side of Percy than in the supernatural. As late as 1790, the humorous
condescension of Burns's treatment of the witches' sabbath in 'Tam o' Shanter'
was representative of the prevailing view that ghost stories were for children and
rustics. During the 1790s, however, interest in the supernatural revived. Fictional
encounters with real or imaginary spirits provided opportunities for representing
feelings excited by fear, horror, madness and even ecstasy. The growth of this taste
has been traced through the decade in the Gothic novel, and it has a poetical
equivalent in the Gothic ballad.[1] Memories of Percy's *Reliques* were refreshed, after
a lapse of fifteen years, by reprintings in 1790 and 1791 and by a new edition in
1794. The infusion of German *Sturm und Drang* writing, which had itself drawn
upon Percy in a distinctive way, seems to have begun with John Aikin's adaptation
of Bürger's ballad in 'Arthur and Matilda' (1791). Schiller's play, *The Robbers*
(*Die Räuber*), was translated in 1792, and was republished six times by 1800.
Goethe's *Sorrows of Werther*, a novel that was famous for the suicide of its hero, was
first translated in 1779, appeared four times in the 1790s and was much admired.
'Lenora' was the tip of an iceberg.

Readers recognized its affinities to Percy at once, but they were more interested
in Bürger's innovations. They complained of the poetic injustice of the moral, but
they were impressed by the wild exhilaration of the night ride, by the slow and
chilling revelation of William's condition, and by the shock of the macabre ending.
For the next five years the press teemed with poems about ghosts, demons,
graveyards, and charnel houses. In 1801 Matthew Lewis gathered the best of them
into two volumes entitled *Tales of Wonder*. He included examples of earlier modern
ballads—by Dryden, Parnell, Mallet, Gray, Percy and Burns—and translations of
the more remarkable German ones—by Goethe and Bürger—as well as a few by
Scott, Southey, and himself. The collection is an attractive one, and the mixture of
old and new as well as the presence of one or two parodies provides a refreshing
antidote to the grotesque excesses of the vogue of 'Lenora'.

But excesses there were. T. J. Mathias, in Part IV of his satirical *Pursuits of
Literature* in 1796, had expressed the older objections of common sense: 'No
German nonsense sways my English heart,/Unus'd at ghosts and rattling bones to
start . . . '. 'Lenora' he dismissed as 'a sort of Blue-Beard story for the nursery'.[2]
The physical transformation of William in Bürger's poem is explicit, but it is

passed over quickly. In Matthew Lewis's 'Alonzo the Brave and the Fair Imogine' (1796) it was exploited with lingering detail. Imogine promises to remain true to Alonzo while he is away on a crusade, but instead marries a rich baron. At the wedding banquet a stranger appears, clad in black armour. Imogine invites him to lay aside his helmet:

> The lady is silent: the stranger complies,
>   His vizor he slowly unclosed:
> Oh! God! what a sight met Fair Imogine's eyes!
> What words can express her dismay and surprise,
>   When a skeleton's head was exposed!   (Vol. 3, p. 65)

Bürger would have been satisfied to leave the rest to our imaginations, but Lewis continues with characteristic brio:

> All present then uttered a terrified shout;
>   All turned with disgust from the scene.
> The worms they crept in, and the worms they crept out,
> And sported his eyes and his temples about,
>   While the spectre addressed Imogine . . . .

He reproaches her for being untrue to him and carries her off; four times a year their ghosts are to be seen dancing wildly around the hall while demons riotously drink toasts from newly dug-up skulls. The incongruous gaiety of the metre[3] suggests that Lewis may have been writing tongue in cheek, but the revolting incident is of a piece with others in *The Monk*—the novel in which the poem first appeared—that seem to be meant to make our flesh creep. Whatever the intention, 'Alonzo' struck many readers as being ludicrous. Nothing is so fatal to the credit of a ghost as laughter, and parodies accompanied the Gothic ballads thenceforth. A comic volume entitled *Tales of Terror* followed close upon the heels of *Tales of Wonder* in 1801. Its authorship is still unknown, though Lewis himself may have had a hand in it. Even *Tales of Wonder* had contained a spoof of 'Alonzo'—'Giles Jollup the Grave and Brown Sally Green'—which in turn acknowledged an earlier parody in 'Pil-Garlic the Brave, and Brown Celestine'; *Tales of Terror* is close enough to the poems it is mocking to be taken for them at times.

With these two collections and some interesting new specimens in Thomas Moore's pseudonymous volume, *The Poetical Works of Thomas Little* (1801), the fashion had passed its zenith. Imitations continued to appear. There are some remarkable revivals such as Thomas Beddoes's 'Albert and Emily' (1821), in which lightning strikes and Emily is left with Albert's charred remains:[4]

>   onward came the white
> And woe-worn EMILY—with vacant face
> That loathsome lump she hastened to embrace,
>   And pressed it to her bosom, and then hid
>   Her soft cheek under it, and, madly gay,

> She called it love, and in quick accent chid
> The lifeless matter for its voiceless play. (p. 27)

And John Greenleaf Whittier grafts the genre effectively to New England witchcraft in his 'The Weird Gathering' (1831). But the macabre continues to appear as a disturbing element in longer poems. It is steadily a feature of Southey's romances, and it is to be found in horrifying scenes in Shelley's *The Revolt of Islam* and *The Cenci*. When traces of this outmoded convention are found in well-known poems, modern readers who are unaccustomed to such gruesomeness pay more attention to it than the poets meant them to.

II

The damaging results may be observed in Keats's 'Isabella or, the Pot of Basil' (1820). In the tale of Lorenzo and Lisabetta in Boccaccio's *Decameron*, Lisabetta reveals her love to the handsome Lorenzo who works in her brothers' shop, and he gives up other amorous liaisons and consummates one with her. Her brothers discover what is going on and murder Lorenzo to preserve their sister's reputation and their own. Keats uses the story in his 'Isabella or, the Pot of Basil', but makes significant alterations in two aspects of it. In the first place, the love of his Lorenzo and Isabella is a bashful first love for both that neither dares declare. They dream of one another and pine helplessly. Lorenzo, seeing that Isabella grows pale and thin, resolves to speak to her:

> So said he one fair morning, and all day
> His heart beat awfully against his side;
> And to his heart he inwardly did pray
> For power to speak; but still the ruddy tide
> Stifled his voice, and puls'd resolve away—
> Fever'd his high conceit of such a bride,
> Yet brought him to the meekness of a child:
> Alas! when passion is both meek and wild! (11. 41–8)

They meet and Isabella, sensing his longing, 'straight all flush'd; so, lisped tenderly,/"Lorenzo!"' (11. 54–5). They kiss and take to meeting secretly in a bower in the evenings. Their love is innocent, natural, and ideal, and we are made to feel that it is worth preserving. The ottava rima and the repetition of phrases Keats borrows from Fairfax's translation of Tasso imbue the whole with an antique flavour.

The second alteration is that Keats introduces Isabella's brothers as rich profiteers from the miseries of others:

> for them many a weary hand did swelt
> In torched mines and noisy factories,

And many once proud-quiver'd loins did melt
   In blood from stinging whip;—with hollow eyes
Many all day in dazzling river stood,
To take the rich-ored driftings of the flood.

For them the Ceylon diver held his breath,
   And went all naked to the hungry shark;
For them his ears gush'd blood; for them in death
   The seal on the cold ice with piteous bark
Lay full of darts; for them alone did seethe
   A thousand men in troubles wide and dark:
Half-ignorant, they turn'd an easy wheel,
That set sharp racks at work, to pinch and peel.   (ll. 107–20)

The point of this interpolation of the evils of commerce into Boccaccio's tale—an interpolation for which Keats is about to apologize—is that Isabella's brothers have nothing to be proud of.[5] And yet, when they discover Lorenzo's love for Isabella, they are

                    well nigh mad
That he, the servant of their trade designs,
   Should in their sister's love be blithe and glad,
When 'twas their plan to coax her by degrees
To some high noble and his olive-trees.   (ll. 164–8)

Since Lorenzo, unlike his prototype in Boccaccio, has done nothing wrong, it is necessary to make his murderers into inhuman villains. The intrusion of this powerful but partisan social comment is a small price to pay for an increase in pathos in the fate of the young lovers.

    Keats is faithful to the rest of Boccaccio's plot. Lorenzo's ghost appears to Isabella explaining that he has been murdered and telling her where he is buried. She finds the place, digs up his body, takes his head home with her and hides it in a pot in which she plants some basil. Her brothers, wondering at her attentions to the plant, investigate, find the head and flee. Isabella wastes away, complaining of the loss of her basil plant, and dies. In this section of the poem, however, the manner of the narration departs significantly from the manner of the source; to explain why, a brief digression is necessary.

    Ghosts, who, like Hamlet's father, complained to friends or relations that they were the victims of foul play, provided a variant on reproachful ghosts. When they appeared to wives or mistresses the feelings evoked were especially poignant. William Hamilton's 'The Braes of Yarrow', in Percy's *Reliques*, is a touching and restrained example in which the ghost's appearance is mercifully brief. Blake's remarkable and horrible 'Fair Elenor' (1783) adopts the morbid explicitness of Jacobean tragedy, and has a murderer thrust a bloody parcel into a wife's hands. The parcel unwraps itself, revealing the severed head of her husband which proceeds to warn her against the love of the 'cursed duke' who has had him killed.

> She sat with dead cold limbs, stiffened to stone;
> She took the gory head up in her arms;
> She kissed the pale lips; she had no tears to shed;
> She hugged it to her breast, and groaned her last. (11. 69–72)

Blake's poem does not seem to have been known outside his own circle. The situation which it describes is horrid enough to have found favour with the writers of Gothic ballads in the 1790s, but it lacks one complicating factor that they usually relied upon—the guilty conscience of the person to whom the ghost appears. Scott, to be sure, with typical narrative ingenuity, has a lover reveal to his mistress that although they had spent the previous night together, her husband, who is sleeping by her side, had slain him three days before. But this solution, in 'The Eve of St. John' (1801), leaves us in some doubt as to where our sympathies should lie. Even the young Byron tried his hand at this genre in 'Oscar of Alva' (1807).

Scott's inclusion of 'The Twa Corbies' in his *Minstrelsy of the Scottish Border* (1802) stimulated James Hogg to write a beautiful but chilling elaboration of it, 'Sir David Graeme' (1807),[6] in which a lady blames the absent Sir David for failing to elope with her as he had promised, and then begins to receive signs that he has met with an untimely end. A dove brings her the lock of hair that she had given Sir David; then it brings back her ring; and finally his dog comes to her and leads her to where his master lies:

> Wi' a wound through his shoulder-bane,
>   An' in his bosom twa or three;
> Wi' flies an' vermine sair o'ergane,
>   An' ugsome to the sight was he
> His piercing een, that love did beet,
>   Had now become the ravens' prey;
> His tongue, that moved to accents sweet,
>   Deep frae his throat was torn away. (p. 11)

We learn that Sir David, who has risked a family feud in courting her, has been killed by her brothers.

The form of the Scottish ballad disguises the resemblance to the story of Lorenzo and Isabella and it may be coincidental. But the interest in the macabre had renewed attention to promising Italian sources. In 1804, Richard Wharton published his *Fables: Consisting of Select Parts from Dante, Berni, Chaucer and Ariosto. Imitated in English Heroic Verse*. The collection was modelled on Dryden's *Fables*, and it contained several gruesome choices: from Dante's *Inferno*, the description of Ugolino gnawing Ruggiero's head; from Berni's *Orlando Innamorato*, Marchino's rape of Stella while she is bound to her husband's putrefying corpse; and from Ariosto's *Orlando Furioso*, Astolfo's scalping of the severed head of Orillo. The *Monthly Review* remarked only that the collection was boring and complained that some of the rhymes were incorrect.[7] In 1807, Charles Kirkpatrick Sharpe brought out his *Metrical Legends, and Other Poems*, which includes several Gothic poems, and among them a translation of Boccaccio's tale of 'Lorenzo and Isabella'. It is possible that Hogg had seen Sharpe's version—both men were in touch with Scott who in turn had links with both their publishers.

Returning to Keats's poem, it is clear that by the time Keats attempted his version of Boccaccio he was writing for a jaded public that had drunk deep of horrors. Hence it is that when his love story requires him to horrify us he seems to cast aside restraint. Lorenzo's ghost is described:

>   the forest tomb
>   Had marr'd his glossy hair which once could shoot
> Lustre into the sun, and put cold doom
>   Upon his lips, and taken the soft lute
> From his lorn voice, and past his loamed ears
> Had made a miry channel for his tears.   (11. 275–80)

When Isabella and her old nurse dig for the body, the poet seems to be aware of the perilous incongruity:

>   Ah! wherefore all this wormy circumstance?
>   Why linger at the yawning tomb so long?
>   O for the gentleness of old Romance,
>   The simple plaining of a minstrel's song!
>   Fair reader, at the old tale take a glance,
>   For here, in truth, it doth not well belong
>   To speak:—O turn thee to the very tale,
>   And taste the music of that vision pale.   (11. 385–92)

But he may really be providing a moment of reflective respite before inflicting worse upon us. 'With duller steel than the Persëan sword' (1. 393) they cut Lorenzo's head off and carry it home:

>   And then the prize was all for Isabel:
>   She calm'd its wild hair with a golden comb,
>   And all around each eye's sepulchral cell
>   Pointed each fringed lash; the smeared loam
>   With tears, as chilly as a dripping well,
>   She drench'd away:—and still she comb'd, and kept
>   Sighing all day—and still she kiss'd, and wept.   (11. 402–8)

The story still requires that her brothers should discover the head in the basil pot—'The thing was vile with green and livid spot,/And yet they knew it was Lorenzo's face . . .' (11. 475–6).

It is difficult not to be distracted by such unpleasant details, and to remember that Isabella's complete unawareness of them really matters more. Her reaction to the loss of Lorenzo is a reaction to the loss of true love. Even before she has learned of his death she is declining visibly towards her own. When his ghost appears to her, she recognizes the cause of his death, but she shows neither resentment nor fear. In her mental derangement she transfers her love for Lorenzo to his corpse, and, in turn, to the basil which she plants above his severed head. The single-minded intensity of her devotion is a fitting parallel to the idyllic happiness she has lost, and the obliqueness of her complaint—'O cruelty,/To steal my basil-pot away from me!' (11. 503—4)—expresses her madness and reminds us that the loss of Lorenzo, like the loss of the plant, meant the loss of all she cared for.

III

In 1817, Coleridge recalled how he and Wordsworth had divided the job of composing *Lyrical Ballads* twenty years before. It was agreed that his endeavours

> should be directed to persons and characters supernatural, or at least romantic; yet so as to transfer from our inward nature a human interest and a semblance of truth sufficient to procure for these shadows of imagination that willing suspension of disbelief for the moment, which constitutes poetic faith.[8]

A criticism of the superficiality of the Gothic fashion is implied here. But whereas a poet who wished to render ordinary experience more truly could react against inadequate literary stereotypes by appealing to life itself, abnormal experience, and particularly experience of the supernatural, could only be judged against literary alternatives. As it turned out, this reform involved the absorption of Gothic ballad materials, reinforced by techniques found in Gothic novels, into the Renaissance romance as represented by authors like Spenser, Ariosto and Tasso, and, as we shall see, the mingling of the Celtic and Nordic materials in epics founded on Milton and Virgil. But the nature of the reform does not seem to have been obvious to the poets who effected it.

Coleridge's unfinished poem 'Christabel' was not published until 1816, but it was begun in 1797 and carried as far as it goes in 1800. Like 'The Rime of the Ancient Mariner'—which will be discussed in Chapter 4—it is a product of the Gothic fashion as well as a reaction against it. Coleridge's wish to confer upon the supernatural 'a human interest and a semblance of truth' comes closest to realization in 'Christabel', and his results transcend the models on which he built. The origins of its plot have been traced plausibly to poems in Percy's *Reliques*—particularly to 'Sir Cauline' and 'The Child of Elle'—and to the novels of Mrs Radcliffe and Matthew Lewis—especially *The Mysteries of Udolpho* (1794), *The Italian* (1797), and *The Monk* (1796). It combines an interest in the psychology of minds made uneasy by contact with supernatural events with a more cheerful enthusiasm for the noble feelings and romantic settings of the age of chivalry. Part I observes the conventions of the Gothic ballad as a maiden worries about the plight of her absent lover and is visited by a stranger who casts a spell over her and reveals a hideous physical deformity. In Part II the conventions have shifted to the Gothic novel as we encounter religious rituals, an ancient family feud, aristocratic pride, failure of communication between parent and child, and a setting of sublime or at least picturesque landscape. The fact that the poem is unfinished has naturally excited curiosity about the intended plot, but it should be a reminder that the appeal of the poem is independent of its story.[9]

When the mysterious Geraldine is discovered behind the old oak tree in Part I, much is made of her beauty:

> a damsel bright,
> Drest in a silken robe of white,
> That shadowy in the moonlight shone:
> The neck that made that white robe wan,
> Her stately neck, and arms were bare;
> Her blue-veined feet unsandal'd were,
> And wildly glittered here and there
> The gems entangled in her hair.
> I guess, 'twas frightful there to see
> A lady so richly clad as she—
> Beautiful exceedingly! (11. 58–68)

The splendour of Geraldine's appearance makes her presence in the woods at night doubly disconcerting. She is unmistakably a 'lofty lady' (1. 223). About what Christabel looks like, beyond the fact that she has blue eyes—a sign of innocence—we are told little, but we are told that she is gentle, mild, sweet, and, repeatedly, that she is 'lovely'. Her loveliness is presented to us in terms of her character. In a slightly earlier poem, 'To the Nightingale' (1796), Coleridge had provided a parallel contrast between physical and moral beauty, when he declared that the notes of the nightingale's song:

> Tho' sweeter far than the delicious airs
> That vibrate from a white-arm'd Lady's harp,
> What time the languishment of lonely love
> Melts in her eye, and heaves her breast of snow,
> Are not so sweet as is the voice of her,
> My Sara—best beloved of human kind!
> When breathing the pure soul of tenderness,
> She thrills me with the Husband's promis'd name! (11. 19–26)

The lover's compliment is combined with a preference for humble domesticity. The natural beauty of the nightingale's song and the 'pure soul of tenderness' breathed by Sara are both preferred to the artful pretence of fashionable beauty. The preference is to be expected from a sentimental egalitarian like the young Coleridge but it is obscured by the apparently medieval and magical context of 'Christabel'.

Christabel herself, however, is carefully drawn as a woman with the 'pure soul of tenderness'. She is not only lovely, she is beloved—by her betrothed knight and by her father—and even Geraldine is obliged to admit 'All they who live in the upper sky,/Do love you, holy Christabel!' (11. 227–8). Her behaviour makes us understand why she is beloved. Her reception of Geraldine is hospitable—she immediately offers refuge and promises her father's help; she assists Geraldine's 'weary weight' over the threshold and revives her with a precious medicinal cordial. She is devout—in her prayers for her absent lover, in her gratitude to the Virgin Mary for Geraldine's deliverance, and in her instinctive appeal to heaven when Geraldine, warring with the unseen ghost of Christabel's mother, seems unwell. Even in sleep she is said to be

> Like a youthful hermitess,
> Beauteous in a wilderness,
> Who, praying always, prays in sleep. (11. 320–2)

The characterization might be cloying were it not that Christabel's good qualities so evidently spring from an unself-conscious sympathy for others. Her concern for a distressed stranger and her habitual piety impress us less than her thoughtfulness about her father's difficulty in sleeping. From the poet's point of view it was important to provide a reasonable pretext for having Geraldine share Christabel's couch, but as readers we take in rather Christabel's unhesitating considerateness in inconveniencing only herself.

Geraldine's account of being abducted by unknown ruffians is conventional, resembling Angelica's predicament in Canto I of the *Orlando Furioso*, for instance; familiarity with the convention prevents us from being much interested in this instance of it, and subsequent events make us doubt its truth. The tribulations of Christabel, however, are more unusual, and we are witnesses of the toils in which she is entangled even if we are uncertain about their nature. The stage directions and asides of the narrator contribute to our sense of ominous events. At the beginning of Part I, particularly, the old ballad device of asking questions and offering speculative answers alerts us to suspicious circumstances. The howling of the mastiff, the moonlight, and Christabel's sighs as she prepares for her unaccustomed venture into the midnight wood alone, prepare us for something supernatural. The moaning behind the oak tree frightens Christabel, and the narrator prompts us to share her fear:

> Hush, beating heart of Christabel!
> Jesu, Maria, shield her well! (11. 53–4)

Her involuntary reaction, as if for protection against the cold, is a natural expression of her uneasiness.

> She folded her arms beneath her cloak,
> And stole to the other side of the oak. (11. 55–6)

She and Geraldine hurry to the castle, but as if in a nightmare their steps 'strove to be, and were not, fast' (1. 113). Geraldine's inability to cross the iron threshold unassisted is observed without comment, as is her inability to pray; the mastiff's angry moan is speculated about, and the reflection of the fire in Geraldine's eye and in the metal boss of Sir Leoline's shield is remarked upon, but we are left to make what we can of the meaning of these unexplained but suspicious details. Even Geraldine's strife with the invisible spirit of Christabel's mother, which seems for the first time to identify Geraldine as an actively evil character, is complicated by renewed appreciation of her beauty—'She was most beautiful to see,/Like a lady of a far countrée' (11. 224–5)—and by her reassuring acquaintance with all those 'who live in the upper sky' (1. 227). When Christabel sees Geraldine undress, the narrator makes it plain that Christabel sees something threatening:

> Behold! her bosom and half her side—
> A sight to dream of, not to tell!
> O shield her! shield sweet Christabel!   (11. 252–4)

But even at this crucial moment in the poem, the sight is left undefined, and the hostility we might feel towards Geraldine is confused by the affliction from which she herself is evidently suffering:

> Ah! what a stricken look was hers!
> Deep from within she seems half-way
> To lift some weight with sick assay,
> And eyes the maid and seeks delay . . . .   (11. 256–9)

Geraldine appears to be a reluctant evildoer. The spell she pronounces over Christabel 'with low voice and doleful look' (1. 265) is merely one that will prevent her from revealing the secret.

The heroes and heroines of Gothic novels are constantly faced with doubts and uncertainties, but their susceptible imaginations people these uncertainties with extravagant improbabilities. In 'Christabel' the imaginings are left to the reader. The effect of the situation on Christabel, however, is explained in the Conclusion to Part I, where her innocent and gentle resignation is contrasted with her condition in Geraldine's arms:

> With open eyes (ah woe is me!)
> Asleep, and dreaming fearfully,
> Fearfully dreaming, yet, I wis,
> Dreaming that alone, which is—
> O sorrow and shame! Can this be she,
> The lady, who knelt at the old oak tree?   (11. 292–7)

After Geraldine's hour is over, Christabel is able to sleep naturally, reassured by her faith:

But this she knows, in joys and woes,
That saints will aid if men will call:
For the blue sky bends over all!   (11. 329-31)

It is usual in discussions of Part II to notice the sudden introduction of scenery from the Lake District, but changes in the narrative technique make more difference. We are no longer teased with foreboding questions; we are made perfectly aware of what is going on and only the characters are puzzled or deceived. The two main mysteries of Part I—the 'sight to dream of' and the nature of Geraldine's intentions—are cleared up for us, and no new ones take their place. The advantage that is gained in dramatic irony as Sir Leoline ignores the significance of Bracy's dream and misjudges Christabel and Geraldine, counts for little because his character has not been established in such a way as to make us expect anything better from him. Furthermore, although in Part II Sir Leoline occupies centre stage rather than Christabel, we are not allowed intimate glimpses of his feelings. Even the acute analysis of the quality of anger we feel towards those we love, that is found in the Conclusion to Part II, appears too late to retrieve our impression that Sir Leoline is a passionate and hasty man. Our interest in Part II depends largely on feelings engendered in Part I; they are so strong that the affections of most readers extend to both.

IV

Part I of 'Christabel' avoids the ominous sublimities of the Gothic novel. Here we have no bats or toads, no worms or charnel houses, no grim dungeons replete with rattling chains. When Coleridge analysed the opening scene of *Hamlet* in which the sentinels greet one another before the entrance of the ghost, he singled out Francisco's answer to the question 'Have you had quiet guard?'—'Not a mouse stirring'—for special praise.[10] His preparation for Geraldine is in the same homely and realistic spirit. The hooting of the owls is accompanied by the drowsy crowing of the cock, the striking of the clock, and the short howls of the watchdog. The traditional full moon is qualified by a thin grey cloud, and the coldness of the night by the observation that 'the Spring comes slowly up this way' (1. 22). With the narrator's daylight knowledge we learn that 'moss and rarest misletoe' are 'green upon the oak' (11. 33-4), that one red leaf hangs 'On the topmost twig that looks up at the sky', and that Christabel has a ringlet curl upon her cheek (11. 46, 49). When Geraldine appears, the plot thickens, but the setting—indoors the open fire, the shield on the wall, the rushes underfoot, the lamp with its angel's feet—is one of increasing charm. The tale is supernatural, but its effect is softened by the romantic surroundings in which it is enacted.

This fusion of beauty and fear conveyed in an unforgettably unfamiliar metre was hard for other poets to resist. Although Coleridge's delay in publishing 'Christabel' might have been expected to prevent it from having any influence, Walter Scott heard parts of it recited early on by a friend who had heard it from

Coleridge himself.[11] In metrical matters Scott never needed more than a hint. In emulating the atmosphere of 'Christabel' he brought to it two older traditions from which no really satisfactory poem had emerged. One was the 'legendary tale', a mildly antiquarian form of ballad that was popularized by Thomas Percy's *The Hermit of Warkworth* (1771), mocked by Samuel Johnson, and imitated unceasingly for the next thirty years.[12] The legendary tale usually involved a pair of ill-starred lovers, a case of mistaken identity, and a vaguely medieval setting in which the clash of arms could be expected at any moment. The other tradition was the romance, a form practised mainly by antiquarians with an unquenchable enthusiasm for Spenser and Ariosto. Two of these were respected countrymen of Scott's, the blind Thomas Blacklock, author of *The Graham* (1774), and John Ogilvie, author of *Rona* (1777); a third, Richard Hole, emphasized the magical rather than the historical elements in *Arthur; or, the Northern Enchantment* (1789). To these precedents Scott brought his own formidable and growing knowledge of Scottish history, and his unerring narrative instinct.

His first experiment, *The Lay of the Last Minstrel* (1805), was a popular success without a precedent. Until quite recently it was so well known to every schoolchild as to make summary superfluous. Suffice it to say that it concerns a young lover's reconciliation of a blood feud in sixteenth-century Scotland, that it involves necromancy, kidnapping, mistaken identity, single combat in sight of the opposed English and Scottish armies, an evil and magical dwarf, a concluding feast at which several tales are sung by rival minstrels, and, of course, the true love of Lord Cranstoun and Margaret. Scott proceeded to write a series of poems with similar appeal—*Marmion; a Tale of Flodden Field* (1808), *The Lady of the Lake* (1810), *Rokeby* (1813), and *The Lord of the Isles* (1815). The spirit in which they were read may be gathered from a diary entry of the period:

> Tuesday, 12th.—I received Walter Scott's *Rokeby*. I gazed at it with a transport of impatience, and began reading it in bed. I am already in the first canto:—my soul has glowed with what he justly terms 'the art unteachable'. My veins have thrilled; my heart has throbbed; my eyes have filled with tears—during its perusal. The poet who can thus master the passions to do his bidding, must be *indeed a poet*.[13]

When he noticed that the public enthusiasm for his poetical romances was beginning to flag, Scott branched out experimentally in two opposite directions. He minimized the risk to his valuable reputation by remaining anonymous. One of his experiments took: *Waverley, or, 'Tis Fifty Years Since* (1814) was the first of the series of novels whose fame eclipsed his poetry; the other experiment, *The Bridal of Triermain, or the Vale of St. John* (1813), a poem in which suspense, characterization and historical circumstances were set aside in favour of fantasy and enchantment, was judged to be a failure. Scott did not profit from it, but the poetry of fantasy and enchantment survived and flourished in other hands. His experiment in evoking atmosphere is worth pausing over as a precedent for subtler successors.

The Bridal of Triermain is a story within a story within a story. It is set in the Lake District and framed by the love of the humble but virtuous Arthur for the beautiful but highborn Lucy. Arthur tells Lucy of the search of Sir Roland de Vaux of Triermain[14] for a beautiful maiden he has seen in a dream. Sir Roland sends his page to ask the seer, Lyulph, whether she exists. Lyulph in turn tells how King Arthur, 501 years ago, found a magical castle in the Vale of St John and fell in love with the half-mortal Gwendolen who lived there. After three months Arthur returned to the duties of the Round Table and promised that if Gwendolen bore him a son he would make him his heir, and that he would marry a daughter to the bravest of his knights. Fifteen years later a maiden named Gyneth appeared claiming his promise. The knights of the Round Table fought so fiercely for her that Merlin was obliged to intervene; he ordained that Gyneth, like the sleeping beauty, should sleep in the Vale of St John until a worthy knight came to wake her. De Vaux accordingly rides to the place, waits until the castle reappears, and then enters to undergo a succession of trials of his courage and skill. He overcomes the temptations of pleasure, wealth and pride in turn and reaches Gyneth's bower:

> And so fair the slumberer seems,
> That De Vaux impeached his dreams,
> Vapid all and void of might,
> Hiding half her charms from sight.
> Motionless a while he stands,
> Folds his arms and clasps his hands,
> Trembling in his fitful joy,
> Doubtful how he should destroy
>   Long-enduring spell;
> Doubtful too, when slowly rise
> Dark-fringed lids of Gyneth's eyes,
>   What these eyes shall tell.
> 'St. George! St. Mary! can it be,
> That they will kindly look on me!'   (III, xxxviii)

De Vaux's approach is devout:

> Gently, lo! the Warrior kneels,
> Soft that lovely hand he steals,
> Soft to kiss, and soft to clasp . . . .   (III, xxxix)

The castle vanishes, Gyneth wakes, and

> In the arms of bold De Vaux,
>   Safe the princess lay!
> Safe and free from magic power,
> Blushing like the rose's flower
>   Opening to the day . . . .   (III, xxxix)

In the preface to the first edition of *The Bridal of Triermain*, Scott distinguishes between the historical requirements of the epic and the freedom from constraint possible in a romance, which he defines as 'a fictitious narrative, framed and combined at the pleasure of the writer . . .'.[15] Scott uses this freedom to depict a world that is magical as well as antique, a world in which abstract virtues flourish, and in which an uncomplicatedly virtuous lover who overcomes dangerous odds in quest of a beautiful maiden seems believable. The conclusion to the poem in which young Arthur addresses Lucy, whom he has married, links the exotic joys of the legendary world to the tender affections of a flesh and blood husband and wife.

In *The Story of Rimini* (1816), Leigh Hunt retells Dante's unhappier tale of the loves of Paolo and Francesca. Hunt is less inhibited by knowledge of the past than Scott, but he is very skilful at bringing scenes before us. The high point of *Rimini* occurs in Canto III when the lovers sit in a bower reading together of Lancelot's illicit love for Queen Guinevere:[16]

> 'May I come in?' said he:—it made her start,—
> That smiling voice;—she coloured, pressed her heart
> A moment, as for breath, and then with free
> And usual tone said, 'O yes,—certainly'.
> There's apt to be, at conscious times like these,
> An affectation of a bright-eyed ease,
> An air of something quite serene and sure,
> As if to seem so, was to be, secure:
> With this the lovers met, with this they spoke,
> With this they sat down to the self-same book,
> And Paulo, by degrees, gently embraced
> With one permitted arm her lovely waist;
> And both their cheeks, like peaches on a tree,
> Leaned with a touch together, thrillingly . . . .
>
> And Paulo turned, scarce knowing what he did,
> Only he felt he could no more dissemble,
> And kissed her, mouth to mouth, all in a tremble.
> Sad were those hearts, and sweet was that long kiss:
> Sacred be love from sight, whate'er it is.
> The world was all forgot, the struggle o'er,
> Desperate the joy.—That day they read no more.   (pp. 77–8)

It is difficult to decide whether Hunt is recreating the past for us or whether he is disguising the present in a flattering fancy dress. In either case, however, the combination helps to convey the consummation of innocent yearning without seeming to lose touch with reality.

The weakness of *The Bridal of Triermain* and *The Story of Rimini* is that while they sacrifice plot and characterization to the creation of magical atmosphere, they have not quite relinquished them. As a consequence, *Rimini* is now known mainly by excerpts and *The Bridal* not at all. The publication of the unfinished 'Christabel' in 1816 renewed the influence of Coleridge's poem and allowed distinctions to be made between it and Scott's popular verse narratives. Byron puffed it in the preface to *The Siege of Corinth* (1816) as 'That wild and singularly original and beautiful poem' and the volume in which it appeared passed through three editions within the year. Traces of its influence are to be found in Keats's 'The Eve of St. Agnes' (1820). It is set, like 'Christabel', in a vaguely defined middle ages, and it takes place on a moonlit night at an aristocratic house. Whereas Coleridge simply stated that the weather was chilly, Keats has us share the fancy of a poor old Beadsman whose fingers are numb with cold as he tells his rosary:

> His prayer he saith, this patient, holy man;
> Then takes his lamp, and riseth from his knees,
> And back returneth, meagre, barefoot, wan,
> Along the chapel aisle by slow degrees:
> The sculptur'd dead, on each side, seem to freeze,
> Emprison'd in black, purgatorial rails:
> Knights, ladies, praying in dumb orat'ries,
> He passeth by; and his weak spirit fails
> To think how they may ache in icy hoods and mails.   (11. 10–18)

The old man's unstinting sympathy conveys the feeling of extreme cold to us indirectly. Within the house the scene is contrastingly rich and comfortable: 'The level chambers, ready with their pride,/Were glowing to receive a thousand guests . . .' (11. 32–3). A splendid ball is in progress.

Porphyro and Madeline, the young hero and heroine of the poem, are separated from these extremes of austere self-denial on the one hand and of haughty self-indulgence on the other. Madeline is present at the dance, but preoccupied with the prospect of a dream she hopes to have that night. She has been told

> how, upon St. Agnes' Eve,
> Young virgins might have visions of delight,
> And soft adorings from their loves receive
> Upon the honey'd middle of the night,
> If ceremonies due they did aright;
> As, supperless to bed they must retire,
> And couch supine their beauties, lily white;
> Nor look behind, nor sideways, but require
> Of Heaven with upward eyes for all that they desire.   (11. 46–54)

Porphyro has come secretly in the hope of catching a glimpse of her at the dance, but at the risk of his life:

> For him, those chambers held barbarian hordes,
> Hyena foemen, and hot-blooded lords,

40

> Whose very dogs would execrations howl
> Against his lineage: not one breast affords
> Him any mercy, in that mansion foul,
> Save one old beldame, weak in body and in soul.   (ll. 85–90)

His thoughts, like Madeline's, are bent on true love.

The situation is obviously reminiscent of Romeo's daring visit to the Capulet ball in Act I of *Romeo and Juliet*. The old beldam, Angela, is a reasonable substitute for Juliet's nurse in her well-meant garrulousness; in place of Tybalt and Old Capulet we have 'dwarfish Hildebrand' and 'old Lord Maurice'; and even the Beadsman makes a possible substitute for Friar Laurence. As the tale progresses it resembles more closely Romeo's later nocturnal visit to Juliet after they have been secretly married (III, v). For Keats's contemporaries the situation was also reminiscent of *The Lay of the Last Minstrel*. The Beadsman is very like the ancient Monk of St Mary's Aisle who, in the moonlit chapel, surrenders the magical book of Michael Scott to young William of Deloraine (II, iii–xxiii). The Beadsman, like the Monk, is found dead the following day. The scene with the Monk is immediately followed in *The Lay* by the clandestine meeting of a pair of young lovers, Baron Henry of Cranstoun and fair Margaret of Branksome, whose families are divided by a 'bloody feud' (II, xxv–xxix). By calling upon our memories of these precedents, Keats is able to borrow feelings associated with them without requiring us to make much effort to grasp a plot.

The focal point of 'The Eve of St. Agnes' is Porphyro's visit to Madeline's bedchamber. He reassures the horrified Angela that his intentions are honourable:

> 'I will not harm her, by all saints I swear',
> Quoth Porphyro: 'O may I ne'er find grace
> When my weak voice shall whisper its last prayer,
> If one of her soft ringlets I displace,
> Or look with ruffian passion in her face . . .'.   (ll. 145–9)

Rather, he wishes to be hidden in a closet:

>   of such privacy
> That he might see her beauty unespied,
> And win perhaps that night a peerless bride,
> While legion'd fairies pac'd the coverlet,
> And pale enchantment held her sleepy-eyed.
> Never on such a night have lovers met,
> Since Merlin paid his Demon all the monstrous debt.   (ll. 165–71)

The reference to Merlin recalls the occasion in *The Faerie Queene* (III, iii) on which he reveals to Britomart and her nurse the identity of Arthegall, the husband destined to found the British race with Britomart. Keats is annexing associations from another well-known work, this time associations of magical power and virtuous love.

When Madeline enters, intent upon her devotions, she kneels and then undresses. In 'Christabel' the moment when Geraldine undresses is an ominous one:

> Then drawing in her breath aloud,
> Like one that shuddered, she unbound
> The cincture from beneath her breast:
> Her silken robe, and inner vest,
> Dropt to her feet, and full in view,
> Behold! her bosom and half her side—
> A sight to dream of, not to tell!
> O shield her! shield sweet Christabel! (11. 247–54)

In 'The Eve of St. Agnes', the moment when Madeline undresses is similarly one of suspense and wonder as Porphyro watches her, but it has no taint of deformity or danger:

> her vespers done,
> Of all its wreathed pearls her hair she frees;
> Unclasps her warmed jewels one by one;
> Loosens her fragrant boddice; by degrees
> Her rich attire creeps rustling to her knees:
> Half-hidden, like a mermaid in sea-weed,
> Pensive awhile she dreams awake, and sees,
> In fancy, fair St. Agnes in her bed,
> But dares not look behind, or all the charm is fled. (11. 226–34)

Geraldine's sinister beauty has been replaced by a loveliness that is serenely quiet and yielding.

Once Madeline is asleep, Porphyro prepares a feast for her and he sings to waken her. The wakening resembles De Vaux's awakening of Gyneth, but it is closer to another awakening that is seldom looked at nowadays. In James Montgomery's biblical epic, *The World Before the Flood* (1813),[17] the troubled young hero, Javan, returns from exile and finds his former sweetheart Zillah sleeping in a bower. In her sleep she utters his name and he, fired by 'pure affection', sits nearby and plays on his flute to waken her gently. A musical voice intrudes upon her dream of him and she wakes:

> but in her solitude
> Found the enchantment of her dream renew'd;
> That living voice, so full, melodious, clear,
> That voice of mystery warbled in her ear . . . . (p. 33)

Javan, who is out of sight, continues to play, inspired anew by her beauty, and Zillah, charmed by his playing, timorously seeks its source:

> Breathless, on tip-toe, round the copse she crept;
> Her heart beat quicker, louder, as she stept,
> Till Javan rose, and fix'd on her his eyes,
> In dumb embarrassment, and feign'd surprise;
> Upright she started, at the sudden view,
> Back from her brow the scatter'd ringlets flew,
> Paleness a moment overspread her face;
> But fear to frank astonishment gave place,
> And, with the virgin-blush of innocence,
> She ask'd,—'Who art thou, Stranger, and from whence?'   (p. 36)

Zillah, although she recognizes Javan in spite of the change exile has wrought in him, refers him decorously to her father's house nearby and returns to watching her sheep. She and Javan are meant to epitomize innocent young love.

Madeline's awakening, like Zillah's, is apprehensive, and she too has difficulty separating her dream from reality:

> 'Ah, Porphyro!' said she, 'but even now
> Thy voice was at sweet tremble in mine ear,
> Made tuneable with every sweetest vow;
> And those sad eyes were spiritual and clear:
> How chang'd thou art! how pallid, chill, and drear!'   (ll. 307–11)

But instead of breaking away, she appeals to him to resume his dream state, and languidly echoes Romeo's line—'O trespass sweetly urged!/Give me my sin again' (I, v, 111–12):

> 'Give me that voice again, my Porphyro,
> Those looks immortal, those complainings dear!
> Oh leave me not in this eternal woe,
> For if thou diest, my Love, I know not where to go'.   (ll. 312–15)

In an early draft of the poem the lines 'See while she speaks his arms encroaching slow/Have zon'd her, heart to heart . . .' are interposed at this point.[18] But, in the final version, Keats omits this repetition of Paolo and Francesca's illicit love. Instead Porphyro rises from his knees:

> Beyond a mortal man impassion'd far
> At these voluptuous accents, he arose,
> Ethereal, flush'd, and like a throbbing star
> Seen mid the sapphire heaven's deep repose
> Into her dream he melted . . . .   (ll. 316–20)

The sleet patters on the window panes, Madeline wakes fully, Porphyro proposes marriage, and they flee away together into the stormy night. The ideal fantasies of

43

love have been rescued from the artificiality of the romance and given a form that is physically imaginable.

V

The possibilities of presenting romantic atmosphere without any plot at all are made apparent in Coleridge's 'Kubla Khan'. Coleridge is believed to have written the poem in 1798. When he published it in 1816 as a 'psychological curiosity'—the fragmentary remnant of a dream—he absolved himself of responsibility for narrative coherence or even meaning.[19] The appeal of the poem has always been a mixture of the incantatory quality of its metre and language and the strange and beautiful scenes and events it conveys.

Coleridge evidently used to recite 'Kubla Khan' to considerable effect; 'so enchantingly', Charles Lamb told Wordsworth, 'that it irradiates and brings heaven and Elysian bowers into my parlour while he sings or says it . . .'.[20] And 'Perdita' Robinson as early as 1800 had praised its 'wondrous witcheries of song'.[21] Coleridge's claim that 'Kubla Khan' was composed in a dream might seem to be sufficient warning that its manner would be different from the manner of more conscious poetry, and yet there were significant anticipations and parallels. If we look at the rhapsodic ending, for example, a ritualistic frenzy or ecstasy of inspiration seems to be described:

> And all who heard should see them there,
> And all should cry, Beware! Beware!
> His flashing eyes, his floating hair!
> Weave a circle round him thrice,
> And close your eyes with holy dread,
> For he on honey-dew hath fed,
> And drunk the milk of Paradise.   (ll. 48–54)

Throughout the latter part of the eighteenth century there had been an interest in poetic renderings of the incantations of people involved in charms, spells, sorcery, or prophecy. The spells uttered by the witches in *Macbeth* were familiar, but tended to be regarded as comical. The growing interest in superstitions, however, encouraged a more respectful curiosity about sorcery, especially the sorcery of the Celtic world and the rituals of Scandinavian mythology. When Gray attempted Nordic odes, he conveyed their wildness with a mixture of deliberately ghastly images and trochaic alliteration reminiscent of Shakespeare's witches:

> Now the storm begins to lower,
> (Haste, the loom of hell prepare,)
> Iron-sleet of arrowy shower
> Hurtles in the darkened air.

Glittering lances are the loom,
Where the dusky warp we strain,
Weaving many a soldier's doom,
Orkney's woe, and Randver's bane.

See the grisly texture grow,
('Tis of human entrails made,)
And the weights that play below,
Each a gasping warrior's head.[22]

Similar experiments were tried by Thomas Penrose, in his 'The Carousal of Odin' (1775), by William Mickle in his ballad, 'The Sorceress; or Wolfwold and Ulla' (1782), and by T. J. Mathias in his *Runic Odes* (1781). The most famous example of such metre is Blake's 'The Tiger' (1794), in which the trochaic beat is reinforced by intervening pauses occasioned by the rhetorical questions:

What the hammer? What the chain?
In what furnace was thy brain?
What the anvil? What dread grasp
Dare its deadly terrors clasp? (11. 13–16)

The associations of such poetry are with the dark aspect of the gods, and, in 'The Tiger', as we have seen, Blake is already able to exploit that expectation with his unexpected question, 'Did he who made the Lamb make thee?'

The use of trochaic lines was particularly striking in a period that was attuned to heroic couplets. Blank verse and Spenserian stanzas, and even the ballad quatrains, also provided an effective contrast. As poets began to experiment more freely with metres at the end of the 1790s, new effects were needed for charms, sorceries and curses. In 'Christabel', Geraldine's spell is marked by the introduction into the loose iambic tetrameter of the poem of a series of anapaestic and then amphibrachic lines:

In the touch of this bosom there worketh a spell,
Which is lord of thy utterance, Christabel!
Thou knowest to-night, and wilt know to-morrow,
This mark of my shame, this seal of my sorrow;
    But vainly thou warrest,
      For this is alone in
    Thy power to declare,
      That in the dim forest
    Thou heard'st a low moaning,
And found'st a bright lady, surpassingly fair;
And didst bring her home with thee in love and in charity,
To shield her and shelter her from the damp air. (11. 267–78)

45

The breakdown of the heavy stresses in the final lines lends an ingenuously antique touch, and the naivety is perhaps in keeping with the simple version of events to which Christabel is to be confined. In Southey's *Thalaba* (1801), the extraordinary freedom of the metre used set a difficult problem for the incantation of Khawla in Book IX. Southey was proud of his solution:

> With spreading arms she whirls around
> Rapidly, rapidly,
> Ever around and around;
> And loudly she calls the while,
> 'Eblis! Eblis!'
> Loudly, incessantly,
> Still she calls, 'Eblis! Eblis!'
> Giddily, giddily, still she whirls,
> Loudly, incessantly, still she calls;
> The motion is ever the same,
> Ever around and around;
> The calling is still the same,
> Still it is, 'Eblis! Eblis!'
> Till her voice is a shapeless yell,
> And dizzily rolls her brain,
> And now she is full of the Fiend.
> She stops, she rocks, she reels!
> Look! look! she appears in the darkness!
> Her flamy hairs curl up
> All living, like the Meteor's locks of light!
> Her eyes are like the sickly Moon!   (Vol. 4, p. 311)

The repetition and the disjointed but monotonous rhythm are used to set off the prophecy that issues from her trance:

> 'Ye may hope and ye may fear,
> The danger of his stars is near.
> Sultan! if he perish, woe!
> Fate hath written one death-blow
> For Mohareb and the Foe!
> Triumph! triumph! only she
> That knit his bonds can set him free'.   (p. 312)

A similar technique is employed for the curse in Southey's *The Curse of Kehama* (1810).

In 'Kubla Khan' a regular iambic framework is used to set off variants, and the entire poem is marked by alliteration and elaborate assonance that reaches back in subtlety to Milton. There is a sense of incantatory elevation throughout, and within the poem a movement of rising excitement that exceeds the gloomier precedents of Gray and Blake.

46

Much of the material in the first thirty-six lines of 'Kubla Khan' has been traced to Milton's Eden. Coleridge opened with the variation on a passage in Purchas, but between lines 131 and 268 of Book IV of *Paradise Lost* we find a walled garden, 'fertile ground', 'All Trees of noblest kind', an underground river, a fountain, rills, a waterfall, a steep glade, brooks running in 'mazy error', lawns, caves, and the 'crystal mirror' of a lake. Lines 280 to 281 add mention of Abassin kings and Mount Amara. The passage would, of course, have been entirely familiar to Coleridge's readers; they must have been struck by his conversion of Eden into a picturesque garden. If one compares the descriptions of Chinese gardens in Sir William Chambers's *A Dissertation on Oriental Gardening* (1772), for instance, the appeal of such scenery becomes more apparent. According to Chambers, 'Their scenes of terror are composed of gloomy woods, deep vallies inaccessible to the sun, impending barren rocks, dark caverns, and impetuous cataracts rushing down the mountains from all parts' (p. 36). By way of variation, 'sometimes, in this romantic excursion, the passenger finds himself in extensive recesses, surrounded with arbors of jessamine, vine and roses, where beauteous Tartarean damsels, in loose transparent robes, that flutter in the air, present him with rich wines . . .' (p. 40). Coleridge and his readers knew Chambers,[23] and we can expect them to share what by the 1790s had become conventional associations of sublime scenery with fear or awe, and beautiful scenery with reassuring pleasure. Coleridge's simile for the 'deep romantic chasm'—'A savage place! as holy and enchanted/As e'er beneath a waning moon was haunted/By woman wailing for her demon-lover' (11. 14–16)—seems so appropriate to the place that many readers have actually pictured her there. She provides a specific link, if one were needed, with the Gothic fantasies of the period.

The overall effect of the rhapsody, however, is that of a glimpse of a world that is more beautiful, more exciting, more portentous, than we shall ever experience. Mary Robinson allowed it to stimulate her imagination in her tribute 'To the Poet Coleridge' (1801):

> SPIRIT DIVINE! with THEE I'll trace
> Imagination's boundless space!
> With thee, beneath thy *sunny dome*,
>   I'll listen to the minstrel's lay,
>   Hymning the gradual close of day;
> In *Caves of Ice* enchanted roam,
> Where on the glitt'ring entrance plays
> The moon's-beam with its silv'ry rays;
>   Or, when glassy stream,
>   That thro' the deep dell flows,
>   Flashes the noon's hot beam;
>   The noon's hot beam, that midway shows
> Thy flaming Temple, studded o'er
> With all PERUVIA's lustrous store!
> There will I trace the circling bounds

> Of thy NEW PARADISE extended!
> And listen to the awful sounds,
> Of winds, and foamy torrents blended![24]

Mrs Robinson's vision of 'Kubla Khan' may not be ours, but she is a useful witness to the way in which the poem stimulated the imaginations of Coleridge's contemporaries to embroider its splendid abstractions.

One of the curious features of 'Kubla Khan' is that its scenery is so critically observed. To the precision of the 'twice five miles' and the orderly exposition of the gardens, must be added the expression of awe in the 'But oh!', and the elaborate similes for the chasm, the fountain, and the vaulting fragments. The appreciative summation of lines 35–6—'It was a miracle of rare device,/A sunny pleasure-dome with caves of ice!'—reveals an awareness of the paradox of the combination of sun and ice that is not typical of dreams. Throughout we are conscious of the presence of an unusual perceiver. When we are addressed in the first person in the second section of the poem, this impression is reinforced and we confer upon him a capacity for rapturous aesthetic response and creative frenzy. A man of feeling has been introduced into a picturesque paradise.

In the poetry of Keats we find the full range of romantic scenery being deployed before mortals who are tremblingly alive to the awe-inspiring splendour of their surroundings. In *Endymion* (1818) the influence of Leigh Hunt keeps the emphasis on descriptions of scenery rather than on reactions to it, but that phase is over by the time of 'Hyperion A Fragment' (1820). In 'The Fall of Hyperion—A Dream', left unfinished at Keats's death in 1821, a dreamer is introduced who finds himself in an Edenic scene and comes upon the remains of a banquet. He eats and drinks appreciatively, but the drink proves to be an opiate.

> Upon the grass I struggled hard against
> The domineering potion; but in vain:
> The cloudy swoon came on, and down I sunk . . . .　　　　(ll. 53–5)

Against his will he sleeps, and when he wakens he finds himself in an enormous building that is like an ancient cathedral. He sees treasures in profusion lying upon the floor:

> Turning from these with awe, once more I rais'd
> My eyes to fathom the space every way;
> The embossed roof, the silent massy range
> Of columns north and south, ending in mist
> Of nothing; then to Eastward, where black gates
> Were shut against the sunrise evermore.
> Then to the west I look'd, and saw far off
> An Image, huge of feature as a cloud,
> At level of whose feet an altar slept . . . .

> Towards the altar sober-pac'd I went,
> Repressing haste, as too unholy there . . . . (ll. 81–9, 93–4)

Keats is answering the question, 'what would it feel like to be in such a situation?', and by doing so he changes our awareness of the situation itself. A voice informs the dreamer that he must either ascend the altar steps before the incense leaves have burned down or die.

> I heard, I look'd: two senses both at once
> So fine, so subtle, felt the tyranny
> Of that fierce threat, and the hard task proposed.
> Prodigious seem'd the toil, the leaves were yet
> Burning,—when suddenly a palsied chill
> Struck from the paved level up my limbs,
> And was ascending quick to put cold grasp
> Upon those streams that pulse beside the throat:
> I shriek'd; and the sharp anguish of my shriek
> Stung my own ears—I strove hard to escape
> The numbness; strove to gain the lowest step.
> Slow, heavy, deadly was my pace: the cold
> Grew stifling, suffocating, at the heart;
> And when I clasp'd my hands I felt them not.
> One minute before death, my iced foot touch'd
> The lowest stair; and as it touch'd, life seem'd
> To pour in at the toes: I mounted up
> As once fair Angels on a ladder flew
> From the green turf to heaven. (ll. 118–36)

The veiled prophetess, Moneta, whose voice the dreamer has heard, is allowed to reveal in her turn feelings that we can understand:

> Then the tall shade, in drooping linens veil'd,
> Spake out, so much more earnest, that her breath
> Stirr'd the thin folds of gauze that drooping hung
> About a golden censer from her hand
> Pendent; and by her voice I knew she shed
> Long-treasured tears. (ll. 216–21)

Together they view the gigantic form of the sleeping Saturn and Thea's sad awakening of him. The poem breaks off at the beginning of Canto II with the arrival of the unfallen Hyperion, but we have already absorbed a treatment of the domain of gods and spirits that is absent in such great antecedents as Virgil, Dante and Milton. The supernatural of the vernacular has been united with the Classical tradition, and a world that never was has been made unforgettably a part of our experience.

49

3   The ambiguities of guilt

Hitherto we have been considering the outer limits of poetic manners, moving in Chapter 1 through various implications of simplicity to the development of fresh perceptions of ordinary experience, and then, in Chapter 2, observing renderings of abnormal experience, from the disturbing and uncanny to the idyllic. Some of the verse discussed in the course of this preliminary survey has been mediocre or even trivial, of interest to us now mainly as typical evidence of the literary environment from which good poems came. A sketch of fashionable poetic manners would be incomplete, however, without one more excursion into a kind of verse that is not much read at present.

In the Romantic period, narrative and dramatic poems fulfilled much the same function as novels do today. The idea of luxuriating in a long poem of an evening has come to seem improbable because when we think of long poems we have in mind ones that are difficult and demanding. But *Paradise Lost* is no more typical of the long poem than *Ulysses* is of the novel, and there are many narrative poems whose principal aim is to involve our feelings in the fascinating experiences of a hero or a heroine. The Romantic period was their heyday. From a critical point of view such poems are something of an embarrassment. They are generally too unpolished and relaxed to stand up well to close scrutiny; they are meant to be read quickly and to have an immediate effect. The fact that they were written in verse was not supposed to imply that they were more serious than they would have been if they had been written in prose, but rather that they would satisfy their readers in a slightly different way. Their prevailing emphasis on rhyme reflects a wish to please us rather than impress us; their recurrent experiments with short four-beat lines reveal the need to find a metre that could be written fluently. For the most part, the narrative poets were content to jog along smoothly, occasionally making a special effort to convey pathos, excitement or dignity as their plots required. They expected their work to be judged as fiction.

Such verse deserves a place in the history of poetry if only because some poems of enduring interest emerged from it and because for a while it provided a norm for long poems against which poets with serious aspirations had to struggle. Fifty years before, respectable publishers had regarded it as their duty to support literature by issuing a few long, serious poems, but, for the twenty years after Scott's success with *The Lay of the Last Minstrel* in 1805, this admirable if unreliable tradition was undermined by the assumption that they should be best-sellers. Byron alone mastered the required facility and survived to enjoy modern approval.

Byron's heroic villains are usually traced back to the vogue for Gothic novels in the 1790s. Typically these novels afford the reader a distressed heroine who is persecuted by an unprincipled and powerful man, a setting redolent of the supernatural, and a plot in which probability is sacrificed to suspense.[1] Modern interest has been concentrated on the persecutors and not their victims, largely because the victims, with their endless pious anxieties, their unfailing benevolence, their passivity and their convenient tendency to swoon in a crisis, are as insipid as they are silly. The Gothic novel set out to engage the sympathies of its readers, however; it differed from other novels in its emphasis on fear—the strongest emotion, according to the view that had been propounded by Edmund Burke's *Essay on the Sublime and Beautiful* in 1757—and it encouraged its readers to share vicariously in the sublime terrors experienced by that most frightenable of creatures, a young, unmarried lady.[2] The villain who frightened her was of secondary interest. In Ann Radcliffe's *The Mysteries of Udolpho* (1794), for instance, we are not given any reasons for the evil Montoni's wickedness, we never share his thoughts or look at the situation from his point of view, and when he dies we are told briefly and matter of factly of the event. Montoni is an occasion for the fears of the lovely Emily and little more.

Fear tends to be assessed in terms of its intensity rather than its quality, and there was, accordingly, a gradual escalation of villainy to satisfy appetites too jaded to relish commonplace forms.[3] Narrative verse with epic pretensions was not immune to the temptations of this easy road to sublimity. Kailyal, the heroine of Southey's ambitious Indian poem, *The Curse of Kehama* (1810), for example, is really a Gothic victim in disguise. Spared at the outset from being ravished by Arvalan, the wicked son of Kehama, she is forced to witness the sufferings of her aged father who for killing Arvalan in her defence is condemned to live eternally with a 'fire' in his brain and to be denied food, water, and sleep. Kehama is a more abstract villain than his Gothic predecessors—although at one point he does offer to rescind his curse if Kailyal will marry him, and then afflicts her with leprosy when she refuses—but he is endowed with correspondingly greater powers. In the religion of the Hindus, so Southey tells us, religious observances have a value independent of the moral state of the worshipper. Kehama, by the elaborateness of his devotions, gains a status that threatens the supremacy of the Gods themselves. Until the very end of the poem it seems possible and even likely that he will become God and that the innocent will no longer have any hope of redress. Kailyal experiences the whole catalogue of Gothic horrors—the repeated threats of a fate worse than death, one of which obliges her to set her bed on fire in an attempt at suicide, the nobler fear of what her father may suffer, the fear of being physically disfigured, and the loss of a virtuous lover—but what makes them more interesting than usual is the possibility that the whole world may at any moment be governed by the forces that inflict them.

We never sympathize with Kehama, and when he is overthrown at last in his

51

moment of triumph our attention passes on immediately to the happy apotheosis of Kailyal. Nevertheless, as the sinister and intelligent embodiment of an unfamiliar belief he is not wholly forgotten. Thomas Moore's Mokhanna, the villain of 'The Veiled Prophet of Khorassan', the first tale in *Lalla Rookh* (1817), lacks this redeeming feature. When he closes a long career of religious fraud and debauchery by poisoning his worshippers at a banquet and then, having mocked them in their dying agonies, plunges into a fiery well and is consumed, the poem seems merely extravagant.

Such careers totter on the brink of absurdity through sheer excessiveness. They are too inventively wicked to sink into lifeless predictability. They are too repulsive to be enjoyed complacently as fantasy, as Charles Lamb maintained that the milder peccadilloes of Restoration comedy should be.[4] We are inclined to pay them the compliment of keeping them at arm's length. Inevitably our interest palls and our sympathies return to their beleaguered victims. The last masterful incarnation of consistent evil in the period appears in Shelley's tragedy *The Cenci* (1820). Count Cenci is a foil to the moral destruction of his daughter Beatrice—the Cenci of the title—but Shelley, writing at the peak of his skill, endows him with a magnificent ferocity that makes him stand head and shoulders above his predecessors.

Count Cenci is self-conscious in his wickedness. He behaves as he believes we would all behave if we were not inhibited by scruples:

> —All men delight in sensual luxury,
> All men enjoy revenge; and most exult
> Over the tortures they can never feel—
> Flattering their secret peace with others' pain.
> But I delight in nothing else. (I, i, 77–81)

He obtains immunity for his crimes by paying fines to the Church.[5] He has the commanding presence required of the Gothic villain—he can quell a crowd of prelates and noblemen with a glance (I, iii, 95–8)—but he prefers to torment the weak and the defenceless. When two of his sons die suddenly by misadventure, he holds a banquet at which their passing is unexpectedly announced as good news—to the horror of the guests. We hear of his past mistreatment of his family—of his forcing Beatrice to look upon her little brother 'when the rust/Of heavy chains has gangrened his sweet limbs . . .' (II, i, 70–1), for instance—but during the action of the play his ambition is fixed upon the rape of his daughter, a crime that will surpass all that has gone before.

Even Cenci is struck with the enormity of his plan:

> 'Tis an awful thing
> To touch such mischief as I now conceive:
> So men sit shivering on the dewy bank,
> And try the chill stream with their feet; once in . . .
> How the delighted spirit pants for joy! (II, i, 124–8)

Incest and rape were the moral unmentionables of the Romantic period—the indirect allusions to them in *The Cenci* precluded performance of the play and endangered its publication. Count Cenci's intentions are made to seem even more wicked by the unblemished character and serious religious devotion of his daughter, and they are unpleasantly complicated by the fact that as an elderly man he no longer has any sexual appetite.[6] His first assault on Beatrice is achieved by revealing to her what he has in mind (II, i, 55–64); the second, in which he carries his threat into effect, leaves her for a time mentally unhinged (III, i, 1–76). Even then he has not done with her, and hopes to complete her ruin by making her a willing partner in his iniquity. Force might be sufficient to quell resistance, but Count Cenci seeks the ultimate refinement:

> Yet so to leave undone
> What I most seek! No, 'tis her stubborn will
> Which by its own consent shall stoop as low
> As that which drags it down.   (IV, i, 9–12)

Only his death two scenes later saves Beatrice from this further trial, and the monstrous figure of her father is allowed to recede from our consciousness, having fulfilled its function by providing an adequate incentive for an innocent young woman to turn to parricide. *The Cenci* is in the end a play about the victims of evil.[7]

As long as the villain was defined primarily as a source of terror for the victim his possibilities were severely limited. The alternative of making the villain the central character was already enshrined in the most popular tragedies and in the novel. Shakespeare's Richard III, Zanga in Young's *The Revenge*, combined with figures from the novel such as Richardson's Lovelace and Fielding's Jonathan Wild, easily encompass the range of immorality achieved by the Gothic villains. But because it was an age in which readers were expected to feel deeply it became exceptionally difficult for them to identify themselves with fictional cut-throats and seducers. Piling wickedness on wickedness was self-defeating. The alternative was to mute the deeds and to make their perpetrator sufficiently likeable for the reader to identify with him. Wordsworth's *The Borderers* (1797) and Coleridge's *Osorio* (1797),[8] plays that were influenced by the popular English translation of Schiller's *The Robbers*, show a clear awareness of the possibilities of examining the conscience of a thoroughly bad man, but both were rejected by the managers of the theatre. Whether by design, or, as seems more likely, because his incurably sunny disposition made it impossible for him to imagine a character who was deliberately cruel, it was Walter Scott who performed the experiment in attractive villainy that proved so popular as to be decisive.

In 1807 Scott was offered the unprecedented sum of a thousand guineas for a new poem, sight unseen. When *Marmion: a Tale of Flodden Field* appeared in 1808, 8,000 copies were sold in four months, and within four years 20,000 more, surpassing even the sales of *The Lay of the Last Minstrel*.[9] Like the *Lay*, *Marmion* was an adventure story set in the distant past, replete with antiquarian lore, supernatural events, chivalric derring-do and lovers' anxieties. It provided Scott's contemporaries with an absorbing form of escapism that was only to be outdone by his *Lady of the Lake* (1810)[10] before being translated, largely through his own exertions, into the ampler sphere of the historical novel. But *Marmion* is of interest here for features that distinguish it from Scott's other verse, features that were to be adopted and developed to a higher level of sophistication by other poets.

The story of *Marmion* is set in 1513 and describes Lord Marmion's attempt, as an English ambassador, to persuade James IV of Scotland not to declare war on England. The king's mind is already made up and Scotland's greatest military catastrophe, the Battle of Flodden, follows. This setting provides an occasion for a magnificent description of the prospect of Edinburgh surrounded by armed encampments (Canto IV) and for a concluding battle-scene that earned even Francis Jeffrey's praise.[11] Marmion, although his mission is unsuccessful, performs his part faithfully and impressively and his death at Flodden is as heroic as could be desired. From his first appearance, riding into Norham castle on his 'red roan charger', he is the commanding figure of the poem, still at the height of his unrivalled physical vigour and respected for his experience and skill in politics and strategy. He is generous to those of lower rank, considerate of his men, able to inspire an unquestioning loyalty in all who follow him. It is gradually revealed, however, that he has a guilty conscience. We learn that he has seduced a nun, Constance de Beverley, and that, having allowed her to follow him for three years disguised as a page, he has betrayed her to the Church. We learn further that his motives for abandoning her were greed—he wished to marry a reluctant heiress, Clare, for her lands—and impatience—Constance wearied him with her objections and even tried to have her rival poisoned. As if this were not enough, Marmion has forged documents to prove that Clare's favoured suitor, De Wilton, was a traitor and he has defeated De Wilton in a consequent trial by combat. De Wilton is believed to be dead, but reappears disguised as a holy palmer and by coincidence becomes Marmion's guide through the Lowlands; Clare, who has become a novice in a nunnery, is for a while entrusted to Marmion's perilous custody. In the end Clare and De Wilton, we are reassured, are happily married.

The unfortunate Constance is tried by the Church for breaking her vows and is condemned to death. The second canto is devoted to her dreadful fate. Much is made of her beauty and her stoical dignity is contrasted with the grovellings of a man who is condemned as her accomplice; but we are spared none of the prospect before her:

> Yet well the luckless wretch might shriek,
> Well might her paleness terror speak!
> For there were seen, in that dark wall,
> Two niches, narrow, deep, and tall;—
> Who enters at such griesly door,
> Shall ne'er, I ween, find exit more.
> In each a slender meal was laid,
> Of roots, of water, and of bread:
> By each, in Benedictine dress,

Two haggard monks stood motionless;
Who, holding high a blazing torch,
Shewed the grim entrance of the porch:
Reflecting back the smoky beam,
The dark-red walls and arches gleam.
Hewn stones and cement[12] were displayed
And building tools in order laid.   (II, xxiii)

The revulsion we feel at discovering that Constance is to be buried alive—a revulsion that our own imaginations are allowed to complete, for Scott does not show us the burial itself[13]—remains with us throughout the rest of the poem and colours our feelings about Marmion even though he does not hear of Constance's death himself until he is dying.

Marmion's crimes are relatively petty and he is never observed to profit from them. We are given no details of his original seduction of Constance. He remembers her affectionately and regretfully after listening to one of the songs she used to sing. His last thoughts, before he hears that she is dead, are of the need to 'redress her woes' (VI, xxxii) and then, although he is in his death throes, he is immediately but impotently afire to avenge her. One could argue that his weakness here was a lawless spontaneity. There is no suggestion that he would have connived at more than Constance's confinement; he is never told how she died. Of the wrongs he has done De Wilton, slander backed by forgery and superior prowess in arms, it is the forgery that seems more repellent, not because it is the more serious,[14] but because it implies a devious meanness that is out of keeping with Marmion's bold and impetuous spirit. Scott admitted as much years later when he said that forgery was 'the crime of a commercial, rather than a proud and warlike age'.[15] Marmion's actual weaknesses are insufficient to make him a thoroughgoing villain and they are unrelated to his character as we know it; as Byron put it, he is 'Not quite a Felon, yet but half a Knight'.[16] At the same time he is associated in our minds with the entombment of Constance, an act of monstrous and cold-blooded cruelty for which he is indirectly though partly and unwittingly responsible, and this association is a substitute of sorts for the terrible crimes that disfigure the characters of previous heroic villains. In trying to eat his cake and have it too, Scott fails to create either a satisfactory hero or a satisfactory villain, but he does manage to involve the reader in the experience of sharing a guilty conscience by engaging him first in an innocent empathy with the public Marmion.

Marmion is not only an adventure story and an analysis of individual conscience, it is a poem with explicit political and social connotations. Each canto is introduced by a verse epistle to one of Scott's friends, and the first epistle lamented the recent deaths of Nelson and of those two great political opponents, William Pitt the younger and Charles James Fox. The tribute to Fox was condemned by suspicious Whigs as inadequate and insincere, but Scott's intention seems to have been to exhort the nation as a whole to rise above party politics and live up to the ideals set by the great men of the past. His introductory epistles interest us in a

55

series of gloomy parallels: age looks back on youth, winter looks back on spring, bleak landscapes recall the luxuriant forests of the past, the ups and downs of human fate are reflected upon. The past, it seems, must be admired and regretted; it cannot be reclaimed. Mixed with such elegiac sentiments are hints that something different and worthwhile may be achieved for the future. An analogy is found in the adoption of Scottish matter for a poem rather than Classical matter, the use of a 'measure wild' rather than one of the old, established metres, and in the choice of a fairy tale rather than 'the lofty strain'. In the Introduction to Canto V, modern Edinburgh is contrasted with the ancient Dun-Edin so glowingly rendered in Canto IV and the moral superiority of the present is asserted:

> So thou, fair City! disarrayed
> Of battled wall, and rampart's aid,
> As stately seem'st, but lovelier far
> Than in that panoply of war.
> Nor deem that from thy fenceless throne
> Strength and security are flown;
> Still, as of yore, Queen of the North!
> Still canst thou send thy children forth.

The optimism and patriotic enthusiasm are unmistakable. Some critics have maintained that the introductory epistles interrupt the narrative flow of *Marmion*, and some editors of the poem silently omit them, but by removing them one removes a dimension that is necessary if we are to understand Scott's protagonist. Marmion vies with other heroic literary villains or flawed literary heroes without being equal to the best of them; but in the minor quality of his sins, the unexpected and disproportionate results of them, and in his clear sense of the high moral road that honour requires of him, he provides a model for every man in an age that has temporarily lost confidence in itself. Scott did not perfect *Marmion* and the social context of his poem has been neglected, but by mingling heroism and guilt and making both of them seem alive to his contemporaries he poured new life into an old convention.

In subsequent poems Scott kept his villains and his heroes apart, although there is something of Marmion in the formidable Roderick Dhu of *The Lady of the Lake*. It was left to the successor to Scott's position as the most popular poet in Britain to develop the noble villain in a slightly different direction. Byron's *The Corsair* (1814) surpassed even Scott's prodigious sales; 10,000 copies were sold on the day of publication.[17] Conrad the corsair resembles the heroes of Byron's earlier oriental tales—Selim in *The Bride of Abydos* (1813) in his faithfulness in love and his reckless opposition to tyranny, and the nameless hero of *The Giaour* (1813) in his misanthropical rancour at an unforgivable wrong. However, we are told as well that Conrad is a villain:

> Feared—shunned—belied—ere youth had lost her force,
> He hated Man too much to feel remorse,
> And thought the voice of Wrath a sacred call,

To pay the injuries of some on all.
He knew himself a villain—but he deemed
The rest no better than the thing he seemed;
And scorned the best as hypocrites who hid
Those deeds the bolder spirit plainly did.   (11. 261–8)

The characterization closely follows that of Schiller's Carl von Moor in *The Robbers*. Conrad is abstemious and aloof, subject to recurrent longings for his lost innocence and inflexibly committed to the pirates' rough code of honour. To this isolated figure, Byron has added Medora, the misanthropist's Lucasta—'I cease to love thee when I love Mankind . . .' (1. 405)—a woman for him to be faithful to. Conrad's mastery or commanding genius is 'The power of Thought—the magic of the Mind!' (1. 182); his men follow him unquestioningly and devotedly.

The action of the poem centres on Conrad's desperate pre-emptive attack on the threatening galleys of the Pacha Seyd. The attack fails, after a fierce struggle against overwhelming numbers, largely because Conrad chivalrously insists on rescuing the inmates of a burning harem. While the imprisoned Conrad awaits public impalement, Gulnare, the grateful queen of the harem, offers to help him escape. When he refuses the opportunity to stab the sleeping Seyd, Gulnare kills the pacha herself. Conrad regrets having been the occasion of her crime, 'Gulnare, the Homicide!' (1. 1631), but he comforts her in spite of his disapproval. On his return home he finds Medora dead and sails away alone, never to be seen or heard of again. One might sum up Conrad's career as one of private virtue and public vice. His actions throughout the poem, like Marmion's, are admirable, and by leaving his wicked past obscure Byron spares us from having to associate the character we admire with deeds we despise. In *Lara* (1814) and *The Siege of Corinth* (1816), Byron repeats this device of an undefined evil past, but in these poems the principals lack Conrad's appealing innocence and concern for others and bear a closer resemblance to the old Gothic villain.

Southey's narrative poems have never been popular. In his own time, however, he was a literary presence to be reckoned with; Shelley borrowed from him respectfully and even Byron admitted that he had '*passages* equal to any thing'.[18] One of Southey's chief faults was his failure to invent characters who were genuinely interesting. His heroes are so unbelievably and unrelievedly good and his villains so impossibly bad that they do not surprise us and are therefore boring. Unsatisfied by his characters, we are inclined to attend instead to his exotic settings, but even these, clever and well informed though they are, pall for want of human interest. His *Roderick, the Last of the Goths: a Tragic Poem* (1814) differs from the rest—from *Thalaba, the Destroyer* (1801), *Madoc* (1805) and *The Curse of Kehama*—in having as its protagonist a man of heroic mould whose personal immorality has caused the overthrow of his country. In Roderick, for the first time, Southey attempts a character of some complexity and places him in an antiquarian setting worthy of Scott.[19] Byron unexpectedly singled the poem out: 'I think Southey's Roderick as near perfection as poetry can be—which considering how I dislike that school I wonder at . . .'.[20]

In *Roderick*, Southey tries to solve the problem of evoking a healthy enthusiasm for a person who has sinned and finds a solution that carries him well beyond the efforts of Scott and the early Byron. Roderick is as dominant a figure as Marmion or Conrad or Lara, and yet we know exactly what his crime has been and we are expected to condemn it. We know the worst at the outset instead of learning it gradually as in *Marmion*, but Roderick himself condemns what he has done even more harshly than we do. His entire career thereafter is devoted to making amends, and in the course of doing so exhibits a consistent heroism that is moral as well as physical.

Roderick has violated the woman he loves, and the memory of his deed haunts him:

> worse than Hell . .
> Yea to his eyes more dreadful than the fiends
> Who flock'd like hungry ravens round his head, . .
> Florinda stood between, and warn'd him off
> With her abhorrent hands, . . that agony
> Still in her face, which, when the deed was done,
> Inflicted on her ravisher the curse
> That it invoked from Heaven . . . . (Vol. 9, p. 5)

The offence is briefly told, but it is complicated by Roderick's circumstances. He is king of Spain; he is married to a queen; Count Julian, the father of Florinda, is one of the most powerful of his countrymen; and Christian Spain is threatened by Moslem invasion from Africa. On a personal level Roderick's remorse is adequate to the private wrong he has inflicted, but when Count Julian indignantly defects to the Moors and Spain is conquered and brutally forced to convert to Moham-medanism, the unanticipated public wrong seems to be beyond what an individual might be expected to redress. The disparity between consequences and intention here is anticipated in *Marmion*, but, while the intention here is worse, the fact that the consequences are national rather than personal makes it possible for Roderick to do something about them. Nations do not fall, of course, because of one man's momentary lapse, and as the story unfolds we learn of other contributing causes: the queen's bad character, the disloyalty of powerful factions in Spain, and even Florinda's awareness of having half tempted Roderick to forget himself. These revelations make us think more tolerantly of him than he does, but at the outset we find him in the depths of misfortune and disgrace, fleeing 'like a thief in darkness from the field' (p. 4). He has experienced defeat in battle for the first time, and is haunted by the memory of his own wickedness; as he flees he becomes aware of the dimensions of his catastrophe:

> leaving their defenceless homes to seek
> What shelter walls and battlements might yield,
> Old men with feeble feet, and tottering babes,
> And widows with their infants in their arms,

Hurried along. Nor royal festival,
Nor sacred pageant, with like multitudes
E'er fill'd the public way. All whom the sword
Had spared were here; bed-rid infirmity
Alone was left behind; the cripple plied
His crutches, with her child of yesterday
The mother fled, and she whose hour was come
Fell by the road.   (pp. 5–6)

Roderick, appalled, is 'unable to endure/This burthen of the general woe . . .' (p. 6).

He finds refuge eventually in a deserted hermitage in company with an aged monk. When the monk dies, he buries him beside the grave of the departed hermit, and then, at his lowest point in the poem, digs his own grave at their feet and realizes that there will be no one to bury him in turn. He is tempted momentarily to commit suicide, but, saved by his 'better mind', prays by the monk's grave for some active form of expiation.

Guided by a vision of his mother, he concludes that it is his duty to free Spain from its Moslem conquerors but to do so without reinstating himself as king or clearing his name from infamy. His career henceforth is to be devoted to setting right the public disaster which his sin has unintentionally precipitated, and it is to be anonymous. Uncertain as to how to proceed in his staggering task, Roderick visits the ruins of Auria, a city that has resisted a Moslem siege by fighting street by street until every citizen is dead. There he meets Adosinda,[21] whose parents, husband and children have all been massacred, and who has survived by killing as he slept the Moslem who set her aside as a concubine. Adosinda personifies the vengeful spirit of a conquered people; Roderick vows to serve her cause and she renames him Maccabee.[22] Soon after, he is ordained as a priest. The fortunes of Spain improve steadily, slowly at first as Roderick enlists Prince Pelayo as the rightful heir to the throne and pockets of resistance are organized in the mountains, but with a gathering speed that comes to a climax in Cantos XXIII to XXV in a battle sequence that outdoes the one in *Marmion*. If there is a fault in the unfolding of Southey's plot, it is that virtue is too punctiliously rewarded, and that although from time to time concern is expressed about, say, the fate of Pelayo's wife and children, or about the effect of the proposed assassination of the traitor, Count Julian, events turn out to be consistently in favour of Roderick and Spain from the moment he re-engages in the struggle.

The transparency of such a national success story matters less than it would if Roderick's own success were identified with the outcome; as it is, however, the success of Spain and of Pelayo provides a series of moral temptations to Roderick that test the depth and integrity of his remorse. The first challenge to his resolution occurs early in the poem when he meets Severian, a faithful family retainer, and resists the urge to escape from his spiritual isolation by revealing his identity. He is tested again when he forces himself to pay homage to Pelayo (pp. 42–3). He is intensely embarrassed in his priestly disguise when Florinda confesses to him (pp. 90–100) and later, when he is obliged to debate the merits of Christianity with the infidel Count Julian (pp. 192–203), but in each case his consistency of purpose sustains him. His most serious trials occur when he is obliged to conceal his identity from his mother and when Pelayo and Severian recognize at last that he is Roderick and express their willingness to see him restored to power. The unbearable strain of the interview with his mother is expressed afterwards in his Odyssean reunion with his dog:

> The watchful dog
> Follow'd his footsteps close. But he retired
> Into the thickest grove; there yielding way
> To his o'erburthen'd nature, from all eyes
> Apart, he cast himself upon the ground,
> And threw his arms around the dog, and cried,
> While tears stream'd down, Thou, Theron, then hast known
> Thy poor lost master, . . Theron, none but thou! (p. 140)

The temptation to profit by his success is expiated in his participation in the crowning of Pelayo. Southey is not inhuman in the fate to which he condemns Roderick. Before the end of the poem he is allowed a private reunion with his mother; he converts the dying Count Julian and is reconciled with him, and he is embraced by Florinda as she dies a moment later. And he has the satisfaction of riding his old warhorse into battle against the Moors once more and uttering his warcry, 'Roderick the Goth! Roderick and Victory!/Roderick and Vengeance!', as he passes through the enemy ranks like an avenging angel. We recognize that such private reliefs are his due; at the public level he remains true to his resolve, and after the final victory his horse and armour are found upon the battlefield as they had been after the defeat at the beginning. Centuries later his 'humble tomb' is discovered in a hermitage.

The reconciliation of sinner and hero in *Roderick* is something of a *tour de force*. Southey has avoided the meanness of Marmion and the social vacuum of Byron's early heroes, and if Roderick's rise from the depths is too steady to engender suspense it has a compelling momentum. The more complex moral possibilities remain untouched. We are not asked to question the rightness of Roderick's rebellion, although it costs thousands of Moslem and Christian lives, even if we are allowed a little doubt about his obligations to an unworthy wife. It was left to Byron to explore these issues in a series of tragedies during his last years. Taking up once again the troubled heroes who had first made him famous, he concentrated upon their consciences rather than their actions and moods.[23] By subjecting accepted codes of social behaviour to a scrutiny that exposed them as an inconsistent mixture of ethical principles, social prejudice and unthinking habit, he tried to undermine the confidence of his contemporaries' moral and political assumptions.

In *Sardanapalus* (1821), Byron examines the character of a king who glories in the motto 'Eat, drink, and love; the rest's not worth a fillip' (I, ii, 252). In a private individual, in Byron's own Don Juan for instance, this hedonistic repudiation of duty and ambition might be harmless, but Sardanapalus is the ruler of a vast empire and his subjects expect more of him than self-indulgence. Instead of distinguishing between Sardanapalus's private life and his public life, Byron develops the reader's awareness of the contradictions between the kind of government that lets subjects live peacefully and contentedly and popular presuppositions about the moral character of successful governors. He allows a parallel to develop between the self-denial of the individual—which he sees as the tyrannical repression of natural desires—and despotic treatment of other people, and by relying upon our disapproval of the latter encourages us to question the values of the former. He makes the upholders of public morality seem less moral than the immoral king they oppose.

The stage direction for Sardanapalus's entrance associates him with such fallen heroes as Achilles, Hercules, and Shakespeare's Mark Antony: 'Enter Sardanapalus effeminately dressed, his Head crowned with Flowers, and his Robe negligently flowing, attended by a Train of Women and young Slaves' (I, ii). Unlike his great predecessors, this 'she-king' has no warlike deeds to look back on and few regrets, but his loyal brother-in-law, Salamenes, the disapproving Enobarbus of the play, perceives his heroic qualities:

> In his effeminate heart
> There is a careless courage which Corruption
> Has not all quenched, and latent energies,
> Repressed by circumstance, but not destroyed—
> Steeped, but not drowned, in deep voluptuousness.
> If born a peasant, he had been a man
> To have reached an empire . . . .   (I, i, 9–15)

This accolade, coming from an experienced general whose sense of public duty is so strong as to make him stifle private resentment at Sardanapalus's adulterous neglect of his sister, helps us to accept from the beginning that the king's misbehaviour is the consequence of choice and not of incapacity. His courage is exhibited before the play ends, and the final suicide, in which he is joined voluntarily on a funeral pyre by his faithful slave and concubine, Myrrha, is proudly heroic.

Sardanapalus's fall, like Roderick's, stems from his adultery. But Byron's hero lacks the excuse of an unsympathetic and vicious wife and his unwavering attachment to Myrrha is devoid of self-reproach. He does regret having injured his wife, however, and in a parting speech slips for a moment into conventionality:

> She loved me, and I loved her.—Fatal passion!
> Why dost thou not expire at *once* in hearts
> Which thou hast lighted up at once? Zarina!
> I must pay dearly for the desolation
> Now brought upon thee. Had I never loved
> But thee, I should have been an unopposed

61

> Monarch of honouring nations. To what gulfs
> A single deviation from the track
> Of human duties leads even those who claim
> The homage of mankind as their born due . . . .   (IV, i, 429–38)

The action of the play is restricted to the twenty-four hours that elapse between Salamenes' warning that rebellion is about to break out and the actual overthrow of the monarchy. Sardanapalus has the ringleaders in his power but forgives them and lets them go. He is as magnanimous as he is gentle.[24] He makes no pretence to be what he is not, condemning the hypocritical pieties of priests and expecting neither the gods nor the stars to be interested in his affairs. He is undeviatingly honest and he is disappointed to find that his subjects are not.

His chief opponents are the veteran soldier Arbaces and the hypocritical soothsayer Beleses. When Sardanapalus spares them, Arbaces is abashed by this generosity and is only induced to resume his rebellion by being persuaded, falsely, that Sardanapalus is plotting against him after all. Salamenes is unsparing in his disapproval of the king's marital infidelity, wanton behaviour and capriciousness, but he remains faithful until he is mortally wounded. Sardanapalus's wife and mistress are both loyal to him. Only Beleses is unreservedly hostile, and he is made out to be an unprincipled and canting rascal. The esteem in which Sardanapalus is held in spite of his violation of certain moral conventions makes the violation seem less important. The king's crucial mistake, as it turns out, is his quixotic insistence on refusing to break his word when it would be practical to do so (II, i, 470–515). Immoral or not, he is seen to be more 'honourable' than the sober Salamenes, and his honesty, generosity and kindness contrast strangely with the devious, self-seeking pretences of the rebels. By mixing together in one man characteristics that are usually attributed separately to either heroes or villains, Byron confuses us and makes us think about the characteristics. He creates a likeable protagonist, surrounds him with unappetizing opponents and strait-laced critics and then has him act as resolutely in adversity as Shakespeare's Macbeth or Richard III, without giving him their careers of serious crime to atone for. We are bound to sympathize with him, in spite of his hedonism.

An absolute monarchy has little political reality for the modern reader. A kingdom is required for Sardanapalus so that public duty may be observed impinging upon private pleasure and so that, when he falls, his fall may be seen to have more than personal significance. As king he, in a sense, personifies the state. But it is not a state like the states of Europe in the early nineteenth century; it has no pretensions to justice, freedom and equality, let alone aspirations to democracy. Byron was living in Venice at the time, and he found materials for a more political treatment of the morality of rulers in the history of the Venetian Republic. In *The Two Foscari* (1821) and *Marino Faliero, Doge of Venice* (1820) he introduced further moral complications.[25] Whereas in *Sardanapalus*, private immorality was contrasted with what purported to be public morality, in these 'historical tragedies' private morality was placed in conflict with public morality in a way that made public duty and virtue seem to be at odds with one another.

In *The Two Foscari*, Byron considers the morality of patriotism. He does not condemn it as the last refuge of a scoundrel, but by offering us extreme examples of it he makes us aware that selfless loyalty to the state is a public virtue only if the state deserves the support of its citizens. Francis Foscari, the Doge of Venice, is titular head of state, but he is responsible to an all-powerful oligarchy, the Council of Ten. Foscari has been in office for thirty-five years and he is now in his eighties. His claim that Venice has prospered during his reign—'I found her Queen of Ocean, and I leave her/Lady of Lombardy . . .' (II, i, 17–18) is assented to. He has been effective and incorruptible. As might be expected, he has had political opponents, and he is wrongly suspected of having had two of them, the father and the uncle of the patrician Loredano, poisoned surreptitiously. Loredano, who becomes a member of the Council of Ten, sets out to destroy the Foscari family by legal means, manipulating the weaknesses of the constitution in the interests of private revenge. Ironically, the patriotism of the Foscari plays into his hands.

Jacopo Foscari, the son, has been falsely accused of murder and because he has withstood trial by torture he has been exiled for life rather than executed. He is separated from his wife and children, but worse than that he has been separated from Venice. He is a sentimental patriot, passionately rather than rationally loyal. In exile he contrives to have himself brought back to Venice to be tried for other crimes of which he is equally innocent, knowing that he will be tortured once more. When the play opens there is a pause in the torture of Jacopo on the rack. One of the members of the presiding Council of Ten remarks to Loredano that 'the poor wretch has suffered beyond Nature's/Most stoical endurance' (I, i, 12–13). Loredano reveals his own implacable hatred, and at the same time we learn that Jacopo's father is obliged as Doge to be present with the Council during the torture of his son. The situation is ingeniously contrived to test the patriotism of the Foscari. We are told that the father, 'With more than Roman fortitude, is ever/First at the board in this unhappy process/Against his last and only son' (I, i, 24–6). A touching reunion at the end of the play reveals how deeply he has felt the experience—'My boy!/Couldst thou but know . . .' (III, i, 342–3)—and yet he is unshaken in his loyalty to the idea of Venice:

> Had I as many sons
> As I have years, I would have given them all,
> Not without feeling, but I would have given them
> To the State's service, to fulfil her wishes,
> On the flood, in the field, or, if it must be,
> As it, alas! has been, to ostracism,
> Exile, or chains, or whatsoever worse
> She might decree.
>
> (II, i, 420–7)

With the torture about to resume, Jacopo is equally firm. When his sympathetic guard asks how he can love the soil that hates him, he replies:

> The soil!—Oh no, it is the seed of the soil
> Which persecutes me: but my native earth

Will take me as a mother to her arms.
I ask no more than a Venetian grave,
A dungeon, what they will, so it be here.   (I, i, 141–5)

Between them, father and son combine the main motives for patriotism. They are heroic in their mastery of mental and physical pain, in their self-sacrifice, and in their unswerving consistency, but our admiration of them is tempered by scepticism and by the conviction that their heroism is being wasted.

The pragmatism of Jacopo's wife, Marina, is placed in opposition to the abstract idealism of the Foscari. By anticipating our scepticism she dissipates it. In her desperation she accuses the Doge of being an unfeeling father—'And this is Patriotism?/To me it seems the worst barbarity' (II, i, 427–8)—and her husband of indifference to her when he longs for death rather than exile (IV, i, 135). Her recognition on each occasion of the injustice of her accusations confirms the genuineness of the Foscari. But her expressions of empirical common sense, informed by instinctive feelings and free of patriotic theory, are closely related to the realities of the world she lives in. The self-sacrifice of the Foscari is thrown away. Jacopo dies as he is waiting to be taken into exile; his father dies as he is being deposed a few hours later; the misguidedly vindictive Loredano is left to triumph in his revenge. The state has proved to be unworthy of its patriots. We are left to ask whether the patriotism of the Foscari is not as culpably blind as it is ineffectual.

In *Marino Faliero* the subject is treachery. Faliero's situation resembles that of the elder Foscari in some respects. He is an old man with an unblemished and distinguished career behind him: as Doge he is more a figure-head than a ruling monarch; the Council of Ten is similarly corrupt; and the Doge is vulnerable in the person of his beautiful young wife, Angiolina, as the elder Foscari had been in the person of his son. There are two crucial differences, however. One is that the Council of Ten is identified as a patrician oligarchy that tyrannizes over the plebeians; the other is that Faliero himself is no cautious stoic, but an imperious and passionate man to whom personal honour is everything.

The action of the play is precipitated by a young patrician's joking about the disparity of age between Faliero and Angiolina by scrawling on the Doge's throne a lampoon about Angiolina's inconstancy. When the Council of Ten sentences the offender to house arrest for a month, Faliero, who has been expecting a sentence of death, regards the sentence as an affront to himself and to his office and is outraged. His obligation as Doge to uphold the law forbids him the conventional Venetian redress of assassination and he is led to look critically at the institution of the Council itself. From this moment on he thinks of himself as having an obligation to the people of Venice rather than to their rulers:

Could I not shatter the Briarean sceptre
Which in this hundred-handed Senate rules,
Making the people nothing, and the Prince
A pageant? . . .

> Oh! but for even a day
> Of my full youth, while yet my body served
> My soul as serves the generous steed his lord,
> I would have dashed amongst them, asking few
> In aid to overthrow these swoln patricians . . . .   (I, ii, 268–71, 274–8)

Having this democratic sympathy arise from a personal grievance makes Faliero less estimable than he might be, but Byron seems to be intent upon the conflict of feelings that ensues rather than upon the cause of them. Faliero soon finds willing conspirators, and it is only when he is placed at the head of a plebeian uprising that he becomes aware of the conflict between this enterprise and his own political habits and social prejudices. When one of the conspirators asks him whether his doubts are dispelled, he replies:

> Not so—but I have set my little left
> Of life upon this cast: the die was thrown
> When I first listened to your treason.—Start not!
> *That* is the word; I cannot shape my tongue
> To syllable black deeds into smooth names,
> Though I be wrought on to commit them.   (III, i, 54–9)

Faliero is painfully aware that he is betraying his patrician ancestry (III, i, 94–102) and as an honourable soldier he is repelled by the need to act by stealth (III, i, 105–17). In his rebellion he has repudiated family pride and loyalty to the state and yet the motives for his rebellion are family pride and loyalty to the state. The confusion of his conscience is complete. When the rebellion fails, self-questioning is forgotten. Faced with the certainty of death and knowing that he has been defeated, Faliero prophesies the fall of Venice and achieves the moral majesty that he has hitherto lacked.

In the preface to *Marino Faliero*, Byron mentions a handful of modern works as being 'full of the best "*matériel*" for tragedy that has been seen since Horace Walpole . . .'.[26] In going back to Walpole as a touchstone he was thinking of *The Mysterious Mother* (1768), a Gothic tragedy famous for the shattering disclosures of its final scene in which the newly-wed hero learns that, owing to an incestuous trick played upon him by his mother in his youth, his bride is also his sister and daughter. Byron seems to have valued the dramatic possibilities of such sudden, horrifying realizations. One of the works he mentions is Henry Hart Milman's very recent dramatic poem, *The Fall of Jerusalem* (1820), which contains a situation of similar potentialities that must have been of special interest to an author who was experimenting with varieties of moral perplexity.[27] Milman's protagonist is Simon the Assassin, military commander of Jerusalem at the time of Titus's siege. Simon, as his nickname suggests, is not a man of moral delicacy, but he differs from a Cenci or a Kehama in believing that so long as his many crimes are committed in Israel's cause, and as long as he observes the ceremonies required by Judaism, God will be with him. At the end, with the walls of Jerusalem breached, the Gentiles in the streets, the Temple itself in flames, and Simon standing unarmed in the midst waiting for judgment to strike, he realizes suddenly that God has deserted him. At this finely achieved moment Milman avoids the searing moral crisis for which he has paved the way and settles instead for the defiant rant of a man who is heroic only in his pride:

> We are then of thee
> Abandon'd—not abandon'd of ourselves.
> Heap woes upon us, scatter us abroad,
> Earth's scorn and hissing; to the race of men
> A loathsome proverb; spurn'd by every foot,
> And curs'd by every tongue; our heritage
> And birthright bondage; and our very brows
> Bearing, like Cain's, the outcast mark of hate .... (p. 152)

The reaction is not worthy of the situation, and Milman's flat characterization does not provide a satisfactory alternative focus of interest. In *Werner* (1822), Byron exploits the device that Milman squanders and uses it to bring moral weakness and virtue as closely into conjunction as seems possible while maintaining the distinction between them.

The central character of Byron's poem is Count Siegendorf. When we first see him he is penniless, and he is avoiding the persecution of an unscrupulous and powerful kinsman by living under the assumed name of Werner. We learn that he was once heir to a great estate, that his father disinherited him because he married honourably but imprudently for love, and that his own son Ulric's inheritance was only secured on condition that he should be brought up by his grandfather. When the play begins the grandfather has died, Ulric has disappeared, and the kinsman, Stralenheim, is about to intercept the inheritance. Fortune has frowned on Siegendorf. His loyal wife accompanies him and he has the satisfaction of a clear conscience, but he chafes at the injustices of poverty and loss of social status. On his way to attempt to reclaim his estates he falls ill and is obliged to put up at a decayed palace. On a tempestuous night the dreaded Stralenheim is rescued from a flooded river nearby and brought to the palace. He is also on his way to claim Siegendorf's estates, and although he is not sure of Werner's true identity he is suspicious. Stralenheim is rescued by two young men, one of whom turns out to be Siegendorf's missing son, the other a Hungarian adventurer.

Siegendorf quite rightly fears Stralenheim, and he takes refuge in a secret passage that leads him unexpectedly to the room where Stralenheim is sleeping. Armed, and with his enemy helpless before him, Siegendorf stifles the temptation to murder him in his sleep, but temporarily overcome by just resentment he appropriates to himself one of several bags of gold lying on the table as a means of escaping from the palace. This unreflecting lapse from his customary honesty is the fateful act that destroys him in the end. He tries to explain the temptation to his son afterwards:

                    —Wait!—
Wait till, like me, your hopes are blighted till
Sorrow and Shame are handmaids of your cabin—
Famine and Poverty your guests at table;
Despair your bed-fellow—then rise, but not
From sleep, and judge! Should that day e'er arrive—
Should you see then the Serpent, who hath coiled
Himself around all that is dear and noble
Of you and yours, lie slumbering in your path,
With but *his* folds between *your* steps and happiness,
When *he*, who lives but to tear from you name,
Lands, life itself, lies at your mercy, with
Chance your conductor—midnight for your mantle—
The bare knife in your hand, and earth asleep,
Even to your deadliest foe; and he as 'twere
Inviting death, by looking like it, while
His death alone can save you:—Thank your God!
If then, like me, content with petty plunder,
You turn aside . . . .   (II, ii, 105–23)

But Werner's sense of honour is unforgiving. As he waits for the carriage that is to
bear him to safety, he bitterly repents:

                    for the last time I
Look on these horrible walls. Oh! never, never
Shall I forget them. Here I came most poor,
But not dishonoured: and I leave them with
A stain,—if not upon my name, yet in
My heart!—a never-dying canker-worm,
Which all the coming splendour of the lands,
And rights, and sovereignty of Siegendorf
Can scarcely lull a moment.   (III, iv, 6–14)

Long after, he gives the offending bag of gold, still unused, to the church, so that
prayers may be said for Stralenheim's soul. This moral crisis is temporarily
overshadowed by an event that secures Werner's safety and inheritance. The
following night, some unknown person does kill the sleeping Stralenheim. The
Hungarian disappears and is blamed for the murder. The Siegendorfs, father and
son, resume their rank and their estates, and Count Siegendorf makes some
amends to his unappeasable conscience by adopting Stralenheim's orphan
daughter and betrothing her to Ulric.
   The other weakness in Siegendorf's position is his ignorance of his son's true
nature. From the age of eight to the age of twenty the boy has been in his
grandfather's care. When he is reunited with his parents, his father is overjoyed:

                                                              67

> Come!
> Come to my arms again! Why, thou look'st all
> I should have been, and was not. Josephine!
> Sure 'tis no father's fondness dazzles me;
> But, had I seen that form amid ten thousand
> Youth of the choicest, my heart would have chosen
> This for my son! (II, ii, 24–30)

The young man is as confident and decisive as he is handsome, and it is remarked upon more than once that he would have made a fine soldier if only the wars were not over. Siegendorf assumes that Ulric's honesty is the equal of his own, and that it is unblemished. When the Hungarian reappears a year later and accuses Ulric not only of being a leader of brigands but the murderer of Stralenheim, Siegendorf is by turns indignant, incredulous, and finally appalled. But when he reproaches Ulric, calling him 'monster', Ulric claims that he only acted on Siegendorf's advice and for his sake. Reminding his father of his earlier apology for theft, he unrepentantly belittles the distance between crime committed and crime contemplated in a way that rounds upon the conscience of anyone who has ever been tempted to do wrong:

> —If *you* condemn me, yet,
> Remember *who* hath taught me once too often
> To listen to him! *Who* proclaimed to me
> That *there were crimes* made venial by the occasion?
> That passion was our nature? that the goods
> Of Heaven waited on the goods of fortune?
> *Who* showed me his humanity secured
> By his *nerves* only? *Who* deprived me of
> All power to vindicate myself and race
> In open day? By his disgrace which stamped
> (It might be) bastardy on me, and on
> Himself—a *felon's* brand! The man who is
> At once both warm and weak invites to deeds
> He longs to do, but dare not. Is it strange
> That I should *act* what you could *think*? (V, i, 439–53)

This diabolical speech plays upon each facet of Siegendorf's own sense of inadequacy, and by assigning to him the chief responsibility for deeds that he regards as abhorrent, deprives him at a stroke of the pretensions to honour that have been his sole resource in life. Byron might have had Siegendorf, deprived of his *raison d'être*, throw in his lot with the criminal suggestion of his son—'We have done/With right and wrong; and now must only ponder/Upon effects, not causes' (V, i, 453–5)—escaping from his embarrassment like Milman's Simon by repudiating its source. Or he might have let him sink weakly into a sublime despair. Instead he has him turn unheroically but practically and selflessly to the predicament of the man who revealed Ulric's crime:

Am I awake? are these my father's halls?
And *you*—my son? *My* son! *mine*! who have ever
Abhorred both mystery and blood, and yet
Am plunged into the deepest hell of both!
I must be speedy, or more will be shed—
The Hungarian's! (V, i, 479–84)

This instinctive reassertion of the common bonds of humanity has little to do with Siegendorf's aristocratic origin or with the grandiose gestures of a tragic protagonist, but it removes any doubts we may have had about the essential goodness of the man. Moral turpitude at this level is convincing, bearable and worth thinking about.

4 The human predicament

As the guilt of the protagonist fades from our recollection and we become absorbed in his disproportionate sufferings, it is difficult not to think of him as a victim of circumstances. The closer his situation is brought to our own, the easier it is to sympathize with him. If his distant crime or sin is omitted altogether, the only impediment to our sympathy is removed, and the unsatisfactoriness with which his case confronts us is the world's and not his. There is no limit to the ways in which we may react to the unsatisfactoriness of the world. We may mock it, defy it, or bear it stoically, according to our respective temperaments and convictions. Prolonged introspection on its unsatisfactoriness, however, encourages gravity and gloom; the implications of the topic are hard to resist.

I

In 'Tam o' Shanter' (1791), Burns keeps gloominess at bay by maintaining a distinction between thoughtless Tam and the moralizing but enthusiastic narrator. The meanness and austereness of the lives of ordinary people lie behind the gathering of 'drouthy' (thirsty) neighbours at the end of the market day as they do behind the forbidding prospect of being scolded if one pauses to satisfy thirst before returning home:

> Whare sits our sulky sullen dame,
> Gathering her brows like gathering storm,
> Nursing her wrath to keep it warm.   (11. 10–12)

Tam's simple pleasures must come to an end—'Nae man can tether time or tide;/The hour approaches *Tam* maun ride . . .' (11. 67–8)—and he must be penalized for his delay. Burns's narrator accepts the gloomy view of the norms of life, and he pays lip service at least to the assumption that violations of the norm will be punished, but he so readily gets caught up in Tam's disreputable preoccupations, and so infectiously, that we have no hesitation in preferring them ourselves.

70

The poem has two high points. The first is Tam's rise through conviviality to joy as drink unites him in sympathy with his companions; he enjoys songs, tales and flirtation, and in short forgets himself and his condition:

> Ae market-night,
> *Tam* had got planted unco right;
> Fast by an ingle, bleezing finely,
> Wi' reaming swats, that drank divinely;
> And at his elbow, Souter *Johnny*,
> His ancient, trusty, drouthy crony;
> *Tam* lo'ed him like a vera brither;
> They had been fou [drunk] for weeks thegither.
> The night drave on wi' sangs and clatter;
> And aye the ale was growing better:
> The landlady and *Tam* grew gracious,
> Wi' favours, secret, sweet, and precious:
> The Souter told his queerest stories;
> The landlord's laugh was ready chorus:
> The storm without might rair and rustle,
> *Tam* did na mind the storm a whistle.
> Care, mad to see a man sae happy,
> E'en drown'd himsel amang the nappy:
> As bees flee hame wi' lades o' treasure,
> The minutes wing'd their way wi' pleasure:
> Kings may be blest, but *Tam* was glorious,
> O'er a' the ills o' life victorious!   (11. 37–58)

When in the end he must return home and the wind blows, 'as 'twad blawn its last' (1. 73), Tam's happiness makes him as oblivious of the weather as we have noticed Martha Ray's misery made her. Fortified by 'Inspiring bold *John Barleycorn*' (1. 105), he is ready for anything, and when he comes upon witches and warlocks dancing to Satan's piping amid the ruins of Kirk Alloway he is surprised and inquisitive but unafraid.

The narrator's affected astonishment that Tam should pause to watch ugly witches dancing is quickly followed by the reassurance that Tam was no such fool; the effect of the narrator's expression of surprise is to assure any reader who may himself have dwindled into a husband that he need not deny his natural inclination to admire a pretty girl:

> Now, *Tam*, O *Tam*! had thae been queans,
> A' plump and strapping in their teens,
> Their sarks [shifts], instead o' creeshie flannen,
> Been snaw-white seventeen hunder linnen!
> Thir breeks o' mine, my only pair,
> That ance were plush, o' gude blue hair,

I wad hae gi'en them off my hurdies,
For ae blink o' the bonie burdies!   (11. 151–8)

As it turns out there is indeed a witch worth watching, 'ae winsome wench and wawlie' (1. 164), wearing a shift that is too short (cutty) for her. The narrator declares that no description of his could do her justice, but Tam's own appreciation suffices:

    But here my Muse her wing maun cour;
    Sic flights are far beyond her pow'r;
    To sing how Nannie lap and flang,
    (A souple jade she was, and strang),
    And how *Tam* stood, like ane bewitch'd,
    And thought his very een enrich'd;
    Even Satan glowr'd, and fidg'd fu' fain,
    And hotch'd and blew wi' might and main:
    Till first ae caper, syne anither,
    Tam tint his reason a' thegither,
    And roars out, 'Weel done, Cutty-sark!'   (11. 179–89)

He has to pay the price for his night out of course; the chase that follows as Tam races for safety across the nearby river Doon with the 'hellish legion' and Nannie herself in hot pursuit is a near thing and costs Tam's mare her tail. But the moral with which the narrator brings his story to a close is amusingly anticlimactic:

    Whene'er to drink you are inclin'd,
    Or cutty-sarks run in your mind,
    Think, ye may buy the joys o'er dear,
    Remember Tam o' Shanter's mare.   (11. 221–4)

One is left in no doubt that it is indiscretions like Tam's that make life worthwhile.

The high spirits of 'Tam o' Shanter' run somewhat against the grain of introspection on the human predicament. The problem is, in part, related to the degree of our identification with the presumed victim. The narrator's presence reminds us that we should waver between the impulse to laugh at Tam and the impulse to sympathize with him. One of the most obvious examples of such ambivalent situations in the period was being run away with by a horse. The experience was a dangerous one, but it was also humiliating and ridiculous. The embarrassing social implications of inept horsemanship were the stuff of comic verse from William Cowper's 'John Gilpin' (1782) to Thomas Hood's 'The Epping Hunt' (1829) — Cowper's linen draper and Hood's cheese and butter merchant are both discomfited while aspiring to the activities of a higher social class. The seriousness of their predicament when it is considered from the rider's point of view is epitomized in Byron's *Mazeppa* (1819), in which the formidable hero is punished by being bound naked to the back of a wild Tartar horse which runs with him for several days before collapsing from exhaustion. Byron light-heartedly has the Emperor Charles XII fall asleep while listening to this gripping tale; a more down to earth public in England, France and the United States received it rapturously when it was presented on stage in the form of equestrian drama.[1] On the Continent the experience of Mazeppa was widely accepted as being emblematic of the situation of mankind in general and of the artist in particular.[2] The theme of helplessness in a situation that was not of one's own making had been exploited with increasing elaborateness in the heyday of sentimentality and Gothicism. It was left to the Romantics to develop poetical examples that would stand for life in general.

II

The one that has fastened the most powerful hold upon successive generations of readers has been Coleridge's 'The Rime of the Ancient Mariner'. Sea yarns are not the best-selling fare they once were, but even so we recognize the pattern with which the mariner's tale begins. The cheerful departure from harbour, the perilous but exhilarating flight before the storm-blast, the arrival in the strangely beautiful but desolate region of the South Pole with its ice, mist and snow, and even the impressive appearance of the friendly albatross, would all seem perfectly in place in voyage literature of the time. It is not until line 79, with the wedding guest's alarmed question: 'God save thee, ancient Mariner!/From the fiends that plague thee thus!—/Why look'st thou so?', that we receive any hint that the account of this voyage is going to be utterly different from any that has gone before. Its difference is partly that the wonders of exploration are soon overshadowed by the wonders of the supernatural, but mainly that the emphasis is steadily on what it felt like to be the mariner and not on what happens to him.

The events that follow after the killing of the albatross, disturbing though they are, do not immediately reinforce the wedding guest's anxiety. The voyage continues through strange seas, the mariner is alternately blamed and praised for his hitherto unexamined deed, the ship is becalmed and the crew suffers from thirst. The simple but memorable stanza—'Water, water, every where,/And all the boards did shrink;/Water, water, every where,/Nor any drop to drink' (11. 119–22)—makes a statement that is perhaps obvious, but that conveys to us succinctly the cruel paradox of the sea. Then the dreams of the avenging Spirit and the hanging of the albatross around the mariner's neck at last begin to bring home to him the unanticipated consequences of what he has done. He is made to feel an outcast.

With the arrival of the spectre ship in Part III, the transition from a mere voyage is complete. The strange vessel with its macabre passengers—Death in his traditional guise of animated skeleton, and the ghastlier Life-in-Death as a woman's corpse revivified—belong to the vogue for tales of terror. Life-in-Death's triumphant cry 'The game is done! I've won! I've won!' (1. 197) is obscurely ominous; as darkness falls the mariner waits to learn what it means:

73

> We listened and looked sideways up!
> Fear at my heart, as at a cup,
> My life-blood seemed to sip!   (11. 203–5)

With the death of his shipmates the mariner is left alone with the recollection of their parting curse and the accusing presence of their bodies. Thereafter, his feelings, physical as well as mental, become increasingly the object of our attention:

> I looked to heaven, and tried to pray;
> But or ever a prayer had gusht,
> A wicked whisper came, and made
> My heart as dry as dust.
>
> I closed my lids, and kept them close,
> And the balls like pulses beat . . . .   (11. 244–9)

When the mariner unthinkingly blesses the water-snakes, the albatross falls from his neck and he is able to sleep; when he awakens his thirst has been relieved. Looking at the poem retrospectively we can see that his condition improves from this point on, but at the time he continues to be subject to unexpected and inexplicable occurrences. He witnesses an extraordinary storm. More frighteningly the dead men on board appear to come to life:

> The body of my brother's son
> Stood by me, knee to knee:
> The body and I pulled at one rope,
> But he said nought to me.   (11. 341–4)

The beauty of their morning hymn is reassuring but unnatural; the 'uneasy motion' (1. 386) of the ship causes the mariner to faint, and while he is unconscious he hears for the first time, from the Two Voices, an explanation of what has been happening to him, and the foreboding statement, 'The man hath penance done,/And penance more will do' (11. 408–9). When he comes to himself, the ship moves more normally, but the dead men with the curse in their glittering eyes are staring at him still, and although he manages this time to turn away from them and look upon the sea, he does so

> Like one, that on a lonesome road
> Doth walk in fear and dread,
> And having once turned round walks on,
> And turns no more his head;
> Because he knows, a frightful fiend
> Doth close behind him tread.   (11. 446–51)

74

His terrible fear remains with him as he doubts the evidence of his eyes—'Oh! dream of joy! is this indeed/The light-house top I see?' (11. 464–5) and 'O let me be awake, my God!/Or let me sleep alway' (11. 470–1). The departure of the angelic spirits and the approach of the pilot's boat suggest that deliverance is near, but he has still to endure the terrifying sinking of the ship—'Stunned by that loud and dreadful sound,/Which sky and ocean smote,/Like one that hath been seven days drowned/My body lay afloat . . .' (11. 550–3). When he reaches shore at last, his cry, to the Hermit, 'O shrieve me, shrieve me, holy man!' (1. 574), is a frantic one. And as he tells his tale again to the wedding-guest, long after, the memory of his suffering is as painful to him as ever:

> O Wedding-Guest! this soul hath been
> Alone on a wide wide sea:
> So lonely 'twas, that God himself
> Scarce seeméd there to be. (11. 597–600)

By some witchery readers too are made to remember that affecting solitude.

Charles Lamb's early testimony to the enchantment of 'The Rime of the Ancient Mariner'—'the feelings of the man under the operation of such scenery dragged me along like Tom Piper's magic whistle'[3]—has been confirmed by readers ever since. The enchantment resists analysis, however; the poem is much easier to describe than explain. The characteristic that strikes us first is the metre and the language. The poem resembles a ballad in its iambic tetrameter-trimeter abcb quatrains; and its spellings and some of its locutions are deliberately old-fashioned in the manner of Percy's *Reliques of Ancient English Poetry* (1765). Coleridge called it 'gipsy jargon' and removed some of it in later editions. The diction is often homely—'With heavy thump, a lifeless lump,/They dropped down one by one' (11. 218–19)—and has a disarming effect of archaic artlessness. At the same time, the liberties taken with the metre—inversion of feet, elaborate alliteration, internal rhymes, extra lines, and deliberately contrived combinations of vowel and consonant sounds within words, verge at times upon incantation. The explanatory gloss which first appeared in 1817 contributes a quaint air of authenticity. The result is that we are put off our guard and hurried unresistingly into the midst of the action.

Coleridge's first readers were confused by the mixture of materials in the poem. The supernatural and macabre elements bore resemblances to the newly popular translations of Bürger's ballads and caused one critic to dismiss 'The Rime' as 'a Dutch attempt at German sublimity'.[4] The concluding moral and the comforting Hermit were familiar from ballads like Goldsmith's 'Edwin and Angelina'.[5] Even sympathetic readers were disorientated by these misleading similarities. Modern readers are not usually plagued by the misleadingly familiar in the poem, but the hybrid quality contributes to the strange atmosphere in which the events take place.

The bewilderments of the reader are, of course, matched by the bewilderments of the mariner. At no point are we allowed to feel better informed than he is;

dramatic irony is wholly absent. From the time the crew change their minds about his guilt at line 91 the mariner is at the mercy of forces over which he has no control, and for most of the poem the identity of these forces and their motives remain unknown to both him and us. The effect is one of a nightmare in which the dreamer finds himself alone, in the wrong, surrounded by terrifying phenomena. The mariner's complete absence of a particular character helps us to experience his dream as if it were our own and allows us to inform that dream with the character that suits us. The enchantment defies analysis because for each reader it is likely to be appreciably different. Coleridge has succeeded in involving our imaginations in his poem.

The narrative framework allows for the dramatic presentation of the story. The wedding-guest begins by seeming rather comical with his ineffectual 'Hold off! unhand me, grey-beard loon!' and his breast-beating, but at important points he provides stage directions to the mariner's behaviour and his incongruous intention to attend a wedding sets off and relieves the tensions of the mariner's account. By the end of the poem when the mariner addresses him we feel that we ourselves are being addressed.

III

A case could be made for considering Byron's *Manfred, A Dramatic Poem* (1817) as a point of transition from the swashbuckling heroes of his early tales to the morally suffering protagonists of his later plays. However, *Manfred* has achieved a status independent of these works that makes it seem more promising to compare it with poems like Coleridge's 'Rime' or even, as Goethe himself did, with *Faust*, Part I.[6]

The reaction of Enoch Wray, aged, penniless, and blind—in Ebenezer Elliott's *The Village Patriarch* (1829)—gives some sense of its early effect on readers:

> And when I read to thee that vision drear,
> The Manfred of stern Byron, thou did'st bend
> Fix'd, to drink in each touching word and tone;
> On thy chang'd cheek I saw strong feeling blend
> Impetuous hues; and tears fell, one by one,
> From thy clos'd eyes, as on the moorland stone
> The infant river drops its chrystal chill.   (IV, st.i)

The suffering of Manfred differs from the suffering of the ancient mariner in that it is always understood and always resisted. We may recognize in his plight, as we do in the mariner's, disturbing affinities with the bleaker elements of our own lives, but whereas the mariner's passiveness makes us pity him, Manfred's indomitable self-possession invites us to admire his conduct and challenges us to live up to it. His example recommends a particular kind of response to fate and, by being positive, risks giving offence.

Manfred's character bears a superficial resemblance to Byron's early protagonists; he is a man of mystery, he remains aloof from society, he has a vaguely wicked past, he is gloomy and careless of life. But the differences are really more significant and the portrait is much more deeply etched. Manfred's ascendancy over others is intellectual, and will bear comparison in this respect with Goethe's Faust, although intellect is more commonly associated in the English tradition with wickedness. In him the conventional youthful enthusiasm for sublime nature—'My joy was in the wilderness' (II, ii, 62)—has been succeeded by rarer pursuits:

> then I dived,
> In my lone wanderings, to the caves of Death,
> Searching its cause in its effect; and drew
> From withered bones, and skulls, and heaped up dust,
> Conclusions most forbidden. Then I passed
> The nights of years in sciences untaught,
> Save in the old-time; and with time and toil,
> And terrible ordeal, and such penance
> As in itself hath power upon the air,
> And spirits that do compass air and earth,
> Space, and the peopled Infinite, I made
> Mine eyes familiar with Eternity . . . .   (II, ii, 79–90)

Here we have not only an explanation of his necromantic skills and a reason for the indifference with which he dismissed the temptation of the seven spirits in Act I—'Kingdom, and sway, and strength, and length of days' (i, 168)—but also for his being aware of the consequences of his actions. His perplexing expressions of misanthropy—'For if the beings, of whom I was one,—/Hating to be so,—crossed me in my path,/I felt myself degraded back to them,/And was all clay again' (II, ii, 76–9), and 'I could not tame my nature down; for he/Must serve who fain would sway; and soothe, and sue,/And watch all time, and pry into all place,/And be a living Lie . . .' (III, i, 116–19)—have an unamiable ring of foolish Gothic pride, but the first is part of a rebellion against the human condition—like Gulliver's after the voyage to the Houyhnhnms—and the second reflects a widespread disgust with Whig politics in the regency period. Against them we find set more forcibly—as with Swift—the deep concern for Tom, Harry and Dick in the 'cautious feeling for another's pain' recognized by the Chamois Hunter (II, i, 80), and in the firm but gentle reception of the Abbot of St. Maurice in the final act.

In *Manfred*, Byron has attempted the difficult task of making us sympathize with a character whose formidable authority might prevent us from identifying with him. He does this by placing him in a predicament which his former awareness of things simply makes worse. Having established that Manfred is ideally fitted by temperament and capacity to resist the slings and arrows of fortune, he provides him with an unbearable and unrelievable sorrow that combines personal loss with remorse. Even the remorse poses a familiar problem, because if Manfred has done something truly wicked our sympathy for him will be lessened, and if he feels deep remorse for anything less he will sacrifice something of our esteem. The solution is a nameless deed in an 'all-nameless hour' whose very lack of definition enlists an imaginative resonance in our minds. We know only that he has destroyed Astarte whom he loved:

> Not with my hand, but heart, which broke her heart;
> It gazed on mine, and withered. I have shed
> Blood, but not hers—and yet her blood was shed;
> I saw—and could not stanch it.   (II, ii, 118–21)

He tells us that she resembled him physically and mentally but was more virtuous (II, ii, 106–16). We are not told explicitly how he wronged her, and his servant Herman is interrupted at the very moment when he might have revealed to us her relationship to Manfred. Officious criticism has supplied the missing particulars, but Byron was uncannily good at knowing where to stop.

Manfred's anguish, unlike the ancient mariner's, is wholly inward. In his contemplation of death and his attempted suicide he is as reflective as Hamlet and as resolute as Gray's Bard; only the accident of the Chamois Hunter's interference preserves him. Once foiled he continues to inquire into the future and to contemplate the present, and as he does so he brings to our attention a view of the world that is bleaker and less fancifully recorded than Hamlet's, one from which readers are inclined to flinch. The contrast he observes between his own misery and the domestic harmony of the Chamois Hunter provides a pastoral norm against which the life of society is set:

> Myself, and thee—a peasant of the Alps—
> Thy humble virtues, hospitable home,
> And spirit patient, pious, proud, and free;
> Thy self-respect, grafted on innocent thoughts;
> Thy days of health, and nights of sleep; thy toils,
> By danger dignified, yet guiltless; hopes
> Of cheerful old age and a quiet grave,
> With cross and garland over its green turf,
> And thy grandchildren's love for epitaph!
> This do I see . . . .   (II, i, 63–72)

But this idyll is as remote from Byron's readers as it is from Manfred. What he sees in the world is rehearsed by the self-congratulatory Destinies of Act II, iii, who improve on the ingenious but small-scale malevolence of the Witches in *Macbeth*—of whom they remind us—by spreading tyranny, slaughter, pestilence, and individual folly across the earth. These followers of Nemesis and their overlord Arimanes are faced boldly by Manfred who knows their power but does not fear it because he does not fear death. In this confrontation, as in his final meeting with death, his situation is potentially that of his readers. At the end he does not die with the bravado of Mozart's Don Giovanni, nor does he rage pitifully and ineffectually against the dying of the light. He is calm and reflective as he rebukes the Spirit:

> What I have done is done; I bear within
> A torture which could nothing gain from thine:
> The Mind which is immortal makes itself
> Requital for its good or evil thoughts,—
> Is its own origin of ill and end—
> And its own place and time . . . .   (III, iv, 127–32)

The echo of Milton's Satan is, of course, deliberate. Not that Byron is indulging in the blasphemous claims of Ahasuerus in Shelley's *Queen Mab* (1813) or in a Blakean paradox, but because, like Burns, he admires Satan's 'manly fortitude in supporting what cannot be remedied—in short, the wild broken fragments of a noble, exalted mind in ruins'.[7]

Manfred moves us to sympathy with the predicament of a man. Having involved our sympathetic and lively acceptance of the world of the drama, it challenges us to apply that world to our own and to match the steadiness of the noble mind that we have so recently pitied. If we had not observed the progress of his distress and experienced its unselfish nature, if we had not witnessed his masterful firmness in the face of supernatural powers, and if we had not been made aware of his capacity for love and his innate gentleness to others, his example would be less affecting. Manfred's final sentence—'Old man! 'tis not so difficult to die' (III, iv, 151)—was omitted from the first edition of the poem. Byron protested to his publisher: 'You have destroyed the whole effect & moral of the poem . . .'.[8] Like old Enoch Wray, we are meant to be moved.

IV

Although Keats's 'Lamia' (1820) ends with disillusionment and death, it is on the whole a rather cheerful and hauntingly beautiful rendering of life in a bower of bliss. The occasional intrusions of an archly non-committal narrator spare us from taking the interesting feelings of the characters too deeply to heart, and we are carried along instead by an evocation of an unreal world that is so vivid that it allows us briefly to share a dream of an idyllic love that is forbidden to man. The poem, in fact, describes three different loves—the love of Hermes for a nymph, the love of Lamia for Lycius, and the love of Lycius for the woman Lamia pretends to be. Only Lycius dies of love, however, and it is with his fate that we are mainly concerned.

Lycius is introduced to us as a serious and dispassionate young man. Lamia first sees him, according to the narrator, 'Charioting foremost in the envious race,/Like a young Jove with calm uneager face . . .' (11. 217–18). When she accosts him by the roadside, he is returning alone from a pilgrimage to Jove's temple, and he passes her 'shut up in mysteries,/His mind wrapp'd like his mantle . . .' (11.

241–2). The contrast with the behaviour of Hermes, who plays truant from Jove while 'bent warm on amorous theft' (1. 8) seems deliberate. Lycius's 'trusty guide and good instructor' is 'Apollonius sage' (1. 375). And although Lamia claims to have seen Lycius musing beside the porch of the temple of Venus, she does so while claiming untruthfully to be a resident of Corinth. Even she calls him a 'scholar' (1. 279). There does not seem to be anything ironical about the characterization, which is broadly drawn.

The irony enters in with Lamia's successful seduction of him. It is a commonplace that serious young men are apt to fall head over heels in love, and while we probably like Lycius the better for conforming to the pattern, the narrator condescends a little to him:

> Lycius to all made eloquent reply,
> Marrying to every word a twinborn sigh;
> And last, pointing to Corinth, ask'd her sweet,
> If 'twas too far that night for her soft feet. (11. 340–3)

Lamia's disguise has all the characteristics that the devotee of reason should shun and that no hot-blooded youth can resist. She is surpassingly beautiful, she longs passionately for Lycius, she is 'A virgin purest lipp'd, yet in the lore/Of love deep learned to the red heart's core' (11. 189–90), and she possesses a magnificent and luxurious palace and unlimited means. Lycius is blinded by the illusion, but even he shrinks instinctively from an encounter with Apollonius—'to-night he seems/The ghost of folly haunting my sweet dreams' (11. 376–7).

The love of Lycius and Lamia is played out seriously enough for us to share Lycius's feelings. For a while, at least, they are happy—'Love, jealous grown of so complete a pair,/Hover'd and buzz'd his wings, with fearful roar . . .' (II, 12–13). And it is not until Lycius begins to come to himself and to be aware again of the world outside their 'purple-lined palace of sweet sin' (II, 31) and wishes to triumph over his friends by showing Lamia off that their happiness is threatened. The idyll has been brief, but it has been attractive enough for us, with the narrator, to regret its passing. The misunderstanding of the lovers as Lamia tries to dissuade Lycius is sufficiently human. And Lycius's inquiry at this point after her name and her family has an amusingly practical air. But Lamia's entreaty that Apollonius be kept away from her is ominous.

The banquet scene renews our sense of Lamia's powers of enchantment. The splendour of the rooms and their appointments is treated at length with inventive and specific detail. The entertainment of the guests is enthusiastically described. And yet, while we picture the scene to ourselves and admire it, we cannot forget the narrator's warning: 'O senseless Lycius! Madman! wherefore flout/The silent-blessing fate, warm cloister'd hours,/And show to common eyes these secret bowers?' (II, 147–9). Nor can we ignore the presence of the uninvited Apollonius. By this stage of the poem, we share the narrator's wish that the dream could continue:

> Do not all charms fly
> At the mere touch of cold philosophy?
> There was an awful rainbow once in heaven:
> We know her woof, her texture; she is given
> In the dull catalogue of common things.
> Philosophy will clip an Angel's wings . . . .　　　　　　　　(II, 229–34)

As Lamia withers before the philosopher's stern but realistic gaze we are moved by Lycius's frenzy of grief because we have responded appreciatively to the beauty of his delusion.

Had the story ended here, as it does in Keats's source, it might have been taken as a simple parable of the respective powers of passion and reason. But the story does not end here. Lycius, far from recovering from his grief and becoming reconciled with the well-meaning Apollonius, dies immediately of a broken heart. The cure for his false love is death. Keats does not comment on the fact, but it provides food for thought. We are also left with mixed feelings about the serpent whom Apollonius has so officiously exorcized. For although Lycius's fate dominates the poem, we are exposed for longer to the fascinating company of Lamia.

When Hermes finds Lamia at the beginning of the poem, she is uttering a complaint at being imprisoned in her serpent form:

> 　　　　　　he heard a mournful voice,
> Such as once heard, in gentle heart, destroys
> All pain but pity: thus the lone voice spake:
> 'When from this wreathed tomb shall I awake!
> 'When move in a sweet body fit for life,
> 'And love, and pleasure, and the ruddy strife
> 'Of hearts and lips! Ah, miserable me!'　　　　　　　　(ll. 35–41)

She is the character with whom we first sympathize. Her beauty even then outdoes the beauty of the serpent in *Paradise Lost* on which it is modelled. Hermes does not question her claim to have been a woman once, and does not hesitate to grant her wish to have a woman's form once more. This wish and her longing for the youth of Corinth seem natural enough, and when she suffers during the transformation we feel sorry for her. It is true that she seems to have magic powers of her own (to conceal the nymph and to foresee the arrival of Hermes), but they are not self-evidently evil.

When she meets Lycius her deceiving ways are treated light-heartedly by the narrator. When she teases her lover with the possibility that she is a goddess, and then reassures him that she is merely flesh and blood, the narrator seems to approve:

> Then from amaze into delight he fell
> To hear her whisper woman's lore so well;

And every word she spake entic'd him on
To unperplex'd delight and pleasure known.
Let the mad poets say whate'er they please
Of the sweets of Fairies, Peris, Goddesses,
There is not such a treat among them all,
Haunters of cavern, lake, and waterfall,
As a real woman, lineal indeed
From Pyrrha's pebbles or old Adam's seed.   (11. 324–33)

Her conduct to Lycius thereafter is tender and attentive and we are given no reason to suppose that if he had been able to match her single-minded devotion his happiness might not have lasted indefinitely. Lamia's attempts to dissuade him from rejoining society seem intended as much to preserve their love as to avoid detection; in so far as an ulterior motive is revealed, it is Lycius's unworthy wish to display her. When Apollonius detects her identity, her beauty fades, and as she vanishes 'with a frightful scream' (II, 306) we are left in doubt as to whether or not the illusion she represents was really a malevolent one. Lycius's death confirms our uncertainty.

A character of similar ambiguity had appeared in a poem three years earlier. Coleridge's unfinished 'Christabel', as we have seen, contains a lady, Geraldine, who gains access to the innocent Christabel and evidently has evil designs on her which begin to be carried into effect. She too is serpent-like. Her likeness to Lamia however is more interestingly the way in which she seems herself to be victim as well as predator. At the moment when she must cast her spell on Christabel, she

                    nor speaks nor stirs;
Ah! what a stricken look was hers!
Deep from within she seems half-way
To lift some weight with sick assay,
And eyes the maid and seeks delay . . . .   (11. 255–9)

The origin of Geraldine's predicament is never revealed to us. But the conflict in her feelings gains her a measure of our sympathy. Keats's characterization of Lamia seems to owe something to the curious conflict of feelings in Geraldine. By attributing them to a creature who is, on the one hand, explicitly a snake, and yet whose ministrations to Lycius, contrary to our expectations, are pleasing while they last, Keats is able to equip his fable with a powerful personification of passionate love, and yet to avoid the pat resolution of Apollonius in which reason compels passion to go away. Keats accepts the incompatibility of ideal passionate love and human life, but he offers it as a human dilemma and is unwilling to reject the ideal.

The tale of Hermes and the nymph, with which 'Lamia' begins, comments on the fates of Lycius and Lamia by anticipation. Hermes's approach to the nymph is complicated by nothing except the need to avoid attracting Jove's attention and the difficulty of finding her. Once Lamia has revealed 'the guarded nymph near-smiling on the green' there is nothing but her innocence to delay or mar their pleasure:

> upon the nymph his eyes he bent
> Full of adoring tears and blandishment,
> And towards her stept: she, like a moon in wane,
> Faded before him, cower'd, nor could restrain
> Her fearful sobs, self-folding like a flower
> That faints into itself at evening hour:
> But the God fostering her chilled hand,
> She felt the warmth, her eyelids open'd bland,
> And, like new flowers at morning song of bees,
> Bloom'd, and gave up her honey to the lees.   (11. 134–43)

Such pleasures are 'the dreams of Gods' (1. 127). They seem remote from ordinary experience and the poem does not dwell upon them. The loves of Lycius and Lamia on the other hand, although they are intense and exotic, involve the expression of feelings by both of them—of being so absorbed in one another as to forget the everyday world, for instance, or of wishing, forgetful of self, only to please another person—that are a part, even if a lamentably fleeting one, of the common experience of love.

V

In Byron's *The Giaour* (1813), a mysterious stranger is observed in a monastery. He remains aloof from the monks and seems to be tormented by memories of a violent and haunting past.

> Dark and unearthly is the scowl
> That glares beneath his dusky cowl:
> The flash of that dilating eye
> Reveals too much of times gone by . . . .   (11. 831–4)

As we put the fragments of the poem together, we learn that he is the Giaour himself—the lover and avenger of the beautiful slave, Leila, who has been drowned in a sack because of her involvement with him. Our curiosity is satisfied. In Shelley's dialogue 'Julian and Maddalo' (written in 1818, but published in 1824), a mysterious stranger is observed in a madhouse. He lives apart from the madmen, he is miserable, he plays sweetly on the piano and talks distractedly and fragmentarily to himself. Julian, the narrator, expresses an interest in his identity and his past, but his friend Maddalo can tell him little about the man. Years later, after the stranger has died, Julian presses Maddalo's daughter for the story and is told it reluctantly. Having thus excited our expectations, he baffles them:

> I urged and questioned still, she told me how
> All happened—but the cold world shall not know.　　　　(11. 616–17)

The framework of mystery and suspense has been used again to engage our vulgar curiosity, but for a different end. It is, in fact, as important for Shelley's poem that the Maniac's past should remain undefined as that he should have a past at all.

Whereas in 'Lamia' Keats undermines the conventional resolution of the conflict of reason and passion by treating passion with unexpected sympathy, Shelley, in 'Julian and Maddalo', turns our attention to the human condition in general. The poem opens with a conversation between two friends reunited after a long absence. As they ride out upon a deserted sand-spit that separates Venice from the Adriatic, they talk cheerfully about old times until, returning as the sun sinks, their mood grows more serious and they begin to think

> Of all that earth has been or yet may be,
> All that vain men imagine or believe,
> Or hope can paint or suffering may achieve . . . .　　　　(11. 43–5)

The time of day and the return homewards—'which always makes the spirit tame' (1. 33)—are deliberately related to the gravity of their discussion. And for Julian, at least, as he describes the occasion, the setting also fits:

> 　　　　I love all waste
> And solitary places; where we taste
> The pleasure of believing what we see
> Is boundless, as we wish our souls to be:
> And such was this wide ocean, and this shore
> More barren than its billows . . . .　　　　(11. 14–19)

The analogies between what Julian and Count Maddalo observe and the course their argument takes are pursued steadily throughout the poem and with increasing complexity.

In the preface, the two friends are described sympathetically but unsparingly. The Venetian Maddalo, despite his genius, his charm, and his kindness, has 'an intense apprehension of the nothingness of human life' (p. 189). Julian, an Englishman, believes passionately in 'the power of man over his own mind, and the immense improvements of which, by the extinction of certain moral superstitions, human society may be yet susceptible' (p. 190). At a time when lovers of freedom were lamenting the decay of the once great republic of Venice and when England, whatever its political backslidings, was still looked to as a cradle of reform, the nationalities of the pessimistic Maddalo and the optimistic Julian must have seemed more significant than they do now.

Their debate is charmingly oblique. Julian is allowed to open it by admiring the magnificent sunset as they wait for Maddalo's gondola:

                              the hoar
And aëry Alps towards the North appeared
Through mist, an heaven-sustaining bulwark reared
Between the East and West; and half the sky
Was roofed with clouds of rich emblazonry
Dark purple at the zenith, which still grew
Down the steep West into a wondrous hue
Brighter than burning gold, even to the rent
Where the swift sun yet paused in his descent
Among the many-folded hills . . . .
And then—as if the Earth and Sea had been
Dissolved into one lake of fire, were seen
Those mountains towering as from waves of flame
Around the vaporous sun, from which there came
The inmost purple spirit of light, and made
Their very peaks transparent.   (11. 67–76, 80–5)

Julian says nothing, but Maddalo guesses what social inferences he must be drawing from this apocalyptic scene, and offers to show him a better one. As they cross the lagoon in the 'funereal' gondola—'Just like a coffin clapt in a canoe', as Byron once put it[9]—Julian leans out and continues to contemplate the sunset beauty of Venice. But Maddalo forestalls his comments on it:

'Look, Julian, on the west, and listen well
If you hear not a deep and heavy bell'.
I looked, and saw between us and the sun
A building on an island; such a one
As age to age might add, for uses vile,
A windowless, deformed and dreary pile . . . .
                              'What we behold
Shall be the madhouse and its belfry tower',
Said Maddalo, 'and ever at this hour
Those who may cross the water, hear that bell
Which calls the maniacs, each one from his cell,
To vespers' . . . .
'And such',—he cried, 'is our mortality,
And this must be the emblem and the sign
Of what should be eternal and divine!—'   (11. 96–101, 106–11, 120–2)

Julian acknowledges the gloomy significance of the scene by commenting morosely on the uselessness of the madmen's prayers. The range of ordinary experience extends from inspiring sights like the mountain sunset to disturbing reminders of the flotsam and jetsam of humanity. Julian's tendency to focus on one end of the scale and Maddalo's to be more aware of the other are symptoms as well as causes of their respective optimism and pessimism.

When Julian visits Maddalo the following morning, the gloomy view seems to persist, for the weather is 'rainy, cold and dim' (1. 141). But as he waits for Maddalo, he sits, 'rolling billiard balls about' with the count's little daughter:

> A lovelier toy sweet Nature never made,
> A serious, subtle, wild, yet gentle being,
> Graceful without design and unforeseeing,
> With eyes—Oh speak not of her eyes!—which seem
> Twin mirrors of Italian Heaven . . . .   (11. 144–8)

Cheered by this reminder of the beautiful possibilities of life, he resumes the debate of the previous evening by offering Maddalo the example of the child when he appears.

> See
> This lovely child, blithe, innocent and free;
> She spends a happy time with little care,
> While we to such sick thoughts subjected are
> As came on you last night—it is our will
> That thus enchains us to permitted ill—
> We might be otherwise—we might be all
> We dream of happy, high, majestical.
> Where is the love, beauty, and truth we seek
> But in our mind?   (11. 166–75)

Maddalo listens tolerantly to the rather extreme political conclusions that follow upon this rhapsody, and then replies that he knew someone recently who talked like this but who has since gone mad, and he suggests that they pay him a visit. Julian agrees.

So far the evidence offered by the two friends has clearly supported one side of their debate or the other and has been unsurprising. The reader has become used to relating what is seen to the issues of the argument. With the visit to the madhouse, however, although we seem to be intended to relate our observation of the Maniac to the argument it is much more difficult to decide what in fact we are observing. The Maniac is said vaguely to have lost a fortune and to have been left by a lady. Maddalo, who has been instrumental in making his life at the madhouse comfortable, knows no more about him. When the friends reach the island they are greeted by the cacophony of the inmates' cries, but these are stilled by a song:

> I saw, like weeds on a wrecked palace growing,
> Long tangled locks flung wildly forth, and flowing,
> Of those who on a sudden were beguiled
> Into strange silence, and looked forth and smiled
> Hearing sweet sounds.   (11. 224–8)

The musician who calms these wretched creatures, as it turns out, is the Maniac himself. Julian and Maddalo are admitted to his presence by a keeper. They witness his pitiable abstractedness and overhear his monologue.

The monologue is disjointed and difficult to follow, as befits the ravings of a demented man, but like the sand-spit, the sunset, the madhouse itself, and Maddalo's child, it is to be considered as evidence that bears upon Julian and Maddalo's difference of outlook.[10] The monologue consists of two distinguishable parts. The first part, lines 300–82, describes in abstract terms the predicament in which the Maniac finds himself; it is addressed to our understandings. The second part, lines 382–510, reveals what it feels like to be so afflicted; it is addressed to our sympathies.

The state of despair which the Maniac describes in the first part is made even more unbearable by his conviction that he has a duty not to divulge its existence. His concern is for his friends:

> Ye few by whom my nature has been weighed
> In friendship, let me not that name degrade
> By placing on your hearts the secret load
> Which crushes mine to dust. (11. 344–7)

He feels obliged to 'live and move, and . . . smile on' (1. 306), although the 'mask of falsehood' (1. 308) is intensely painful to him, because he would otherwise be the cause of 'more changed and cold embraces,/More misery, disappointment, and mistrust . . .' (11. 313–14). He does not feel responsible for his own misery, at least not wholly responsible; it is not the consequence of vicious self-indulgence. His seemingly belligerent question, 'What Power delights to torture us?' (1. 320), is merely a reflection of his sense of injustice. The defiant spirit that remains with him, even if he is, as he admits, 'subdued', is steadfast in the belief that justice is not chimerical. He reassures his friends that he is still unalterably opposed to tyranny, gain, ambition, revenge, avarice, misanthropy, and lust, and that while he waits eagerly for death he will not flinch from poverty or shame or martyrdom. The Maniac's resolve seems wholly admirable in its selflessness; the cause of his mania, however, is still obscure. King Lear, when he encounters mad Tom a Bedlam, asks immediately, 'What! have his daughters brought him to this pass?' (III, iv, 63). But we, unless we can recall an experience that merits such despair, are bound to wonder what on earth has happened to the man.

In the second part the Maniac reveals what it was, or seems to. He does not forget his duty to keep the secret to himself—we must remember that he is unaware of the presence of Julian and Maddalo—rather he is examining his own pain. As he looks unsparingly into his memory he seems to resist a series of complaints or accusations that proceed from a mistress who has cast him off. The verse paragraphs suggest fragments of thought. The first, which seems to imply that she has killed herself to escape from him—'at the grave's call/I haste, invited to thy wedding-ball/To greet the ghastly paramour, for whom/Thou hast deserted me . . .' (11. 386–9)—is reminiscent of Manfred's meeting with the spirit of

87

Astarte. The remainder are devoted to the charges made against him. He reminds her that it was she who first wooed him; he asserts that if, when he speaks, his lip 'is tortured with the wrongs which break/The spirit it expresses . . .' (11. 409–10), this is not a symptom of pride, but rather the involuntary writhing of the trampled worm. He remembers her expressions of loathing at the thought of their past union, and points out how cruel it would be to punish even the most cruel by returning hatred for their love, and how much crueller it is to treat him so, 'Who loved and pitied all things, and could moan/For woes which others hear not . . .' (11. 444–5). He rejects the suggestion that his own unattractiveness is any greater now than formerly. He is not vengeful—'I give thee tears for scorn and love for hate' (1. 496)—; he abstains from suicide so that her lot 'may be less desolate' (1. 497). But he warns her of the reciprocal relationship there is between those who inflict pain and those who suffer it, and says regretfully, from the vantage point of a sufferer, 'O child!/I would that thine were like to be more mild/For both our wretched sakes . . .' (11. 484–6).

When the Maniac concludes his monologue and falls asleep, Julian and Maddalo are moved to sympathetic tears. They agree that

>   his was some dreadful ill
> Wrought on him boldly, yet unspeakable,
> By a dear friend; some deadly change in love
> Of one vowed deeply which he dreamed not of;
> For whose sake he, it seemed, had fixed a blot
> Of falsehood on his mind which flourished not
> But in the light of all-beholding truth;
> And having stamped this canker on his youth
> She had abandoned him—and how much more
> Might be his woe, we guessed not—he had store
> Of friends and fortune once . . . .　　　　　　　　　　　(11. 525–35)

This solution to the mystery is more circumstantial than Maddalo's original information about the loss of fortune and a lady. The causes of madness—disappointment in love and money—are wholly worldly. But it leaves a great deal unexplained and seems to ignore the first part of the monologue. Julian says, ingenuously, that 'our argument was quite forgot . . .' (1. 520). We, as readers, however, are not expected to have forgotten it, and if we have his remark serves to remind us of it.

One of the Maniac's statements in the first part of his monologue serves as an aid in deciphering the second. In his address to his friends he offers a word of advice:

>   There is one road
> To peace and that is truth, which follow ye!
> Love sometimes leads astray to misery.　　　　　　　　(11. 347–9)

If one applies this statement to Julian and Maddalo's debate, and if we recall Maddalo's assertion that the Maniac talked in Julian's manner shortly before he went mad, it would seem appropriate to see Maddalo as a follower of truth—a person who looks clearly at things as they are—and Julian as a follower of love—a person who sees things as they might be. The Maniac appears to have been a man who found himself able to contemplate both the actual and the ideal simultaneously, who seeing things as they might be is overwhelmed by the perception of them as they are. It is the choice of the word 'love' as an alternative to truth that is confusing. The point of it, however, becomes apparent when we turn to the second part of the monologue.

The experience of an idealist living in a world that is far from ideal is an unusual one. Most of us are not passionately moved by ideas or theories. In order to make us understand how terrible the comparison of what is and what might be is to an awakened mind, Shelley is obliged to use a metaphor for passion that is familiar—disappointed love. The love the Maniac describes is of the world as he thought it might be. The conviction that this ideal world is impossible is the unutterable secret he is unwilling to share. His perception of reality which destroyed the ideal was a measure of the intensity of his belief that the real and the ideal were the same. Now the reality seems to reproach him. He points out that the beauty of the world attracted his enthusiasm in the first place, and that enthusiasm seems only to have given pain. The reality of the world is tortured by the false alternatives of the idealist, and it accuses him of having done it a terrible wrong.[11]

Julian and Maddalo are each familiar with a different side of the Maniac's outlook. His example seems to tip the scales in Maddalo's direction. But the poem, having dramatized the painful dilemma, refrains from taking sides. Indeed Maddalo's last words on the subject are singled out by Julian as memorable:

> He said: 'Most wretched men
> Are cradled into poetry by wrong,
> They learn in suffering what they teach in song'.   (11. 543–5)

The agony of the idealist who faces reality may be great, but the music that he produces out of his suffering may still the ravings of the madmen in the mortal madhouse of the world, as the Maniac calmed his fellow inmates on the island. The implications for the poet are clear enough. In 'Julian and Maddalo' the nightmare of the human predicament which had been experienced in 'The Rime of the Ancient Mariner' is subjected to creative analysis.

5 Meditations of sympathy

The short reflective poems of the Romantic period exhibit several of the preoccupations we have been considering in previous chapters. An interest in simplicity is apparent in the effort to make reflections seem informal and spontaneous; the exploration of troubled states of mind and emphasis on sympathetic participation in the feelings of others encouraged the reflective author to imagine the reflections of others; and realism was challenged to provide convincing settings and occasions. Poets extended the liberties that had been taken with the elegy, the monody and the epistle in the eighteenth century, and they even pressed the ode into service, but their sense of constraint makes them adopt new terms such as 'conversation poem' and 'effusion'.[1] The fact is that the dramatic rendering of a spontaneous sequence of thoughts and feelings was at odds with any settled convention and did not give rise to one. Like most good poems, furthermore, Romantic meditations are irreducibly individual; they are grouped together in this chapter so that a kinship in intention and technique may be traced behind their disparate forms.

In 1779, when Samuel Johnson traced what he called 'local poetry' back to Denham's *Cooper's Hill* and praised the poet for inventing a new 'species of composition', he was recognizing a kind of popular verse that was already in decline. According to his definition, 'the fundamental subject is some particular landscape to be poetically described, with the addition of such embellishments as may be supplied by historical retrospection or incidental meditation'.[2] Although the aesthetic appreciation of landscape increased and altered during the eighteenth century, the abstracting and generalizing tendency of language denied poetry the range of expression that was available to painting. Writers nourished on Pope's *Windsor-Forest* and Thomson's *The Seasons* could not help seeming stale by comparison. Even the incorporation of historical associations and incidental meditation allowed little room for manoeuvre with readers who resented obscurity and expected a poet's reflections to awake an echo in their own.

One solution was to write for a local audience. Every reader was familiar with John Dyer's *Grongar Hill* (1726), but were there not scenes of equal interest and beauty nearer to hand? Henry Pye's *Faringdon Hill* (1774), William Combe's *Clifton* (1775), William Crowe's *Lewesdon Hill* (1788), and Joseph Cottle's *Malvern*

90

Hills (1798), are all honourable examples of this line of experiment, but their emphasis on features peculiar to the places they described limited their appeal.[3]

Indifference to the identity of the landscape coincided with a growing interest in the character of the figure contemplating it. Dyer, while he retained the convention he had inherited from Milton's 'L'Allegro' and 'Il Penseroso' of speaking in the first person, described his speaker as sitting on a flowery bank and reclining on the mountain turf, but he did not attempt to endow him with a personality.[4] Here the influence of Gray's enormously popular 'Elegy Written in a Country Churchyard' (1751) was decisive. In it the landscape convention was combined with the elegiac and Gray introduced as his first-person observer the 'youth to fortune and to fame unknown'. The character of this young man communing gloomily but self-absorbedly with nature owes much to Milton's Penseroso; Gray adds his humble birth, virtue, and early death. The personality formed by this unlikely combination of characteristics haunted reflective verse for more than a century.

Historical retrospections in landscape poems had made it possible to comment upon the contrast between past and present. This practice was severely limited, however, by the fact that relatively few scenes have historical associations that are widely known. When Goldsmith wrote *The Deserted Village* (1770), in which the idyllic past and desolate present of 'sweet Auburn' are contrasted, he was obliged to choose a place that was unknown to his readers and to describe it at such length and in such human terms that it would come to life for them. As we have seen, his success sparked a wave of imitations, and it showed how the sense of the passage of time could be made interesting without being weighed down by a recitation of past public events. Its method was reinforced when Samuel Rogers adopted it in *The Pleasures of Memory* (1792), a poem that was sufficiently well liked to go through nine editions within four years. In it the author, returning after a long absence to the village where he grew up, wanders about and the deserted ruins remind him agreeably of the happinesses of his childhood. The contrast is clearly in favour of the past, but Rogers admits the possibility that memory plays us false:

> What soften'd views thy magic glass reveals,
> When o'er the landscape Time's meek twilight steals!
> As when in ocean sinks the orb of day,
> Long on the wave reflected lustres play;
> Thy temper'd gleams of happiness resign'd
> Glance on the darken'd mirror of the mind. (p. 8)

These implications about the contrast between past and present in the experience of the observer are even plainer in William Lisle Bowles's 'Monody, Written at Matlock' (1791):

> Once more I meet the long neglected Muse,
> As erst when by the mossy brink, and falls
> Of solitary WENSBECK, or the side

91

> Of CLYSDALE's cliffs, where first her voice she tried,
> We wandered in our youth—Since then the thralls
> That wait life's upland road, have chill'd her breast . . . .　　　(11. 4–9)

It was no longer necessary to revisit the same place, the experience of the reflecting mind had become independent of any particular landscape.

I

These precedents were familiar to the first readers of Wordsworth's 'Lines Composed a Few Miles Above Tintern Abbey, On Revisiting the Banks of the Wye During a Tour. July 13, 1798'.[5] The return to a scene previously enjoyed, melancholy reflections on the losses incurred by human mutability, observations in the first person by a figure reclining beneath a tree, the very picturesqueness of the landscape—for the Wye Valley was much visited by tourists in the period—all these were poetical commonplaces. And yet the conventions were being strained powerfully and consciously towards new ends.

The circumstantiality of Wordsworth's title implies that the composition of the poem and the experience it records were almost simultaneous—a claim is being made to ingenuousness. The stately blank verse, although it sounds formal to modern ears, contrasted then with the more customary heroic couplets, and invited comparison with the comfortable meditations of Cowper's *The Task* (1785). The hesitations of the opening description as the author links each element observed to a thought and deliberates over the apt choice of a term—'These hedge-rows, hardly hedge-rows, little lines/Of sportive wood run wild' (11. 15–16)—and the indulgence in fanciful speculation about the presence of gipsies and a hermit, are calculated to bring before us the spontaneous mental workings of a sensitive man.

When, in the second section, we are told what the scene has meant to him during his absence, we are offered the conventional pleasures of memory, down to the recollections of good deeds reminiscent of Rogers's 'bending beggar'. The metaphysical speculation that begins at line 35: 'Nor less, I trust,/To them I may have owed another gift,/Of aspect more sublime' is much more striking. The experience it records, however, while it is difficult to describe, is one that we are meant to recognize. Hence the author's successive attempts to describe it. The attribution of special value to the experience—'We see into the life of things' (1. 49)—is offered more apologetically. The author admits that it may be an illusion.

Having described what the scene has meant to him during his absence, Wordsworth conventionally should now have complained that it has changed for the worse. Instead, using his carefully observed experience of the difference between his cherished memory of the place and the actuality before him, he is led to consider a change that has taken place in himself.[6] Here too he shares an experience that most of us have, even if in a different degree, of growing out of a period of 'thoughtless youth' and regretting its 'aching joys' and 'dizzy raptures'. The particular joys and raptures that he mentions are those of an appreciator of sublime scenery, and they are appropriate to his enthusiastic response to the Wye Valley. The description of his former self is a compelling compression of the enthusiasm for wild nature attributed to young Edwin in Beattie's popular poem *The Minstrel* (1771–4).[7] Edwin's taste for craggy cliffs, foaming torrents, and encircling groves is reiterated by Wordsworth, and even the 'bounding fawn' and 'wild deer sporting' find an echo in 'when like a roe/I bounded o'er the mountains' (11. 67–8). The difference is that Wordsworth does not merely describe what he liked—in fact his account is remarkably abstract; he does not vie with Beattie's hyperbole—but tells us how he liked it, and by doing so he makes it possible for us to feel involved in the experience. It is important for him to convince us that he valued his experience because he wishes to impress us with the fact that he has got over the loss of it.

The author is struck by the difference in himself, by the loss of his capacity for enjoying nature heedlessly, but like the traditional elegist he finds a comfort or recompense for that loss in an appreciation of nature that links it to mankind and to God. Here the metaphysical passage of the second section is recalled. The elegiac pattern is complete at line 111, and at that point it is revealed that the observer is not alone. His address to his sister creates a frame for the entire experience that we tend to anticipate in subsequent readings of the poem. The combination of affectionate feelings for someone who still can react with the spontaneous joy he himself once felt and his wish that she should find the same comfort as himself, saves him from the unattractive self-concern of the melancholy man and lessens the impersonal aloofness of the poem.

II

By the time Coleridge came to write 'Frost at Midnight' (1798) he too had already experimented with reflections in a landscape setting. In his 'Eolian Harp' and 'This Lime-tree Bower My Prison' the emphasis was upon the meditator's thoughts and feelings and upon the affectionate company of his wife and close friends. The setting of 'Frost at Midnight' by a cottage fireside was a departure that had been prepared for by Cowper's fire-gazing idyll in *The Task* (IV, 267–310). Cowper contrasted the humble pleasure of his hearth with the glitter of fashionable drawing rooms, and explains how he indulges his fancy as he pores over the 'red cinders'.

> Nor less amus'd have I quiescent watch'd
> The sooty films that play upon the bars,
> Pendulous, and foreboding, in the view
> Of superstition, prophesying still,
> Though still deceiv'd, some stranger's near approach.   (11. 291–5)

Coleridge adopts the modest cottage setting, the fire with its sooty film and superstition of the stranger, the contrast of winter raging outside, and the blank verse (in which he came closer to matching Cowper's ease and variety than any other imitator). To these he added the sentimental domestic relationship of father to infant, recollections of the past and hopes for the future, and the dramatic representation of his reflections as they occur. The progress of the meditation is from the impression of silence and calm of the winter night, through a series of thoughts stimulated by the surroundings within the cottage and back to the silent coldness of the night. The simple structure of the poem, moving from the present to the past to the future, involves a most ingenious substitution for the changed landscape or changed observer upon which it usually depended.

Coleridge is writing the equivalent of a cradle poem, in which good wishes are expressed for an infant's future. The genre had notable precedents in poems about Christ's nativity—one thinks especially of Crashaw and Milton—and less memorable ones in the recurrent complimentary verses written for the children of the great.[8] But it was gaining currency as an expression of domestic bliss. In his *Poems* (1792), George Dyer had extolled the pleasures of baby-minding:

> How sweet beside the cradle's brink
> In musing state to sit and think!
> No daisy'd bank, no green hill's side,
> So shines in nature's decent pride. (p. 49)

Dyer was describing a mother's delight. The same mood in a father—to be found, for instance, in the 'female service' performed by Wordsworth's Michael—is felt to be even more touching. The poor man's chore is transformed into a privilege. Since Coleridge's meditator is characterized as a plain man living contentedly in plain circumstances, it would be unsuitable for him to wish for worldly success for his child, or to contrast his own misery with the child's glowing future. Instead he compares the experience of his own past childhood with the childhood that he imagines for his child. Cowper's previous association of the sooty film with the visit of a stranger provides the fire-gazer with an excuse for the recollections of homesickness at school and for a depiction of day-dreaming in the classroom that would be familiar to every reader. The child's delicious recollection of his village home and longing to rejoin the domestic circle from which he had been torn is offered as a reminder of the past of the average man, and not as an appeal for pity on the part of someone who has been unusually deprived. The child's 'gentle breathings' divert this strain of reflection to him. His schooling is to be quite different. The stern preceptor is to be replaced by God, the 'Great universal Teacher', moulding the child's spirit in the midst of a sublime landscape. The seemingly natural transitions of the thoughts lend realism to the scene; the description of the schoolboy recalls our childhood and involves our sympathy; we are made receptive to the Rousseauistic upbringing by its contrast with the unwholesome constraint of the traditional school. We accept the loving and generous nature of the father as if it were our own.

94

III

Reflections on the loss of past happiness in 'Tintern Abbey' were tempered by the belief that a different and perhaps nobler sort of happiness had taken its place. In Coleridge's 'Dejection: An Ode' (1802), on the contrary, we encounter the thoughts and feelings of a mind that is still numbed by misery and afflicted with a consciousness of moral impurity. Neither the conviction nor the wretchedness to which it gives rise is foreign to common experience, but to find it enshrined in a poem and yet unresolved is disturbing and moving. A lament in which the only comfort was the thought of someone else who is untouched by sorrow, although edifying, would be depressing were it not for the evident vitality of the mourner's state of mind.

Coleridge builds his poem around a night storm.[9] The first-person convention no longer requires an elaborate physical setting and he can plunge into reflections with an informal abruptness worthy of Pope's 'Epistle to Dr. Arbuthnot'. The opening is deceptively matter of fact as he wishes for the storm that the appearance of the moon foretells. It is not until the end of the first stanza that he alludes to a change in himself, the grief upon which he expatiates to his correspondent in the second stanza. The beauties of the sky that once moved him, although they are as beautiful as ever, now do not touch him. He can see as well as ever, and he particularizes what he sees for us, but he can no longer feel. 'I may not hope from outward forms to win/The passion and the life, whose fountains are within' (11. 45–6). In stanzas IV and V he explains not a theory of perception—although students of criticism are fond of extracting the implications of one—but the way in which we feel joy in observing nature. What he describes is of great value but it is not a special preserve of the talented or the learned: 'O pure of heart! thou need'st not ask of me/What this strong music in the soul may be!' (11. 59–60). The echo of the beatitude ('Blessed are the pure in heart, for they shall see God') is probably intentional, and because he is determined that the rare experience he is referring to shall be recognizable he describes it in various ways:

> This light, this glory, this fair luminous mist,
> This beautiful and beauty-making power.
>   Joy, virtuous Lady! Joy that ne'er was given,
> Save to the pure, and in their purest hour,
> Life, and Life's effluence, cloud at once and shower ....   (11. 62–6)

The 'new Earth and new Heaven' provided for us by the combination of Joy and Nature are denied to 'the sensual and the proud' (11. 69–70).

Stanza VI returns to the self-analysis of the meditator who recalls how formerly such joy in him turned even misfortunes to dreams of happiness. Now, he adds, more obscurely, his experience has rendered this joy useless and has suspended the 'shaping spirit of Imagination' that, as he had said in the previous stanza, was the gift of the pure.

In stanza VII our attention is drawn again to the setting and to the storm that has come up. The Eolian harp whose moaning he had complained of in the opening stanza is now emitting 'a scream/Of agony by torture lengthened out . . .' (11. 97–8). Here we might expect whimsical fantasizing on the sounds made by the harp, after the manner of James Thomson or William Mason,[10] but instead Coleridge muses on the sounds of the wind itself, imagining first a scene of battle and then, as the wind diminishes, the cry of a lost child, playfully summoning up familiar associations with those outworn literary fashions for the terrible and the pathetic—an auditory equivalent to fire-gazing.

But although 'Dejection' leaves the thinker as bereft of joy as when we found him, the effect of the poem is not negative. The concluding stanza, in which he addresses his lady and imagines her far away and hopes that this storm and this experience may not touch her, leaves us with her happiness fresh in our minds. The expression of his own loss, so difficult to contrive without an unseemly mawkishness, steals upon our sympathy because of his ready interest in someone else. The conclusion is calm, even hymn-like in its final lines, and we are made to feel that the fit of despondency, like the storm, has passed.

Discussion of 'Dejection: An Ode' has been complicated most interestingly by the existence of a much longer version (340 lines rather than 139) written as a letter to Coleridge's friend Sara Hutchinson. Some critics prefer the longer version which when coupled with the circumstances of Coleridge's life at the time is a noble and affecting document. The public version, which was first published in a newspaper on Wordsworth's wedding day and addressed to 'Edmund' rather than to a Lady, when placed beside its private predecessor, shows one of the stages by which private experience can be transformed into something that affects us all.[11] The reappearance of the poem in Coleridge's collection of *Sibylline Leaves* in 1817 brought it to the attention of younger poets and coincided with renewed interest in meditative verse.

IV

The meditating figure in Keats's 'Ode to a Nightingale' (1820) lacks a past and is devoid of personality. We know nothing of his circumstances or his social connections. His meditation, by way of compensation, is idiosyncratically bookish. The thoughts move from one well-worn literary motif to another, stirring his readers' memories of previous flights on 'the viewless wings of Poesy'. The frame for his reflections, like the setting for 'Dejection: An Ode', is independent of the physical appearance of his surroundings, and the surrounding darkness suits the elegiac theme.

Keats's poem also turns upon a contrast in happinesses. It is a meditation that springs from the difference observed between the surpassing beauty of a nightingale's song and the sadness of the observer. The experience is expressed by a series of comparisons—with the feelings of someone who, like Socrates, has tasted the slow poison of hemlock and awaits death, or, less melodramatically and more helpfully, with the feelings of someone who has taken a sleeping potion and drifts towards sleep. When he longs to share instead the happiness expressed by the bird,[12] his thoughts turn by a convincingly natural train of association from drinks that will destroy or drug him to ones of an utterly different kind that will stimulate and uplift him. He imagines a wine to end all wines, a wine indeed that is more than wine, 'the true, the blushful Hippocrene' (1. 16)—referring here to the fountain sacred to the Muses. In fact it will be no mere wine, it will be 'the viewless wings of Poesy' (1. 33)—an escape not into oblivion but into a world of the imagination. Young had also had recourse to poetry when he addressed yet another nightingale in his *Night Thoughts*—'How often I repeat their rage divine,/To lull my griefs, and steal my heart from woe'.[13]

The train of thought from poison and sleeping potion through wine to Hippocrene and the flight of the mind possible to us when we read, brings the meditator closer to the winged nightingale and to escape. We share in the gradual process of finding the right metaphor to an even greater degree here than in 'Tintern Abbey'. By the time the process is complete in stanza IV the cause of the meditator's melancholy has been revealed—it is the unhappiness of the human condition:

> The weariness, the fever, and the fret
>   Here, where men sit and hear each other groan;
> Where palsy shakes a few, sad, last gray hairs,
>   Where youth grows pale, and spectre-thin, and dies . . . .   (11. 23–6)

The mourner is not lamenting the loss of a friend, or even of a capacity that all may share but some do not, but disease, old age and death, the mutability that deprives us of those we love and which awaits each of us. The cause of the grief is universally shared; the proposed remedy of escape from grief through the beguilements of art is available to all, but in the end even it is insufficient. Coming back to himself in the darkness, he catalogues appreciatively the flowers he cannot see, luxuriates in the music of the bird's song and toys with the feeling that at such a moment 'seems it rich to die' (1. 55). He thinks of others who have been charmed by the song in the past and singles out the case of Ruth: 'Perhaps the self-same song that found a path/Through the sad heart of Ruth, when, sick for home,/She stood in tears amid the alien corn . . .' (11. 65–7). Leaving for a moment his own feelings of melancholy he is able to distil a tender though remote sympathy for her, makes us share it, and by the exercise of pity helps us to face the sorrow he has hitherto shunned and relieves it. Finally, maintaining the apparent spontaneity and natural sequence of reflection, the word 'forlorn' brings him out of his reverie. There is no escape, the nightingale's song fades in the distance, and we, with him, waken from our reverie.

V

The reflecting mind can become an object of fascination in its own right. Shelley's cheerful verse epistle in heroic couplets, 'Letter to Maria Gisborne' (1820), conveys no readily extractable theme or moral, but it dramatizes the value of experiences shared with friends and admits us to a rare circle of intimacy.[14] The epistle is written to the owner of the Italian house in which the author is staying during her absence in England, and it is assumed that her son Henry will have it shared with him. The contrivance is a challenging one, providing for a three-sided monologue, an invitation to imagine two different places, and shifts between past, present and future. Its complexity is increased by the fact that although the Gisbornes have gone from home, the place they have gone to is 'home' for the readers of the poem, and in a slightly different sense for the author and his correspondents too. As a letter from a house-sitter, this one by describing a familiar room in detail is well calculated to bring it nostalgically before Mrs Gisborne, and at the same time to introduce it to us. The room he chooses, Henry's workshop, seems incongruous enough, like a modern laboratory or photographic dark-room perhaps, and its very oddness permits him to use it as an occasion for fancies that we might cavil at had he only been sitting by a Cowperian fireside in the neighbourhood of everyday chairs and tables.

The poem opens with the ingratiating modesty of the author's comparisons of himself, 'a thing whom moralists call worm', to a spider and to a silkworm, whose thoughts spin his own winding sheet (11. 1–5). His ambitions extend only to being remembered by friends. But after that bow to mutability and recognition of its bleakness, he sportively develops the spectacle of himself surrounded by scientific instruments and equipment of whose significance he affects to know nothing. He supposes he must look like an awe-inspiring inventor:

> Whoever should behold me now, I wist,
> Would think I were a mighty mechanist,
> Bent with sublime Archimedean art
> To breathe a soul into the iron heart
> Of some machine portentous . . . .   (11. 15–19)

The instruments on the walls, 'dread engines', remind him of instruments of torture, and they carry his thoughts from the sufferings of Ixion and Prometheus, to the inventions of the Spanish Inquisition—there he permits himself a sarcastic snap at the godly St. Dominic—and thence to the remains of the Spanish armada washed up on the shores of Cornwall, as evidence of the wickedness of such so-called Christians. The movement of reflection from the strange furnishings of the room to England 'an island of the blest' (1. 32) has sensibly diminished the distance in thought between the correspondents. He turns to the objects on the floor—'Magical forms', 'shapes of unintelligible brass' (11. 44 ff.)—and to the litter on the table. He has even ventured to float a wooden screw in a bowl of quicksilver, 'A rude idealism of a paper boat' (1. 75)—and here he reassures the supposedly anxious Henry that his meddling with equipment has gone no further. He singles out a teacup, a half-burnt match, and other such fragments in company with scientific and mathematical tomes. Throughout, all is observed as if by an outsider whose lack of knowledge excuses any fanciful excess and who nevertheless pokes affectionate fun at the clutter left behind by the scientific virtuoso:'I'll leave, as Spenser says, with many mo,/This secret in the pregnant womb of time,/Too vast a matter for so weak a rhyme' (11. 103–5).

And how is he living up to these mysterious surroundings? The contrast is deftly introduced:

> here like some weird Archimage sit I,
> Plotting dark spells, and devilish enginery,
> The self-impelling steam-wheels of the mind
> Which pump up oaths from clergymen, and grind
> The gentle spirit of our meek reviews
> Into a powdery foam of salt abuse,
> Ruffling the ocean of their self-content . . . .   (11. 106–12)

The indignation of his critics, he implies, would be justified only by the weird Archimage. In fact he is interested, not in his critics, but in the sublime fury of a mountain storm outside his window: 'while such things are,/How could one worth your friendship heed the war/Of worms?' (11. 128–30).

Having summoned up for them the room and himself sitting in it, he recalls how they all used to sit there together, and fearing lest that pleasure may never be renewed lingers over the memory of it—the experiences they shared: walks, meals, high talk, his own poetical efforts and the great poems of the past, and Mrs Gisborne's Spanish lessons. But his friends are far from him. He imagines them in London, doing the things he remembers doing there, and talking to his friends. He characterizes each friend in turn. The poem gains considerably from the chance that the friends he chose are still people of interest to us—we can set his descriptions of Godwin, Coleridge, Hunt, and Peacock against our own conceptions of them. Even Thomas Jefferson Hogg and Horace Smith are not utterly unknown to fame. But the vignettes are long enough to convey a character by themselves:

> You will see Coleridge—he who sits obscure
> In the exceeding lustre and the pure
> Intense irradiation of a mind,
> Which, with its own internal lightning blind,
> Flags wearily through darkness and despair—
> A cloud-encircled meteor of the air,
> A hooded eagle among blinking owls.   (11. 202–8)

They are all presented as people who are worth talking to in one way or another, worth sharing time with, valued in Shelley's recollection in somewhat the same way as the Gisbornes are.

Then Shelley comes back to himself, and, looking out upon the night sky, asks the Gisbornes to do likewise, and in a manner reminiscent of 'Dejection: An Ode',

compares their surroundings. The beauty of the sky is the same. For them he
imagines:

> a shabby stand
> Of Hackney coaches—a brick house or wall
> Fencing some lonely court, white with the scrawl
> Of our unhappy politics;—or worse—
> A wretched woman reeling by, whose curse
> Mixed with the watchman's, partner of her trade,
> You must accept in place of serenade .... (11. 265–71)

The scene before him, however, is richly pastoral and the only sounds are a distant
peasant's song and a sweetly singing bird. 'Now—Italy or London, which you
will!' (1. 291). The contrast is calculated to woo them back. He closes by
promising them delights for the coming winter—cheerful gatherings at his house,
temperate but delicious meals, good reading, and, above all, talk.

The tone of pleasant banter, the attractiveness of the scenes described, and the
interest of the thoughts they inspire do not quite conceal a darker awareness, one
that haunts about Shelley's idyll like the frost outside Coleridge's warm cottage, or
Wordsworth's 'weary weight/Of all this unintelligible world', or Keats's 'weariness, the fever, and the fret'. The elegiac strain is only kept at bay as Shelley
concentrates on the remediable loss caused by his friends' absence. The world to
which they have gone is the one from which the vindictive reviews emanate, in
which great figures like Godwin and Coleridge are fallen and impotent, in which
the condition of the poor and the state of government are shameful; one that it
plays havoc with his 'nerves' to think of:

> —well, come,
> And in despite of God and of the devil,
> We'll make our friendly philosophic revel
> Outlast the leafless time; till buds and flowers
> Warn the obscure inevitable hours,
> Sweet meeting by sad parting to renew;—
> 'To-morrow to fresh woods and pastures new'. (11. 317–23)

The frets of the world are linked directly to the decay and change with which the
poem opened, and the closing line from Milton's 'Lycidas' repeats its necessary
resolution in the face of inevitable death.

VI

The occasional political allusions in the 'Letter to Maria Gisborne' are in keeping
with a powerful tradition in eighteenth-century reflective poetry, and one that had
not been forgotten as poets experimented with the immediately recognizable

sympathies of domestic circles. Throughout the period, which was from a political point of view a troubled and interesting one, attempts were made to transfer the impulse of freshly observed sympathy for individuals to sympathy for whole sections of society.

Coleridge's 'Fears in Solitude' (1798), written at a time when a French invasion was expected daily, begins with an idyllic rural landscape and the familiar image of the author reclining contentedly in the sunshine, thinking generous thoughts and inspired by the nearness of his beloved wife and child in his 'lowly cottage'. Beside this happy scene—similar in many of its details to the setting in his 'Eolian Harp'—he places the contrast of countries that have been visited by war. This contrast in turn is used to reproach the nation—and the author tactfully includes himself—for its immorality and for its insensitivity in having inflicted the horrors of war on other nations in the past. The disparity between domestic virtue and international vice is made simply but perfectly explicit:

> Boys and girls,
> And women, that would groan to see a child
> Pull off an insect's leg, all read of war,
> The best amusement for our morning meal! (11. 104–7)

Coleridge's tone in the political passage shifts uncomfortably from the conversational to an emphatic exhortation more in keeping with the enthusiasms of his 'France: An Ode' (1798), and the analogy of the night storm that coincides with the shift in 'Dejection: An Ode' is missing here. To appreciate such a poem fully we need to share the poet's concern for national depravity; non-political meditations are spared this inconvenient requirement.

The imaginative leap from family circle and familiar countryside to the idea of the nation is taken for granted in Thomas Moore's series of epistles from America (1806). These poems might be better known if they had not had the bad luck to express contempt for the American experiment in democracy and a preference for an aristocratic status quo. They are of interest as examples of the meditation of sympathy practised at the level of international politics.

Moore's 'Epistle VII. To Thomas Hume, Esq., M. D., from the City of Washington' is one of the most effective. Its opening parodies the convention of the domestic felicity of the simple rustic:

> 'Tis evening now; the heats and cares of day
> In twilight dews are calmly wept away.
> The lover now, beneath the western star,
> Sighs through the medium of his sweet segar,
> And fills the ears of some consenting she
> With puffs and vows, with smoke and constancy!
> The weary statesman for repose hath fled
> From halls of council to his negro's shed,
> Where blest he woos some black Aspasia's grace,
> And dreams of freedom in his slave's embrace! (pp. 209–10)

101

The exposure of American hypocrisy, ignorance and bad manners continues throughout the poem; only George Washington is allowed to be an exception. But the physical surroundings of the city provide a contrast that makes the behaviour of its people even harder to excuse:

> And look, how soft in yonder radiant wave,
> The dying sun prepares his golden grave!—
> Oh great Potowmac! oh yon banks of shade!
> Yon mighty scenes, in nature's morning made,
> While still, in rich magnificence of prime,
> She pour'd her wonders, lavishly sublime . . . .　　　　(p. 211)

Americans are represented in this gorgeous setting as the dregs of Europe. The liberty of America is as false as the liberty of France, and a horrid warning to the free-born Englishman.[15] The combination of human folly, architectural pretentiousness and scenic grandeur, is brought into sharp relief at the end of the poem when we are reminded of Moore's correspondent's simpler English situation:

> 　　　　—and now, my HUME! we part:
> But oh! full oft in magic dreams of heart,
> Thus let us meet, and mingle converse dear
> By Thames at home, or by Potowmac here!
> O'er lake and marsh, through fevers and through fogs,
> Midst bears and yankees, democrats and frogs,
> Thy foot shall follow me, thy heart and eyes
> With me shall wonder, and with me despise!
> While I, as oft, in witching thought shall rove
> To thee, to friendship, and that land I love,
> Where, like the air that fans her fields of green,
> Her freedom spreads, unfever'd and serene;
> Where sovereign man can condescend to see
> The throne and laws more sovereign still than he!　　　　(p. 215)

Moore was able to rely here upon his readers' familiarity with the conventions of the poetical meditation, and to evoke an unattractive alternative to make a political point. With the passage of time this poetical short cut has robbed his poem of its original force.

VII

At a first reading, Shelley's 'Lines written among the Euganean Hills' (1819) may seem to be more like Gray's 'The Bard' than like any of the meditations we have considered hitherto. The obtrusive beat of its trochaic tetrameter couplets conveys a sense of excitement, enthusiasm and involvement that aligns it with odes like Coleridge's 'Dejection' rather than with the conversation poems. As we have noticed, the forms overlap considerably. Metre apart, however, Shelley's 'Lines' have most of the characteristics of the traditional meditation. His opening is distinctively Shelleyan with its abrupt introduction of an allegory of human life:

> Many a green isle needs must be
> In the deep wide sea of Misery,
> Or the mariner, worn and wan,
> Never thus could voyage on—
> Day and night, and night and day,
> Drifting on his dreary way,
> With the solid darkness black
> Closing round his vessel's track . . . .   (11. 1–8)

It provides an elegant substitute for the conventional elegiac reflections on human mutability and avoids the old contrast of childish happiness with adult melancholy on the one hand and the Wordsworthian serenity of a more mature contentment on the other. The emphasis on scepticism about an after-life—'Senseless is the breast, and cold,/Which relenting love would fold . . .' (11. 36–7)—and on the general bleakness of experience befits an atheistical political protester. The counterbalancing affirmation is directly related to the meditator's beautiful surroundings:

> Ay, many flowering islands lie
> In the waters of wide Agony:
> To such a one this morn was led,
> My bark by soft winds piloted:
> 'Mid the mountains Euganean
> I stood listening to the paean
> With which the legioned rooks did hail
> The sun's uprise majestical . . . .   (11. 66–73)

The magnificence of the view that he proceeds to unfold replaces the forebodings of his introduction, until, pursuing his image of voyage and sea to the island city of Venice set in the 'waveless plain of Lombardy' (1. 91), he reveals that the island's appearance of loveliness is misleading:

> Those who alone thy towers behold
> Quivering through aëreal gold,
> As I now behold them here,
> Would imagine not they were
> Sepulchres, where human forms,
> Like pollution-nourished worms,
> To the corpse of greatness cling,
> Murdered, and now mouldering . . . .   (11. 142–9)

The reader is brought up sharply by this revelation because the significance of the imagery has been reversed. Having begun with beautiful islands in a sea of misery, we are suddenly confronted with a corrupt island in a sea of beauty. For Shelley's contemporaries the surprise must have been increased by the way in which the foreign idyll is wrenched into the context of British politics with the assertion that Lord Castlereagh, the foreign minister,[16] is directly responsible for the loss of Venetian liberty:

> But if Freedom should awake
> In her omnipotence, and shake
> From the Celtic Anarch's hold
> All the keys of dungeons cold,
> Where a hundred cities lie
> Chained like thee, ingloriously,
> Thou and all thy sister band
> Might adorn this sunny land . . . .   (11. 150–7)

Venice might yet be a 'green isle', and so, he goes on to say, might Padua. We are back in the world of radical patriotism that we encountered in 'Fears in Solitude'.

Shelley's patriotism is more unforgiving than Coleridge's; his voice is reproachful rather than conciliatory. In place of the domestic virtue that Coleridge finds in England, he turns to a vestige of the greatness that was once characteristic of Venice, her hospitality to an outcast from English narrowness, Lord Byron:

> Perish—let there only be
> Floating o'er thy hearthless sea
> As the garment of thy sky
> Clothes the world immortally,
> One remembrance, more sublime
> Than the tattered pall of time,
> Which scarce hides thy visage wan;—
> That a tempest-cleaving Swan
> Of the songs of Albion,
> Driven from his ancestral streams
> By the might of evil dreams,
> Found a nest in thee; and Ocean
> Welcomed him with such emotion
> That its joy grew his . . . .   (11. 167–80)

In the wake of *Childe Harold's Pilgrimage* and the publicity that surrounded Byron's voluntary exile, there was no need to name him. And the thought of his presence and vitality in Venice as Shelley gazes upon the city provides the poem with that sympathy between the meditating mind and another person that gives the abstract elements of these meditations a steadying anchor in individual experience.

The poem ends with hope—'Other flowing isles must be/In the sea of Life and

Agony' (11. 335–6)—but it is a hope for life in general and not for an improvement in the political or social conduct of Britain. The conscience of the contemporary reader might have been stirred, but his modern counterpart is not oppressed by a sense of political partisanship gone by.

VIII

Political issues usually limit our admiration of such poems; the way in which they take us by surprise is more enduring. In Wordsworth's 'Resolution and Independence' (1807), reflections on the sad lot of man are remembered for us from an occasion in the past. The movement of thought does not flit from topic to topic or from metaphor to metaphor but weaves steadily back and forth from assertions of contentment to assertions of sadness to the assertion, finally, of contentment. When the poet meets the leechgatherer, their conversation and the eddying to which it gives rise in the poet's mind are presented dramatically. The expressions of mood depend largely on the force of two extended metaphors. The first is the simile for joy with which the poem begins. The time, a sunny morning after a night storm, is chosen as the most strikingly happy of all, the sun shines, birds sing, and then:

> on the moors
> The hare is running races in her mirth;
> And with her feet she from the plashy earth
> Raises a mist; that, glittering in the sun,
> Runs with her all the way, wherever she doth run.   (11. 10–14)

The author sees the hare and shares its happiness. The second metaphor is the appearance of the old leechgatherer, compared at first to a huge stone:

> Such seemed this Man, not all alive nor dead,
> Nor all asleep—in his extreme old age:
> His body was bent double, feet and head
> Coming together in life's pilgrimage;
> As if some dire constraint of pain, or rage
> Of sickness felt by him in times long past,
> A more than human weight upon his frame had cast.   (11. 64–70)

The author is by this time feeling downcast and he supposes that the man's appearance is a true reflection of despondency. Readers of Burns's 'Man was made to mourn' (1786) with its 'rev'rend Sage' 'whose aged step/Seem'd weary, worn with care' (11. 10, 5–6), might have been forgiven for expecting yet another round of pessimism concluding in an apostrophe to 'Death! the poor man's dearest friend . . .'. But Wordsworth as usual has imitated in order to differ and he thwarts our expectations. The leechgatherer is feeble, aged, poor, experiencing hardship,

105

and yet the only complaint that occurs to him is that leeches are not so plentiful as they used to be.

In *Measure for Measure*, when Barnardine rises from his condemned cell and refuses to be hanged, the Duke's frustration and the audience's surprise and delight are caused by the inconsequentiality of the refusal and the lack of awareness of his predicament that it implies. The poet's encounter with the leechgatherer is surprising and amusing in much the same way. Wordsworth exploits the humour of the situation by making himself the butt of the joke—while letting off his readers who are uneasily aware that they too have been taken by surprise—to press home the moral that causeless melancholy is a self-indulgent weakness.

The poet at cross purposes with the leechgatherer is the central experience of the poem. The more unhappy the figure can be made to appear, the more remarkable his firmness of mind will seem. The circumstances of the poet are happy:

> Even such a happy Child of earth am I;
> Even as these blissful creatures do I fare;
> Far from the world I walk, and from all care . . . .   (11. 31–3)

The happier his circumstances are made to appear, the more perverse his gloomy forebodings will be. In fact, the gloomy forebodings need to be read with caution. The poet—and the first-person figure identifies himself explicitly as a poet, rather unusually—thinks self-pityingly of other poets who died young, Chatterton and Burns—'Him who walked in glory and in joy/Following his plough, along the mountain-side' (11. 45–6)—being the famous recent examples of poetical youths 'to fortune and to fame unknown'. I do not think that when Wordsworth adds 'We Poets in our youth begin in gladness;/But thereof come in the end despondency and madness' (11. 48–9) he has forgotten Shakespeare, Spenser and Milton, or that he expects our assent to be any more than the willing suspension of disbelief—it is rather his figure of the melancholy poet whose memory is so conveniently selective. At this self-indulgent nadir the leechgatherer is mercifully sighted.

The dramatic meditations of the poem do not really begin until after the leechgatherer begins to speak. Then we are permitted to share the poet's bewilderment as he accommodates himself to the unexpected. As in the uncertain moment in 'Tintern Abbey', the 'somewhat of a sad perplexity', he loses track of what is before him, casting the old man as someone 'from some far region sent', perhaps like the ancient mariner. He questions him again, clinging to his prejudice that the man must be miserable, and once more he is surprised.

> and when he ended,
> I could have laughed myself to scorn to find
> In that decrepit Man so firm a mind.   (11. 136–8)

The poet has learned his lesson and is unsparing in his contempt for his previous folly. We are not offended by a homily or left with a trite moral at the end; instead we have shared the chastening experience of the poet without incurring the blame that he good-humouredly takes upon himself.

IX

When Coleridge published his picture-poem, 'The Garden of Boccaccio', in *The Keepsake* in 1829, it was accompanied by Stothard's engraving of the picture. Readers were expected to look from the picture to the poem and back again and to be moved to a subtler or at least different awareness of it by the poet's response. Similarly, when Letitia Landon's 'Poetical Sketches of Modern Pictures' (1825) appeared, her readers were assumed to have seen the pictures. Keats's 'Ode on a Grecian Urn' (1820) is one of the earlier responses to increased public interest in the fine arts, but it is a quite different sort of poem.[17] In the conventional picture-poem, the poet and the reader both observe a picture and then the poet shares his more perceptive or more fanciful experience of it with the reader. We are invited to contrast our experience with his. In the 'Ode on a Grecian Urn' there is no expectation that we have seen the urn or that we shall ever see it. The experience that the poet assumes we share with him is the 'heart high sorrowful and cloy'd', the 'burning forehead' and the 'parching tongue', and the certain prospect of old age (11. 29–30). The experience is so commonplace that it is quickly and easily identified, but it is an experience that is deeply interesting to us. The urn by contrast is an extended metaphor for the ideal of a nobler, happier existence of which we are frustratingly able to conceive.

The focus for reflection might have been one of his own nightingales, or a Wordsworthian rock, but the urn as he describes it provides an admirable point of comparison with human experience. He characterizes it at the outset in terms of its silence, ancientness and remoteness. Its age makes it seem impervious to the passage of time, its Greek origin makes it seem alien and exotic—more so then than now. His personification of it as an 'unravish'd bride' introduces the note of gentle longing that prevails through the poem, a longing that is replaced in the final stanza with regretful but placid acquiescence.

We are given our first hints about the physical appearance of the urn as questions are asked about a picture on it of a pastoral, possibly a Bacchic, revel that prompts an abstract and paradoxical comment on the greater sweetness of melodies unheard. But the reflections turn quickly to a participation in the feelings of the piper and the bold lover, which, although they are fixed in the timelessness of art, are feelings which we too are likely to have shared, however fleetingly, and which are calculated to find corroboration in our memories. It is at this point that Keats reflects on what music and love are capable of being and places them in telling conjunction with what mutability makes of them. The fourth stanza does not develop this trenchant observation. Instead, asking a new series of questions it introduces us to another scene, and as it extends the generous impulse of sympathy even farther, it introduces us to a consequence of the fixed moment in time to the unseen but deduced little town.

Here I think we are being offered an extravagance of fancy from which the author draws back. 'Thou, silent form, dost tease us out of thought/As doth eternity . . .' (11. 44–5). Such reflections resolve nothing and lead nowhere. We should be content with the simple if inexplicable significance of the urn: 'Beauty is truth, truth beauty . . .' (1. 49).[18] But giving up the train of speculation does not imply that the poem in which it appears is pointless. The poet concludes with a serenity and acceptance of the human condition that is compelling because he has been so richly appreciative of the loveliness that life denies us. He has faced the disagreeableness of reality. He does not maintain that reality is in any sense preferable to the ideal he has portrayed, nor does he comfort us with a vision of an after-life. Instead he makes us value our transitory happinesses more by showing us so beguilingly that it would be heaven to have them for ever.

From a formal point of view, the meditations of sympathy may be thought of as the aftermath of, say, the elegy, or as forerunners of the dramatic monologue.[19] The poets themselves cared more about interesting their readers in thoughts and feelings that would comfort, enlighten and perhaps inspire them, than about experimenting with form for its own sake. We shall see in the chapter that follows that meditations were incorporated into much longer poems as an effective element in works that were more obviously didactic.

6 Testimonies of individual experience

On 27 June 1777, a London clergyman was hanged for forgery. His name was William Dodd, and his misfortune is chiefly remembered for having occasioned Samuel Johnson's quip, 'Depend upon it, Sir, when a man knows he is to be hanged in a fortnight, it concentrates his mind wonderfully'.[1] His claim to our attention is that during his confinement in Newgate he composed a long poem in blank verse entitled *Thoughts in Prison* (1777). It went through several editions, but its main interest is that it anticipates a number of characteristics that have come to be associated with later poets and that it exhibits them in a usefully unsophisticated form.

Thoughts in Prison is a reflective poem. It is divided into five 'weeks' ('The Imprisonment', 'The Retrospect', 'Publick Punishment', 'The Trial', and 'Futurity'). The choice of blank verse, the use of the first person throughout, and the structure all follow the famous precedent of Edward Young's *The Complaint: or Night Thoughts* (1743–5) in which the various sections are called 'nights'. In its mixture of religious, moral and social reflections, it more closely resembles James Foot's tedious *Penseroso, or the Pensive Philosopher in His Solitudes* (1771). Given Dodd's situation one might have expected him to capitalize on the public appetite for the last thoughts of condemned malefactors, but he presents himself instead in the guise of a repentant sinner whose experience may be a warning to others. In doing so he adopts a pose typical of Dissenting spiritual autobiography from at least as far back as Bunyan's *Grace Abounding* (1666).[2] Looking into the future, *Thoughts in Prison* may be seen as a revealing precedent for Cowper's *The Task* (1785), Wordsworth's *The Prelude* (1850), and Byron's *Childe Harold's Pilgrimage* (1812–18).

I *The Task*

In the prefatory 'Advertisement' to *The Task*, William Cowper explains that a lady had asked him to write a poem in blank verse on the subject of the sofa. His method was appropriately casual:

> He obeyed; and, having much leisure, connected another subject with it;
> and, pursuing the train of thought to which his situation and turn of

109

mind led him, brought forth at length, instead of the trifle which he at first intended, a serious affair—a Volume.

The archness of this preamble is sustained in the opening lines:

I sing the Sofa. I, who lately sang
Truth, Hope, and Charity, and touch'd with awe
The solemn chords, and with a trembling hand,
Escap'd with pain from that advent'rous flight,
Now seek repose upon an humbler theme;
The theme though humble, yet august and proud
Th'occasion—for the Fair commands the song.

The structure of the poem bears out Cowper's intimations of inconsequentiality. Lamb and Coleridge both praised his 'divine chit-chat',[3] and although Cowper himself later claimed that he had given the several parts 'that sort of slight connection which poetry demands',[4] a pleasing impression of spontaneous informality remains.

Cowper had already written a number of poems of an improving kind. In addition to 'Truth', 'Hope', and 'Charity', his *Poems* (1782) had contained 'Expostulation', and 'The Progress of Error'. All of these are in heroic couplets, and it was natural for readers to associate them with the dominant satirical tradition. In *The Task* Cowper encourages different expectations. A precedent was afforded by Young's *Night Thoughts*, in which the author declared that 'the method pursued in it was rather imposed, by what spontaneously arose in the author's mind . . . than meditated or designed . . .'.[5] But whereas Young's intention seems to have been to reassure his readers that he was serious and sincere, Cowper, whose intentions were just as earnest, disarms us with the promise of a lighter touch. The model for his blank verse, happily, is Milton rather than Young, and in his mixture of matters grave and cheerful a dissenting conscience is effectively combined with a taste for happiness. Satire, he tells us in Book II, is insufficient:

It may correct a foible, may chastise
The freaks of fashion, regulate the dress,
Retrench a sword-blade, or displace a patch;
But where are its sublimer trophies found?
What vice has it subdu'd? whose heart reclaim'd
By rigour, or whom laugh'd into reform?
Alas! Leviathan is not so tam'd:
Laugh'd at, he laughs again . . . .   (II, 316–23)

The subject matter of *The Task* is much the same as the subject matter of the 1782 *Poems*—the wickedness of nations, the corruptness of institutions, the follies of fashionable life—but it is disguised by the titles of the various books—'The Sofa', 'The Time-piece', 'The Garden', 'The Winter Evening', 'The Winter Morning

Walk', and 'The Winter Walk at Noon'—and balanced against irresistible descriptions of the beauties of nature and the blessings of domestic peace.

In James Beattie's unfinished poem *The Minstrel* (1771–4) the idealistic young Edwin overhears a hermit soliloquizing on the wickedness of the world. He is shocked and later returns to the hermit who advises him to put his trust in philosophy. Men who had withdrawn from the world after having tasted its pleasures and having been disappointed in them were a popular feature of eighteenth-century verse. Their age and indifference to fortune made them acceptable advisers to the young, and their experience of the world gave them a certain gloomy authority. They had no more pretensions to reality than the Gothic ruins that were erected on country estates; they were a convention of the picturesque and of romance. As Cowper's contemporaries were aware, the personality behind the advice in *The Task* resembles these hermits in several respects, but he is a hermit with a difference.

The similarity is most obvious in a famous passage in Book III:

> I was a stricken deer, that left the herd
> Long since; with many an arrow deep infixt
> My panting side was charg'd, when I withdrew
> To seek a tranquil death in distant shades.
> There was I found by one who had himself
> Been hurt by th'archers. In his side he bore,
> And in his hands and feet, the cruel scars.
> With gentle force soliciting the darts,
> He drew them forth, and heal'd, and bade me live.
> Since then, with few associates, in remote
> And silent woods I wander, far from those
> My former partners of the peopled scene;
> With few associates, and not wishing more.
> Here much I ruminate, as much I may,
> With other views of men and manners now
> Than once, and others of a life to come.
> I see that all are wand'rers, gone astray
> Each in his own delusions . . . . (III, 108–25)

Cowper's denunciations of the world in Books II and III gained force from his claim to have had unhappy experience of it, and his recommendations came more palatably from someone who admitted weakness.

In the impersonal context of polite literature of the period, the note of religious conviction sounds uncomfortably genuine, and Cowper was probably wise to reserve it for the middle of his poem. By the time we encounter the passage, our confidence and sympathy have been gained. A character has been developed who shares many of our own tastes and attitudes and whose differences from us are ones that make us feel a protective affection for him. In Book I, for instance, the author's age is referred to when he recommends walking as a way of preserving health:

111

> scenes that sooth'd
> Or charm'd me young, no longer young, I find
> Still soothing and of pow'r to charm me still.
> And witness, dear companion of my walks,
> Whose arm this twentieth winter I perceive
> Fast lock'd in mine, with pleasure such as love,
> Confirm'd by long experience of thy worth
> And well-tried virtues, could alone inspire—
> Witness a joy that thou hast doubled long.   (I, 141–9)

And the infirmity of healthy old age is engagingly admitted—'Descending now (but cautious, lest too fast)' (I, 266). But age is represented here as contented with life rather than indifferent to it, and the testimony to the pleasure of long shared experience contrasts even further with the voluntary isolation of the hermit. His early youth is recalled:

> For I have lov'd the rural walk through lanes
> Of grassy swarth, close cropt by nibbling sheep,
> And skirted thick with intertexture firm
> Of thorny boughs; have lov'd the rural walk
> O'er hills, through valleys, and by rivers' brink,
> E'er since a truant boy I pass'd my bounds
> T'enjoy a ramble on the banks of Thames;
> And still remember, nor without regret
> Of hours that sorrow since has much endear'd,
> How oft, my slice of pocket store consum'd,
> Still hung'ring, pennyless and far from home,
> I fed on scarlet hips and stony haws,
> Or blushing crabs, or berries, that emboss
> The bramble, black as jet, or sloes austere.
> Hard fare! but such as boyish appetite
> Disdains not . . . .   (I, 109–24)

We are invited to recall analogies in our own experience not only to the ramble but to the truancy. Other commonplace enjoyments are lovingly described. The vicarious excitements of reading the newspaper of a winter evening (IV, 23–119), the pleasures of wool-gathering while gazing into the parlour fire (IV, 272–310), the well-loved walk (I, 154–361), all these confirm the feeling that we are being addressed by someone like ourselves. Even his regrets, when he pauses to give them a name, are ones we can share:

> How readily we wish time spent revok'd,
> That we might try the ground again, where once
> (Through inexperience, as we now perceive)
> We miss'd that happiness we might have found!

Some friend is gone, perhaps his son's best friend!
A father, whose authority in show
When most severe, and must'ring all its force,
Was but the graver countenance of love . . . .
How gladly would the man recall to life
The boy's neglected sire! a mother too,
That softer friend, perhaps more gladly still,
Might he demand them at the gates of death.
Sorrow has, since they went, subdu'd and tam'd
The playful humour; he could now endure,
(Himself grown sober in the vale of tears)
And feel a parent's presence no restraint.   (VI, 25–32, 42–9)

These reassurances are helpful when Cowper offers us, as he so often does, a finer awareness of the beauties of ordinary life. He avoids giving the impression of superior perceptiveness and reminds us of insignificant everyday trifles that are so familiar that we have stopped noticing them. In Thomson's *The Seasons* domestic animals had been described as they waited to be fed on a winter day:

The cattle from the untasted field return,
And ask, with meaning low, their wonted stalls,
Or ruminate in the contiguous shade.
Thither the household feathery people crowd,
The crested cock, with all his female train,
Pensive and dripping . . . .[6]

In Book V of *The Task*, Cowper, fully aware of his predecessor, shifts the emphasis away from scene painting to the presumed feelings of the animals: 'The cattle mourn . . . and seem half petrified to sleep/In unrecumbent sadness' (V, 27–9). In the deep snow, 'Resign'd/To sad necessity, the cock foregoes/His wonted strut; and . . . seems to resent/His alter'd gait and stateliness retrench'd' (V, 72–5). A robin is sensitively observed:

The redbreast warbles still, but is content
With slender notes, and more than half suppress'd:
Pleas'd with his solitude, and flitting light
From spray to spray, where'er he rests he shakes
From many a twig the pendent drops of ice,
That tinkle in the wither'd leaves below.   (VI, 77–82)

One of the most pleasing of these vignettes is of a woodman starting out for work with his dog on a winter morning:

Forth goes the woodman, leaving unconcern'd
The cheerful haunts of man; to wield the axe

> And drive the wedge, in yonder forest drear,
> From morn to eve his solitary task.
> Shaggy, and lean, and shrewd, with pointed ears
> And tail cropp'd short, half lurcher and half cur—
> His dog attends him. Close behind his heel
> Now creeps he slow; and now, with many a frisk
> Wide-scamp'ring, snatches up the drifted snow
> With iv'ry teeth, or ploughs it with his snout;
> Then shakes his powder'd coat, and barks for joy.
> Heedless of all his pranks, the sturdy churl
> Moves right toward the mark; nor stops for aught,
> But now and then with pressure of his thumb
> T'adjust the fragrant charge of a short tube
> That fumes beneath his nose . . . .   (V, 41–57)

The indifference of the pipe-smoking master to the frolicsome antics of his mongrel contrasts amusingly with the author's lively appreciation, but we are made to understand and sympathize with the woodman's insensibility. Cowper is careful to remind us that the woodman's work is hard and lonely and implies that we should respect his uncomplaining pursuit of it. Human circumstances, and labour especially, will sometimes blind us to the beauties around us; Cowper does not blame the woodman, or us.

When Cowper tells us about the behaviour of Tiney, his pet hare, the experience described is a more singular one, but the ingenuous appreciativeness is the same:

> Innocent partner of my peaceful home,
> Whom ten long years' experience of my care
> Has made at last familiar; she has lost
> Much of her vigilant instinctive dread,
> Not needful here, beneath a roof like mine.
> Yes—thou may'st eat thy bread, and lick the hand
> That feeds thee; thou may'st frolic on the floor
> At evening, and at night retire secure
> To thy straw couch, and slumber unalarm'd;
> For I have gain'd thy confidence, have pledg'd
> All that is human in me to protect
> Thine unsuspecting gratitude and love.
> If I survive thee I will dig thy grave;
> And, when I place thee in it, sighing, say,
> I knew at least one hare that had a friend.   (III, 337–51)

The curious inversion of thought, not only seeing the situation from the hare's point of view, but reducing himself to the hare's level, surpasses Uncle Toby's apostrophe to the fly in *Tristram Shandy* or even Christopher Smart's tribute to his cat Jeoffry in *Jubilate Agno*, but it reveals a lovable, sentimental eccentricity that is

114

akin to theirs. Cowper's disquisition a few lines later on the growing of cucumbers also has a quaint ring to it. He realizes the oddity of his topic and pokes elaborate fun at it:

> To raise the prickly and green-coated gourd,
> So grateful to the palate, and when rare
> So coveted, else base and disesteem'd—
> Food for the vulgar merely—is an art
> That toiling ages have but just matur'd,
> And at this moment unassay'd in song.
> Yet gnats have had, and frogs and mice, long since,
> Their eulogy; those sang the Mantuan bard,
> And these the Grecian, in ennobling strains;
> And in thy numbers, Phillips, shines for aye
> The solitary shilling. Pardon then,
> Ye sage dispensers of poetic fame,
> Th'ambition of one, meaner far, whose pow'rs,
> Presuming an attempt not less sublime,
> Pant for the praise of dressing to the taste
> Of critic appetite, no sordid fare,
> A cucumber, while costly yet and scarce.   (III, 446–62)

The account which follows, with its Miltonic description of the use of a 'stercoraceous heap' is often said to be mock heroic in its tone, and it does remind one of the opening history of the sofa. But the foibles of such a gardener, let alone of such a fancier of hares, are difficult to calculate. When it is said of the gardener that 'Cautious he pinches from the second stalk/A pimple, that portends a future sprout,/And interdicts its growth' (III, 528–9), we may be forgiven for suspecting that an unself-conscious gravity worthy of Isaac Walton has set in. These foibles are harmless and amusing. They help us to imagine the author, and they make us feel comfortable in his presence.

It is important that we should feel comfortable, because *The Task*, for all its conversational informalities, has serious designs upon our way of life. As one reads through the poem an alternating structure gradually emerges; we are offered satirical comments on the prevailing vices and follies and, in about equal measure, vivid and persuasive accounts of domestic virtue. The satire is fairly systematic in its choice of subject matter. International affairs are discussed, with particular emphasis on the immorality of wars and the wickedness of slavery (II, 1–74). The decline of institutions is deplored. Politicians are represented as corrupt and frivolous (II, 222–84); the clergy are scorned as venal and hypocritical (II, 326–573); and the universities are castigated for having abandoned discipline (II, 699–832). Various less official aspects of the social order are examined and found wanting. Cities are said to be sinks of sin (I, 678–774, and III, 811–48); wickedness in the countryside is blamed on drink, military experience, and the bad influence of the towns (IV, 429–658); and French despotism is held up as a terrible warning of what may happen in England if liberty is neglected (V, 379–537). With the exception of a diatribe against cruelty to animals (III, 306–51), the topics of Cowper's jeremiad are conventional, and they are treated abstractly enough to sound modern. Their abstractness lessens their force, and the bitterness of Cowper's attack is mitigated by his frequent reminders that English institutions have behaved better in the past and by his recurrent expressions of patriotism.

When he turns to mere follies his indignation is replaced by specific descriptions of the excesses he condemns, and he devotes his energies to showing how miserable fashionable people really are. We have the pathetic picture of elderly card players:

> The paralytic, who can hold her cards,
> But cannot play them, borrows a friend's hand
> To deal and shuffle, to divide and sort,
> Her mingled suits and sequences; and sits,
> Spectatress both and spectacle, a sad
> And silent cypher, while her proxy plays.
> Others are dragg'd into the crowded room
> Between supporters; and, once seated, sit,
> Through downright inability to rise,
> Till the stout bearers lift the corpse again.   (I, 472–81)

In answer to the question, 'Whom call we gay?', Cowper mocks the beau monde for preferring art galleries to nature, and for suffering from the spleen (I, 409–505). He dismisses ambition, whether frivolous or serious, as vain, and disapproves of public recognition (III, 124–90, and VI, 632–728). He makes fun of such fashionable pastimes as chess, billiards, and attendance at auctions (VI, 262–94), and of theatre-going, card-playing, again, and travelling (IV, 194–242). One has no doubt about his familiarity with the activities he describes, and he appears to be reassuring those who yearn for them from a distance that the game is not worth the candle.

The great strength of *The Task* lies not in its dismissal of fashionable life, but in its recommendation of a plausible alternative in the second half of the poem. The attractions of a retired life in the country were familiar to readers of Horace or even of Pomfret's *The Choice* (1700), but these were the idylls of a privileged minority. Few could expect to command villas and Salernian wine, but what Cowper recommended was within the reach of everyone. To him the preoccupations of the worldly were a kind of lunacy:

> So many maniacs dancing in their chains.
> They gaze upon the links that hold them fast
> With eyes of anguish, execrate their lot,
> Then shake them in despair, and dance again!   (II, 663–6)

The alternative he proposes is a compromise between the paradise that has been lost and the heaven that is to come:

116

> O, friendly to the best pursuits of man,
> Friendly to thought, to virtue, and to peace,
> Domestic life in rural leisure pass'd!
> Few know thy value, and few taste thy sweets . . . .   (III, 290–3)

One of the few metaphysical principles enunciated in *The Task* is the theory that
'By ceaseless action all that is subsists' (I, 367). The statement is prompted by the
sight of a thresher working with his flail, and Cowper moralizes:

> Come hither, ye that press your beds of down
> And sleep not: see him sweating o'er his bread
> Before he eats it.—'Tis the primal curse,
> But soften'd into mercy; made the pledge
> Of cheerful days, and nights without a groan.   (I, 362–6)

When he speaks of rural leisure, then, he is not thinking of idleness. The
satisfactions of moderate industriousness are clearly set out in Book III. Work
allows us to relish life, and Cowper is concerned to remind us how much there is to
relish, and how independent it is of wealth or social station. The point of the
famous description of Catherine the Great's ice palace in Book V is the inferiority
of this imperial folly to the frozen spray thrown off by a mill wheel:

> And see where it has hung th'embroider'd banks
> With forms so various, that no pow'rs of art,
> The pencil or the pen, may trace the scene!
> Here glitt'ring turrets rise, upbearing high
> (Fantastic misarrangement!) on the roof
> Large growth of what may seem the sparkling trees
> And shrubs of fairy land. The crystal drops
> That trickle down the branches, fast congeal'd,
> Shoot into pillars of pellucid length,
> And prop the pile they but adorn'd before.
> Here grotto within grotto safe defies
> The sun-beam; there, emboss'd and fretted wild,
> The growing wonder takes a thousand shapes
> Capricious, in which fancy seeks in vain
> The likeness of some object seen before.   (V, 107–21)

Such sights are available to us all if only we take the trouble to notice them. The
pleasures of gazing into the embers of a fire are accessible to everyone, and so are
the pleasures of God's landscape even though some mortal may have temporary
possession of them:[7]

> He looks abroad into the varied field
> Of nature, and, though poor perhaps compar'd

117

> With those whose mansions glitter in his sight,
> Calls the delightful scen'ry all his own.
> His are the mountains, and the vallies his,
> And the resplendent rivers. His t'enjoy
> With a propriety that none can feel,
> But who, with filial confidence inspir'd,
> Can lift to heaven an unpresumptuous eye,
> And smiling say—My Father made them all!   (V, 738–47)

Although the democratic assumptions behind this point of view were a reflection of Cowper's religious sentiments rather than of levelling political opinion, they were gratefully adopted by the young radicals of the following decade. *The Task* could just as well be read as an argument for the preservation of the old order. Cowper maintains that the ingredients of true happiness are already available to us all. His demonstration of the vanity of some human wishes differs from, say, Johnson's, in that he insists that there are other human wishes that are intrinsically more sensible and that need not be vain. By presenting to us delights that are within our grasp even if we have not valued them, he puts us more truly in possession of what is our own. His summation of the good life sounds very much like paradise regained:

> He is the happy man, whose life ev'n now
> Shows somewhat of that happier life to come;
> Who, doom'd to an obscure but tranquil state,
> Is pleas'd with it, and, were he free to choose,
> Would make his fate his choice; whom peace, the fruit
> Of virtue, and whom virtue, fruit of faith,
> Prepare for happiness; bespeak him one
> Content indeed to sojourn while he must
> Below the skies, but having there his home.   (VI, 906–14)

And the religious enthusiasm, which is given its head in the remarkable anticipation of the second coming with which the poem concludes, reminds us again of the hermit strain in him. Unworldly though he is, Cowper offers an account of the simpler satisfactions of this world that make it a better place to live in regardless of one's religious convictions. For the next generation of poets *The Task* was a central text.

II *The Prelude*

At the beginning of Wordsworth's *The Prelude* (1805)[8] the author comes upon us abruptly with his thoughts. Before we know anything about his identity we have shared his exhilaration at escaping to the open countryside from the uncongenial confines of the city, and his joy at the prospect of months of liberty to do as he pleases. Towards the end of the preamble he reveals what such an opportunity means to him:

> Enough that I am free; for months to come
> May dedicate myself to chosen tasks . . . .
> Nay more, if I may trust myself, this hour
> Hath brought a gift that consecrates my joy;
> For I, methought, while the sweet breath of Heaven
> Was blowing on my body, felt within
> A corresponding mild creative breeze,
> A vital breeze which travell'd gently on
> O'er things which it had made, and is become
> A tempest, a redundant energy,
> Vexing its own creation. 'Tis a power
> That does not come unrecogniz'd, a storm,
> Which, breaking up a long-continued frost
> Brings with it vernal promises, the hope
> Of active days, of dignity and thought,
> Of prowess in an honorable field,
> Pure passions, virtue, knowledge, and delight,
> The holy life of music and of verse.   (I, 33–4, 39–54)

We learn of the earnestness of his enthusiasm and of his belief that the creative energy within him will rise to the occasion.

When he turns to address his friend (I, 55 ff.) he reveals that the prophetic moment of confidence and dedication which he has recorded took place some time before, and that as yet its promise has not been fulfilled. He complains of finding himself unable to settle upon a subject and confesses to an unsettled and discontented state of mind. Recalling Shakespeare's extravagant analogy of 'The lunatic, the lover, and the poet', he wrily admits to weakness:

> But, O, dear Friend!
> The Poet, gentle creature as he is,
> Hath, like the Lover, his unruly times;
> His fits when he is neither sick nor well,
> Though no distress be near him but his own
> Unmanageable thoughts . . . .   (I, 144–9)

In his despondency he takes stock of himself but can find no excuses for his inaction. He runs over a series of heroic or romantic themes and characters without feeling able to fix upon any one of them. He is clear about his ambition:

> last wish,
> My last and favourite aspiration! then
> I yearn towards some philosophic Song
> Of Truth that cherishes our daily life . . . .   (I, 228–31)

119

But he does not feel ready for it yet. He reproaches himself for being a 'false steward' of his talents and his mind reverts to the extraordinary advantages he has had in his upbringing, with a sense of having wasted them.

Intent upon the debt he has incurred and eager to do justice to the advantages he has enjoyed, Wordsworth introduces the long account of his early life that occupies most of his poem. As he does so, we find ourselves insensibly embarked upon the 'noble theme' that he has been seeking. It is nothing less than the meaning of the experience of human life, but the autobiographical form is so successful in its own terms that its wider implications seem to be almost an afterthought. It is a mark of Wordsworth's success that it should be commoner to compare *The Prelude* to Rousseau's *Confessions* than to *Paradise Lost*, and yet Wordsworth's matter is really closer to Milton's. He too addresses himself to the central paradox of the presence of evil in a world presided over by a benevolent God. But in a secular age he cannot simply 'assert Eternal Providence,/And justify the ways of God to men' and expect a patient hearing. In place of the great story of the fall of Adam, backed as it was by tradition and authority, he relies audaciously and vulnerably on the unfamiliar but authentic experiences of a modern man.

Wordsworth stresses the unusual advantages of growing up in the Lake District. The area was well known for its sublime landscapes, and childhood in such a place provided an effective contrast to the urban upbringing of the friend to whom he addresses himself, and, incidentally, to that of most of his readers. The boyhood that Wordsworth describes is reassuringly boisterous and sociable and utterly unlike that of the 'model of a child' he deplores in Book V:

> We were a noisy crew, the sun in heaven
> Beheld not vales more beautiful than ours,
> Nor saw a race in happiness and joy
> More worthy of the ground where they were sown. (I, 505–8)

A wide enough range of pastimes is recorded to remind most of us of our own childhoods. Bathing in the river, basking in the sun, and running through fields of flowers, may have seemed more paradisal then than now, but fishing, skating, boating, riding, picnicking, and playing at cards, skittles and noughts and crosses strike the common touch. Wordsworth's descriptions are memorable not because his activities were out of the way, but because he manages to recreate the intense absorptions of childhood and makes us aware of unappreciated experiences in our own lives. In the skating scene, the children's make-believe merges easily with the poet's metaphors:

>   clear and loud
> The village clock toll'd six; I wheeled about,
> Proud and exulting, like an untired horse,
> That cares not for its home.—All shod with steel,
> We hiss'd along the polish'd ice, in games
> Confederate, imitative of the chase

And woodland pleasures, the resounding horn,
The Pack loud bellowing, and the hunted hare.
So through the darkness and the cold we flew,
And not a voice was idle; with the din,
Meanwhile, the precipices rang aloud,
The leafless trees, and every icy crag
Tinkled like iron . . . .   (I, 457–69)

When he shifts to quieter moments the particulars of the skater's movements are
exactly conveyed:

Not seldom from the uproar I retired
Into a silent bay, or sportively
Glanced sideway, leaving the tumultuous throng,
To cut across the image of a star
That gleam'd upon the ice: and oftentimes
When we had given our bodies to the wind,
And all the shadowy banks, on either side,
Came sweeping through the darkness, spinning still
The rapid line of motion; then at once
Have I, reclining back upon my heels,
Stopp'd short, yet still the solitary Cliffs
Wheeled by me . . . .   (I, 474–85)

The dizziness is true to our own experience, and the simile that follows—'even as if
the earth had roll'd/With visible motion her diurnal round' (I, 485–6)—is not
attributed to the child. It is the settings that are exceptional. Rowing home after a
day of mirth during which 'shouts we sent/Made all the mountains ring', has
picturesque possibilities:

But ere the fall
Of night, when in our pinnace we return'd
Over the dusky Lake, and to the beach
Of some small Island steer'd our course with one,
The Minstrel of our troop, and left him there,
And row'd off gently, while he blew his flute
Alone upon the rock; Oh! then the calm
And dead still water lay upon my mind
Even with a weight of pleasure, and the sky
Never before so beautiful, sank down
Into my heart, and held me like a dream.   (II, 170–80)

The author does not distinguish himself from the group, but vouches for the
impression the scene made on him. He is one observer among many, and not the

121

minstrel. Had we been there, he implies, we should have been similarly moved. Another child with special talents is recalled in Book V:[9]

> There was a Boy, ye knew him well, ye Cliffs
> And Islands of Winander! many a time
> At evening, when the stars had just begun
> To move along the edges of the hills,
> Rising or setting, would he stand alone
> Beneath the trees, or by the glimmering Lake,
> And there, with fingers interwoven, both hands
> Press'd closely, palm to palm, and to his mouth
> Uplifted, he, as through an instrument,
> Blew mimic hootings to the silent owls,
> That they might answer him.—And they would shout
> Across the watry Vale, and shout again,
> Responsive to his call, with quivering peals,
> And long halloos, and screams, and echoes loud,
> Redoubled and redoubled; concourse wild
> Of mirth and jocund din! And when it chanced
> That pauses of deep silence mock'd his skill,
> Then sometimes, in that silence, while he hung
> Listening, a gentle shock of mild surprize
> Has carried far into his heart the voice
> Of mountain torrents; or the visible scene
> Would enter unawares into his mind,
> With all its solemn imagery, its rocks,
> Its woods, and that uncertain Heaven, receiv'd
> Into the bosom of the steady Lake.   (V, 389–413)

His feelings are so intimately and convincingly rendered that it is hard to believe that they are not the poet's own, but Wordsworth immediately informs us that the child of whom he speaks died young, and, as if to remove any doubt from our minds, gives us the details of his grave.

Wordsworth was faced with a tactical problem in *The Prelude.* He wished to comfort and encourage people who had experienced disillusionment by reassuring them that he had experienced it too and recovered. From a purely rhetorical point of view it was important that his credentials as an optimistic adviser should depend upon the accident of superior opportunities and not upon any superiority of mind or rank. In his account of childhood he makes himself one of a crowd as much as possible, but at the same time the peculiarities of unique experience were a mark of the authenticity essential to his argument. His solution of the problem was to present some unique experiences as samples of his own and to recognize that other people had different ones.

Wordsworth tells us of several occasions on which he became aware of what he calls 'Presences of Nature'. His first notices of them seem to be connected with guilty conscience. He tells of snaring woodcocks, and concludes:

> Sometimes it befel
> In these night-wanderings, that a strong desire
> O'erpower'd my better reason, and the bird
> Which was the captive of another's toils
> Became my prey; and, when the deed was done
> I heard among the solitary hills
> Low breathings coming after me, and sounds
> Of undistinguishable motion, steps
> Almost as silent as the turf they trod.   (I, 324–32)

Stealing birds' eggs was also attended with disturbing but inspiring premonitions:

> Oh! when I have hung
> Above the raven's nest, by knots of grass
> And half-inch fissures in the slippery rock
> But ill sustain'd, and almost, as it seem'd,
> Suspended by the blast which blew amain,
> Shouldering the naked crag; Oh! at that time,
> While on the perilous ridge I hung alone,
> With what strange utterance did the loud dry wind
> Blow through my ears! the sky seem'd not a sky
> Of earth, and with what motion mov'd the clouds!   (I, 341–50)

And there was the famous 'act of stealth/And troubled pleasure' when he made off with someone else's boat at night:

> She was an elfin Pinnace; lustily
> I dipp'd my oars into the silent Lake,
> And, as I rose upon the stroke, my Boat
> Went heaving through the water, like a Swan;
> When, from behind that craggy Steep, till then
> The bound of the horizon, a huge Cliff,
> As if with voluntary power instinct,
> Uprear'd its head. I struck and struck again,
> And, growing still in stature, the huge Cliff
> Rose up between me and the stars, and still,
> With measur'd motion, like a living thing,
> Strode after me. With trembling hands I turn'd,
> And through the silent water stole my way
> Back to the Cavern of the Willow tree.
> There, in her mooring-place, I left my Bark,
> And, through the meadows homeward went, with grave
> And serious thoughts . . . .   (I, 401–17)

It is difficult to be sure whether Wordsworth is claiming to have had such experiences only when doing things that he should not have done, or whether he chooses incidents deliberately to set himself in an unflattering and therefore more congenial light. The meaning of the experiences is deliberately left obscure. As Wordsworth explains:

>   Of Genius, Power,
> Creation and Divinity itself
> I have been speaking, for my theme has been
> What pass'd within me. Not of outward things
> Done visibly for other minds, words, signs,
> Symbols or actions; but of my own heart
> Have I been speaking, and my youthful mind.
> O Heavens! how awful is the might of Souls,
> And what they do within themselves, while yet
> The yoke of earth is new to them, the world
> Nothing but a wild field where they were sown.
> This is, in truth, heroic argument,
> And genuine prowess; which I wish'd to touch
> With hand however weak; but in the main
> It lies far hidden from the reach of words.
> Points have we all of us within our souls,
> Where all stand single; this I feel, and make
> Breathings for incommunicable powers.
> Yet each man is a memory to himself,
> And, therefore, now that I must quit this theme,
> I am not heartless; for there's not a man
> That lives who hath not had his godlike hours,
> And knows not what majestic sway we have,
> As natural beings in the strength of nature.   (III, 171–94)

He claims a bond with his readers, inviting them to recognize the greatness within themselves.

Wordsworth's description of his encounter with society occupies Books III to VIII. Once the unusual circumstances of his early life have been established, the chronological progress is less rigorous. He feels free to use flashbacks, to omit periods that do not contribute to his theme, and to expatiate digressively on favourite topics when he finds an opening for them. The traditional characteristics of the reflective poem begin to reassert themselves. Knowledge of the world, of course, was something that Wordsworth shared with his readers. Instead of telling them about experiences they have missed, he is obliged to remind them of what they already know. If we find the shift towards representative catalogues of social life or of the experience of reading less interesting at first than the fully realized incidents with which we have been regaled hitherto, we come to appreciate that the course of Wordsworth's argument requires the sacrifice. By way of making

124

amends, he intersperses the vacations in the Lake District and among the Alps in which he is freer to follow his own bent.

Cowper, it will be recalled, castigated the universities for repudiating their worthy past by abandoning discipline. Wordsworth begins more persuasively by emphasizing his high expectations of Cambridge, and admitting the many genuine charms of the place. His first glimpse of an undergraduate captures the ingenuous excitement of the newcomer:

> Soon afterwards, we espied upon the road,
> A student cloth'd in Gown and tassell'd Cap;
> He pass'd; nor was I master of my eyes
> Till he was left a hundred yards behind. (III, 6–9)

His first impressions of his new surroundings and companions are utterly uncritical:

> I was the Dreamer, they the Dream; I roam'd
> Delighted, through the motley spectacle;
> Gowns grave or gaudy, Doctors, Students, Streets,
> Lamps, Gateways, Flocks of Churches, Courts and Towers:
> Strange transformation for a mountain Youth,
> A northern Villager. (III, 28–33)

He relishes his new status as a man of means and takes his part in the social whirl (III, 33–43), acknowledges that he did not apply himself to his studies, and even records an occasion when having become tipsy at a party held in a room that had once been Milton's he ran 'Ostrich-like' through the streets to the compulsory chapel service:

> Up-shouldering in a dislocated lump,
> With shallow ostentatious carelessness,
> My Surplice, gloried in, and yet despised,
> I clove in pride through the inferior throng
> Of the plain Burghers, who in audience stood
> On the last skirts of their permitted ground,
> Beneath the pealing Organ. (III, 316–22)

Looking back he is ashamed of such antics and speaks of 'the weakness of that hour/In some of its unworthy vanities,/Brother of many more' (III, 326–8). But the effect of mentioning them is to stress his likeness to the average young man. Again he appears as one of a crowd:

> if a throng was near
> That way I lean'd by nature; for my heart
> Was social, and lov'd idleness and joy. (III, 234–6)

Wordsworth felt that Cambridge had let him down as it had let down many of his generation, and he takes great care to explain why. Although, as he admits, he did not apply himself to his studies, he did respond to the inspiring traditions of the place:

> I could not print
> Ground where the grass had yielded to the steps
> Of generations of illustrious Men,
> Unmov'd; I could not always lightly pass
> Through the same Gateways; sleep where they had slept,
> Wake where they wak'd, range that enclosure old
> That garden of great intellects undisturb'd.   (III, 261–7)

He revered the memories of such great men as Newton, Chaucer, Spenser and Milton, and respected the devout austerities of ancient learning. Their modern counterpart, however, was unworthy of those 'homely days':

> The surfaces of artificial life
> And manners finely spun, the delicate race
> Of colours, lurking, gleaming up and down
> Through that state arras woven with silk and gold;
> This wily interchange of snaky hues,
> Willingly or unwillingly reveal'd
> I had not learn'd to watch . . . .   (III, 590–6)

And the elders of the place, 'Men unscour'd, grotesque/In character' (III, 574–5), appeared at a disadvantage when compared with the simple dignity of the aged shepherd swains of his own region. Wordsworth's disillusionment with Cambridge, then, is not allowed to imply either his personal superiority or an indifference to the ideals of learning and piety.

When he returns home for the summer vacation, it is with a livelier sense of the valuableness of the place and of the people. He renews old acquaintances—among them a terrier whom Cowper would have liked—and revisits favourite scenes, and has his memorable meeting with the discharged veteran, a variant on the 'old Cumberland beggar'. Back at Cambridge he is sustained by feelings and interests that have been reinforced by his return to the Lake District, and he begins, 'detached/Internally from academic cares' (VI, 29–30), to indulge poetic ambitions. Lonely evening walks replace the earlier conviviality, and from this solitariness at least one singular set-piece survives:

> A single Tree
> There was, no doubt yet standing there, an Ash
> With sinuous trunk, boughs exquisitely wreath'd;
> Up from the ground and almost to the top
> The trunk and master branches everywhere

> Were green with ivy; and the lightsome twigs
> And outer spray profusely tipp'd with seeds
> That hung in yellow tassels and festoons,
> Moving or still, a Favourite trimm'd out
> By Winter for himself, as if in pride,
> And with outlandish grace. Oft have I stood
> Foot-bound, uplooking at this lovely Tree
> Beneath a frosty moon.   (VI, 90–102)

Wordsworth claims no more personal credit for such perceptions than for the philosophical satisfactions of his rather casual incursions into geometry; they are satisfactions merely incidental to attending university.

Reading, that more private and yet more universal educational resource, had to be accorded its due. In some ways it belongs with the influence of Nature rather than with encounters with the world, but it too is an experience that Wordsworth must assume is familiar to his audience. Further, it is an experience that—as a critic is humiliatingly aware—withers in the retelling. Book V entitled 'Books' pays a tribute without which the account of the growth of an individual mind would be incomplete, but little is made of individual works. Wordsworth is satisfied with a general acknowledgment to the power of simple tales:

> Why call upon a few weak words to say
> What is already written in the hearts
> Of all that breathe? what in the path of all
> Drops daily from the tongue of every Child,
> Wherever Man is found? The trickling tear
> Upon the cheek of listening Infancy
> Tells it, and the insuperable look
> That drinks as if it never could be full.   (V, 185–92)

Having impressed upon us the preciousness of human art and science in his allegorical dream of the Arab with the stone and the shell (V, 49–165), he uses the opportunity to argue for books as stimulators of youthful imaginations. He inveighs against the stultifying influence of books designed to 'improve' children—expressing a distaste here that was shared by many of his contemporaries—and speaks out instead for the *Arabian Nights*, legends and romances, with all their extravagance, as fitter fare for 'simple childhood'. He adds the diffident assertion 'From heart-experience, and in humblest sense/Of modesty' (V, 609–10) that those who have grown up in the midst of 'living Nature' gain an additional pleasure from the 'great Nature that exists in works/Of mighty Poets' (V, 618–19).

Two further encounters with the world remain—with foreign countries and with the great city. The journey on foot through the Alps occupies much of Book VI. The purposes of the journey were twofold, to admire the sublime scenery and to experience the heady new emancipation of revolutionary France. Wordsworth stresses the picturesqueness and the sociableness of meetings with unknown

127

strangers. The famous sights are duly registered—Mont Blanc and the Vale of Chamonix, the monastery at Chartreuse, and, in Italy, Lake Locarno and Lake Como. All these were expected to inspire a young man. There is one disappointment, however. Hurrying to rejoin their guide after lingering behind over a meal, Wordsworth and his companion are surprised to find that their path leads downwards. The significance of the discovery is that they have crossed the Alps without being aware of it. The contrast between their experience of the act and its tremendous historical associations in his mind suddenly brings home to him a dimension that has been missing from his tour:

> Imagination! lifting up itself
> Before the eye and progress of my Song
> Like an unfather'd vapour; here that Power,
> In all the might of its endowments, came
> Athwart me; I was lost as in a cloud,
> Halted, without a struggle to break through.   (VI, 525–30)

London too is full of promise. Wordsworth recalls his childish fantasies of it, and his description of the city is sufficiently detailed and appreciative to gladden even a Londoner's heart, and yet it too falls short of Wordsworth's expectation. He records faithfully the variety of people, occupations, and pastimes, concluding with the confusion of Bartholomew Fair as 'a type not false/Of what the mighty City is itself/To all except a Straggler here and there,/To the whole Swarm of its inhabitants . . .' (VII, 695–8). He visits and describes the law courts, parliament and the theatre, and he listens disapprovingly to fashionable preachers. But out of all this 'perpetual flow/Of trivial objects' (VII, 701–2) emerge the moving sights of a 'rosy Babe' in the midst of dissolute spectators at Sadler's Wells (VII, 365–411), and of a blind beggar, 'propp'd against a Wall' with a label on his chest (VII, 610–22), both of which are reminders of aspects of humanity that the city obscures.

The disappointment of these encounters with the world was not enough to shake Wordsworth's confidence in 'what we may become' (VIII, 807). Cowper's response had been a contented retirement, but Wordsworth was young, he had not been wounded personally, and he had faith in the potentialities of society. It was natural for him to consider possibilities of political reform, natural but dangerous. The French Revolution was not only the most momentous example of a political experiment in modern times, but it and the ensuing war against France had also divided Englishmen as they had not been divided since the Civil War. Southey once confided in a younger poet one of the bitter lessons learned by Wordsworth's generation: 'to feel *against* our own country can only be right upon great and transitory occasions, and none but our contemporaries can feel with us,—none but those who remember the struggle and took part in it'.[10] When Wordsworth grasped this nettle he knew that the issues were still alive. In treating them explicitly, as he was to do again in *The Excursion* (1814), he could be sure of an interested hearing, but he ran the risk of offending readers upon whom he wished to impress more

128

general truths. His own first-hand experience in revolutionary France gave him the excuse he needed.

Books IX to X are not wholly political. They contain not only the abbreviated version of the story of Vaudracour and Julia, which it is now customary to associate with Wordsworth's love of Annette Vallon, but a convincing and sympathetic rendering of the feelings of a young man steeping himself in the life of a foreign country. In *The Task* Cowper had said of the Bastille, 'There's not an English heart that would not leap/To hear that ye were fall'n at last . . .' (V, 389–90). Yet a few years later Wordsworth portrays himself as being more interested in a sentimental painting by Le Brun than in the ruins of the infamous prison:

> Where silent zephyrs sported with the dust
> Of the Bastile, I sate in the open sun,
> And from the rubbish gather'd up a stone
> And pocketed the relick in the guise
> Of an Enthusiast, yet, in honest truth
> Though not without some strong incumbences;
> And glad, (could living man be otherwise)
> I look'd for something that I could not find,
> Affecting more emotion than I felt . . . .   (IX, 63–9)

The confession is ingenuous and true to the experience of many travellers, but it also allays the suspicion that this young visitor to France was a political zealot. Again Wordsworth emphasizes his ordinariness in the midst of exceptional circumstances:

> I scarcely felt
> The shock of these concussions, unconcerned,
> Tranquil, almost, and careless as a flower
> Glassed in a Green-house, or a Parlour shrub
> When every bush and tree, the country through,
> Is shaking to the roots; indifference this
> Which may seem strange; but I was unprepared
> With needful knowledge, had abruptly pass'd
> Into a theatre, of which the stage
> Was busy with an action far advanced.
> Like others I had read, and eagerly
> Sometimes, the master Pamphlets of the day;
> Nor wanted such half-insight as grew wild
> Upon that meagre soil, help'd out by Talk
> And public News; but having never chanced
> To see a regular Chronicle which might shew,
> (If any such indeed existed then)
> Whence the main Organs of the Public Power

> Had sprung, their transmigrations when and how
> Accomplish'd, giving thus unto events
> A form and body, all things were to me
> Loose and disjointed, and the affections left
> Without a vital interest. (IX, 85–107)

His first associations were with military members of the upper class who were opposed to the course of political events and who tried to enlist him in their cause, but their passionate devotion to royalism and hierarchical society merely seemed alien to the humble democracy of the Lake District, where 'wealth and titles were in less esteem/Than talents and successful industry' (IX, 234–5).

Beaupuy is an outcast among these aristocratic officers because of his democratic views, but Wordsworth is drawn to him because of his saintly qualities:

> By birth he rank'd
> With the most noble, but unto the poor
> Among mankind he was in service bound
> As by some tie invisible, oaths profess'd
> To a religious Order. Man he lov'd
> As Man.... (IX, 308–13)

Their earnest discussions of social justice are carried on in a mood of gentle tolerance as master and pupil walk along the banks of the Loire. And, as if to assure us that they were not oblivious of the romantic old associations of the place, Wordsworth mentions the recollections of Ariosto, Tasso, and others that came to mind. It is, however, in these beautiful surroundings that the most individual scene in this part of *The Prelude* occurs:

> when we chanc'd
> One day to meet a hunger-bitten Girl,
> Who crept along, fitting her languid self
> Unto a Heifer's motion, by a cord
> Tied to her arm, and picking thus from the lane
> Its sustenance, while the Girl with her two hands
> Was busy knitting, in a heartless mood
> Of solitude, and at the sight my Friend
> In agitation said, ''Tis against *that*
> Which we are fighting', I with him believed
> Devoutly that a spirit was abroad
> Which could not be withstood, that poverty
> At least like this, would in a little time
> Be found no more.... (IX, 510–23)

The incident would not have been out of place among Southey's eclogues in the *Annual Anthology*. Set in a foreign country it can be looked at with less sense of self-reproach, and it would be hard to withhold sympathy for their wish however unrealistic one might think it. Wordsworth's involvement with the hopes of France, stemming as it does from his actual presence there, from friendship, charitable feeling and the optimism of youth, captures the essence of the idealism of the young and it is quite untouched by the doctrinaire intolerance that is so offensive to honest opponents of reform.

Wordsworth's hopes were doomed to disappointment. Returning to Paris after the declaration of the Republic he had premonitions of the carnage to come and, compelled by lack of money, returned reluctantly to England. The great personal trials lay ahead. The English declaration of war seemed to him a betrayal of the English faith in liberty, and in a passage that he did not see fit to alter in more conservative years he speaks out against this shock to the better instincts of the young:

> Oh! much have they to account for, who could tear
> By violence at one decisive rent
> From the best Youth in England, their dear pride,
> Their joy, in England; this, too, at a time
> In which worst losses easily might wear
> The best of names, when patriotic love
> Did of itself in modesty give way
> Like the Precursor when the Deity
> Is come, whose Harbinger he is, a time
> In which apostacy from ancient faith
> Seem'd but conversion to a higher creed . . . .　　　　　(X, 276–86)

The reproach is not an individual one and it is not even primarily political. Following upon the account of his own disinterested idealism, it sums up majestically the grievance of Wordsworth's contemporaries. England's failure to stand by her principles is a stimulant to the forces of wickedness in France and the Terror begins. Even the death of Robespierre, which brings about an eager revival of hope temporarily, is insufficient. Wordsworth emphasizes the paradigmatic significance of these events:

> It was a lamentable time for man
> Whether a hope had e'er been his or not,
> A woeful time for them whose hopes did still
> Outlast the shock; most woeful for those few,
> Who still were flattered, and had trust in man.　　　　　(X, 356–61)

In Book XI, when he recapitulates the course of his political development, Wordsworth explains that loss of hope in France meant for him loss of hope in mankind. Bereft of his confidence in man he turns temporarily to the less disappointing abstractions of mathematical thought:

131

> I lost
> All feeling of conviction, and, in fine,
> Sick, wearied out with contrarieties,
> Yielded up moral questions in despair,
> And for my future studies, as the sole
> Employment of the enquiring faculty,
> Turn'd towards mathematics, and their clear
> And solid evidence . . . .   (X, 898–905)

The blackness of his despair seems all the darker for the sunshine of the earlier books. The fall is complete without being the product of a moral act. The final act of the spiritual autobiography remains to be played out.

Political events and Wordsworth's own political idealism were the immediate cause of his miserable condition. But if we look back over *The Prelude* we find that the first wrong turning had taken place long before when he was at Cambridge. Of his arrival there he was able to say:

> . here, O Friend! have I retrac'd my life
> Up to an eminence, and told a tale
> Of matters which, not falsely, I may call
> The glory of my youth.   (III, 168–71)

Although, as we have seen, his early advantages protected him from being seriously misled by his experiences as a young man, he had admitted to a significant alteration from the start:

> I had made a change
> In climate; and my nature's outward coat
> Changed also, slowly and insensibly.
> To the deep quiet and majestic thoughts
> Of loneliness succeeded empty noise
> And superficial pastimes . . . .   (III, 207–12)

Abrupt though his despair after the failure of his hopes for France may have seemed, he represents it as the last stage of a long decline. His recovery, in the final books of the poem, is not merely from the political shock but from the entirety of that decline, from Book III on.

Looking retrospectively at what had happened to him, Wordsworth proceeds by analogies rather than analysis, as a poet should. He considers an alternative to his own habit of mind:

> I knew a Maid,
> Who, young as I was then, conversed with things
> In higher style, from Appetites like these
> She, gentle Visitant, as well she might,

132

> Was wholly free, far less did critic rules
> Or barren intermeddling subtleties,
> Perplex her mind; but, wise as Women are
> When genial circumstance hath favor'd them,
> She welcom'd what was given, and craved no more.
> Whatever scene was present to her eyes,
> That was the best . . . .   (XI, 199–209)

And he recognizes the resemblance to his own early youth:

> Even like this Maid before I was call'd forth
> From the retirement of my native hills
> I lov'd whate'er I saw . . . .   (XI, 224–6)

An appreciation of natural surroundings that is not inhibited by the connoisseur's comparing habit is what seems to be implied here, but an appreciation that is not wholly dependent either upon the surroundings themselves. At this point Wordsworth introduces his famous passage about the 'spots of time' in order to press his meaning home. The term has been applied by some commentators to the more vivid episodes in the early part of the poem, and the beginning of Wordsworth's definition may seem to sanction this view:

> There are in our existence spots of time,
> Which with distinct pre-eminence retain
> A vivifying Virtue, whence, depress'd
> By false opinion and contentious thought,
> Or aught of heavier or more deadly weight,
> In trivial occupations, and the round
> Of ordinary intercourse, our minds
> Are nourished and invisibly repair'd . . . .   (XI, 258–65)

He goes on to fit it more narrowly, however, to two incidents that he is about to describe for the first time:

> A virtue by which pleasure is enhanced
> That penetrates, enables us to mount
> When high, more high, and lifts us up when fallen.
> This efficacious spirit chiefly lurks
> Among those passages of life in which
> We have had deepest feeling that the mind
> Is lord and master, and that outward sense
> Is but the obedient servant of her will.   (XI, 266–73)

Of the childhood incidents that follow—the encounter with the girl carrying the pitcher, and the occasion when he sat waiting between the sheep and the hawthorn tree—the first may have taken on an unintended picturesqueness for the modern reader, but Wordsworth's intention is unequivocal. 'It was', he says, 'in truth,/An ordinary sight . . .' (XI, 308–9). The significance of such sights lies in the strong feelings of the observer. And it is this capacity of the mind to transcend experience and make something memorable out of unprepossessing materials that Wordsworth makes the corner-stone of his account of man's potentiality.

In Book XIII he describes an occasion on which as a young man he climbed Mount Snowdon at night with a friend in order to see the sunrise from its summit. A taste for such sights was normal for nature lovers of the period, and Wordsworth would have expected his readers to remember Beattie's depiction of young Edwin's enthusiasm in *The Minstrel*:

> And oft the craggy cliff he loved to climb,
> When all in mist the world below was lost.
> What dreadful pleasure! there to stand sublime,
> Like shipwreck'd mariner on desert coast,
> And view th' enormous waste of vapour, tost
> In billows, lengthening to th' horizon round,
> Now scoop'd in gulfs, with mountains now emboss'd!
> And hear the voice of mirth and song rebound,
> Flocks, herds, and waterfalls, along the hoar profound!
>
> (I, st. xxii)

Wordsworth gives his own experience the necessary particularity by describing the effort of the climb and mentioning the noisy excitement when their guide's dog came upon a hedgehog. The homeliness of the interruption sets off the suddenness of their emergence from the mist:

> a Light upon the turf
> Fell like a flash: I looked about, and lo!
> The Moon stood naked in the Heavens, at height
> Immense above my head, and on the shore
> I found myself of a huge sea of mist,
> Which, meek and silent, rested at my feet:
> A hundred hills their dusky backs upheaved
> All over this still Ocean, and beyond,
> Far, far beyond, the vapours shot themselves,
> In headlands, tongues, and promontory shapes,
> Into the Sea, the real Sea, that seem'd
> To dwindle, and give up its majesty,
> Usurp'd upon as far as sight could reach.
> Meanwhile, the Moon look'd down upon this shew
> In single glory, and we stood, the mist
> Touching our very feet; and from the shore
> At distance not the third part of a mile

Was a blue chasm; a fracture in the vapour,
A deep and gloomy breathing-place through which
Mounted the roar of waters, torrents, streams
Innumerable, roaring with one voice.
The universal spectacle throughout
Was shaped for admiration and delight,
Grand in itself alone, but in that breach
Through which the homeless voice of waters rose,
That dark deep thoroughfare had nature lodg'd
The Soul, the Imagination of the whole.   (XIII, 39–65)

Wordsworth makes a symbol of this scene, as he had of his dream of the mounted
Arab in Book V, and if it is a more difficult symbol to interpret it is mainly because
it stands for something that can only be conjectured at. Looking back upon the
experience, he tells us that

      it appear'd to me
The perfect image of a mighty Mind
Of one that feeds upon infinity,
That is exalted by an under-presence,
The sense of God, or whatsoe'er is dim
Or vast in its own being . . . .   (XIII, 68–73)

The lighter world above the level of the mist, glorious but attentive, seems to stand
for the mind in Wordsworth's analogy. The voices from beneath, heard through
the rift in the mist, are the appearances of the world. Such a mind is the ideal
representation of the actuality referred to in the 'spots of time' in Book XI:

              the mind
Is lord and master, and that outward sense
Is but the obedient servant of her will.   (XI, 271–3)

In its ideal state such a mind can only be imagined of God, but human beings in
their best moments may be thought of as approaching it.

    Summing up his life in Book XIII, Wordsworth sees himself in spite of his great
initial advantages as having been 'careless then/Of what was given me' and
describes his present self modestly as 'a meditative, oft a suffering Man . . .' (XIII,
124–6). His recovery from his disillusionment and his ability once again to have
faith in his fellow creatures has come about as a result of his healing association
with his sister—the 'gentle Visitant' of Book XI—which reminds him of his own
happier beginnings. He resumes his former habits of mind:

            Above all
Did Nature bring again that wiser mood
More deeply re-established in my soul,

135

> Which, seeing little worthy or sublime
> In what we blazon with the pompous names
> Of power and action, early tutor'd me
> To look with feelings of fraternal love
> Upon those unassuming things, that hold
> A silent station in this beauteous world. (XII, 44–52)

He takes no credit for the recovery, and he concludes the poem with expressions of gratitude to the various friends who helped to restore him to himself. His aim is to encourage and sustain others whose circumstances must necessarily have been less happy than his own, and who were therefore almost bound to miss what he had so fortuitously found.

Falling back on hopes closer to those expressed in *The Task*, Wordsworth turns from the abstraction of the state towards the observable individuals within it:

> having gain'd
> A more judicious knowledge of what makes
> The dignity of individual Man,
> Of Man, no composition of the thought,
> Abstraction, shadow, image, but the man
> Of whom we read, the man whom we behold
> With our own eyes; I could not but inquire,
> Not with less interest than heretofore,
> But greater, though in spirit more subdued,
> Why is this glorious Creature to be found
> Only one in ten thousand? What one is,
> Why may not many be? What bars are thrown
> By Nature in the way of such a hope? (XII, 81–93)

His answer can be much more optimistic than Cowper's.

Even the visionary moments, however, are not to be valued for their own sakes. Wordsworth has recorded his own experience of the aspect of mind that is independent of sense, and he calls it 'imagination'. In Book XIII, he offers a series of explanatory definitions of it:

> Imagination, which, in truth,
> Is but another name for absolute strength
> And clearest insight, amplitude of mind,
> And reason in her most exalted mood. (XIII, 167–70)

He has come to realize that this form of insight has always been his source of strength, and that his period of disillusionment came about when he stopped relying on it:

> This faculty hath been the moving soul
> Of our long labour: we have traced the stream

From darkness, and the very place of birth
In its blind cavern, whence is faintly heard
The sound of waters; follow'd it to light
And open day, accompanied its course
Among the ways of Nature, afterwards
Lost sight of it, bewilder'd and engulph'd,
Then given it greeting, as it rose once more
With strength, reflecting in its solemn breast
The works of man and face of human life,
And lastly, from its progress have we drawn
The feeling of life endless, the great thought
By which we live, Infinity and God.   (XIII, 171–84)

The value of imagination, then, in the sense in which Wordsworth defines it in this poem, is that it reconciles us with the lot of man by reassuring us that however untoward circumstances may be a benevolent Power persists. To revert to the comparison with *Paradise Lost*, Wordsworth may be said to have provided a secular substitute for the authority of Revelation. Addressing his friend, Coleridge, in the concluding lines of the poem, he sums up their ambition as poets to share with others the haven they have found. They hope the testimony of their experience will strengthen their readers:

                    we to them will speak
A lasting inspiration, sanctified
By reason and by truth; what we have loved,
Others will love; and we may teach them how;
Instruct them how the mind of man becomes
A thousand times more beautiful than the earth
On which he dwells, above this Frame of things
(Which, 'mid all revolutions in the hopes
And fears of men, doth still remain unchanged)
In beauty exalted, as it is itself
Of substance and of fabric more divine.   (XIII, 442–52)

The mind of the individual is the unfailing source of faith. Wordsworth makes this claim as an ordinary but fortunate man speaking to other men. It is a religious claim, with moral and political implications.

  The Prelude has often been interpreted more narrowly as a poet's discussion of literary imagination. The full title of the poem — *The Prelude, or Growth of a Poet's Mind: An Autobiographical Poem* — seems to encourage such a view. And Wordsworth certainly represents himself as a poet and speaks of his literary ambitions at various points. But the title of the poem was supplied by Mrs Wordsworth after her husband's death in 1850 at a time when it was natural to be more interested in him as a poet than merely as a man. The only manuscript title-page bore the inscription 'Poem/Title not yet fixed upon/by/William Wordsworth/Addressed to/S. T. Coleridge'. And over the years since it had been completed the Wordsworth household referred to it simply as 'the poem to Coleridge'. The 'persona' of the poet in *The Prelude* is undeniable, but it should be kept in perspective. Impersonal as this autobiography is—we find out much less about Wordsworth's character than we do about Cowper's in *The Task*, although we learn more about the events of his life—we expect to be told the narrator's occupation. If he is to be persuasive he must be seen to be disinterested, and yet the confident and sociable purport of *The Prelude* would make it inappropriate for him to be portrayed as a recluse. The occupation of poet is true to life, but because of its classlessness and freedom from an externally imposed routine it is also rhetorically convenient. To make it the centre of the poem is a distortion and one that loses sight of a grander and nobler theme.

III *Childe Harold's Pilgrimage*

It is appropriate to think of Lord Byron's *Childe Harold's Pilgrimage* as a trilogy whose parts differ considerably from one another in character. Cantos I and II (1812) constitute the first part, Canto III (1816) the second, and Canto IV (1818) the third. When the volume containing the first two cantos appeared, it was offered to the public as a book of travels through Portugal, Spain, and Greece. After four years of news reports of the uneven progress of the Peninsular War, the place names of Portugal and Spain were familiar to every English reader. They were associated with battles, sieges and treaties, and Byron's descriptions of the settings (Lisbon, Cintra, Seville, and Cadiz) were deliberately topical and lost nothing from his eye-witness account of troop movements. The place names of the eastern Mediterranean, by contrast, were known through Classical literature. The idea of describing the relics of ancient Greece had already been tried out in Walter Wright's *Horae Ionicae : A Poem, Descriptive of the Ionian Islands, and Part of the Adjacent Coast of Greece* (1809), [11] a work to which Byron had referred respectfully in *English Bards and Scotch Reviewers* (1809). His own tour also catered to an interest in the past, but it stressed the modern and the practical. He provided a facsimile of modern Greek writing as a frontispiece, included a list of colloquial expressions with their English counterparts in an appendix, and made much of his journey into the primitive and relatively untravelled regions of Albania.

Byron's decision to introduce a fictitious traveller 'for the sake of giving some connection to the piece', has come to seem more significant than it did at the time. The chivalric connotations of Childe Harold's name, and the antique ring of the title of the poem and of its sub-title, 'a Romaunt', may have led some readers to expect a narrative poem after the manner of Scott's newly popular romances, but they were derived from Byron's decision to write in Spenserian stanzas. According to his preface, he chose the stanza because it was adaptable to various moods, and he cited the authority of James Beattie, James Thomson and Ariosto. The recent success of Thomas Campbell's *Gertrude of Wyoming* (1809)—which Byron disliked and might well have wished to spare his readers—seems to have reminded poets of

138

the possibilities of the Spenserian stanza. Scott, for instance, adopted it in his own Portuguese poem, *The Vision of Don Roderick* (1811), but found it uncongenial. For Byron the complexities of the stanza acted as a welcome stimulus to the digressive reflections characteristic of much of his best writing. The archaic vocabulary that marks the opening of Canto I and reappears from time to time is also part of the Spenserian fancy dress, and together with lines such as 'Ah me! in sooth he was a shameless wight', with its echo of Beattie's *The Minstrel*, it lends a touch of playfulness to the poem.

The character of Childe Harold has become a focus for commentary. In the first place, as the irregularities of Byron's life became public knowledge it became common to identify him with his hero, a habit confirmed by subsequent biographers. In the second place, the appearance of a series of men of mystery in the poems that Byron published in the next few years—*The Giaour* (1813), *The Corsair* (1814), *Lara* (1814)—made it seem appropriate to confer their command-ing characteristics upon the much less explicitly defined Childe Harold. Childe Harold has a character in Cantos I and II that emerges from the poem itself, and Byron's first readers responded to it directly; modern readers have to make an effort.

In Canto I (ii–viii), Childe Harold is introduced to us as a young man of rank who has wasted his youth in debauchery and lost his capacity to enjoy life. It is said of him that 'he through Sin's long labyrinth had run' (I, v), but only his addiction to 'concubines and carnal companie' (I, ii) is specifically mentioned. 'Sick at heart', he chooses exile as the next best thing to suicide:

> Apart he stalked in joyless reverie,
> And from his native land resolved to go,
> And visit scorching climes beyond the sea;
> With pleasure drugged, he almost longed for woe,
> And e'en for change of scene would seek the shades below.　　(I, vi)

Childe Harold differs from the conventional sinner in his failure to repent, but his unhappiness and his renunciation of his former way of life are acceptable substitutes for penance. The Childe's worldly experience makes him a sophisti-cated observer, his rank accounts for his independent means, his lack of social connection frees him from company and responsibility, his withdrawal from society establishes his disinterestedness, and his relative youth fits him for arduous and dangerous travel. In character he is quite unlike the first-person observers of *The Task* and *The Prelude*, but from a rhetorical point of view he is useful in much the same way.

Once Childe Harold's weakness has been established we may be permitted to sympathize with him. His loneliness is impressed upon us—his unrequited love (I, v), his lack of genuine friends (I, ix), his estrangement even from the mother and sister whom he leaves behind (I, x). And yet, in 'Childe Harold's Good Night' his ability to understand the feelings of his homesick servants shows that he is no misanthropist. His sense of personal loss is returned to on several occasions—the death of a friend in battle (I, xci), and of another friend towards the end of Canto II (xcv–xcvi)—and his capacity to suffer is made explicit:

> None are so desolate but something dear,
> Dearer than self, possesses or possessed
> A thought, and claims the homage of a tear;
> A flashing pang! of which the weary breast
> Would still, albeit in vain, the heavy heart divest.   (II, xxiv)

It is often difficult to distinguish the author's reactions from Childe Harold's— Byron is agreeably casual—but the tribute 'To Inez' (following I, lxxxiv) is certainly the Childe's and it shows his appreciation of beauty and virtue in other people even if, like the 'fabled Hebrew Wanderer' (stanza 5), he feels cut off from them for ever. We are told that Childe Harold has been wicked, but it is impossible to keep company with him for long without feeling that although he is unhappy, he is essentially generous, kind, and upright. Byron's friend Samuel Rogers is reported as saying: 'I knew two old maids in Buckinghamshire who used to cry over the passage about Harold's "laughing dames" that "long had fed his youthful appetite", &c'.[12] The reaction is sentimental, but it is understandable.

Half-way through Canto I, Byron pauses in his account of Spain to mention that he is actually in sight of Mount Parnassus as he writes, and he reflects upon the difference between seeing a place and imagining it 'in the fabled landscape of a lay' (I, lx) as so many poets have had to in the past. This short digression provides an apt metaphor for the series of comparisons of Childe Harold's experiences with popular expectations that is offered throughout the poem. Byron emphasizes the discrepancies and uses them as an opening for comment on various differences between ideas and actuality.

On arriving in Portugal he pays a tribute to the beauty of 'Cintra's glorious Eden':

> The horrid crags, by toppling convent crowned,
> The cork-trees hoar that clothe the shaggy steep,
> The mountain-moss by scorching skies imbrowned,
> The sunken glen, whose sunless shrubs must weep,
> The tender azure of the unruffled deep,
> The orange tints that gild the greenest bough,
> The torrents that from cliff to valley leap,
> The vine on high, the willow branch below,
> Mixed in one mighty scene, with varied beauty glow.   (I, xix)

The grandeur of this prospect is out of keeping with the abject character of the people who live beside it. They are depicted as dirty, servile and treacherous—'Why, Nature, waste thy wonders on such men?' (I, xviii) From the wooden crosses that mark where assassinations have taken place, Childe Harold passes

140

almost immediately to the scene of the Convention of Cintra. The transition from Portuguese baseness to British folly serves notice that when the Childe disparages foreigners his remarks will have a discomfiting way of coming home to the reader.

A mere 'silver streamlet' separates Spain from Portugal (I, xxxiii), but Byron makes no bones about his feeling that the two countries are utterly different from one another. His view was shared by his contemporaries. In 1810 and 1811 the eyes of Europe were upon Spain as the first country to offer serious resistance to a Napoleonic invasion. The enthusiasm that Byron expresses for Spain's glorious past (I, xxxv) would have been just as appropriate to the past of Portugal, but in Spain there was the exciting possibility of a revival. Freedom from tyranny was the cause, and some allowance is made for patriotic feeling in the treatment of the pyrrhic victories of Talavera and Albuera (I, xl–xliii), but the emptiness of military glory is stressed:

> Three hosts combine to offer sacrifice;
> Three tongues prefer strange orisons on high;
> Three gaudy standards flout the pale blue skies;
> The shouts are France, Spain, Albion, Victory!
> The Foe, the Victim, and the fond Ally
> That fights for all, but ever fights in vain,
> Are met—as if at home they could not die—
> To feed the crow on Talavera's plain,
> And fertilise the field that each pretends to gain. (I, xli)

From stanza xliv to the end of Canto I Byron's attention is devoted to the people on whose behalf this campaign is being waged. The contrast between the heedless gaiety of Seville and the sullen apprehensiveness of the country folk provides a civil counterpart to the illusions of war. The image of women in combat appealed to Romantic sensibilities and the Maid of Saragoza was one of the sights of Seville. Byron stresses her womanly qualities by way of reminding us of the terrible sacrifices required by an invasion (I, liv–lix). His description of Cadiz, however, is the most extensive in the canto and it is designed to present his readers with a Spanish counterpart to English society. His enthusiasm for the beauty of the city is perfectly genuine, but he concentrates on that quintessential target of English disapproval, bull-fighting on Sundays. Southey had treated the topic amusingly from a Spanish point of view in Don Espriella's *Letters from England* in 1807, but Byron's purpose is not so much to tease his readers into an awareness of their own weaknesses as to make them feel how much the Spanish are like themselves. By arousing a livelier sympathy for the victims he hopes to impress upon us the hideousness of war, especially of ineffectual war.

In Canto II, different scenes prompt different reflections, and yet similar motifs emerge. The ruins of Athens illustrate the decay of civilizations and remind us of human mutability (II, i–x), but their magnificence and historical associations are lost upon the people who live near them: 'Yet these proud Pillars claim no passing sigh;/Unmoved the Moslem sits, the light Greek carols by' (II, x). This

141

indifference pales into insignificance beside the mischievous enthusiasm of the British Lord Elgin (II, xi–xv). The transition from abject native to disgraceful countryman is as tellingly easy and topical in Athens as it was at Cintra (II, xvii–xviii). The voyage calls for mention if only because the romance of shipboard life had reached a new height in the years following the death of Nelson—as even homely poems such as Ireland's *The Sailor-Boy* (1809) show. The passing of Calypso's Isles allows for the mention of the disappointed Florence as a modern counterpart to Calypso, and as a sequel to Childe Harold's appreciativeness of Spanish women and a reminder of his aloofness (II, xxix–xxxv). The great battle scenes—Actium, Lepanto, Trafalgar—serve for another expression of contempt for military fame, ancient or modern (II, xl).

As with Canto I, the longest section is devoted to an account of an unfamiliar society—the Albanians under Ali Pasha. Byron offers it for its contrast to England and to Christian civilization.

> Land of Albania! let me bend mine eyes
> On thee, thou rugged Nurse of savage men!
> The Cross descends, thy Minarets arise,
> And the pale Crescent sparkles in the glen,
> Through many a cypress-grove within each city's ken.   (II, xxxviii)

The relativity of religions is rather daringly implied as part of a rebuke to Christian hypocrisy (II, xliv). The account of Tepalen during the Fast of Ramazan would have been wholly novel to Byron's readers, and he makes the most of the mixture of exotic races, and, in their midst, of the inscrutable despot Ali Pasha. Ali's appearance belies his character:

> In marble-paved pavilion, where a spring
> Of living water from the centre rose,
> Whose bubbling did a genial freshness fling,
> And soft voluptuous couches breathed repose,
> ALI reclined, a man of war and woes:
> Yet in his lineaments ye cannot trace,
> While Gentleness her milder radiance throws
> Along that agéd venerable face,
> The deeds that lurk beneath, and stain him with disgrace.   (II, lxii)

The Suliote warriors, on the other hand, savages though they might be, are not only brave and loyal but hospitable and considerate to strangers in distress. Childe Harold's dread of being shipwrecked upon their shores proves groundless:

> Vain fear! the Suliotes stretched the welcome hand,
> Led them o'er rocks and past the dangerous swamp,
> Kinder than polished slaves though not so bland,
> And piled the hearth, and wrung their garments damp,

> And filled the bowl, and trimmed the cheerful lamp,
> And spread their fare; though homely, all they had:
> Such conduct bears Philanthropy's rare stamp:
> To rest the weary and to soothe the sad,
> Doth lesson happier men, and shames at least the bad. (II, lxviii)

The Suliotes are not to be compared with Wordsworth's 'statesmen' of Cumberland, but the contrast of unpolished generosity of nature with the meaner habits of city people similarly implies a reproach and supports a faith in the noble capacities of men.

In the closing stanzas, Byron turns to the condition of the Greeks themselves, subject to the tyranny of a foreign people, and reflects upon their proud past as he had in Canto I on the past of Spain. Unlike the Spaniards, the Greeks have not risen to free themselves, but Byron expresses his faith in them and exhorts them to rebel:

> Hereditary Bondsmen! know ye not
> *Who* would be free *themselves* must strike the blow?
> By their right arms the conquest must be wrought?
> Will Gaul or Muscovite redress ye? No!
> True—they may lay your proud despoilers low,
> But not for you will Freedom's Altars flame.
> Shades of the Helots! triumph o'er your foe!
> Greece! change thy lords, thy state is still the same;
> Thy glorious day is o'er, but not thine years of shame. (II, lxxvi)

To the Spaniards and to the Greeks Childe Harold's encouragement might seem to have a limited and attainable political objective; to English readers his views were rather vivid expressions of faith in values—freedom, courage, honesty, and generosity—that were thought to be characteristic of England. Throughout Cantos I and II it is implied that these values have been deserted.

Byron had an instinctive sense of what was interesting and colourful. He was free of cant and only slightly encumbered with singular opinions. He was direct and enthusiastic. His metrical fluency allows him to triumph over the straitjacket of the Spenserian stanza as no other writer had been able to before. This combination of qualities gave his travels, which would have been attractive even in prose, an unprecedented freshness. As he recorded in his journal the day after publication, 'I awoke one morning and found myself famous.'[13]

The distinction between the author and Childe Harold is uncertainly maintained in Cantos I and II. In Canto III, its purpose of providing an excuse for a disenchanted way of looking at the world having been fulfilled, the Childe is virtually discarded. The author reminds himself of his presence in stanza viii, but only to explain that he is no longer as invulnerable to human sympathies as before: 'Harold, once more within the vortex, rolled/On with the giddy circle, chasing Time . . .' (III, xi). In stanza liv it is remarked that Harold 'had learned to

143

love . . . The helpless looks of blooming Infancy', and this sentiment is perfectly in accord with the verses addressed by the narrator to his own daughter Ada at the opening and close of the canto. Thereafter, Harold's character, more tolerant and without a trace of his former profligacy, is merged in the narrator's.

The Battle of Waterloo is still the most famous of British victories. When Byron wrote it was fresh in his readers' minds. His decision to treat the event in elegiac terms was conventional enough: where he differs in spirit from commemorations such as Scott's *The Field of Waterloo* (1815) and Southey's *The Poet's Pilgrimage to Waterloo* (1816) is in his inability to believe that anything has been gained by the sacrifice. He uses the unmarked appearance of the battlefield as a metaphor for the inconsequentiality of the victory:

> Stop!—for thy tread is on an Empire's dust!
>   An Earthquake's spoil is sepulchred below!
>   Is the spot marked with no colossal bust?
>   Nor column trophied for triumphal show?
>   None; but *the moral's truth* tells simpler so.—
>   As the ground was before, thus let it be;—
>   How that red rain hath made the harvest grow!
>   And is this all the world has gained by thee,
> Thou first and last of Fields! king-making Victory?   (III, xvii)

Byron's answer in the affirmative is calculated to ruffle the feelings of the establishment, but it is not merely an unsympathetic provocation.

Having asked the telling question 'is Earth more free?' (III, xix), he launches into his stirring description of the Duchess of Richmond's ball on the eve of the battle:

> There was a sound of revelry by night,
>   And Belgium's Capital had gathered then
>   Her Beauty and her Chivalry—and bright
>   The lamps shone o'er fair women and brave men;
>   A thousand hearts beat happily; and when
>   Music arose with its voluptuous swell,
>   Soft eyes looked love to eyes which spake again,
>   And all went merry as a marriage bell;
> But hush! hark! a deep sound strikes like a rising knell!   (III, xxi)

The unlooked-for intrusion of death upon a fashionable assembly was a familiar theme—indeed it had recently been treated in crude contemporary terms by William Combe and Rowlandson in *The English Dance of Death* (1815). But whereas Combe unmasks hypocrites in his 'Masquerade' ball, Byron's dancers are good and beautiful and young. Their reluctance to hear the sounds of war is presented as natural and charming: 'On with the dance! let joy be unconfined;/No sleep till morn, when Youth and Pleasure meet/To chase the

144

glowing Hours with flying feet . . .' (III, xxii). And when the roar of the cannon can no longer be ignored, the sorrow of parting is described in terms that Keats could hardly have bettered:

> Ah! then and there was hurrying to and fro—
>   And gathering tears, and tremblings of distress,
>   And cheeks all pale, which but an hour ago
>   Blushed at the praise of their own loveliness—
>   And there were sudden partings, such as press
>   The life from out young hearts, and choking sighs
>   Which ne'er might be repeated; who could guess
>   If ever more should meet those mutual eyes,
> Since upon night so sweet such awful morn could rise! (III, xxiv)

Byron leaves no doubt as to the liveliness of his sympathy with such cruel partings, and he invites us to share it. With similar intensity he conveys the excitement and resoluteness of the soldiers going into battle:

> And there was mounting in hot haste—the steed,
>   The mustering squadron, and the clattering car,
>   Went pouring forward with impetuous speed,
>   And swiftly forming in the ranks of war—
>   And the deep thunder peal on peal afar . . . . (III, xxv)

The paradox of martial splendour and the horrors of war had already been memorably expressed in Thomas Campbell's battle song, 'Hohenlinden' (1801); Byron's treatment of it, as befits the illustration of a more comprehensive theme, acquaints us with the sufferers and endows his summation with a greater poignancy:

> Last noon beheld them full of lusty life;—
>   Last eve in Beauty's circle proudly gay;
>   The Midnight brought the signal-sound of strife,
>   The Morn the marshalling in arms,—the Day
>   Battle's magnificently-stern array!
>   The thunder-clouds close o'er it, which when rent
>   The earth is covered thick with other clay
>   Which her own clay shall cover, heaped and pent,
> Rider and horse,—friend,—foe,—in one red burial blent! (III, xxviii)

Byron's initial coolness to the victory is temporarily forgotten, and we are swept along by his awareness of the greatness of the sacrifice.

Byron's claim to be trusted by orthodox feeling is confirmed by his muted tribute to a man he knew (III, xxix–xxxi). He recognizes that those who have lost people

145

who were close to them cannot be comforted, and compares the stoical survivors to a series of broken, empty or decaying objects (III, xxxii–xxxiii). When he poses the disillusioned question: 'Did man compute/Existence by enjoyment, and count o'er/Such hours 'gainst years of life,—say, would he name threescore?' (III, xxxiv), such people, 'Living in shattered guise' (III, xxxiii), might well agree. The grim reality of Waterloo has been linked with the condition of life in general.

The treatment of Napoleon (III, xxxvi–xlv) is another instance of a topical specific case that is developed into one of general significance. Some of Napoleon's few votaries in England felt chagrin at his unheroic withdrawal from the battlefield and subsequent tame submission to captivity. For Byron, however, the incongruity—'Battling with nations, flying from the field' (III, xxxviii)—made him a truer emblem of mankind. His admiration is clear:

> There sunk the greatest, nor the worst of men,
> 　Whose Spirit, antithetically mixed,
> 　One moment of the mightiest, and again
> 　On little objects with like firmness fixed . . . .　　　　　(III, xxxvi)

The characterization is developed in general terms, and where we might have expected a rival to Dryden's dangerous Achitophel, we find instead a figure who is closer to Pope's representative man—'Great lord of all things, yet a prey to all . . ./ The glory, jest, and riddle of the world!'[14] Napoleon's capacity for greatness is diagnosed as a longing for the unattainable rather than as base ambition:

> 　　　　　there is a fire
> And motion of the Soul which will not dwell
> In its own narrow being, but aspire
> Beyond the fitting medium of desire . . . .　　　　　(III, xlii)

It is a longing that typifies the leaders among men:

> This makes the madmen who have made men mad
> 　By their contagion; Conquerors and Kings,
> 　Founders of sects and systems, to whom add
> 　Sophists, Bards, Statesmen, all unquiet things
> 　Which stir too strongly the soul's secret springs,
> 　And are themselves the fools to those they fool;
> 　Envied, yet how unenviable! what stings
> Are theirs! . . . .　　　　　(III, xliii)

The example of Napoleon has been used to introduce the theme of the vanity of human ambition, as the example of Waterloo had previously been used to introduce the uselessness and pain of human unhappiness. The point of view reminds one of Childe Harold's in Cantos I and II, but he is not mentioned; instead the predicament is disconcertingly presented as the reader's own.

Stanza xlv, with its comment on mankind's ingratitude to those who try to improve its condition, may be taken as the depth of misanthropic disillusionment. It corresponds to Wordsworth's loss of faith in *The Prelude*; the rest of Canto III is devoted to thoughts that, however tentatively they are argued, display feelings that are redolent of ardent optimism. The shift of mood is not immediately obvious. We are reminded of Childe Harold again, and his journey continues. As he passes through the Rhine Valley, natural beauties seem to be a relief from human inadequacies, and the castles of the robber barons, the battlefields and the memorials to the dead, rub in the lesson that Waterloo by contrast was pointless. At the same time a welcome vein of affirmation begins to emerge, ushered in by the admission of the Childe's capacity for affection (III, lii–lv) and by the charming if facile lyric of 'The castled Crag of Drachenfels'. Marceau's heroism is celebrated (III, lvi–lvii), Ehrenbreitstein is hailed as a 'Tower of Victory' (III, lviii), the battlefield of Morat is compared with that of Marathon (III, lxiii–lxiv), and the vain effort of Julia Alpinula to save her father is approvingly recorded (III, lxvi). This chronicle of 'deeds which should not pass away' (III, lxvii) revives something of the enthusiasm of the stanzas leading up to Waterloo.

With the arrival at Lake Leman (III, lxviii), a transitional passage on the experience of living apart from society, the focus of the Canto shifts from the analysis of human life and human nature in general to the unrepresentative but absorbing introspection of an individual. In stanzas lxix to lxxv, Byron expounds in the first person the rationale of the man who withdraws from society because he feels unsuited to it. The withdrawal he describes resembles the hermit's in its ambition to live more spiritually.

> And when, at length, the mind shall be all free
>   From what it hates in this degraded form,
>   Reft of its carnal life, save what shall be
>   Existent happier in the fly and worm,—
>   When Elements to Elements conform,
>   And dust is as it should be, shall I not
>   Feel all I see less dazzling but more warm?
>   The bodiless thought? the Spirit of each spot?
> Of which, even now, I share at times the immortal lot?   (III, lxxiv)

The 'fire/And motion of the Soul' attributed earlier (III, xlii) to 'the madmen who have made men mad/By their contagion' (III, xliii), which will 'aspire/Beyond the fitting medium of desire' (III, xlii) is claimed here as a personal experience. Napoleon was an instance of the incompatibility of such aspirations with society; beside Lake Leman, Rousseau comes appositely to mind as another who found that the actuality was at odds with his ideals. The terrible effects of such conflict were seen in the French Revolution and its bloody aftermath. Byron hints obscurely at the possibility that society is capable of improvement and that a time will come when passionate ideals may be carried into practice:

> in his lair
> Fixed Passion holds his breath, until the hour
> Which shall atone for years; none need despair:
> It came— —it cometh— —and will come . . . .   (III, lxxxiv)

But the prospect of the millennium is remote; in the meantime solitude must serve.

The night scene that follows (III, lxxxvi–xcvii) provides a soothing contrast. But, like the battlefield of Waterloo and the characters of Napoleon and Rousseau, it is presented as an extended metaphor for something else. It ranges from the picturesque calm observed from a boat—'on the ear/Drops the light drip of the suspended oar' (III, lxxxvi)—with the awe-inspiring stillness of the starry sky overhead, through the sublime disturbance of the thunderstorm, to the cheerful morning that follows. The remarkable feature of Byron's treatment of the storm is his choice of human emotions as analogues for it. The stars—'the poetry of Heaven' (III, lxxxviii)—are made a reminder 'That in our aspirations to be great,/Our destinies o'erleap their mortal state . . .' (III, lxxxviii). The loveliness of the coming of the storm is compared, riskily, to 'the light/Of a dark eye in Woman' (III, xcii); the cloven banks of the Rhône are likened to parted lovers—a simile that was probably borrowed from Coleridge's 'Christabel'—and the gathering parallel is made explicit in the question, 'But where of ye, O Tempests! is the goal?/Are ye like those within the human breast?/Or do ye find, at length, like eagles, some high nest?' (III, xcvi) The sustained metaphor of the sublime energies of the thunderstorm arising in the serene infinitude of the night sky provides the poet with an indirect way of communicating feelings for which conventional language seems inadequate. The metaphor is applied to himself at last:

> Could I embody and unbosom now
>   That which is most within me,—could I wreak
>   My thoughts upon expression, and thus throw
>   Soul—heart—mind—passions—feelings—strong or weak—
>   All that I would have sought, and all I seek,
>   Bear, know, feel—and yet breathe—into *one* word,
>   And that one word were Lightning, I would speak;
>   But as it is, I live and die unheard,
> With a most voiceless thought, sheathing it as a sword.   (III, xcvii)

The confession that his feelings cannot be adequately expressed conveys a fitting humility, but following a passage of such magnificence it adds to the extraordinariness of the feelings.

Love is personified as haunting the beautiful morning scene at Clarens that follows (III, xcviii–civ). The place is presented as a paradise away from the world, and again every aspect of the landscape is related to human emotions. The sentimentality of the setting seems less mawkish beside contemporary sentimentalities like Thomas Moore's 'Paradise and the Peri' (1817) or Leigh Hunt's *Story of Rimini* (1816):

148

> A populous solitude of bees and birds,
>   And fairy-formed and many-coloured things,
>   Who worship him with notes more sweet than words,
>   And innocently open their glad wings,
>   Fearless and full of life: the gush of springs,
>   And fall of lofty fountains, and the bend
>   Of stirring branches, and the bud which brings
>   The swiftest thought of Beauty, here extend
> Mingling— —and made by Love— —unto one mighty end.   (III, cii)

It works as a contrast to the fierce energy of the night scene and by analogy reveals the other extreme of human aspiration as it was conceived of in an age that perceived love as a 'tender mystery' (III, ciii).

In the first half of Canto III, the morals of Waterloo and Napoleon were expounded and they led to a despairing nihilism. In the second half, the experiences of being present at the night storm and the beauties of Clarens are described, but analysis is avoided. The effect is one of joyful and reassuring affirmation. Byron does not say in so many words that although rational observation of the world will lead to pessimism, our feelings belie it, but in Canto III he acts upon that assumption. Expecting more of the disillusionment of the jaded Childe Harold we are effectively taken by surprise by his mature successor.

Canto IV commences in Venice (i–xxiv), passes on to Arqua, Ferrara and Florence (xxx–lxi) and then to the natural beauties of Lake Trasimene, Clitumnus and the waterfall at Velino (lxii–lxxiv), before concluding in Rome (lxxviii–clxiii). The unequal proportions of the itinerary are a measure of its subservience to the reflections it purports to occasion. Although Childe Harold is mentioned, the distinction between him and the narrator is not kept up. The relics of the Italian past prompt the decision:

> To meditate amongst decay . . .
>   there to track
> Fall'n states and buried greatness, o'er a land
> Which *was* the mightiest in its old command,
> And *is* the loveliest . . . .   (IV, xxv)

The elegiac theme of the transience of empires dominates the canto, and it is used in turn for moralizations on human nature and human destiny.

For Byron and his readers, the spell of Venice was derived from their literary tradition; and the eclipse of the Venetian Republic first under French and then under Austrian rule had been a topic of concern during the Napoleonic period for all who cared about the cause of liberty:

> Venice, lost and won,
> Her thirteen hundred years of freedom done,
> Sinks, like a sea-weed, unto whence she rose!   (IV, xiii)

Byron wishes to disturb the complacency of his readers with the uncomfortable parallel with the shorter-lived freedom of their own island nation:

> thy lot
> Is shameful to the nations,—most of all,
> Albion! to thee: the Ocean queen should not
> Abandon Ocean's children; in the fall
> Of Venice think of thine, despite thy watery wall.   (IV, xvii)

The inspiring associations of Venice and its strategic similarity made it an appropriate focus for English reflections on national mutability.

The greatness of Rome made its fall—outlined so persuasively in Gibbon's *Decline and Fall of the Roman Empire* (1776–88)—the epitome of imperial catastrophe. There the double perspective of Servius Sulpicius's observations on the chastening sight of ruined cities in the Piraeus (IV, xliv–xlv) is multiplied.

> The Goth, the Christian—Time—War—Flood, and Fire,
> Have dealt upon the seven-hilled City's pride;
> She saw her glories star by star expire,
> And up the steep barbarian Monarchs ride,
> Where the car climbed the Capitol; far and wide
> Temple and tower went down, nor left a site:
> Chaos of ruins! who shall trace the void,
> O'er the dim fragments cast a lunar light,
> And say, 'here was, or is,' where all is doubly night?   (IV, lxxx)

It is our detailed acquaintance with the achievements of Rome and our sense of their scale that make the obliteration of them so impressive. Beside such ruin, the proud careers of Sylla and Pompey prompt the question 'have ye been/Victors of countless kings, or puppets of a scene?' (IV, lxxxvii). The scale of Julius Caesar's greatness is defined by comparing him favourably with Napoleon (IV, xc–xcii). The ruins of the Palatine defy identification:

> Cypress and ivy, weed and wallflower grown
> Matted and massed together—hillocks heaped
> On what were chambers—arch crushed, column strown
> In fragments—choked up vaults, and frescos steeped
> In subterranean damps, where the owl peeped,
> Deeming it midnight:—Temples—Baths—or Halls?
> Pronounce who can: for all that Learning reaped
> From her research hath been, that these are walls—
> Behold the Imperial Mount! 'tis thus the Mighty falls.   (IV, cvii)

The massive tomb of Cecilia Metella is paradoxically all that is known of her (IV, xcix–ciii), and the impressive shell of the Coliseum survives transformed by time into a thing of beauty that bears no relation to its original barbaric purposes (IV, cxxviii–cxxxi). Both are evidence of the inevitability of being forgotten.

If even Rome could pass away, the ultimate frustration of the ambitions and achievements of all human societies is implied—a limitation to the meaning of human existence that is more damaging than the failure of individuals. The implications of mortality had traditionally been countered by faith in a compensatory after-life; lacking that, Byron admits the force of a nihilistic pessimism:

> What from this barren being do we reap?
>   Our senses narrow, and our reason frail,
>   Life short, and truth a gem which loves the deep,
>   And all things weighed in Custom's falsest scale;
>   Opinion and Omnipotence,—whose veil
>   Mantles the earth with darkness, until right
>   And wrong are accidents, and Men grow pale
>   Lest their own judgments should become too bright,
> And their free thoughts be crimes, and Earth have too much light.
>
> (IV, xciii)

But he does not surrender to it. Limits to human existence there may be, but we should not be too hasty about defining them. The experience of trying to adjust to the enormous size of St. Peter's is used as an example:

> Our outward sense
>   Is but of gradual grasp—and as it is
>   That what we have of feeling most intense
>   Outstrips our faint expression; even so this
>   Outshining and o'erwhelming edifice
>   Fools our fond gaze, and greatest of the great
>   Defies at first our Nature's littleness,
>   Till, growing with its growth, we thus dilate
> Our spirits to the size of what they contemplate.   (IV, clviii)

The statues of Laocoön and the Apollo Belvedere in the Vatican are juxtaposed as alternative heroic symbols of man's condition. In the former we see 'A Father's love and Mortal's agony/With an Immortal's patience blending:—Vain/The struggle . . .' (IV, clx); in the latter, 'The Sun in human limbs arrayed, and brow/All radiant from his triumph in the fight;/ . . . in his eye/And nostril beautiful Disdain, and Might/And Majesty, flash their full lightnings by,/Developing in that one glance the Deity' (IV, clxi).

Canto IV is not an argument in favour of one alternative rather than the other; the elegiac form might seem to tip the balance in favour of the stoicism of Laocoön, and yet this view is undermined steadily in two ways. The first is that a distinction is made between human behaviour and human capacity. The value of Petrarch's poetry, for instance, is contrasted with his city's indifference to him while he was alive (IV, xxx–xxxiii, lvi), and a similar case is made with regard to Tasso, Ariosto, Dante and Boccaccio (IV, xxxv–xli, lvi–lx). The scanty memorials of these great men anticipate the contrast of the Roman self-assertion later in the canto, but they are also an affirmation of human achievement that survives. Byron does not suggest that society cannot help neglecting genius.

The second way in which the elegiac is undermined is by the employment of contrasting impressions. Throughout the canto, depressing reflections are followed by encouraging ones. Our reaction to the decay of Venice is softened by our literary recollections of it; the stanzas on the misery of the human condition (IV, xx–xxiv) are followed by a description of the splendour of an Italian evening (IV, xxvii–xxix). The failures of Florence and the slaughter at Trasimene are countered by the loveliness of natural settings (IV, lxv–lxxiv). Even the overwhelming testimony of Rome is alleviated by positive sentiments—thoughts on the mind's independence of ruin arise from the contemplation of Metella's tomb (IV, civ–cvi), the wreckage of the Palatine (IV, cvii–cxv) finds an antidote in the testament to the power of love in the Grotto of Egeria (IV, cxv–cxix); the heartless slaughter of the Coliseum (IV, cxxxviii–cxxxix) is set against the sentimental homesickness of the dying gladiator (IV, cxl–cxli); Roman cruelty is contrasted with the moving tale of the Roman matron suckling her imprisoned father (IV, cxlvii–cli); and even the unregretted prospect of Childe Harold's death (IV, clxiv–clxvi) is compared to the unexpected and unfitting death of Princess Charlotte (IV, clxvii–clxxii). No sustained argument is offered, and the reflections shift in accordance with the objects reflected upon. But the cumulative effect on the reader is akin to that of an unresolved dialogue. We come to have a stronger understanding of both points of view and are confirmed in a state of doubt.

It is at this point that the character of Childe Harold, or rather of the narrator, plays its part. Critics of Canto III had complained that its visionary passages were as obscure as Wordsworth's *Excursion*. In Canto IV, a homelier narrator avoids such flights of inspiration and concentrates instead upon experiences that are immediately comprehensible. The personality he presents is that of a man who has suffered and who has been wronged. The stanzas on sorrow (IV, xx–xxiv) imply that the experience of suffering continues still; the reference to himself as a 'ruin amidst ruins' (IV, xxv) and the unsparing self-examination of stanzas cxxxii to cxxxvii testify to a mind that has suffered from the weaknesses of human nature and has nevertheless tempered a justifiable resentment into forgiveness. When we come to the closing apostrophe to the sea (IV, clxxv–clxxxiv) the note is unmistakably misanthropic:

> Roll on, thou deep and dark blue Ocean—roll!
> Ten thousand fleets sweep over thee in vain;
> Man marks the earth with ruin—his control
> Stops with the shore;—upon the watery plain
> The wrecks are all thy deed, nor doth remain
> A shadow of man's ravage, save his own,
> When, for a moment, like a drop of rain,

He sinks into thy depths with bubbling groan—
Without a grave—unknelled, uncoffined, and unknown.　　　(IV, clxxix)

Here, as in a preceding stanza—'Oh! that the Desert were my dwelling-place'—the hermit's avoidance of society is apparent. But the recollection of childhood love of the sea—'from a boy/I wantoned with thy breakers' (IV, clxxxiv)—leads to a form of comfort—'For I was as it were a Child of thee,/And trusted to thy billows far and near,/And laid my hand upon thy mane—as I do here' (IV, clxxxiv). We are left with the feeling that the society he abjures is that of man as he is and has been and not man as he might be.[15]

7 Reappraisals of society

For the experiences of a sadder and wiser individual to provide a persuasive case for an unorthodox view of life, it is necessary that they be generalized to the point where we can recognize analogies between them and our own. The whole tendency of such writing is towards abstract recommendations of optimism, stoicism, patriotism, and the like, which may well be more palatable to readers in later generations. For poets who aimed at an immediate and practical effect upon the behaviour of their contemporaries, there was bound to be an ambition to treat life at a more particular level and to base their case on the experience of people in general by reminding them of it convincingly. Such precedents as there were for doing this, however—one thinks of works like Pope's *Moral Essays* or perhaps Chaucer's *Canterbury Tales*—though they might expose the weaknesses of actual human behaviour, did not take issue with accepted opinion as to what it ought to be. It may seem perverse to use general experience to substantiate a point of view that is at variance with what people generally believe, but the poet with a message to communicate had no alternative. In Crabbe's *The Borough* (1810), Words-worth's *The Excursion* (1814), and Byron's *Don Juan* (1819–24) this problem is solved in related but distinctive ways.

I *The Borough*

The search for an appropriate form is apparent in *The Borough*. The poem is arranged as a series of twenty-four letters written by a resident of a provincial town to an acquaintance in the country. Crabbe explains in his preface that his adoption of this 'man of straw' is a mere expedient: 'When the reader enters into the Poem, he will find the author retired from view, and an imaginary personage brought forward to describe his Borough for him: to him [the author] it seemed convenient to speak in the first person . . .' (p. xiv). But Crabbe had already employed the first person in 'The Parish Register' (1807) and had identified himself there as a country parson. Further, 'when, with this point, was considered what relations were to be given, what manners delineated, and what situations described, no method appeared to be so convenient as that of borrowing the assistance of an ideal friend . . .' (p. xv). The difficulty of creating the character of an impartial and

154

well-informed observer was not to be got over easily, and, in fact, after Letter I, in which the idyllic rural surroundings of the imagined correspondent are used for contrast, the fiction is conveniently discarded.

Crabbe's choice of an urban setting is unusual in the Romantic period, and it is also unusual for him. He had attempted vignettes of town life years before in *The Candidate* (1780) and *The Newspaper* (1785), but his name was made in 1783 with *The Village*. When he resumed publication in 1807, after a twenty-year silence, 'The Parish Register' was set in the country; subsequent volumes—his *Tales* in 1812 and *Tales of the Hall* in 1819—were predominantly about life in the country. *The Borough* may be thought of as an 'unpoetical' choice, but it is also a very practical one. In 'The Parish Register', Crabbe had depicted the whole social range of a village. His arrangement of it into the 'Baptism', 'Marriage' and 'Burials' of the parish records is rational enough, but adds even less to the materials so arranged than did Cowper's attempt in his 1782 volume of *Poems* to group his observations within topics such as 'The Progress of Error', 'Truth', 'Hope', and 'Retirement'. In *The Borough*, each of the various letters is devoted to a topic, and these vary from institutions—'The Church', 'Inns', 'The Alms House', 'The Hospital', 'Prisons', 'Schools'—to prominent members of society—'The Vicar, the Curate',—to groups of people—'Law', 'Physic', 'Trades', 'Players', 'The Inhabitants of the Alms House', 'The Poor'—to less easily grouped ones like 'Sects and Professions in Religion', 'Elections', 'Amusements', and 'Clubs and Meetings'. The shift from one kind of category to another makes the organization seem unsystematic and this impression is increased by the disproportionate share of the poem—altogether about a third—devoted to the inhabitants of the alms house and the poor.

By 1810, didactic surveys in heroic couplets, which had been a staple of the 1780s, were having a revival. Erasmus Darwin's *Botanic Garden* (1789–91) was in its fourth edition by 1799, and publishers, encouraged perhaps by its example and responding to a general thirst for information among the reading public,[1] issued a number of works of similar scale. Many of these looked back to Virgil's *Georgics* and Thomson's *The Seasons*—Luke Booker's *The Hop Garden* (1799), Darwin's own *The Temple of Nature* (1803), John Evans's *The Bees* (1806–13), William Tighe's *The Plants* (1808–11), James Grahame's *The Birds of Scotland* (1806) and his *British Georgics* (1809). A number of them were devoted depressingly to potted history—Richard Payne Knight's *The Progress of Civil Society* (1796), Henry James Pye's *Naucratia; or Naval Dominion* (1798), and Bowles's relatively respectable *The Spirit of Discovery* (1804). A few examined social organizations, generally in a nostalgic Goldsmithian or moral Cowperian spirit—Richard Polwhele's *Old English Gentleman* (1797), James Hurdis's *The Favourite Village* (1800) and Grahame's *The Sabbath* (1804). In addition, the interest in realistic accounts of the lives of the poor was well established, as we have noticed in Chapter 1, and it provided Crabbe with a precedent for descriptive detail that would have seemed eccentric or tendentious twenty years before. Together, the didactic survey of society and the minute description of particular walks of life provided Crabbe with a structure and a procedure upon which to build a moral poem. The conventions from which he borrowed were so lack-lustre that they have sunk out of sight, conferring a spurious uniqueness on Crabbe's manner and subject matter that distracts our attention from his genuine claims to distinction.

One of his general strategies may be observed in his account of a seaside picnic on an island of sand left by the ebbing tide ('Amusements', Letter IX). The expedition begins satisfactorily enough:

> —Gay the Friends advanc'd,
> They walk'd, they ran, they play'd, they sang, they danc'd;
> The Urns were boiling, and the Cups went round,
> And not a grave or thoughtful Face was found;
> On the bright Sand they trod with nimble Feet,
> Dry shelly Sand that made the Summer-seat;
> The wondering Mews flew fluttering o'er the Head,
> And Waves ran softly up their shining Bed. (p. 127)

But when it is discovered that the boat that is their only link with dry land has drifted away, and that the tide is turning, heedless enjoyment is replaced abruptly by alarm and despair. Their efforts to attract the attention of those on shore are frustrated by fog:

> They shout once more, and then they turn aside,
> To see how quickly flow'd the coming Tide;
> Between each Cry they find the Waters steal
> On their strange Prison, and new Horrors feel;
> Foot after foot on the contracted Ground
> The Billows fall, and dreadful is the sound;
> Less and yet less the sinking Isle became,
> And there was Wailing, Weeping, Wrath and Blame. (p. 128)

In this terrible situation all are afraid. Some pray, some complain loudly, angry reproaches are exchanged; a few attempt to calm their companions; but at the sinking of the sun

> the most lively bade to Hope adieu;
> Children by Love, then lifted from the Seas,
> Felt not the Waters at the Parents' knees . . . . (p. 129)

In the end they are rescued by chance by sailors who have noticed the drifting boat, and 'the most giddy, as they reach the Shore,/Think of their Danger, and their GOD adore' (p. 130).

In several respects this incident epitomizes the character of *The Borough*. While the human nature it displays is unheroic and may seem to be viewed ironically, the cause for fear is genuine and it is presented graphically enough for us to appreciate it sympathetically. Crabbe certainly does not imply that, in the same circumstances, he, or we, would have behaved better. His emphasis falls rather on the way in which events take us by surprise and on the vulnerable condition of our happiness. This moral is confirmed repeatedly in *The Borough*, and it provides a background for one that is more particular and about which more can be done.

In the eighteenth century, the men who made quick fortunes in the East Indies were regarded as figures of fun. The 'nabobs', as they were called, were condescended to by the gentry, envied by the middle classes, and admired like sweepstake winners by the poor.[2] Crabbe's account of a dejected nabob among a crowd of holiday-makers at the seaside departs significantly from this pattern:

> Lo! where on that huge Anchor sadly leans
> That sick tall Figure, lost in other Scenes;
> He late from India's clime impatient sail'd,
> Where, as his Fortune grew, his Spirits fail'd;
> For each Delight, in search of Wealth he went,
> For Ease alone, the Wealth acquir'd is spent—
> And spent in vain; enrich'd, aggriev'd, he sees
> The envied Poor possess'd of Joy and Ease:
> And now he flies from Place to Place, to gain
> Strength for Enjoyment, and still flies in vain:
> Mark! with what Sadness, of that pleasant Crew,
> Boist'rous in Mirth, he takes a transient View;
> And fixing then his Eye upon the Sea,
> Thinks what has been and what must shortly be:
> Is it not strange that Man should Health destroy,
> For Joys that come when he is dead to Joy? (p. 121)

The conventional moral that one cannot buy happiness is present here, but Crabbe has applied it in such a way as to encourage us to think about it. The modern reader may miss the oddness of treating a nabob seriously, but the pathetic nature of the case remains obvious. The man has taken a calculated risk to gain a prize; has succeeded but lost his health in the process; and now he finds that he cannot enjoy the prize he has won. There is no suggestion that he is a bad man, or that his disappointment is an appropriate one; rather he is treated sympathetically as a victim of misguided ambition. *The Borough* is full of similar case histories, but Crabbe, like Cowper, does not encourage us to adopt an attitude of stoical resignation by implying that all human wishes are vain; instead he concentrates on showing which ones are, in the hope that his readers will be helped to avoid them.

There are several instances in *The Borough* of people who have been made miserable by achieving the means to an end at the cost of the end itself—Walter, the merchant whose intolerance of human weakness helps him to become rich, but costs him the affection of his wife, children and friends (Letter VIII); Blaney, the wastrel, who having run through two fortunes is reduced in his old age to running errands for prostitutes (Letter XIV); the self-righteously puritanical parish clerk,

Jachin, who observes that only the well-to-do are accorded the respect he longs for and is detected augmenting his meagre income by stealing from the collection plate (Letter XIX). Others are merely rendered ineffectual—the cautious Vicar, who confuses virtue with abstinence from vice, and the impoverished curate who strives vainly to support his growing family by employing his useless learning upon an edition of Euripides (Letter III); the fashionable but flirtatious Clelia, who sinks to the bottom of the social ladder before being offered refuge in an alms house (Letter XV); and Benbow, the sociable tippler, who fails in trade (Letter XVI). Crabbe records their weaknesses matter of factly, and he concentrates on making us aware of their unhappiness. Our sympathy with their misfortunes makes the recognition of kindred weaknesses in ourselves less uncomfortable and more likely.

While Crabbe deals gently with the foolish mistakes of misguided people, implying that we must all be on our guard against them and that they are one of the natural hazards of life, he has no hesitation in identifying and condemning those who prey on the weaknesses of others and mislead them unnecessarily. His harshest comments are reserved for false preachers, false doctors and false lawyers. Letter IV contains an account of 'Sects and Professions in Religion' and rounds out the account of the established church in Letters II and III. Crabbe treats the various forms of dissent sceptically on practical rather than doctrinaire grounds. He punctures the pretensions of other churches to greater virtue, but he is no friend to bigoted intolerance. Of the Church of Rome he can say, 'Use not triumphant rail'ry, or at least/Let not thy Mother be a whore and beast . . .' (p. 49); of the Swedenborgians' mysterious idea of the after-life, he says, 'The view is happy, we may think it just,/It may be true—but who shall add, it must?' (p. 52). He contrasts the Jews severely with their biblical predecessors, but allows that 'A part there are whom doubtless Man might trust,/Worthy as wealthy, pure, religious, just . . .' (pp. 53–4), and he mimics the more enthusiastic flights of Wesleyan Methodists with telling but gentle irony (p. 54). His indignation is reserved for Calvinistic Methodists with their promises of instantaneous conversion and faith without works, and, later, in the story of Abel Keene (Letter XXI) the dangerous effects of their teachings are shown. This nervous usher retreats from the uncongenial boisterousness of a schoolroom to become a merchant's clerk. His younger colleagues lightheartedly undermine his religious assumptions and turn him into an antiquated devil-may-care fop. He loses his job and is reduced to beggary; in his distress and conscious of his wickedness he turns to a Calvinistic preacher for help.

'What must I do', I said, 'my Soul to free?'
—'Do nothing, Man; it will be done for thee'.—
'But must I not, my reverend Guide, believe?'
—'If thou art call'd, thou wilt the Faith receive:'—
'But I repent not': —Angry he replied,
'If thou art call'd, thou needest nought beside:
Attend on us, and if 'tis Heaven's Decree,
The Call will come,—if not, ah! woe for thee'. (p. 295)

But the call does not come, and in despair the wretched Abel,—whose very name is presumably meant to remind us of Cain's original murder—hangs himself.

Legal and medical practice are the subjects of Letters VI and VII respectively. Crabbe allows that there are such things as honest lawyers and competent physicians, but he makes them out to be rare. The law itself he regards as having lapsed from its ancient simplicity, and he sees the proliferation and wealth of modern lawyers as proof of its venal nature. The career of the devious attorney, Swallow,—'An hard bad Man, who prey'd upon the Weak' (p. 89)—is told by way of illustration. Crabbe's criticism of medical practice centres on the disquieting prevalence of quacks who recommend useless and often dangerous patent medicines. The success story of Neddy with his nostrum, 'Oxymel of Squills', is offered:

> Now see him Doctor! yes, the idle Fool,
> The Butt, the Robber of the Lads at School;
> Who then knew nothing, nothing since acquir'd,
> Became a Doctor, honour'd and admir'd . . .'.   (p. 102)

The mischievous activities of such men are to be exposed and prevented.

It is one thing to contemplate the foolish hopes and predictable disappointments of others, and quite another to be brought to question our own basic expectations of life. In *The Borough*, Crabbe tries to make us do both. A direct assault on our assumptions would probably have been intolerable. As it is, Crabbe's tactful solution offended his contemporaries by its 'pessimism' and its indecorous renderings of low life just as it has pleased some modern readers by its 'realism'. But these are only the symptoms of a central argument that is conducted as a series of asides about the differences between appearances and the actualities they hide. *The Borough* is full of comments on these discrepancies. Some, such as the contrast between the complimentary inscriptions on gravestones and the indifferent lives they commemorate (Letter II), escape notice as the stock in trade of moralizing verse. Some, such as the foolish practice of painting weather stains on church towers to make them look picturesquely aged (Letter II), have taken on a distracting historical interest. A few, like the compliant 'sisters' at the Boar Inn (Letter XI), were felt at the time to be in bad taste.[3] The theme is brought to a head, however, in Letter XX, with a discussion of the difference between real life and literary renditions of it—an example in which an author could claim to be criticizing his own trade.

Objections to the falsifications of literature in the Romantic period are usually offered as an occasion for the reform of writing rather than the abandonment of it, and the reform is generally represented as being a return to a valuable tradition that has been forgotten rather than as a progressive innovation. In his preface to *Lyrical Ballads* (1800), Wordsworth concentrated on the vindication of a style that was close to the 'real language of men' and objected to the inflated 'poetic diction' that was fashionable. 'I have', he confided, 'wished to keep my Reader in the company of flesh and blood, persuaded that by so doing I shall interest him.'[4] In

The Borough, Crabbe, whose literary ambitions included the novel, complained analogously of falsification of human experience and expresses his surprise:

> That Books, which promise much of Life to give,
> Should show so little how we truly live.
> To me it seems their Females and their Men
> Are but the Creatures of the Author's Pen;
> Nay, Creatures borrow'd and again convey'd
> From Book to Book—the Shadows of a Shade:
> Life, if they'd search, would show them many a change . . . .
>
> (pp. 269–70)

Crabbe's objection, like Wordsworth's, is not so much to the failure of literary skill as to the misapplication of it. Where Wordsworth is anxious to avoid the stultifying effect of figures of speech that are employed automatically and without any relation to the sort of experience from which they might naturally arise, Crabbe is concerned to combat the employment of escapist plots whose happy endings defy probability.

In fact, Crabbe goes so far in his support of probability as to question the validity of poetic justice.[5] The tale of Ellen Orford (Letter XX) follows his ironic summary of romance plots and is offered explicitly as a contrast to them:

> These let us leave and at her Sorrows look,
> Too often seen, but seldom in a Book;
> Let her who felt, relate them:—on her chair
> The Heroine sits—in former Years, the Fair,
> Now ag'd and poor . . . .
>
> (pp. 273–4)

The story which follows is told simply and in the first person, giving an impression of verisimilitude. When Ellen's widowed mother remarries unhappily and then dies, Ellen, who has been looking after her younger brothers and sisters, is seduced by a young man of property who deserts her when she is found to be pregnant and marries another. Ellen is expelled from her home. Her daughter turns out to be an idiot and for her sake ('true, my Heart denied') she marries an honest tradesman by whom she has five sons. Her husband fails in trade, turns to a gloomy Calvinism for comfort, and, like Abel Keene, hangs himself. Ellen's four elder sons are taken from her by the parish, while she is left with her daughter and one son who is sickly. Three of her sons die young, and her favourite is hanged for some unspecified crime. Her eldest son is drowned leaving numerous children. Her idiot daughter dies in childbirth and the sickly half-brother who dies soon after is suspected of being the father. For a while Ellen maintains herself by keeping a school, and then she goes blind. She concludes, resignedly:

> And as my Mind looks cheerful to my end,
> I love Mankind and call my God my Friend.
>
> (p. 281)

Summarized so baldly this appalling catalogue of woe reminds one of the worst excesses of Mrs Robinson's *Lyrical Tales*, but Ellen Orford retains our interest by her complete freedom from self-pity or resentment and because of Crabbe's understatement and circumstantiality. Her tale is no less improbable than the escapist fiction it combats, but its grimness seems to be intended as a corrective to them rather than as a norm.[6]

Ellen is on the whole an innocent sufferer. The fisherman, Peter Grimes, whose story is told in Letter XXII, is a wicked and violent man. Having rebelled against his father, he leaves home and keeps himself by a combination of fishing and stealing. To satisfy his longing 'for one to trouble and controul' he buys a workhouse boy to bully. After three years the child dies. A second is killed at sea, but nothing can be proved against his master. When a third dies, Grimes is ostracized. He begins to be troubled by guilty dreams and finally goes mad. On his deathbed he raves of being haunted by his father and the boys, and he dies crying out, 'Again they come.' No cause is given for Grimes's wickedness; he has no good qualities; his crimes are not punished by law, and his regrets, such as they are, are devoid of repentance.[7]

In their subject matter the stories of Ellen Orford and Peter Grimes resemble the radical verse that was prevalent in the 1790s, and to that extent they may remind us in turn of Wordsworth's more familiar uses of the genre. Like Wordsworth, Crabbe avoids linking his stories to any campaign for reform of the social structure, but his abstinence is much more thoroughgoing. The crucial difference between Ellen Orford and a figure such as Wordsworth's Michael is not so much their respective lives as the fact that Crabbe claims absolutely no significance for Ellen, whereas Wordsworth transforms the memory of Michael into something worthwhile. Peter Grimes finds a parallel in Wordsworth's *Peter Bell* (1819, but written in 1798), a violent man who is brought to an awareness of his depravity by seemingly supernatural experiences; Grimes, whose hauntings are not explained away, learns nothing. The point of Crabbe's avoidance of a moral is that he believes that the morals drawn in literature are too facile. His method is to forgo the convention of poetic justice for the moment, on the grounds that readers make themselves miserable unnecessarily by expecting the equivalent of poetic justice in life itself. *The Borough* is a humane and temperate exposé of the various illusions that embitter human life unnecessarily, and the contributory illusions of poetry are singled out as an example because our feelings about them are likely to be less intense than our feelings about, say, the seven deadly sins, and because an attack upon poetry comes most acceptably from a poet.

II *The Excursion*

In *The Excursion*, the author spends three days with an old friend, the sage and experienced pedlar whom he calls the Wanderer. On the first day he is told the sad story of Margaret and the ruined cottage; the following day he is taken on a walk to a beautiful but lonely valley to meet a disillusioned recluse, the Solitary; and on the third day all three proceed to the next valley where they encounter the Pastor who tells them exemplary stories of people buried in his churchyard and then invites the travellers to join him and his family for refreshment and recreation. Wordsworth's poem, like Crabbe's, is meant to provide a defence against personal and social despair. It is almost as unflinching in its record of human misery and it warns similarly of the dangers of relying on worldly hopes. Both poems exhibit conservative political instincts, seeing advantages to social hierarchy and stability that are independent of theories then current about the importance of equal opportunity. Crabbe implies that we should live resignedly in a society that is unavoidably a mixture of good and evil. Wordsworth leaves room for the visionary possibility that the happiness that has been within the capacity of a few favoured individuals may be within the capacity of society as a whole, but he emphasizes the importance of living usefully in a pre-millennial world and the satisfactions of doing so. Differences in setting and idiom obscure the considerable agreement of the two poets, as they obscure less important formal similarities of the poems such as their use of the social organization as a way of arranging the argument and their reliance on exemplary anecdotes to reinforce a point of view; their shared practical concern to bring immediate comfort and strength to afflicted contemporaries is harder to miss.

In *The Borough*, as we have seen, the fiction that we are reading a series of letters from a town burgess to a friend in the country serves to introduce the series of lively and detailed accounts of human experience and is then conveniently laid aside. The three days' ramble of *The Excursion* provides an occasion for a prolonged conversation on the central problems of belief in which an attempt is made to rescue the Solitary from his despondency. The Wanderer sums these problems up when the Pastor joins the group:

> 'Is Man
> A child of hope? Do generations press
> On generations, without progress made?
> Halts the individual, ere his hairs be grey,
> Perforce? Are we a creature in whom good
> Preponderates, or evil? Doth the will
> Acknowledge reason's law? A living power
> Is virtue, or no better than a name,
> Fleeting as health or beauty, and unsound?
> So that the only substance which remains,
> (For thus the tenor of complaint hath run)
> Among so many shadows, are the pains
> And penalties of miserable life,
> Doomed to decay, and then expire in dust!'   (V, 465–78)

The scale of such enquiries might well prompt the fear that Wordsworth was about to address himself to the subject—to which Milton devoted an epic—with a confident directness more appropriate to Pope's derivative outline in *The Essay on*

162

Man. Wordsworth was writing for an age in which scepticism was more widespread, a scepticism that he himself had passed through, and his treatment of these overwhelming questions gives doubts their due.

In the eighteenth century the prose dialogue had been a popular form for philosophical discussions of the relative merits of materialism and belief in God, Berkeley's *Hylas and Philonous* (1713) and Shaftesbury's *Characteristics* (1711) being familiar examples, and in Wordsworth's time the form was still being used in theoretical books such as Horne Tooke's treatise on language, *The Diversions of Purley* (1786, 1798). Wordsworth's adaptation of the form is truer to the best of the Platonic originals in being genuinely dramatic and offering interlocutors who are more than mere mouthpieces, but he wisely refrains from conducting a systematic argument. At the end of *The Excursion*, the Solitary is not convinced, he has only agreed to continue the discussion. As the Wanderer summarizes the Pastor's views

> the mind's repose
> On evidence is not to be ensured
> By act of naked reason. Moral truth
> Is no mechanic structure, built by rule;
> And which, once built, retains a stedfast shape
> And undisturbed proportions; but a thing
> Subject, you deem, to vital accidents . . . .   (V, 560–6)

Accordingly, the contributions of the Solitary, the Wanderer, and the Pastor to the discussion depend less on theories or arguments than on the conclusions to be drawn from their experience of life. And at the end of the poem, when the Solitary agrees that 'Another sun . . . shall shine upon us, ere we part . . .', there is a sense of victory in the very fact that a man who has so many good reasons for despair should be willing to acknowledge that discussion was worth pursuing.

The Solitary is the central character of *The Excursion* because he is a surrogate for the reader. If we are as complacently cheerful as the gregarious self-taught Wanderer in his single state, or as at peace with ourselves as the Pastor with his fixed abode, gentle origin and education and contented family, we do not need *The Excursion*. It is a poem written to give comfort. The Solitary's life, considered event by event, is not improbable, but in its accumulation of catastrophe it is exceptional. His marriage to a beautiful, virtuous lady of adequate means, and their idyllic retirement with one son and one daughter, lasts for seven years, and is then obliterated by the swift sequence of the deaths of both children and his wife:

> In privacy we dwelt, a wedded pair,
> Companions daily, often all day long;
> Not placed by fortune within easy reach
> Of various intercourse, nor wishing aught
> Beyond the allowance of our own fireside,
> The twain within our happy cottage born,
> Inmates, and heirs of our united love;

> Graced mutually by difference of sex,
> And with no wider interval of time
> Between their several births than served for one
> To establish something of a leader's sway;
> Yet left them joined by sympathy in age;
> Equals in pleasure, fellows in pursuit.
> On these two pillars rested as in air
> Our solitude.   (III, 584–98)

This epitome of domestic happiness is suddenly swept away by the illness and deaths of his wife and children. As a cause for despair this disaster replaces the traditional anguish of the frustrated romantic lover with one that is graver and perhaps rarer, one that involves the realities of virtuous happiness experienced rather than the unfulfilled dreams of the young. The Solitary is roused from the depths of his grief by the outbreak of the French revolution with its promise of social paradise:

> —My heart rebounded;
> My melancholy voice the chorus joined;
> —'Be joyful all ye nations; in all lands,
> Ye that are capable of joy be glad!
> Henceforth, whate'er is wanting to yourselves
> In others ye shall promptly find . . .'.   (III, 726–31)

This illusion of millennium, seeming to provide an escape from the misery of his personal experience, occupies him for a time, and when the bubble of French hopes bursts he still clings to the political illusions that have kept despair at bay. He emigrates to the new world, that last refuge of romantic political hope, but finding there only 'Big passions strutting on a petty stage' (III, 900), he continues across the continent in search of man as he should be:

> So, westward, tow'rd the unviolated woods
> I bent my way; and, roaming far and wide,
> Failed not to greet the merry Mocking-bird;
> And, while the melancholy Muccawiss[8]
> (The sportive bird's companion in the grove)
> Repeated o'er and o'er his plaintive cry,
> I sympathised at leisure with the sound;
> But that pure archetype of human greatness,
> I found him not. There, in his stead, appeared
> A creature, squalid, vengeful, and impure;
> Remorseless, and submissive to no law
> But superstitious fear, and abject sloth.   (III, 944–55)

The frustration of his attempt to find a social Eden to make up for the domestic paradise he has lost is too much for the Solitary, and he retires from society and refrains from hoping, believing or fearing as he waits indifferently for death.

Although the details of the Solitary's experience seem to be defined by a wish to endow him with causes for disillusionment that will exceed those that any likely reader might have, Wordsworth does not stop short at a mere abstraction of suffering. The Solitary has a character as well as experiences, and, as the Wanderer remarks from time to time, that character leads him to act better than he is willing to admit. The Wanderer first describes the Solitary's life for us, explaining that like himself he came of 'lowly parentage/Among the wilds of Scotland . . .' (II, 165–6), and how, being studious and clever, he was ordained and became a military chaplain. How during the period of the French revolution he became an eloquent and persuasive preacher, for 'The cause of Christ and civil liberty' (II, 221), until disillusionment made him renounce his faith; and how at last, in his retirement

> he dwells,
> And wastes the sad remainder of his hours,
> Steeped in a self-indulging spleen, that wants not
> Its own voluptuousness;—on this resolved,
> With this content, that he will live and die
> Forgotten,—at safe distance from 'a world
> Not moving to his mind'.   (II, 309–15)

This severe verdict, pronounced before we have had an opportunity to observe the Solitary for ourselves, expresses the concerned impatience of old and intimate friendship. When the Wanderer and the author enter the Solitary's valley, they encounter a funeral that they fear may be his; his sudden appearance follows hard upon our being introduced to the idea of his death, and is accordingly even more vigorous by contrast:

> Vivid was the light
> That flashed and sparkled from the other's eyes;
> He was all fire: no shadow on his brow
> Remained, nor sign of sickness on his face.
> Hands joined he with his Visitant,—a grasp,
> An eager grasp; and many moments' space—
> When the first glow of pleasure was no more,
> And, of the sad appearance which at once
> Had vanished, much was come and coming back—
> An amicable smile retained the life
> Which it had unexpectedly received,
> Upon his hollow cheek. 'How kind', he said,
> 'Nor could your coming have been better timed;
> For this, you see, is in our narrow world
> A day of sorrow. I have here a charge'—

165

And, speaking thus, he patted tenderly
The sun-burnt forehead of the weeping child—
'A little mourner, whom it is my task
To comfort . . .'.   (II, 514–32)

The instinctive courtesy and friendliness of the Solitary, and the tenderness of his
concern for the child, are confirmed for us by the simple hospitality he dispenses
'with more ardour than an unripe girl' (II, 654). It becomes apparent that the
difference between him and the Wanderer is not one of intellectual capacity or of
goodness of heart, but one of outlook. To borrow an expression from *The Prelude*, he
looks at the darker side of life, the Wanderer at the golden.

The ensuing debate between the Wanderer and the Solitary is a contest between
equals. The Wanderer is allowed the lion's share of the discussion as he argues for
the practical necessity of belief in God (IV, 10–12), expatiates in terms that
remind us of *The Prelude* upon the unworldly essentials of human life (IV, 66 ff.),
and, attacking the causes of the Solitary's despondency more directly, points to
Heaven as a comfort for loss through death (IV, 186–238) and recommends
strenuous physical activity as a remedy for social disappointment (IV, 466–504).
The Solitary from time to time deflates the Wanderer's optimistic raptures,
attacking not so much their accuracy as their applicability to his own scepticism,
and revealing a critical awareness of the limitations of the Wanderer's case that is
not evinced by the ingenuous figure of the author in the poem. It is the Wanderer
who develops the argument for God from the analogy of the ordered splendour of
nature (IV, 332–50, 373–504), and asserts that it is in the power of the human soul
to transform what it perceives (IV, 1058–77). But we have learned earlier of the
Solitary's perceptive capacities, from his account of a glimpse he has had of clouds
seen once as the mist cleared:

The appearance, instantaneously disclosed,
Was of a mighty city—boldly say
A wilderness of building, sinking far
And self-withdrawn into a boundless depth,
Far sinking into splendor—without end!
Fabric it seemed of diamond and of gold,
With alabaster domes, and silver spires,
And blazing terrace upon terrace, high
Uplifted; here, serene pavilions bright,
In avenues disposed; there, towers begirt
With battlements that on their restless fronts
Bore stars—illumination of all gems.   (II, 834–45)

It is not the eye for natural beauty that is wanting, nor the willingness to be
convinced that there is a God, but the confidence that the existence of the former is
in any way related to the latter. As he says at the end of the Wanderer's
166

disquisition, 'Alas! such wisdom bids a creature fly/Whose very sorrow is, that time hath shorn/His natural wings!' (IV, 1083–5).[9]

From a theological point of view the Solitary's position is more orthodox than the Wanderer's. Blake's objection to *The Excursion* was presumably directed at the argument for God from what we perceive, and even a devoted reader like Wordsworth's friend Henry Crabb Robinson was disturbed by the force with which the Wanderer's Deistical case was presented.[10] Wordsworth himself seems to have intended the points of view of both the Wanderer and the Solitary to be insufficient, and he retreats from them to the less assertive orthodoxy of the Church of England by entrusting the remaining discussion to the Pastor's reliable hands. In response to the Wanderer's request for the confirming experience of society observed by him in his parish—'Give us, for our abstractions, solid facts;/For our disputes, plain pictures' (V, 637–8)—he agrees to tell the experiences of those who are buried in his churchyard, on the prudent ground that in their case 'The future cannot contradict the past . . .' (V, 664). What follows may be thought of as arising ultimately from the graveyard poetry of the mid-eighteenth century. Certainly there is a formal resemblance, and Gray's assumption in the 'Elegy written in a Country Churchyard', that great talents in obscure places must often pass unregarded, is shared. But the old theme of mutability and of the levelling effect of death has been replaced by stories that like Crabbe's are meant to represent a wide range of human experience. The churchyard merely provides a plausible setting for abrupt transitions from one anecdote to another.

Early in his exhortation to the Solitary in Book IV, the Wanderer emphasizes the importance of religious faith:

> One adequate support
> For the calamities of mortal life
> Exists—one only; an assured belief
> That the procession of our fate, howe'er
> Sad or disturbed, is ordered by a Being
> Of infinite benevolence and power;
> Whose everlasting purposes embrace
> All accidents, converting them to good.   (ll. 10–17)

As the Solitary later points out, however, this is cold comfort to a person whose affliction is that he has lost his faith. It is noticeable that the Wanderer does not press the point and that even the Pastor does not rely upon it although he obviously agrees with it. *The Excursion* is specially tailored for those who have lost their faith, and while the recovery of that faith is the end in view, the means depend more upon our common experience than upon our religious convictions.

The story of Margaret in Book I is of a fall from domestic contentment into misery unconnected with moral failure on the part of the people involved. It shares most of the characteristics of the political eclogue, except that little more is made of the baneful effect, of foreign wars than of failed harvests and sickness. At first we have the happy life of Margaret and her small family. Then her 'keenly

167

industrious' weaver husband is left out of work and falls ill; their savings are exhausted and her husband decides to enlist in the army rather than watch his family starve, departing silently and leaving her the money he has received. She ekes out a living, but gradually her spirit is broken. From having been 'a Woman of a steady mind,/Tender and deep in her excess of love' (I, 513–14), she becomes a negligent housekeeper and mother, wandering along the roadside dejectedly seeking news of her husband. Her cottage and garden reflect her decline in their own deterioration into disorder and unkemptness. Her infant dies; the decay of the cottage exposes her to the inclemency of a long winter, and she too sickens and dies.

The author is moved by this affecting tale and gloomily contemplates her ruined cottage and the tangled, weedy state of its garden until the Wanderer interrupts his melancholic reverie:

> Why then should we read
> The forms of things with an unworthy eye?
> She sleeps in the calm earth, and peace is here.
> I well remember that those very plumes,
> Those weeds, and the high spear-grass on that wall,
> By mist and silent rain-drops silvered o'er,
> As once I passed, into my heart conveyed
> So still an image of tranquillity,
> So calm and still, and looked so beautiful
> Amid the uneasy thoughts which filled my mind,
> That what we feel of sorrow and despair
> From ruin and from change, and all the grief
> That passing shows of Being leave behind,
> Appeared an idle dream, that could maintain,
> Nowhere, dominion o'er the enlightened spirit
> Whose meditative sympathies repose
> Upon the breast of Faith. I turned away,
> And walked along my road in happiness.   (I, 939–56)

The Wanderer attributes this characteristically vigorous cheerfulness to his belief in God, without taking anything away from the experience he has described. And in the Pastor's stories later on we are allowed to share an experience of being reconciled to misfortune that is consistent with faith but does not depend upon it. Ultimately Wordsworth's argument is allowed to rest on practical experience rather than theoretical debate.

It is easier to categorize the Pastor's tales according to the morals that may be drawn from them than by the events themselves or by the characters who are involved in them. Their educative purpose is unmistakable. As with the life of the Solitary whose misfortunes so exceed our own, the lives of the Pastor's flock are deprived in ways that when added together are likely to make our own disappointments with life seem rather petty. In fact their misfortunes differ from the Solitary's mainly in lacking the contrasting moments of great happiness that he has enjoyed. A few of the cases bear particularly on the disappointment of the Solitary's social hopes—the story of Sir Arthur Irving who withdrew from a rapidly changing Elizabethan society to live in contented obscurity in the valley, for example (VII, 923 ff.), and the amusing account of the formerly rebellious Jacobite and the unsuccessful Hanoverian politician who retired there and after repeated political arguments found that they had come to rely upon one another's company. Most of them have a more general application. The contented and useful deaf man (VII, 395–481) and the animated and knowledgeable blind man (VII, 481–536) live satisfying lives in spite of handicaps that are familiar and easy to imagine. The more interesting tale of the 'wedded pair in childless solitude' (V, 670–837), their lonely cottage amid desolate surroundings and long hours of work apart and rare hours of daylight together, introduces us to a kind of physical deprivation that is in some ways beyond anything in Crabbe, and which nevertheless results in an enviable mutual support and cheerfulness.[11] Even the Solitary can apply the moral:

> The untutored bird may found, and so construct
> And with such soft materials line, her nest
> Fixed in the centre of a prickly brake,
> That the thorns wound her not . . . .   (V, 840–3)

But he distances himself from it by referring to 'those, who, not contending/Nor summoned to contend for virtue's prize,/Miss not the humbler good at which they aim . . .' (V, 855–7).

Closer to his own situation are instances of talents thwarted or misplaced—the woman 'surpassed by few/In power of mind, and eloquent discourse' (VI, 676–7), who married unfortunately and in overcoming poverty and caring for her dissolute son became the slave of avarice and maternal doting (VI, 675–777); the hedonistic man of talents who wasted them and lived like a prodigal, returning home from time to time as to a place of refuge (VI, 275–383); the joyous account of young Oswald, the born leader who is cut off by a chill on the eve of his departure for the war against France (VII, 695–816); and the cruel loss to a family of seven sons of the infant sister who was a 'precious boon' to them (VII, 632–94). The Pastor does not conceal the waste that such cases involve, but his placid record of them makes it plain that the fate of these people has been observed and their qualities have been reflected upon by the little community in which they lived.

There is comfort of a more personal kind in the recoveries of the sorrowful: the story of the widower left with six young daughters whose loss is never quite forgotten but who finds contentment—'Mild man! he is not gay, but they are gay;/And the whole house seems filled with gaiety' (VI, 1186–7); the story of the disappointed lover who takes up botany as a cure for his injured feelings and finds peace of mind (VI, 95–211) is balanced against the perseverant miner, who after twenty years of unrewarding toil finds his precious ore and dies soon after unable to adapt himself to the joy of his discovery and the loss of his occupation (VI,

212–61)—both show how the absorbing power of the mind can alter our original outlook on the world. A parson, disappointed in his hopes of preferment and seemingly unfitted for his calling by his restless ambition and choleric temper, is soothed by his surroundings and by his family's influence and attains old age 'A man of hope and forward-looking mind . . .' (VII, 274). And even the tale of gentle Ellen, the 'weeping Magdalene' who pines when she is made to give up her child when she finds employment as a wet nurse, reminiscent though it is of the story of Margaret, concludes on a note of stoical devotion (VI, 787–1052).

The presence of the listeners who have already differed on the conclusions to be drawn from human experience concentrates our attention upon the implications of the Pastor's anecdotes, and this awareness is refreshed from time to time by the listeners' interruptions and comments. The sequence of the narratives is made to seem natural and unpremeditated, drawing upon the technique of meditation of sympathy, and Wordsworth avoids straining our credulity with tales which though true are improbable.

Our knowledge of *The Prelude* reveals one further aspect of *The Excursion* that may have its effect upon us without our being wholly conscious of it. The moral struggle and the experience of despondency chronicled in *The Prelude* parallel the political experience of the Solitary to some extent, while the healthier state of mind of the Wanderer resembles the healed self with which *The Prelude* concludes. The idea that the Solitary and the Wanderer are personifications of two contrary states of mind—representing faith in intellect and faith in experience, and the Pastor as a mediating personification of faith in God, is an oversimplification that should not be rigidly applied, but it does have some justification in the overall strategy of *The Excursion*.[12] The deep consistency of its presence emerges more strongly and more satisfyingly with repeated re-readings.

With Book VII the dialogue is in a sense complete. In Book VIII, interspersed with the cheering description of family life at the parsonage and the beauties of the surrounding landscape, the Solitary and the Wanderer unite in qualifying the complacent tenor of the poem with a keen indictment of the unnecessary forms of degradation in Britain. The Wanderer introduces the bleaker side of the industrial revolution with its night shifts in terms that should almost have satisfied Blake when he was young:

> in full many a region, once like this
> The assured domain of calm simplicity
> And pensive quiet, an unnatural light
> Prepared for never-resting Labour's eyes
> Breaks from a many-windowed fabric huge;
> And at the appointed hour a bell is heard,
> Of harsher import than the curfew-knoll
> That spake the Norman Conqueror's stern behest—
> A local summons to unceasing toil!
> Disgorged are now the ministers of day;
> And, as they issue from the illumined pile,

A fresh band meets them, at the crowded door—
And in the courts—and where the rumbling stream,
That turns the multitude of dizzy wheels,
Glares, like a troubled spirit, in its bed
Among the rocks below. Men, maidens, youths,
Mother and little children, boys and girls,
Enter, and each the wonted task resumes
Within this temple, where is offered up
To Gain, the master idol of the realm,
Perpetual sacrifice. (VIII, 165–85)

To this condemnation of mills that were soon to become even more satanic, the Solitary adds a catalogue of deprivation that preceded the industrial revolution and maintains that such miseries are inseparable from the human condition:

Yet be it asked, in justice to our age,
If there were not, before those arts appeared,
These structures rose, commingling old and young,
And unripe sex with sex, for mutual taint;
If there were not, *then*, in our far-famed Isle,
Multitudes, who from infancy had breathed
Air unimprisoned, and had lived at large;
Yet walked beneath the sun, in human shape,
As abject, as degraded? (VIII, 337–45)

The Wanderer and the Solitary agree in their observations of life, and they agree in their fervent dissatisfaction with the various forms of social unhappiness they see around them. The Wanderer parts company with his friend in refusing to believe that such conditions are necessary or permanent. He is an optimist, to be sure, but not an unthinking one. His enthusiasm about the possibility of material progress and the potential usefulness of technical knowledge is coupled with an insistence that both must be subject to moral standards if they are to be beneficial.

The Wanderer's vision of the future in Book IX calls for progress and reform on an international scale. Beginning with a statement of faith in the capacities of every individual, he describes the way in which such capacities may be fulfilled even in humble rural circumstances, using the boy who plays with the Pastor's young son as an example. Current social conditions permit such fulfilment and it should be regarded as a national duty to ensure that the necessary education is provided.

O for the coming of that glorious time
When, prizing knowledge as her noblest wealth
And best protection, this imperial Realm,
While she exacts allegiance, shall admit
An obligation, on her part, to *teach*
Them who are born to serve her and obey;

> Binding herself by statute to secure
> For all the children whom her soil maintains
> The rudiments of letters, and inform
> The mind with moral and religious truth,
> Both understood and practised . . . .   (IX, 293–303)

This call for universal literacy and for religious instruction is in keeping with the prevailing practical attempt to improve the lot of the poor in Wordsworth's time.[13] Had the Wanderer stopped here the social message of *The Excursion* might have seemed wholly unexceptionable, but he goes on to describe the benefits of British progress being conferred upon the world at large.

> —Vast the circumference of hope—and ye
> Are at its centre, British Lawgivers;
> Ah! sleep not there in shame! Shall Wisdom's voice
> From out the bosom of these troubled times
> Repeat the dictates of her calmer mind,
> And shall the venerable halls ye fill
> Refuse to echo the sublime decree?
> Trust not to partial care a general good;
> Transfer not to futurity a work
> Of urgent need.—Your Country must complete
> Her glorious destiny.   (IX, 398–408)

What was meant by Wordsworth as a call to his countrymen to extend the benefits of their patriotism to other countries in a spirit of altruism is sometimes read sceptically and anachronistically in the light of the actual experiences of the British Empire in the century that followed. But the internationalism of the Wanderer's conscience is what is unusual for Wordsworth's time; his confidence in the relatively favourable political situation of England was commonplace.[14] His call is for general human progress, not for the aggrandisement of Britain.

To those of us who are uninspired, such dreams of the future as the Wanderer's, for all their beauty, seem so remote from our experience that, although we are reluctant to part from them, we cannot easily hold them in our minds, and are obliged to let them go. The Pastor's wife remarks when observing the beautiful reflection in the lake of a snow-white ram on a grassy bank:

> Ah! what a pity were it to disperse,
> Or to disturb, so fair a spectacle,
> And yet a breath can do it!   (IX, 452–4)

She adds, referring to the Wanderer:

> While he is speaking, I have power to see
> Even as he sees; but when his voice hath ceased,

Then, with a sigh, sometimes I feel, as now,
That combinations so serene and bright
Cannot be lasting in a world like ours . . . .   (IX, 465–9)

Although the dream may seem too good to be true and although it may be difficult
even to remember it in any detail, we can remember that for a time we were
permitted to share in it. If that recollection plays its part in strengthening our
resolution in the face of adversity, Wordsworth would have felt, I think, that *The
Excursion* had had the effect he hoped for.

III   *Don Juan*

In 1817 Byron's fancy was caught by J. H. Frere's curious burlesque of epic verse,
The Monks and the Giants. The first two cantos of this *jeu d'esprit* bore the
cumbersome title *Prospectus and Specimen of an Intended National Work . . . Intended to
Comprise the Most Interesting Particulars Relating to King Arthur and His Round Table*,
and they appeared under the pseudonyms William and Robert Whistlecraft.[15]
Byron immediately attempted Frere's irreverent and digressive form in *Beppo, A
Venetian Tale* (1818). This departure from the sustained gravity of *Childe Harold's
Pilgrimage* preserved the habit of reflective digression that he had developed there.
In *Beppo*, the plot, which depends upon a rather simple-minded and mildly ribald
joke, is merely the excuse upon which amusing and sometimes penetrating social
comment is hung, and the form allowed Byron to exploit his extraordinary
metrical fluency and variety in an ottava rima that was genuinely colloquial and
entirely free of artificial pompousness. Francis Jeffrey summed the poem up in the
Edinburgh Review:

> It is, in itself, absolutely a thing of nothing—without story, characters,
> sentiments, or intelligible object—a mere piece of lively and loquacious
> prattling, in short, upon all kinds of frivolous subjects,—a sort of gay and
> desultory babbling about Italy and England, Turks, balls, literature and
> fish sauces.[16]

The mixture was favourably received by the reading public.

When Byron committed himself to his next long poem, he chose the *Beppo* style.
The manner of *Don Juan* is so natural and easy and its matter is often so
extravagant, so comical and even so indecent, that comparisons with *The Borough*
or *The Excursion* seem incongruous. And yet for all the differences in his solution,
Byron was addressing himself to much the same literary problem that Crabbe and
Wordsworth had faced. He sought a form that would allow him to comment on a
broad range of human experience. Like them he believed that devotion to false
values made people unhappier than they needed to be. Like them he avoided
preaching directly and instead furnished his readers with accounts of individual
cases from which they could draw their own conclusions. Crabbe anatomized a
provincial town and distinguished between those who deceive others with false

173

hopes and those who are deceived. Wordsworth, more abstractly, placed the views of a pessimist and an optimist on personal and national experience in conflict with one another and mediated between them with the view of religious orthodoxy. Byron, choosing the wider and more exotic canvas of social life in several countries, distinguished between the virtuous and the respectable. The impartial and impersonal narrative voice of the letter-writer which Crabbe introduces and then abandons in *The Borough*, and which Wordsworth uneasily preserves in the person of the author throughout *The Excursion*, is deftly provided in *Don Juan* by a narrator with a genuine story to expound and a presence whose impartiality is vouched for by mockingly candid direct addresses to the reader after the manner of Fielding's *Tom Jones*. Whereas Crabbe's classifications of profession, institution, and so on and Wordsworth's device of the country graveyard provide pretexts for a series of moral tales, the continuing adventures of Don Juan, unfolded by a tale-teller who had lost none of the instinct for mystery and suspense that had made *The Corsair* so popular, are so interesting in themselves that one is scarcely aware that the experiences threaded upon the strand of Juan's career may have a cumulative moral significance. It is the assumption that what is expressed facetiously cannot be meant to be taken seriously that isolates Byron's great poem from the moral works of his more conventional contemporaries.

The plot of *Don Juan* is as rich as anyone could wish. In his teens (to use an expression current long before Byron's day) the handsome Juan is seduced by Donna Julia, a young married woman. He is discovered in her bedroom by her husband; she is committed to a convent, but he is sent abroad with a tutor to mend his ways. He is the only survivor of a shipwreck and is washed up on the shore of an island belonging to one Lambro, a pirate. In Lambro's absence, Juan and the pirate's beautiful daughter Haidée fall in love and, believing her father to be dead, settle down together in domestic bliss. Their idyll is interrupted by Lambro's return, Haidée dies of a broken heart and Juan is shipped off into slavery. He is bought by a sultana, smuggled into her harem in female attire, and makes his escape the following morning. He participates in the Russian siege of Ismail, rescues a little girl from the slaughter, and is sent to St Petersburg to carry the news of victory to Catherine the Great. Catherine immediately enrols him among her lovers, but when, after a prolonged period of dissipation, he shows signs of ill health, she sends him on an embassy to England to recuperate. There he encounters and kills a footpad and is courted by high society. He is invited to a country house where three women set their caps at him. At this point the poem breaks off, left unfinished at the time of Byron's death. Readers sometimes complain of digressive longueurs, of characters introduced and then abruptly abandoned, and of complicated situations that turn out unaccountably to have been resolved, but on the whole *Don Juan* is a gripping tale.[17]

The manner in which the tale is told is both satisfying and disturbing. Byron's capacity for the sentimental is exhibited on the grand scale:

> They looked up to the sky, whose floating glow
>   Spread like a rosy Ocean, vast and bright;

They gazed upon the glittering sea below,
    Whence the broad Moon rose circling into sight;
They heard the waves' splash, and the wind so low,
    And saw each other's dark eyes darting light
Into each other—and, beholding this,
    Their lips drew near, and clung into a kiss . . . .   (II, clxxxv)

It seems to belong to a different world from the slangy realism of the footpad's last words:

But ere they could perform this pious duty,
    The dying man cried, 'Hold! I've got my gruel!
Oh! for a glass of *max*! We've missed our booty;
    Let me die where I am!' And as the fuel
Of Life shrunk in his heart, and thick and sooty
    The drops fell from his death-wound, and he drew ill
His breath,—he from his swelling throat untied
A kerchief, crying, 'Give Sal that!'—and died.   (XI, xvi)

And the mood of passages like these is set off by others of a worldly and bantering tone, such as the following anecdote:

An English lady asked of an Italian,
    What were the actual and official duties
Of the strange thing some women set a value on,
    Which hovers oft about some married beauties,
Called 'Cavalier Servente?'—a Pygmalion
    Whose statues warm (I fear, alas! too true 't is)
Beneath his art:—the dame, pressed to disclose them,
Said—'Lady, I beseech you to *suppose them*'.   (IX, li)

These stanzas might be used as instances of Byron's metrical variety; at the same time they exemplify a range of narrative temper that is sustained throughout *Don Juan* and that keeps surprising the reader by its independence of the events described. We are never permitted to relax our attention and feel confident that we are of one mind with our author.

The very events themselves jostle one another in ways that make us feel uneasy. In the shipwreck incident in Canto II the pitiable condition of the survivors whose sufferings drive them to draw lots and eat one another is vividly described. Four stanzas (II, lxxxvii–xc) are devoted to the experience of two fathers helplessly watching their sons die; the horror of cannibalism is recognized and the subsequent symptoms of madness in the cannibals are presented in frightful detail. Incongruous elements accompany these descriptions. The pieces of paper drawn to decide who is to be eaten first are taken from Donna Julia's farewell letter to Juan. Juan refrains from eating his tutor, Pedrillo, because he had previously objected to

eating his own pet dog (II, lxxviii). The fat master's mate is spared because he is
indisposed as a consequence of 'a small present made to him at Cadiz,/By general
subscription of the ladies' (II, lxxxi). The summary of the crew's condition is
accurate enough:

> Famine—despair—cold—thirst and heat, had done
> Their work on them by turns, and thinned them to
> Such things a mother had not known her son
> Amidst the skeletons of that gaunt crew;
> By night chilled, by day scorched, thus one by one
> They perished, until withered to these few . . . .   (II, cii)

But the jesting couplet that concludes the stanza—'But chiefly by a species of self-
slaughter,/In washing down Pedrillo with salt water' (II, cii)—seems heartless.
Consistent irony in a burlesque makes for more relaxed reading. We are at ease
with Samuel Butler's *Hudibras* because, though it has a serious relationship to the
world we live in, we can rely upon Butler's mockery throughout. InThackeray's
'Little Billee'—to choose a parallel to the shipwreck incident—the decision 'We
have no wittles, so we must eat *we*' is merely, and pleasingly, amusing. In *Don Juan*,
however, Byron characteristically involves the sympathies of his readers in
affecting and sometimes terrible events and then spurns at them with his fun.

The line between pathos and bathos is not an easy one to draw. Byron's
deliberate transitions from the one to the other do not, as some of his
contemporaries maintained they did,[18] reveal a contempt for human sympathy,
but rather a highly critical view of the objects upon which it is fashionable to lavish
it. Consistent burlesque might have drawn these to our attention; in *Don Juan* the
shifts of tone force us to take stock of our own feelings as well.

Don Juan was published in parts over a period of five years.[19] The effect of
reading it in sections, as it was published and as it was written, is to lessen our sense
of lapses in the continuity of the narrative and to increase our awareness of an
author replying indirectly in the later cantos to public reactions to earlier ones. In
Canto XII he can turn the outcry against his immorality to good account by
threatening to resume it and immediately associating the word with truthfulness in
such a way as to embarrass his critics:

> But now I'm going to be immoral; now
> I mean to show things really as they are,
> Not as they ought to be . . . .   (XII, xl)

The immorality objected to by his detractors, he argues, is the immorality of the
world they live in. The episodic quality of the poem tilts the balance of our
attention away from the successive adventures and towards the generally
consistent point of view that informs the reflective comments that continually
intrude upon the narration.

Byron plays with the reader's sense of the kind of poem *Don Juan* is. In Canto I

we are informed 'My poem's epic, and is meant to be/Divided in twelve books . . .'
(I, cc). In Canto XII he reveals that 'These first twelve books are merely
flourishes,/*Preludios* . . .' and adds 'I thought, at setting off, about two
dozen/Cantos would do; but at Apollo's pleading,/If that my Pegasus should not
be foundered,/I think to canter gently through a hundred' (XII, liv–lv).[20] The
uncertainties of purpose revealed by such remarks reflect Byron's own lack of a
firm plan for the poem. The outline he sent to his publisher after finishing
Canto V, to be taken with a grain of salt perhaps, differs substantially from the
poem as we have it:

> The 5th is so far from being the last of D. J., that it is hardly the
> beginning. I mean to take him the tour of Europe, with a proper mixture
> of siege, battle, and adventure, and to make him finish as Anacharsis
> Cloots[21] in the French revolution. To how many cantos this may extend,
> I know not, nor whether (even if I live) I shall complete it; but this was
> my notion: I meant to have made him a *Cavalier Servente* in Italy, and a
> cause for divorce in England, and a Sentimental 'Werther-faced man' in
> Germany, so as to show the different ridicules of the society in each of
> those countries, and to have displayed him *gaté* and *blasé* as he grew
> older, as is natural. But I had not quite fixed whether to make him end
> in Hell, or in an unhappy marriage, not knowing which would be the
> severest.[22]

The presiding rationale seems to be to have Juan mingle with various European
societies and expose the frailties of each; the hero's character may develop in
response to his experiences but it is of secondary importance and is left undefined.

Perceptive readers noticed from the start that the unique value of *Don Juan* was
not related directly to its plot. Juan's encounters with unfamiliar societies interest
us not so much because we care about Juan, even though at times we do, but
because they involve conflict between behaviour that is convincingly good-
natured and spontaneous and social conventions that are arbitrary. In *Childe
Harold's Pilgrimage* the sacrifices required by empire and war are made to seem
futile by being placed in the context of the inevitable decay and oblivion that
await even the greatest empires. By a somewhat similar technique, in *Don Juan*
social conventions are made to seem relative by being shown to differ from one
country to another.

Byron's choice of Don Juan as the catalyst that will transform our estimate of
social conventions is extraordinarily apt. It may have owed something to
Coleridge's recent treatment of the traditional Don Juan's career as the necessary
consequence of atheism. At any rate, Coleridge's summary of the atheist's
creed—'Obedience to nature is the only virtue: the gratification of the passions
and appetites her only dictate: each individual's self-will the sole organ through
which nature utters her commands . . .'—expresses a distrust of natural human
feelings when they are unsupported by religious belief.[23] *Don Juan* consistently
undermines this point of view. Where Coleridge admits the attractiveness of Don

177

Juan in order to point out how dangerous such a person is, Byron surrenders to it. Byron's charming Don Juan owes little to the Spanish original. He is no seducer, but he yields to seduction. Byron accepts Coleridge's analysis and rejects its consequences. As befits a materialist he has the loftier view of nature.

So many aspects of national, social and individual behaviour are exposed and made fun of in *Don Juan* that it is tempting to treat the poem primarily as a satire and compile catalogues of its targets. But the overall effect is neither satirical nor negative but prevailingly energetic and full of faith in human beings. The idyll of Juan and Haidée in Cantos II and III is the least complicated in its assertiveness. Byron compares the young lovers to Adam and Eve before the fall:

> Alas! for Juan and Haidée! they were
> So loving and so lovely—till then never,
> Excepting our first parents, such a pair
> Had run the risk of being damned for ever . . . .   (II, cxciii)

He makes no bones about his enthusiasm for their mutual infatuation, but the conditions it requires suggest how rare a thing it is. Juan and Haidée meet apart from their respective societies; they cannot speak one another's languages; Juan's distress makes introductions unnecessary. Haidée is untaught. She

> spoke not of scruples, asked no vows,
> Nor offered any; she had never heard
> Of plight and promises to be a spouse,
> Or perils by a loving maid incurred;
> She was all which pure Ignorance allows,
> And flew to her young mate like a young bird;
> And, never having dreamt of falsehood, she
> Had not one word to say of constancy.   (II, cxc)

The joy of first love so feelingly presented here is natural, Byron implies, and might be a general experience if it were not interfered with by social conventions. Byron's enthusiasm does not prevent him from indulging in occasional ironic asides even in this section of the poem; they are designed to qualify sentimental falsifications of love. Before he is interested in Haidée, Juan must be fed: 'Love must be sustained like flesh and blood' (II, clxx), and, 'Juan, after bathing in the sea,/Came always back to coffee and Haidée' (II, clxxi). Byron's young lovers are ideal but they are endowed with a physical reality that the ideal lovers of fiction usually lack. Above all they are unaffectedly natural:

> Haidée was Nature's bride, and knew not this;
> Haidée was Passion's child, born where the Sun
> Showers triple light, and scorches even the kiss
> Of his gazelle-eyed daughters; she was one
> Made but to love, to feel that she was his

178

> Who was her chosen: what was said or done
> Elsewhere was nothing. She had nought to fear,
> Hope, care, nor love, beyond,—her heart beat *here*.　　　　(II, ccii)

Such prelapsarian enthusiasm for nature owes something to a climate of opinion informed by Rousseau's *Emile* and *La nouvelle Héloïse*.[24] In *Don Juan* it provides a counterbalance to theories of education that are in turn linked directly to prevailing forms of delusion in social life.

Juan's blue-stocking mother, Donna Inez, is often compared by commentators to Byron's estranged wife and sometimes to his mother. In *Don Juan* Byron compares her to a bevy of fashionable educators and sums her up as 'Morality's prim personification . . .' (I, xvi). Her plans for educating Juan provide the first expression of the theory that lies behind the social conventions that are pilloried in the rest of the poem. After the death of her easy-going but philandering husband, she is determined that Juan shall turn out differently. Her scheme allows for the 'accomplishments of chivalry' in case he has to go to war—'He learned the arts of riding, fencing, gunnery,/And how to scale a fortress—' (I, xxxviii). Byron, unable to refrain from anticipating events, adds 'or a nunnery'. Her chief concern, however, is her son's moral education.

> Much into all his studies she inquired,
> 　And so they were submitted first to her, all,
> Arts, sciences—no branch was made a mystery
> To Juan's eyes, excepting natural history.　　　　(I, xxxix)

The consistently impractical bias of the curriculum, which may still be detected feebly resisting the educational reforms of our own day, culminates in a self-defeating attempt to deny human nature:

> The languages, especially the dead,
> 　The sciences, and most of all the abstruse,
> The arts, at least all such as could be said
> 　To be the most remote from common use,
> In all these he was much and deeply read:
> 　But not a page of anything that's loose,
> Or hints continuation of the species,
> Was ever suffered, lest he should grow vicious.　　　　(I, xl)

Byron has some fun with the difficulties of avoiding such topics when studying classical and even religious texts, and he points out that such education does not reflect Donna Inez's own experience—she is said to have a peccadillo in her past (I, lxvi–lxxvii)—or the experience of the authors she requires Juan to study. What is implied here is not so much Donna Inez's hypocrisy, although there is a hint of that too, as the typical blindness of those who prescribe moral behaviour for other people. It is a blindness shared by Haidée's father when, forgetting that he himself

179

lives by piracy, he complains of Juan's taking ways and ships him into slavery (IV, xxxix–li). The frustration of such moralists is inevitable. Lambro's Haidée dies of grief, but Donna Inez's Juan merely falls prey to Donna Julia who is 'married, charming, chaste, and twenty-three' (I, lix). When Juan has to select a tutor for his ward, Leila, in Canto XII, and chooses Lady Pinchbeck, it is because, though elderly and respectable, she does not pretend to have been a paragon of virtue in her youth. The author remarks:

> That ladies in their youth a little gay,
>   Besides their knowledge of the World, and sense
>   Of the sad consequences of going astray,
> Are wiser in their warnings 'gainst the woe
> Which the mere passionless can never know.   (XII, xliv)

If the aims of education are often at odds with life, so are the conventions of social behaviour that they are designed to support. At one point or another most aspects of social behaviour are touched on in *Don Juan*; the tendency of the poem to focus on contradictions, inconsistencies and absurdities provides the basis for an awareness of differences between what is respectable and what is done and between what is respectable and what is good.

Discrepancies between virtue and respectability have always been readily apparent in the double standards applied by society to the behaviour of men and women respectively. It is, for instance, acceptable for a man to be promiscuous but not for a woman to be. It is acceptable for a woman to burst into tears or run away when frightened but not for a man to do so. Byron uses Don Juan, a man famous for his relations with women, as a device for revealing the realities concealed behind such stereotypes of the sexes. Near the beginning of Canto VII, he begins a stanza with a quotation: ' "Fierce loves and faithless wars"—I am not sure/If this be the right reading—'t is no matter;/The fact's about the same, I am secure . . .' (VII, viii). This allusion to Spenser's line, 'Fierce warres and faithfull loves shall moralize my song',[25] serves notice of his rejection of the chivalric assumptions of romance and draws attention to the two themes with which the characters of man and woman are to be tested. Throughout the poem the action may be said to alternate between scenes of love and scenes of war, with women having the larger share of the former and men of the latter.

In recent years public discussion of the promiscuity of women and the prevailing affectation of being shocked by nothing has lessened the initial impact of *Don Juan*, but even the jaded modern can be brought up short by the way in which Byron's women combine the outlook of cloistered innocence with the behaviour of the experienced. Like cynical Don Alfonso in Mozart's *Così fan tutte*, the narrator of *Don Juan* understands women's frailty without losing his respect for them. In his own time Byron gave particular offence by maintaining that love and marriage were incompatible and that adultery was the rule. Marriage was a touchy subject for a man who had been socially ostracized after the very public failure of his own.

180

Some of his more outrageous sallies may have been provoked by hostile criticism, but for the most part his indictment of the institution follows traditional lines.

The marriage of Donna Julia, with whom Juan serves his apprenticeship in love, has one feature in common with many marriages of the period. Her husband, Don Alfonso, is more than twice her age. In other respects her situation is distinctive. Donna Julia is unusually beautiful, there is a trace of Moorish blood in her Spanish pedigree, and, according to the narrator, 'What men call gallantry, and gods adultery,/Is much more common where the climate's sultry' (I, lxiii). Having provided these excuses for Donna Julia, the author shows how her acquaintance with Juan the boy develops almost imperceptibly into acquaintance with Juan the young man. Juan is unaware of the reasons for the change in their relationship, although he is aware of the change itself and turns melancholy. Donna Julia, who knows perfectly well what is what, tries to resist temptation, but she does not try very hard. The seduction scene is presented in detail but with great delicacy (I, cii–cxvii), concluding with the lines: 'A little still she strove, and much repented,/And whispering "I will ne'er consent"—consented'. When she is accused of the affair by Don Alfonso, but before he has proof, Donna Julia reveals a more worldly side to her nature, but her letter of farewell to Juan before she enters a convent mixes false sentiment and genuine grief in a way that seems vulnerable and appealing.

Juan's next encounter with a married woman occurs when he is bought as a slave by the sultana Gulbeyaz. Her marriage, like Donna Julia's, is to a man much older than herself, with 'fifty daughters and four dozen sons', and three other wives and 1500 concubines. To the disparity of his age may be added his necessary neglect of her. At the advanced age of twenty-six, the inhabitant of a Moslem harem has none of Donna Julia's hesitancies or inhibitions. She is passionate but not affectionate. Byron categorizes her type:

> a headlong, headstrong, downright She,
>   Young, beautiful, and daring—who would risk
> A throne—the world—the universe—to be
>   Beloved in her own way—and rather whisk
> The stars from out the sky, than not be free
>   As are the billows when the breeze is brisk— . . . .   (VI, iii)

When Juan appears to hesitate she is direct: 'Christian, canst thou love?' And when it turns out the following morning that after failing her he has spent the night with one of the concubines after all she orders that both of them be put to death without more ado.

Gulbeyaz is more self-possessed than Donna Julia. She illustrates a theory propounded in Canto III:

> In her first passion Woman loves her lover,
>   In all the others all she loves is Love,
> Which grows a habit she can ne'er get over,

181

> And fits her loosely—like an easy glove,
> As you may find, whene'er you like to prove her:
> One man alone at first her heart can move;
> She then prefers him in the plural number,
> Not finding that the additions much encumber. (III, iii)

This view, so contrary to the terms of Christian marriage, is developed in a disquisition on the incompatibility of love and marriage (III, iv—xi)—'that moral centaur, man and wife' (V, clviii)—and hence the near certainty of adultery. But at least such behaviour is surreptitious. Juan's liaison with Catherine the Great on the contrary is as public as any of the Prince Regent's liaisons with mistresses—Byron interpolates an apparently innocent reference to George IV a stanza or so before Catherine appears (IX, xxxix). Juan's beauty is described and he is compared to Cupid (IX, xliii—xlvii):

> Her Majesty looked down, the youth looked up—
> And so they fell in love;—she with his face,
> His grace, his God-knows-what . . . . (IX, lxvii)

Juan's feelings for the middle-aged empress are based rather on his own vanity than upon her beauty:

> Her sweet smile, and her then majestic figure,
> Her plumpness, her imperial condescension,
> Her preference of a boy to men much bigger
> (Fellows whom Messalina's self would pension),
> Her prime of life, just now in juicy vigour,
> With other *extras*, which we need not mention,—
> All these, or any one of these, explain
> Enough to make a stripling very vain. (IX, lxxii)

This example of the behaviour of a woman who can have her own way is made into a general rule by Byron's division of love into three kinds, 'love Platonical', 'love canonical' or marriage, and a third sort 'flourishing in every Christian land,/... when chaste matrons to their other ties/Add what may be called *marriage in disguise*' (IX, lxxvi). The affront to English readers is completed by the gratuitous indecency of having Juan led away to be tested beforehand by Miss Protasoff the 'Éprouveuse' (IX, lxxxiv).

Byron goes on to assess the modesty of women in England. The trio at Lady Adeline Amundeville's country house (XIII and ff.) provides English counterparts to each of the types of women encountered previously abroad: Aurora Raby, the beautiful virgin who is a potential substitute for the lost Haidée; Lady Adeline herself, whose middle-aged husband takes her for granted, whose self-deceiving good intentions resemble Donna Julia's, and whose confidence in arranging the affairs of others reminds us of Gulbeyaz; and finally the attractive counterpart to

182

Catherine, 'her frolic Grace' the Duchess of Fitz-Fulke. It is pointless to speculate about an unfinished plot, but the possibilities for examining and dismissing female pretensions to respectability are obvious enough. The duchess makes an auspicious beginning by finding her way into Juan's bedroom by the third night of his visit, on her second attempt.

Love in *Don Juan* is made to seem more important to women than to men and they are presented throughout as the predators. Their advances are not objected to as those of men in similar fictional situations usually are. Juan is usually receptive and appreciative, even on very short notice. The only instance of ardour being repelled by anything remotely like chastity or bashfulness occurs when Juan bursts into tears on being challenged by Gulbeyaz. The point of this touching scene is to show that his love for the lost Haidée means something to him.[26] The opinion that every woman is at heart a rake has been a recurrent minority view since the time of Tiresias at least; in *Don Juan* the implications of it are borne in upon the reader by the skilful detail of domestic situation and sure psychological insight, and are made subversively attractive.

Society is always preoccupied with love, but only now and then with glory. Byron's attack upon the ideal of military glory in his account of 'faithless wars' is consistent with his treatment of battle in *Childe Harold's Pilgrimage* Canto III, but it is less idiosyncratic. The aftermath of the defeat of Napoleon at Waterloo, like the aftermath of victory in the Second World War, might be characterized as a period of unthinking jingoism in which political reaction masqueraded as patriotism. By the time *Don Juan* was written, disillusionment was widespread. The Peterloo Massacre of 1819 was so named in mockery of a Waterloo whose significance had come to be continued repression at home instead of national salvation abroad. Byron's liberal sympathies lent his account a political edge that is no longer easy to appreciate;[27] the mixed feelings of the public, mingling scepticism of the political aims of war with a lingering nostalgia for the acts of heroism with which they had been regaled, provided him with an opportunity to reveal to an interested public the reality that lay behind the illusion of glory:

> I want a hero: an uncommon want,
> When every year and month sends forth a new one,
> Till, after cloying the gazettes with cant,
> The age discovers he is not the true one . . . . (I, i)

He follows this declaration with a catalogue of famous contemporaries the very length of which belittles them.[28] The inadequacy of fame is shown in an amusing light by a parody of the newspaper bulletins that record deeds of valour (VII, xiv–xxii, VIII, xviii and XIII, lii–liv), and, by way of providing a longer view, by an allusion to current doubts about the locations of the graves of the Homeric heroes (IV, lxxvi). But Byron's account of the heroism of men, like his treatment of the chastity of women, relies primarily upon the force of particular example: Juan passes through scenes of danger as he passes through scenes of seduction, willing, unaffected and spontaneous in his actions.

183

By contrast with the abject behaviour of most of his companions, Juan's often seems worthy of a hero. When the crew and passengers panic in the shipwreck, it is Juan who coolly prevents them from breaking open the rum and dying drunk (II, xxxiv–xxxvii). When the ship founders and the crew rush for the lifeboats, Juan manages to save his tutor, and his spaniel, while 200 people drown (II, lii–lxi). His defiance of Haidée's father, if ultimately ineffectual, is resolute (IV, xxxix–l). The contrast between Juan and the English veteran John Johnson, whom he meets in slavery soon after, is one of impracticality rather than bravery, however. Johnson has survived military campaigns and marriages and has on the whole found marriage to be the more frightening experience. When Juan suggests that they try to escape, Johnson replies, 'In Heaven's name let's get some supper now,/And then I'm with you, if you're for a row' (V, xlvii). Food takes precedence over heroics as it had earlier over love. In the assault upon Ismail, Juan, 'following Honour and his nose,/Rushed where the thickest fire announced most foes' (VIII, xxxii) and found himself alone. His 'virgin valour never dreamt of flying,/From ignorance of danger . . .' (VIII, xxxvi); the more genuinely brave Johnson 'Knew when and how "to cut and come again". . .' (VIII, xxxv). A distinction is being developed between useful courage and naive bravado. And yet the distinction does not lower Juan in our esteem, and his similarly impulsive action in rescuing little Leila in the thick of the fray, while equally impractical, succeeds and exemplifies the apothegm offered earlier in the canto: 'The drying up a single tear has more/Of honest fame, than shedding seas of gore' (VIII, iii). The courage of the soldier turns out to be an inglorious, common-sense quality; heroism seems to be more closely related to a generous and self-forgetting sympathy for others.

The analysis of military glory in *Don Juan* extends to those who supervise the conduct of war as well as to the men who wage it hand to hand. The siege of Ismail is depicted as a bloody and desperate affair, carried on for the most part with roughly equal incompetence by both sides. When the Russian general, Suwarrow, takes command the situation is transformed. His arrival is sufficiently unportentous:

> For, on the sixteenth, at full gallop, drew
>   In sight two horsemen, who were deemed Cossacques
> For some time, till they came in nearer view:
>   They had but little baggage at their backs,
> For there were but *three* shirts between the two;
>   But on they rode upon two Ukraine hacks,
> Till, in approaching, were at length described
> In this plain pair, Suwarrow and his guide.   (VII, xliii)

His behaviour in the camp sustains the first impression. Stripped to his shirt this 'little—odd—old man' (VII, xlix) attends to everything, even the training of recruits, himself. Byron's description of him as 'Hero, buffoon, half-demon and half-dirt' (VII, lv) recalls the description of Napoleon in Canto III of *Childe Harold's Pilgrimage*. For all his military genius, and stripped of the ceremonial

184

trappings that might conceal the true nature of his trade, he presides over butchery on a grand scale. Byron provides a profusion of detail that is made more horrible by being interspersed with asides on spelling, rhymes, vulgar nicknames, taxes and national debt. By presenting the gruesome facts of battle on a level with such comparative trivialities, he exaggerates the state of mind that lies behind the complacent acceptance of war.

> Oh, blood and thunder! and oh, blood and wounds!
>   These are but vulgar oaths, as you may deem,
> Too gentle reader! and most shocking sounds:—
>   And so they are; yet thus is Glory's dream
> Unriddled . . . .   (VIII, i)

If war is inglorious in itself, the only excuse for it must be the cause for which it is fought. Suwarrow's blasphemous message to Catherine the Great is indignantly recorded:

> With bloody hands he wrote his first despatch;
>   And here exactly follows what he said:—
> 'Glory to *God* and to the Empress!' (*Powers*
> *Eternal! such names mingled!*) 'Ismail's ours.'   (VIII, cxxxiii)

Byron's objection prepares the way for Canto IX in which he turns from analysis of the conduct of a relatively remote foreign war to English militarism as it is personified by the Duke of Wellington. The contrast in personal character is useful here. Wellington's ostentation and luxurious way of life and his presence in the social establishment seem to be at odds with his earthy occupation. In fact he is 'the best of cut-throats' (IX, iv) and morally very much on a level with the butcher Suwarrow. And he differs from the generals who were great statesmen (Cincinnatus, Epaminondas, Washington) in having accepted a fortune from the public for his services and continuing to take an active part in public life. Wellington makes an admirable example of war made respectable and he is therefore an appropriate target. Byron's pun—'Oh Wellington! (or "Villainton"—for Fame/Sounds the heroic syllables both ways . . .)' (IX, i)—is spiced with partisan political animus, but the real charge against Wellington is the timeless one, that he has presided over an unjustifiable war. After a war allegedly against a tyrant, Europe remains enslaved. Fame and fortune gained on such terms 'Are nothing but a child of Murder's rattles' (VIII, iv).

The ultimate responsibility, however, lies with the rulers whom generals obey. In despotic Russia, Catherine the Great's frivolity may be blamed for Suwarrow's prowess:

> Great joy was hers, or rather joys: the first
>   Was a ta'en city, thirty thousand slain:
> Glory and triumph o'er her aspect burst . . . .   (IX, lix)

185

The blame for a British general's misapplied zeal must lie closer to home. Catherine at least makes no pretence and 'looked on the match/Between these nations as a main of cocks . . .' (IX, xxix). Despotism on a national scale, with tyrants enforcing on others disagreeable conditions that they themselves do not share, has a domestic counterpart in the petty tyrannies of mothers like Donna Inez and fathers like Lambro. In England, the humiliation of the unwed mother in her scarlet cloak (XVI, lxi–lxviii) in the same house where the infidelities of Fitz-Fulke pass unnoticed and the 'two poachers caught in a steel trap' (XVI, lxi) wait to be committed to gaol by a Lord Henry fresh from legal plundering in property (XVI, lx), introduce the despotism of one class in its dealings with another. Whether these analogies would have been pursued in later cantos of *Don Juan* we cannot know, but their presence helps to unite the poem as we have it.

8 Unfamiliar ideas

During the Romantic period the reading public seems to have forgotten about the vein of poetry in the English tradition that conveyed unfamiliar ideas or expressed common ones in an unfamiliar way. Their unawareness was a legacy of the indifference of the eighteenth century, expressed cogently in Samuel Johnson's strictures on the metaphysicals,[1] and reflected more tellingly by his omission of Donne from *The Lives of the English Poets*. Broadly speaking, metaphysical poetry was ignored. The poets themselves read widely and had access not only to the few whom Johnson and subsequent anthologists such as Chalmers and Anderson had admitted into their collections, but also to Platonists like Henry More, to Spenser's *Hymnes*, and, with the revival of interest in the middle ages, to an allegorical tradition expressed in its most elaborate form in the poetry of Dante. They also had direct access to Plato and Plotinus, and to the allegorical turn of dissenting interpretations of the Bible and of nature from Jakob Boehme to Emmanuel Swedenborg. When the need arose there were sufficient precedents to fall back on; the difficulty was that readers were baffled by conventions they neither expected nor understood.

If the Romantics had confined their poems to a coterie of adepts, a larger audience might gradually have been cultivated, but the assumption that poetry should be accessible to all had taken such a hold that this possibility seems hardly to have been considered. Blake, by producing very few copies of his beautiful illustrated poems and thinking of them as being works of art as much as they were poems, restricted his work to a small circle and seems to have been content. The cost to posterity has been that no one can now be sure how he meant them to be interpreted, and that by feeling free of interaction with any representative group of readers he may have become even more idiosyncratic in his isolation than his ideas required. Shelley engaged defiantly with publishers who preferred the narrative verse of Scott and Byron, but even he was denied the helpful sense of the nature of the reader's difficulties that a more sympathetic reception might have given him. The characteristic problem that still makes the reading of Romantic poems of ideas difficult is that they do not constitute an easily recognizable genre. Deprived of a convention that readers could identify the poets were forced to use conventions that were usually differently employed. Typically, the best poems of ideas were disguised as something else, and the disguise was rarely penetrated with patience.

I

When Wordsworth arranged his poems in groups for a collective edition in 1815, he included his 'Ode: Intimations of Immortality from Recollections of Early Childhood' (1807) among the 'Epitaphs and Elegiac Pieces' along with 'Elegiac Stanzas Suggested by a Picture of Peele Castle' (1807), rather than among 'Poems of the Imagination' along with 'Tintern Abbey', or even among 'Poems Referring to the Period of Childhood' along with 'The Idle Shepherd-boys' (1800). This decision and the title of the ode itself are useful hints that although celebrations of childhood are characteristic of Wordsworth, he was prepared at times to use them as a means rather than an end. A conventional elegy mourns the death of an individual, meditates upon the unhappy condition of mankind, and finds comfort in the realization that the dead person must be happier in Heaven. 'Intimations' omits the occasion of a particular death, begins with an aspect of the unhappy condition of man, and develops an ingenious relationship between it and the happiness of heaven that attempts to reconcile us to the inevitability of growing old and dying.

In the first two stanzas the author contrasts his sense of the beauty of the natural world with the livelier sense he had of it when he was younger:

> There was a time when meadow, grove, and stream,
> The earth, and every common sight,
>   To me did seem
>   Apparelled in celestial light,
> The glory and the freshness of a dream.
> It is not now as it hath been of yore;—
>   Turn wheresoe'er I may,
>   By night or day,
> The things which I have seen I now can see no more.   (11. 1–9)

He can still recognize and appreciate beauty—'The Rainbow comes and goes,/And lovely is the Rose...' (11. 10–11)—but it is no longer what it was—'But yet I know, where'er I go,/That there hath past away a glory from the earth' (11. 17–18).

We have been given no reason for the change he describes, and that the range of possibilities is considerable will seem more obvious if we consider the model upon which these opening stanzas are based. In 1800 the following lines had appeared in the *Morning Post*:

> There was a time when earth, and sea, and skies,
>   The bright green vale, and forest's dark recess,
> With all things, lay before my eyes
>   In steady loveliness:
> But now I feel, on earth's uneasy scene,
>   Such sorrows as will never cease;—

I only ask for peace;
If I must live to know that such a time has been.

They are spoken by a madman who has jealously murdered the woman he loved, and they are part of a rather melodramatic poem entitled 'The Voice from the Side of Etna; or the Mad Monk: An Ode in Mrs. Ratcliff's Manner' that is usually attributed to Coleridge. The lyrical intensity and irregularity are occasioned by the disturbed state of the speaker's mind. Wordsworth preserves the verse form and improves it, and yet the borrowing retains a generalizing quality and an impersonality that are unusual in his poetry.

In stanzas iii and iv the author's complaint is provided with a setting—a beautiful May morning in which young animals and children celebrate the season in pastoral surroundings. The author is alone in his sorrow, has found some relief in expressing it, and willingly joins the children—'Thou Child of Joy,/Shout round me, let me hear thy shouts, thou happy Shepherd-boy!' (11. 34–5)—and goes some way towards joining sympathies with them—'I see/The heavens laugh with you in your jubilee;/My heart is at your festival,/My head hath its coronal,/The fulness of your bliss, I feel—I feel it all' (11. 37–41). The effort is sincere and unselfish—'Oh evil day! if I were sullen/While Earth herself is adorning . . .' (11. 42–3)—but it is only partly successful, and again the contrast between the present and the past intrudes itself upon the author:

> —But there's a Tree, of many, one,
> A single Field which I have looked upon,
> Both of them speak of something that is gone:
>   The Pansy at my feet
>   Doth the same tale repeat:
> Whither is fled the visionary gleam?
> Where is it now, the glory and the dream?   (11. 51–7)

The sense of loss is plain, and it is clear enough that the gulf that separates the author from the children is one of age as well as of feelings, and yet questions remain unanswered.

Wordsworth satisfies our curiosity indirectly by turning suddenly to a new topic, the pre-existence of the soul. It is usual to observe that the theory which he propounds has Platonist origins:

> Our birth is but a sleep and a forgetting:
> The Soul that rises with us, our life's Star,
>   Hath had elsewhere its setting,
>   And cometh from afar:
>   Not in entire forgetfulness,
>   And not in utter nakedness,
> But trailing clouds of glory do we come
>   From God, who is our home . . . .   (11. 58–65)

Furthermore, in these lines Wordsworth seems to be qualifying a version of this tradition that was to be found in Dodsley's popular anthology, *A Collection of Poems*,[2] Abel Evans's 'Pre-existence: A Poem, In Imitation of Milton'. In this lugubrious but once well-known piece, God sentences the minor angels who assisted in Satan's rebellion to life on earth:

> Hither compell'd, each soul must drink long draughts
> Of those forgetful streams, till forms within,
> And all the great ideas fade and die:
> For if vast thought should play about a mind
> Inclos'd in flesh, and dragging cumbrous life,
> Flutt'ring and beating in the mournful cage,
> It soon would break its grates and wing away:
> 'Tis therefore my decree, the soul return
> Naked from off this beach, and perfect blank,
> To visit the new world . . . .   ([1782], Vol. I, p. 177)

Wordsworth departs from the Lockean implications of a *tabula rasa*, and contends that when we are born we do not forget entirely:

> Heaven lies about us in our infancy!
> Shades of the prison-house begin to close
>   Upon the growing Boy,
>   But He
> Beholds the light, and whence it flows,
>   He sees it in his joy;
> The Youth, who daily farther from the east
>   Must travel, still is Nature's Priest,
>   And by the vision splendid
>   Is on his way attended;
> At length the Man perceives it die away,
> And fade into the light of common day.   (ll. 66–77)

This 'vision splendid', recollected from a previous existence, is to be related to the puzzling 'visionary gleam' and 'the glory and the dream' of stanzas i, ii, and iv.

By this point the author's sense of loss has been identified with an experience that, even if we are imperfectly aware of it, is common to us all. In stanzas vi–vii Wordsworth affectionately outlines the development of a representative child as a familiar paradigm, and fancifully personifies Nature as a foster mother gradually winning her child away from 'the glories he hath known'. The child devotes his attention to learning the ways of the world, 'As if his whole vocation/Were endless imitation' (ll. 107–8).

It is in stanzas viii and ix that Wordsworth's account of childhood departs from common experience. He appears merely to be pursuing his theory about the recollections of the soul when he apostrophizes the wisdom of the child:

190

> Thou, whose exterior semblance doth belie
>   Thy Soul's immensity;
> Thou best Philosopher, who yet dost keep
> Thy heritage, thou Eye among the blind,
> That, deaf and silent, read'st the eternal deep,
> Haunted for ever by the eternal mind,—
>   Mighty Prophet! Seer blest!
>   On whom those truths do rest,
> Which we are toiling all our lives to find . . . . (11. 109–17)

But his own experience of childhood is out of the common path, and the theory, which unsupported by observation might seem to be extravagantly expressed here, is really a counterpart to an unusual perception of childhood. It is not the happiness of childhood to which he looks back so gratefully:

>   not indeed
> For that which is most worthy to be blest;
> Delight and liberty, the simple creed
> Of Childhood, whether busy or at rest,
> With new-fledged hope still fluttering in his breast . . . . (11. 135–9)

Rather he thinks of occult capacities of children that are necessarily difficult to describe, and he conveys them in a series of definitions:

>   those obstinate questionings
>   Of sense and outward things,
>   Fallings from us, vanishings;
>   Blank misgivings of a Creature
> Moving about in worlds not realised,
> High instincts before which our mortal Nature
> Did tremble like a guilty Thing surprised:
>   But for those first affections,
>   Those shadowy recollections . . . . (11. 142–50)

It is in large part owing to the missionary endeavours of Wordsworth and of like-minded pioneers from Rousseau to Jung that most of us can attach some reality to these compelling phrases.

    They are so striking that we must remind ourselves again that the perception of childhood is not presented here as an end in itself. What we observe, or what we recall, is important here as an augury of immortality. As we grow older and farther from childhood we can look back upon our own pasts by observing children:

> Hence in a season of calm weather
>   Though inland far we be,
> Our Souls have sight of that immortal sea

191

> Which brought us hither,
> Can in a moment travel thither,
> And see the Children sport upon the shore,
> And hear the mighty waters rolling evermore.   (11. 162–8)

At last solace is found for the lament of stanzas i and ii, and the author is able to contemplate his loss without a diminution of joy. Although 'the hour/Of splendour in the grass, of glory in the flower' (11. 178–9) is gone forever, we can recall something of what it was like. It was a recollection of immortality, and as it fades from us we, ageing, approach death and the prospect of renewal of immortality itself.

When the 'Intimations Ode' first appeared it contained bleak hints about death that were later removed. A comment on immortality originally followed after line 120:

> To whom the grave
> Is but a lonely bed without the sense or sight
> Of day or the warm light,
> A place of thought where we in waiting lie . . . .

The removal of these lines, out of deference to less stoical sensibilities, made the comfort of the final stanzas less general in their application. In stanza xi the author describes how he now appreciates natural beauties in a different way. In stanza x he speaks of 'the faith that looks through death,/In years that bring the philosophic mind' (11. 186–7). The significance of the new enjoyment is not spelled out for us, and it takes some getting used to. But it is that death and immortality are nearer:

> The Clouds that gather round the setting sun
> Do take a sober colouring from an eye
> That hath kept watch o'er man's mortality . . . .   (11. 197–9)

It is, as Southey told Scott, 'a dark subject darkly handled', but who would wish it otherwise?[3]

II

Shelley, in his 'Hymn to Intellectual Beauty' (written in 1816), reworks the materials of the 'Intimations Ode' from a different point of view. His account of his boyish recognition of an existence beyond the natural world modifies Wordsworth's memory of the child's 'first affections' and 'shadowy recollections' but confirms it, and although Shelley rejects the Christian framework upon which his predecessor had relied, he too finds solace for mortality in the Platonist conviction that something immutable and desirable survives. His dilemma, like Wordsworth's, is that it is difficult to convince others of the value of an unfamiliar idea when one can only describe the idea indirectly.

The idea is introduced in the opening lines ('The awful shadow of some unseen Power/Floats though unseen among us . . .') and it is buttressed by the name 'Intellectual Beauty' in the title and the apostrophe 'Spirit of BEAUTY' at the beginning of the second stanza; but definition is gradually approached by analogies with ordinary experience as the poem proceeds. We are told that it appears transitorily, but to everyone (11. 4–7), and its transitoriness is complained of as correspondent to the general condition of mutability:

> —where art thou gone?
> Why dost thou pass away and leave our state,
> This dim vast vale of tears, vacant and desolate?
>   Ask why the sunlight not for ever
>   Weaves rainbows o'er yon mountain-river,
> Why aught should fail and fade that once is shown,
>   Why fear and dream and death and birth
>   Cast on the daylight of this earth
>   Such gloom,—why man has such a scope
> For love and hate, despondency and hope?   (11. 15–24)

To the questions arising from such anxious circumstances there has been no answer from a 'sublimer world' (1. 25); ineffectual notions such as 'Demon, Ghost, and Heaven' (1. 27) (the tendentious parallel was meant to be provocative) are all that 'sage or poet' (1. 26) have been able to conceive. In the face of 'Doubt, chance, and mutability' (1. 31) the only reassurance is the light of the unseen power. The persuasive analogies follow, generalizing the definition, lending weight to it and describing its effect:

> Thy light alone—like mist o'er mountains driven,
>   Or music by the night-wind sent
>   Through strings of some still instrument,
>   Or moonlight on a midnight stream,
> Gives grace and truth to life's unquiet dream.

The symptoms of its presence are as fleeting:

> Love, hope, and Self-esteem, like clouds depart
>   And come, for some uncertain moments lent . . . .
>   Thou messenger of sympathies,
>   That wax and wane in lovers' eyes—
> Thou—that to human thought art nourishment,
>   Like darkness to a dying flame!   (11. 32–8, 42–5)

The circle of analogies has been drawn widely enough to embrace the finer experiences of every reader, and they are used as a counterbalance to the prospect of death—'lest the grave should be,/Like life and fear, a dark reality' (11. 47–8).

193

In stanzas v and vi the poet records the circumstances in which he first encountered the spirit of which he speaks. In the aftermath of puerile attempts to raise ghosts by necromancy, he is taken by surprise while more sociably employed on a beautiful spring day:

> When musing deeply on the lot
> Of life, at that sweet time when winds are wooing
>   All vital things that wake to bring
>   News of birds and blossoming,—
> Sudden, thy shadow fell on me;
> I shrieked, and clasped my hands in ecstasy! (11. 55–60)

It has been his constant effort ever since to make others share his vision:

> never joy illumed my brow
> Unlinked with hope that thou wouldst free
>   This world from its dark slavery,
>   That thou—O awful LOVELINESS,
> Wouldst give whate'er these words cannot express. (11. 68–72)

The consequences, he believes, are of paramount importance, for, as he has stated in stanza iv:

> Man were immortal, and omnipotent,
> Didst thou, unknown and awful as thou art,
> Keep with thy glorious train firm state within his
>   heart. (11. 39–41)

The prospect is not, literally, of immortality after death, but of a state of mind during life that is comparable to our conceptions of heaven.

The Wordsworthian experience, or one very like it, has been adapted to a creed that is content with life as an end in itself. The poem, as befits a hymn, concludes with a prayer rather than an assertion; faith in intimations of intellectual beauty, like faith in those of immortality, nourishes contentment:

> The day becomes more solemn and serene
>   When noon is past—there is a harmony
>   In autumn, and a lustre in its sky,
> Which through the summer is not heard or seen,
> As if it could not be, as if it had not been!
>   Thus let thy power, which like the truth
>   Of nature on my passive youth
> Descended, to my onward life supply
>   Its calm—to one who worships thee,

> And every form containing thee,
> Whom, SPIRIT fair, thy spells did bind
> To fear himself, and love all human kind. (ll. 73–84)

But faith in intimations of intellectual beauty, and reverence of beautiful objects for the spirit within them is offered as a persuasive substitute for faith in an after-life as a defence against decay and death.

III

With the publication of Thomas Sedgwick Whalley's *Mont Blanc: An Irregular Lyric Poem* in 1788, a rich new setting was introduced into the English tradition. Whalley drew upon the French prose account of M. C. Bourrit and upon his own experience.[4] He emphasized the sublime aspects of the mountain, including a description of a terrifying mountain storm, the savage attack of an eagle upon the chamois, and the danger of avalanches and glaciers, as well as the serener beauties of the place. Mont Blanc itself he singled out as 'greatest . . . the works of GOD among' and preferred over classical mountains like Olympus, Ida and Aetna and as worthy of comparison even with Biblical Mount Sinai (pp. 5–6 and 15). By the time of Wordsworth's *Descriptive Sketches* (1793), the contrast of the Arcadian tranquillity of the Vale of Chamonix —'A scene more fair than what the Grecian feigns . . .' (1. 684)—and the dangerous magnificence of lofty Mont Blanc with its destructive glaciers had begun to pass into stock poetic vocabulary. Wordsworth uses the beauty of the scene for its incongruity with the abject political state of Savoy.[5] In his 'Hymn before Sun-rise, in the Vale of Chamouni' (1802), Coleridge, who unlike Whalley and Wordsworth had never seen Mont Blanc, follows and expands upon Friederika Brun's short poem 'Chamouny Beym Sonnenaufgange' in using the rarest of its beauties as an opportunity for praising the varieties of God's creation.[6]

In 'Mont Blanc: Lines Written in the Vale of Chamouni' (1817), Shelley combines the experience of visiting the famous scene with an awareness of the poetical commonplaces. Coleridge had remarked, in a prose preface to his 'Hymn', 'Who *would* be, who *could* be an Atheist in this valley of wonders!'[7] Shelley, and indeed the older Coleridge himself, might well have felt the inadequacy of such a simple-minded expression of religious enthusiasm, and he goes far beyond mere counter-statement in a prolonged meditation upon the relationship of the human mind to the natural world it perceives.

He acknowledges at once the splendour and variety of the natural world and its influence upon the mind:

> The everlasting universe of things
> Flows through the mind, and rolls its rapid waves,
> Now dark—now glittering—now reflecting gloom—
> Now lending splendour . . . . (ll. 1–4)

And without making undue claims for the observer's contribution, he nevertheless mentions its presence:

> where from secret springs
> The source of human thought its tribute brings
> Of waters,—with a sound but half its own,
> Such as a feeble brook will oft assume
> In the wild woods, among the mountains lone,
> Where waterfalls around it leap for ever,
> Where woods and winds contend, and a vast river
> Over its rocks ceaselessly bursts and raves.   (11. 4–11)

Great though the disparity is admitted to be, the 'feeble brook' is introduced into the midst of such sublime surroundings.

In Section II the wonderful appearance (that unparalleled example of the 'everlasting universe of things') of the Ravine of Arve is described appreciatively in terms of power, noise, ancientness and endless movement:

> awful scene,
> Where Power in likeness of the Arve comes down
> From the ice-gulfs that gird his secret throne,
> Bursting through these dark mountains like the flame
> Of lightning through the tempest . . . .   (11. 15–19)

The state of mind induced by this scene and indeed some of the attributes of the scene itself, are curiously reminiscent of 'Kubla Khan'. The feelings examined as he looks at the ravine are confused but exalted:

> when I gaze on thee
> I seem as in a trance sublime and strange
> To muse on my own separate fantasy,
> My own, my human mind, which passively
> Now renders and receives fast influencings,
> Holding an unremitting interchange
> With the clear universe of things around . . . .   (11. 34–40)

The mental activity stimulated by this tremendous experience is represented as a search for adequate analogies. Shelley converts Plato's fable of the cave of human perception, in which shadowy images of the external world are cast upon the interior walls,[8] into a cave of poetry:

> One legion of wild thoughts, whose wandering wings
> Now float above thy darkness, and now rest
> Where that or thou art no unbidden guest,
> In the still cave of the witch Poesy,

Seeking among the shadows that pass by
Ghosts of all things that are, some shade of thee,
Some phantom, some faint image . . . .   (11. 41–7)

The subjectiveness of this experience is stressed, and the word 'witch' seems calculated to remind us that it is deceptive as well as beguiling.

   In Section III the idea of an immutable life beyond mortal life is introduced:

Some say that gleams of a remoter world
Visit the soul in sleep,—that death is slumber,
And that its shapes the busy thoughts outnumber
Of those who wake and live.   (11. 49–52)

Mont Blanc itself—'still, snowy, and serene' (1.61)—might seem an adequate image for this idea:

              —I look on high;
Has some unknown omnipotence unfurled
The veil of life and death?   (11. 52–4)

And yet, when it is examined, it is a disquieting image rather than a reassuring one. The mountain and the peaks that surround it are desolate and inhospitable:

A desert peopled by the storms alone,
Save where the eagle brings some hunter's bone,
And the wolf tracks her there—how hideously
Its shapes are heaped around! rude, bare, and high,
Ghastly, and scarred, and riven.   (11. 67–71)

Shelley's interpretation of what he sees may be regarded as an emphasis upon the terrifying aspect of the sublime, but set beside the treatment of Mont Blanc that preceded him it becomes a comment comparable to Blake's on the tiger—'Did he who made the Lamb make thee?' Such scenes, he seems to say, are in themselves ambiguous:

The wilderness has a mysterious tongue
Which teaches awful doubt, or faith so mild,
So solemn, so serene, that man may be,
But for such faith, with nature reconciled . . . .   (11. 76–9)

The majesty of the scene is self-evident. Its significance is harder to fathom.

   In Section IV the counterpart of immortality, the mutability of life on earth, is examined. Mutability is the condition of nature:

The fields, the lakes, the forests, and the streams,
Ocean, and all the living things that dwell

197

> Within the daedal earth; lightning, and rain,
> Earthquake, and fiery flood, and hurricane, ...
> All things that move and breathe with toil and sound
> Are born and die; revolve, subside, and swell.　　　　(11. 84–7, 94–5)

The waste and destruction involved are compared to the waste and destruction caused by the remorseless progress of the glaciers:

> 　　　　　　a flood of ruin
> Is there, that from the boundaries of the sky
> Rolls its perpetual stream; vast pines are strewing
> Its destined path, or in the mangled soil
> Branchless and shattered stand; the rocks, drawn down
> From yon remotest waste, have overthrown
> The limits of the dead and living world,
> Never to be reclaimed. The dwelling-place
> Of insects, beasts, and birds, becomes its spoil
> Their food and their retreat for ever gone,
> So much of life and joy is lost.　　　　　　(11. 107–17)

From this compelling image of inevitable decay, 'The race/Of man flies far in dread . . .' (11. 117–18).

Yet something survives the wreck and is unaffected by it. In Section V the presiding supremacy of Mont Blanc is recalled for us, unchanging, silent and alone. The idea we expect it to represent, comfortingly, is the idea of God, the idea to which Coleridge's 'Hymn' with its much less disturbing representation of mountain and valley had returned so insistently. Shelley refrains from facile interpretation of something we cannot know. Emphasizing the fact that the summit of the mountain is beyond the bounds of human experience,[9] he imagines for a moment what it must be like:

> 　　　　　　the snows descend
> Upon that Mountain; none beholds them there,
> Nor when the flakes burn in the sinking sun,
> Or the star-beams dart through them:—Winds contend
> Silently there, and heap the snow with breath
> Rapid and strong, but silently!　　　　　　(11. 131–6)

Remote from man and alien as it is, it is natural to us to imagine that it must be inhabited. Shelley admits to sharing this human tendency to confer mysterious existence upon the unknown:

> 　　　　The secret Strength of things
> Which governs thought, and to the infinite dome
> Of Heaven is as a law, inhabits thee!　　　　　(11. 139–41)

And yet, subject as he is to this impulse, he has sufficient resolution to contemplate the alternative. Retiring, as he does so, to the formulation of the relationship with which he began, of the human mind to its environment, he asks the disturbing question:

> And what were thou, and earth, and stars, and sea,
> If to the human mind's imaginings
> Silence and solitude were vacancy?   (11. 142–4)

The question is not atheistical in its tendency, but it is a reproach to the unthinking arguments from design that complacent believers took for granted.[10]

IV

Shelley sub-titled *Adonais* (1821) 'An Elegy on the Death of John Keats, Author of Endymion, Hyperion, Etc.' For his contemporaries the identification was nec-essary. In the preface Shelley made no claims to close acquaintance with Keats, and his guarded praise of 'Hyperion' as 'second to nothing that was ever produced by a writer of the same years' was balanced as a proof of impartiality against a reference to his own 'known repugnance to the narrow principles of taste on which several of his [Keats's] earlier compositions were modelled . . .'.[11] Shelley's subject matter was the death of a promising young poet at the hands of unprincipled reviewers. Had Keats, like Milton's Edward King, slipped from public memory, the poem would be less perplexing. Instead he has become almost as famous as Mont Blanc, and it is inevitable that we should be predisposed to regard *Adonais* as the worthy tribute of one great author to another.

Adonais is sufficiently removed from events to be applicable to any poet who has died young. The injury imputed to the *Quarterly Review* in the preface is not treated literally in the poem—Adonais is described variously as 'pierced by the shaft which flies/In darkness' (11. 11–12) and as having drunk poison (1. 316)—and was in any case untrue. In one respect Keats's identity did tell, and that was in the propriety of Shelley's choice of the myth of Adonis.[12] In Keats's *Endymion* (II, 384–533), the hero comes upon Adonis sleeping in an arbour, surrounded by flowers and ministered to by attentive Cupids, and he is informed that Venus has 'Medicined death to a lengthened drowsiness . . .' (II, 484). Keats's scene was a development of the well-known 'garden of Adonis' section of Spenser's *Faerie Queene* (III, vi, 29–51), but his use of it made it particularly appropriate to apply the conventional lament of Adonis to him.

It was common in the early eighteenth century to publish English versions of satirical Latin poems with the Latin text alongside. The reader could enjoy the witty substitution of the names of his contemporaries for their Roman counter-parts and appreciate significant departures from the original. By the Romantic period this practice had virtually died out,[13] but the habit and expectation of such comparison survived in satire and in other forms of verse.

199

The formal models for *Adonais* were two short Greek poems: Bion's 'Lament for Adonis' and Moschus's 'Lament for Bion'.[14] In 'The Lament for Adonis', Venus is summoned to weep over the blood-stained corpse of her young lover. She is wandering distractedly 'unkempt, unslippered' and briers tear at her, drawing blood. When she comes, she tries to revive him with a kiss and reproaches him for rashly risking his life with a wild beast. Flowers are strewn upon the body and weeping Cupids lay it out. Shelley preserves these elements, endowing them with greater physical realism, and he repeats the refrain 'I weep for Adonais'. On to this material he splices 'The Lament for Bion' from which his Greek epigraph is taken.[15] In 'The Lament for Bion', which is itself an imitation of Bion's, nature and mankind are represented as mourning the poet's death, and the deaths of previous great poets are remembered. The River Meles is reminded how it had mourned the death of Homer previously, and Cupids weep beside the body. Shelley preserves these details while modifying somewhat the single-mindedness of sorrow that Moschus had expressed. Shelley achieves the union of the two forms by introducing Urania—Milton's heavenly successor to the pagan nine muses in *Paradise Lost* (VII, 1–20)—in the place of Bion's Venus, making her a mother rather than a mistress, and as a substitute for Moschus's Sicilian muses and River Meles.

The effect of Shelley's use of these conventions was to draw the attention of his readers to the innovations he was introducing. The identity of the bereaved goddess and her new relationship with Adonais, for instance, requires explanatory emphasis in stanza ii:

> Where wert thou, mighty Mother, when he lay,
> When thy Son lay, pierced by the shaft which flies
> In darkness? where was lorn Urania
> When Adonais died? (11. 10–13)

But the recollection of a previous poet's death, which prompts expectations of Moschus's blind Homer, is incendiary rather than expository. Milton is substituted and, by implication, offered as worthy of comparison:

> —He died,
> Who was the Sire of an immortal strain,
> Blind, old, and lonely, when his country's pride,
> The priest, the slave, and the liberticide,
> Trampled and mocked with many a loathèd rite
> Of lust and blood . . . . (11. 29–34)

These lines, like Byron's praise of Cromwell in *Childe Harold*, had a political edge to them in 1821. The royalist reviewers of the Tory *Quarterly Review* who had just expressed enthusiasm for the coronation of the libertine George IV in 1820 and had yet condemned Adonais are compared to the venal courtiers of Charles II who did not appreciate what Milton stood for.

200

Stanzas vi to xxvii (11. 46–243) rework the death scene and the mourning of Shelley's sources. The attendant Cupids are transformed into Dreams, Thoughts and Feelings, as is suitable for a dead poet.[16] The futile encounter with Death in stanza xxv seems both to acknowledge the tradition of Venus's partial redemption of Adonis and to reject it.

Urania's closing words, in stanzas xxviii–xxix, mark a significant departure from the Greek originals. Her characterization of the destroyers of Adonais, identified in the preface as reviewers, is an open attack on a part of the literary establishment:

> The herded wolves, bold only to pursue;
> The obscene ravens, clamorous o'er the dead;
> The vultures to the conqueror's banner true
> Who feed where Desolation first has fed,
> And whose wings rain contagion . . . .　　　　　　　　(11. 244–8)

And they are adroitly separated in the readers' minds from Lord Byron, the one worthwhile author whom they have praised, by the loaded observation that it was only after he had mocked them in *English Bards, and Scotch Reviewers* (1809) that they acknowledged him:

> 　　　　　　　　　　　how they fled,
> 　When, like Apollo, from his golden bow
> 　The Pythian of the age one arrow sped
> 　And smiled!—The spoilers tempt no second blow,
> They fawn on the proud feet that spurn them lying low.　　(11. 248–52)

Urania concludes with the prophetic comparison of men to reptiles and ephemeral insects on the one hand, and to 'immortal stars' on the other (stanza xxix).

The visit of the mountain shepherds to the bier of their friend has a precedent in 'The Lament for Bion' in which Theocritus, the chief of the Bucolic poets, is accompanied by the humble author himself:

> Thou too, dear Bard, THEOCRITUS bewails,
> The sweetest warbler of Sicilia's dales!
> And I, who suit to sorrow's melting tone
> The *Ausonian* verse, but mimic music own.[17]

Shelley includes four mourners, of whom two are famous. The 'Pilgrim of Eternity' was unmistakably the author of *Childe Harold's Pilgrimage*. The second—'from her wilds Ierne sent/The sweetest lyrist of her saddest wrong . . .' (11. 268–9)—was easily recognized as the author of *Irish Melodies*, Thomas Moore. In 1821 these two were not only the most popular living poets, but both were known to live in exile, Moore to escape creditors, through no fault of his own, and Byron to avoid social

ostracism. With the third, 'A pardlike Spirit beautiful and swift . . .', begins one of
the most difficult passages in the poem.

As we have seen, Moschus included himself as a mourner in 'The Lament for
Bion'. Shelley's description of the third mourner is identified with himself only by
the conventional humility of its opening—'Midst others of less note, came
one frail Form' (1. 271)—and by similarities that may be observed between
the extraordinary character he presents in the next four stanzas and his conception
of himself as it is known from our knowledge of his life. But Shelley could not expect
his readers to have any such knowledge, and it seems likely that our having it has
led to neglect of more typical clues to the mourner's identity. In Keats's *Endymion*,
Venus turns from Adonis to sympathize with Endymion's grief at the sight of her
happiness, and she speaks to Adonis about him:

> My child,
> Favour this gentle youth; his days are wild
> With love—he—but alas! too well I see
> Thou know'st the deepness of his misery.
> Ah, smile not so, my son: I tell thee true,
> That when through heavy hours I used to rue
> The endless sleep of this new-born Adon',
> This stranger ay I pitied. For upon
> A dreary morning once I fled away
> Into the breezy clouds, to weep and pray
> For this my love: for vexing Mars had teaz'd
> Me even to tears: thence, when a little eas'd
> Down-looking, vacant, through a hazy wood,
> I saw this youth as he despairing stood:
> Those same dark curls blown vagrant in the wind;
> Those same full fringed lids a constant blind
> Over his sullen eyes: I saw him throw
> Himself on wither'd leaves, even as though
> Death had come sudden; for no jot he mov'd,
> Yet mutter'd wildly. I could hear he lov'd
> Some fair immortal . . . .   (II, 548–68)

In *Adonais*, 'sad Urania scanned/The Stranger's mien, and murmured: "Who art
thou?"' (11. 302–3). The resemblance to Endymion is pointed by her question,
and may be traced in other attributes of the mourner—his weakness, his
unhappiness, his loneliness. Instead of a 'fair immortal' it is surmised that he

> Had gazed on Nature's naked loveliness,
> Actaeon-like, and now he fled astray
> With feeble steps o'er the world's wilderness . . . .   (11. 275–7)

And here Peona's guess that Endymion has glimpsed Diana's 'naked limbs among
the alders green' (I, 513) is echoed. We know that he is a poet—'of that crew/He
202

came the last, neglected and apart . . .' (11. 295–6)—but this affinity with the dead Adonais as a brother poet is increased into a parallel with the ill-treated Keats by the link made between the mourner and Endymion. In stanza xxxiii his Bacchic garb seems to be too much for him. His fellow-mourners recognize him as yet another sufferer from the blighting effects of criticism. In response to Urania's question

> He answered not, but with a sudden hand
> Made bare his branded and ensanguined brow,
> Which was like Cain's or Christ's—oh! that it
>   should be so! (11. 304–6)

The 'curse of Cain' was pronounced earlier upon the man responsible for Adonais's death (1. 151); its mention here suggests bitterly that it has fallen on the victim rather than the persecutor, and the ambivalence of the suffering is neatly emphasized by the alternatives 'like Cain's or Christ's'.

It seems probable that we are meant to regard the third mourner as the 'poet', if only because of Moschus's precedent. The extent to which we should identify him with Shelley, with consequences that make even biographical critics wince, is much less clear. The mourner, whoever he is, is a living proof that the literary corruption that destroys poets of promise is as active as ever. The fourth mourner too is unnamed, but no reader of the *Quarterly*'s attack on *Endymion* could fail to recognize that Leigh Hunt, whose 'simple neophyte' Keats is there said to be, is intended.[18] Shelley's commemoration of him in terms of his character rather than his art—'gentlest of the wise'—is a public answer to the *Quarterly*'s savage prediction that 'he will live and die unhonoured in his own generation, and, for his own sake it is to be hoped, moulder unknown in those which are to follow'.[19]

The final reproach to the reviewer (stanzas xxxvi–xxxvii) provides a transition in the poem from the theme of the unsatisfactoriness of the literary world to the unsatisfactoriness of life in general. The traditional comfort of imagining the bliss of heaven is given added force by an unqualified denigration of human experience:

> Peace, peace! he is not dead, he doth not sleep—
> He hath awakened from the dream of life—
> 'Tis we, who lost in stormy visions, keep
> With phantoms an unprofitable strife,
> And in mad trance, strike with our spirit's knife
> Invulnerable nothings.—*We* decay
> Like corpses in a charnel; fear and grief
> Convulse us and consume us day by day,
> And cold hopes swarm like worms within our living clay.   (11. 343–51)

The supposed advantages of the after-life are here carried to their logical consequence; our day is called 'our night' (1. 352), and 'that unrest which men miscall delight' is bracketed with 'Envy and calumny and hate and pain . . .' (11.

353–4). The Platonist interpretation of life is carried far beyond the mild and sympathetic sense given by the 'Intimations Ode' that something is missing:

> From the contagion of the world's slow stain
> He is secure, and now can never mourn
> A heart grown cold, a head grown gray in vain;
> Nor, when the spirit's self has ceased to burn,
> With sparkless ashes load an unlamented urn. (11. 356–60)

In the 'Ode to a Nightingale', as we have seen, Keats was led by the contrast between the happiness of the bird's song and his own weariness of a world in which 'men sit and hear each other groan;/Where palsy shakes a few, sad, last grey hairs . . .' to indulge a fancy:

> Darkling I listen; and, for many a time
>   I have been half in love with easeful Death,
> Call'd him soft names in many a mused rhyme,
>   To take into the air my quiet breath;
> Now more than ever seems it rich to die . . . . (st. vi)

The world is depicted in *Adonais* much more darkly and specifically, and death as the ultimate alternative to a miserable life is taken more seriously. Having exposed the corruptness of contemporary life, Shelley invites his readers to consider two aspects of death—our rather vague notions of life after death, and our more mundane but instinctive revulsion at the prospect of physical decay and annihilation.

Shelley advances upon a representation of an ideal life after death, the immortality that Wordsworth had stopped short of in 'Intimations', with a series of analogies. Adonais is said to be 'made one with Nature' (1. 370), and to be 'a portion of the loveliness/Which once he made more lovely . . .' (11. 379–80). Urania's prophecy about the re-awakening of the 'immortal stars' (1. 256) is revived as 'The inheritors of unfulfilled renown', young poets such as Chatterton, Sidney and Lucan, cut off in their prime, are imagined upon thrones 'built beyond mortal thought,/Far in the Unapparent' (11. 398–9). They welcome Adonais when he takes his place as Vesper, the evening star. Shelley asks the reader to imagine this scene in metaphysical terms:

> Clasp with thy panting soul the pendulous Earth;
> As from a centre, dart thy spirit's light
> Beyond all worlds, until its spacious might
> Satiate the void circumference: then shrink
> Even to a point within our day and night . . . . (11. 417–21)

This appeal, with its mixture of feelings, antiquated cosmology and space travel, is difficult to follow. As if aware of the likelihood that we may be unequal to the task, Shelley relieves us with a more traditional analogy for life after death:

Go thou to Rome,—at once the Paradise,
The grave, the city, and the wilderness . . . .   (11. 433–4)

In *Childe Harold's Pilgrimage* (Canto IV) the city had been the ultimate example of
the ruin and frustration of human hopes, and the beauty of Nature's incongruous
transformation of the Colosseum had been admired. Shelley superimposes upon
such historical images of mutability a scene that is less remote from our feelings, the
new memorials of death in the Protestant cemetery:

Here pause: these graves are all too young as yet
To have outgrown the sorrow which consigned
Its charge to each . . . .   (11. 451–3)

Standing beside the very grave, the question 'What Adonais is, why fear we to
become?' is not one to which we are expected to have a ready answer. The fact is
that we do fear death. The sustaining ideal of an after-life is beautifully and
Platonically expressed:

The One remains, the many change and pass:
Heaven's light forever shines, Earth's shadows fly;
Life, like a dome of many-coloured glass,
Stains the white radiance of Eternity,
Until Death tramples it to fragments.   (11. 460–4)

With that prospect before us and disappointment behind, death should seem
desirable, and yet even the author who has described these two poles of existence so
movingly is uncertain:

Why linger, why turn back, why shrink, my Heart?
Thy hopes are gone before: from all things here
They have departed; thou shouldst now depart! . . .
'Tis Adonais calls! oh, hasten thither,
No more let Life divide what Death can join together.
     (11. 469–71, 476–7)

Novel though it would have been to make an elegy so comforting that it ended in
suicide, Shelley, having posed the question, resolves it in terms of what is and what
might be, rather than crudely in terms of life and life after death. Even in life we
perceive benevolent forces that seem impervious to the shortcomings of society:

That Light whose smile kindles the Universe,
That Beauty in which all things work and move,
That Benediction which the eclipsing Curse
Of birth can quench not, that sustaining Love
Which through the web of being blindly wove

By man and beast and earth and air and sea,
Burns bright or dim, as each are mirrors of
The fire for which all thirst; now beams on me,
Consuming the last clouds of cold mortality.   (11. 478–86)

The release from mortality is metaphorical not literal. The author has parted from
the 'trembling throng/Whose sails were never to the tempest given . . .'
(11. 489–90); he has not joined the soul of Adonais which 'Beacons from the abode
where the Eternal are' (1.495). Repelled by the one and attracted by the latter he is
in an unfamiliar unknown region, 'borne darkly, fearfully, afar . . .' (1. 492).

V

The difficulties involved in interpreting these poems are the result of our
uncertainties about the conventions they employ. Some of the most interesting
poems continue to resist interpretation to the point where critics disagree flatly
with one another about their meaning. William Blake's *Book of Thel* (1789) is one
of the most accessible of his so-called 'prophetic books', achieving at some points a
simplicity and clarity worthy of his *Songs of Innocence*. At the beginning of the poem,
however, characters are introduced who have never been identified, and the
conclusion takes an unexpected turn that has been interpreted in mutually
contradictory ways.

The poem appears to be about a girl who laments the fact that while she, like
other living things, grows older and will die, she seems, unlike them, to perform no
useful function. Her name, Thel, has never been convincingly explained; she is
described as the youngest of 'The daughters of Mne Seraphim', and no one has been
able to show who they are; and she mourns beside an unidentified river, the
Adona. Later the Vales of Har and someone called Luvah are mentioned without
any explanation.[20] Thel's lament for mutability seems straightforward enough,
and her subsequent conversations with the lily of the valley, a cloud, a worm and a
clod of clay, furnish her with a contrasting point of view in which her interlocutors
explain their own humble usefulness and try to share their contentedness with her.
In the accompanying illustrations the lily is depicted symbolically, or perhaps
merely analogically, as a woman, the cloud as a man naked but for some flowing
drapery that preserves his modesty, the worm as an infant, and the Clod of Clay as
an attentive mother to the child. The third section of the poem concludes with the
Clod of Clay's invitation to Thel:

Wilt thou, O Queen, enter my house—'tis given thee to enter
And to return. Fear nothing; enter with thy virgin feet.   (pl. 5)

In the fourth and final section, our expectation that Thel will be comfortingly
reassured that her life is not really useless and that she too should be contented is
disappointed. Surprise seems to be intended; as a result of her visit to the house of
the Clod of Clay, Thel is shocked rather than reassured:

> The virgin started from her seat, and with a shriek
> Fled back unhinderd till she came into the vales of Har. (pl. 6)

But what the 'house' is remains unclear. While she is within it, Thel visits her own grave and hears a voice issuing from it. Its words are aphoristic but obscure:

> Why cannot the ear be closed to its own destruction,
> Or the glistening eye to the poison of a smile?
> Why are the eyelids stored with arrows ready drawn,
> Where a thousand fighting men in ambush lie?
> Or an eye of gifts and graces, showering fruits and coined gold?
> Why a tongue impressed with honey from every wind?
> Why an ear a whirlpool fierce to draw creations in?
> Why a nostril wide inhaling terror, trembling and affright?
> Why a tender curb upon the youthful burning boy?
> Why a little curtain of flesh on the bed of our desire? (pl. 6)

These are the questions that put Thel to flight. For explanations of their significance, commentators have searched the rest of Blake's works for analogous expressions or opinions and have examined his acquaintance with the occult and the esoteric. A convincing literary context has yet to be found, and in the meantime the beauty of the letter makes us regret deeply our uncertainty as to its spirit.

VI

When an unfamiliar or obscure idea is conveyed in a fashionable form, there is a risk that deliberate departures from the norm will be mistaken for clumsiness and that the poem will be dismissed summarily as a failure. Wordsworth's *The White Doe of Rylstone; or the Fate of the Nortons* (1815) is a case in point. Wordsworth himself claimed in later life that it was 'in conception, the highest work he had ever produced',[21] but although the poem has found a secure if modest place in the affections of Wordsworthians, it has never received the critical attention that he implied it deserves.

The public appetite for historical verse was whetted by Scott's *Lay of the Last Minstrel* (1805). If *The White Doe* had appeared in 1808 when it was completed, it would have been natural and instructive to compare it with Scott's *Marmion* (1808), set half a century earlier. By delaying publication until 1815, Wordsworth entered his poem in a field that had been pre-empted by Scott and of which the public, sated by *The Lady of the Lake* (1810) and *Rokeby* (1813), was growing tired. Comparison with *The Lord of the Isles* (1815) was inappropriate, and yet the comparison with Scott was inescapable. *The White Doe*, like Scott's poems, was set in a chivalric past, written in his characteristic rhymed iambic tetrameters, embellished with antiquarian and topographical notes, and printed in a handsome quarto. What it signally lacked was Scott's gripping narrative and vivid characterization.

In his notes, Wordsworth explained that he had based his poem on a ballad in Percy's *Reliques* about the rebellion of the Nortons of Rylstone, 'The Rising of the North', and combined with it a tradition from the same period that a white doe from Rylstone used regularly to visit the precinct of Bolton Abbey during divine service. 'The Rising of the North' describes how the Nortons joined Earl Percy, a Roman Catholic, in insurrection against Queen Elizabeth; how Francis Norton, one of Norton's nine sons, advised against rebellion, was reviled for cowardice by his father, and resolved to follow his father unarmed; how the rebellion failed and Norton and his eight sons were captured and executed.

To these materials Wordsworth added the character of Emily, a Norton daughter who survives the destruction of her family, and the death of Francis. Old Norton's domestic intransigence in his vigorous old age may remind us of King Lear, or of one of Wordsworth's 'statesmen', and Francis may combine the activities of Cordelia, Edgar and Kent, but these unequal resemblances only remind us how one-dimensional Wordsworth's characters are. The story is in fact merely a vehicle for Emily's experience. Wordsworth's dedication to the poem hints at his true subject:

> it speaks
> Of female patience winning firm repose;
> And, of the recompense that conscience seeks,
> A bright, encouraging, example shows . . . .　　　　　　　(11. 49–52)

As the uninviting triteness of this formulation suggests, it is a theme that, if it is worth communicating at all, requires to be shared rather than stated.

It is the additions to the story that matter. The painful dilemma in which Francis finds himself, for instance, is carefully developed. His rebellion against his father is an altogether affectionate and understanding one and his death, inconsistently defending his father's banner, comes as a release to 'a suffering Spirit', 'Whose self-reproaches are too strong' (11. 1474–5). Our sense of Francis's reasonable and conscientious character enlivens our sympathy for Emily's loss of him—it means more than estate or family or even belief. Their moral affliction is about as great as could be contrived for people who are not in fact guilty. Emily is left without any enemy to forgive or accomplice with whom to share. Francis has one other function in the poem. His rational and unflinching outlook inflicts a stoical pessimism upon Emily. On his departure from Rylstone he tells her:

> 'Hope nothing, if I thus may speak
> To thee, a woman, and thence weak:
> Hope nothing, I repeat . . .'.　　　　　　　　　　　　　(11. 530–2)

And he adds:

> 'Weep, if that aid thee; but depend
> Upon no help of outward friend;

> Espouse thy doom at once, and cleave
> To fortitude without reprieve.'   (11. 542–5)

Set against this grim counsel is Emily's later prayer to the vision of her mother that she should comfort Francis:

>   'nor forbear
> To greet him with a voice, and say;—
> "If hope be a rejected stay,
> Do thou, my christian Son, beware
> Of that most lamentable snare,
> The self-reliance of despair!"'   (11. 1051–6)

These differing responses to calamity are not to be tried by argument, but by the progress of Emily's experience in the rest of the poem we are better able to form an opinion of them. Her experience may not be reasonable, and it may be surprising, but it is Wordsworth's purpose to make us feel that it rings true.

Emily's grief accumulates gradually from the 'foreboding thought' with which she embroiders her father's banner (1. 347), through her father's declaration, Francis's attempt to dissuade him, and her father's repudiation of him. She and Francis are at one in their tender concern for the family (11. 461 ff.), but she is left behind to mourn restlessly but inactively. Her loneliness has begun before she hears news of the failure of the rebellion. The report that Francis has survived and survived with honour, reassures her and, incidentally, permits us to sense how deeply she feels the loss of the rest of the family. But Francis does not appear and when his body is found, the tenantry, understanding the magnitude of her loss, decide to bury him without telling her:

> —How desolate is Rylstone-hall!
> This was the instant thought of all;
> And if the lonely Lady there
> Should be; to her they cannot bear
> This weight of anguish and despair.   (11. 1511–15)

Emily's own unquietness brings her to the scene to find that her last hope is gone:

>   she sees the knot
> Of people, sees them in one spot—
> And darting like a wounded bird
> She reached the grave, and with her breast
> Upon the ground received the rest,—
> The consummation, the whole ruth
> And sorrow of this final truth!   (11. 1544–50)

In other hands Emily might have been allowed to die of a broken heart, providing a pathetic coda to the fall of the Nortons. In Canto Seventh, however, we are

209

introduced to the remarkable experience that Wordsworth is most anxious that we should share and which was the point of his poem. Rylstone is deserted, the Nortons are forgotten, and Emily has wandered afar clad humbly as a pilgrim. When she returns, she seems to have come to terms with grief, but her emotional stability differs little from despair:

> The mighty sorrow hath been borne,
> And she is thoroughly forlorn:
> Her soul doth in itself stand fast,
> Sustained by memory of the past
> And strength of Reason; held above
> The infirmities of mortal love;
> Undaunted, lofty, calm, and stable,
> And awfully impenetrable.   (11. 1621–8)

This is a stoicism worthy of Francis's advice.

But now the white doe reappears, the beautiful creature that had been brought to her by her youngest brother years before, 'A spotless Youngling white as foam' (1. 1806), and it leaves its herd and comes to her:

> So to her feet the Creature came,
> And laid its head upon her knee,
> And looked into the Lady's face,
> A look of pure benignity . . . .[22]   (11. 1653–6)

The effect of this mute appeal is to pierce the armour of Emily's painfully acquired indifference:

> The pleading look the Lady viewed,
> And, by her gushing thoughts subdued,
> She melted into tears . . . .   (11. 1660–2)

Thereafter the doe follows Emily, who at first shrinks from it and feels obliged to wander once more. But gradually this companionship, with all the desolating memories of past happinesses it revives, becomes bearable to her, and she is able to return to her old haunts. The church-bells comfort her, and she finds a 'milder doom' than Francis had predicted:

> That she, of him and all bereft
> Hath yet this faithful Partner left;
> This one Associate that disproves
> His words, remains for her, and loves.   (11. 1787–90)

Together the two visit Francis's grave, laying the foundation for the habit that first draws our attention to the doe.

The moral at the close defines the significance of Emily's experience; we are supposed already to have grasped its nature. Although 'Distress and desolation spread/Through human hearts . . .' (11. 1842–3), it is possible to recover and live once more. Like the faith expressed in the 'Intimations Ode' in a human experience worthy of our notion of heaven, the recovery here is expressed suggestively in terms of a re-birth:

> Dead—but to live again on earth,
> A second and yet nobler birth;
> Dire overthrow, and yet how high
> The re-ascent in sanctity!
> From fair to fairer; day by day
> A more divine and loftier way! (11. 1844–9)

Emily finds peace in life of such quality that for her, as for a saint, the transition to death is made easy:

> thus faintly, faintly tied
> To earth, she was set free, and died. (11. 1864–5)

The ruined tower of Bolton Priory is imagined speaking the haunting closing couplet to the doe with a smile:

> that seems to say—
> 'Thou, thou art not a Child of Time,
> But Daughter of the Eternal Prime!' (11. 1908–10)

The thought is enigmatic and sibylline, but it seems to hint at the abiding presence of sources of comfort like the doe for those in trouble who do not steel themselves against their aid.

VII

In the *Vita Nuova*, Dante describes how he saw Beatrice and fell in love with her when they were both nine years old, how he searched for her, how when he was eighteen he was greeted by her and composed his first poem, how she subsequently died and how in his grief a sympathetic lady (philosophy) consoled him. In Shelley's *Epipsychidion* (1821), a poet who is represented as having died tells us that when he was young he became aware of the existence of an ideal being and searched for her, encountering substitutes earthly and heavenly who did not satisfy him, and how he found his ideal at last in Emily, to whom he addresses his poem.

Shelley draws the likeness of his poem to Dante's to our attention in the preliminary 'advertisement': his poem, 'like the *Vita Nuova* of Dante', he says, 'is sufficiently intelligible to a certain class of readers without a matter-of-fact history

211

of the circumstances to which it relates . . .'. His poem, in short, is meant to be read as an allegory.²³ In this expectation Shelley was to be disappointed, for three reasons. The first was that for his contemporaries, as for most modern English readers, the *Vita Nuova* was not a familiar work. When Shelley wrote *Epipsychidion* he was living in Italy, soaking up Italian literature, and was fresh from an exchange of letters with one of the leading English Danteans.²⁴ He knew that a warning was needed, but the comparison he chose, though apt, was ineffectual. A second reason for the misreading of the poem was that Shelley wished his readers to respond emotionally rather than intellectually to his ideas and therefore made his metaphor, the longings of the lover, so vivid and realistic that it begins to vie with the ideas it conveys. The third reason, for which his contemporaries had more excuse than we do, was that he was notorious in England as an atheistical advocate of free love who had abandoned one woman, eloped with another and was living in a 'community of incest' with Lord Byron. The facts of the case were otherwise;²⁵ but, given his reputation, Shelley's decision to convey his thought in the guise of a radical expression of love for yet another woman, and one in a convent at that, seems rash. It was all very well for him to chide one of his literal-minded friends that 'As to real flesh & blood, you know that I do not deal in those articles,—you might as well go to a ginshop for a leg of mutton, as expect any thing human or earthly from me'.²⁶ The public was otherwise convinced, and the subterfuge of presenting the poem as the work of another and recently dead person fooled nobody.²⁷

Once we take the hint about the *Vita Nuova*, however, a complex and fascinating experience is unfolded for us. *Epipsychidion* is easier to explicate, though not to read, if one begins with lines 190 to 344 in which the author summarizes his life in terms reminiscent of Dante.

> There was a Being whom my spirit oft
> Met on its visioned wanderings, far aloft,
> In the clear golden prime of my youth's dawn . . . .   (11. 190–2)

This being, spoken of as female, is sensed but not seen. Her nature is apprehended in the experience of solitary and beautiful places, of nature and of literature (11. 193–215) and summed up as 'the harmony of truth' (1. 216). Filled with longing, and unable to understand the advice offered him—'O thou of hearts the weakest,/The phantom is beside thee whom thou seekest' (11. 232–3)—he seeks for her 'with hope and fear/And every gentle passion sick to death . . .' (11. 246–7). He comes upon a woman whose sinister physical beauty has a blighting effect (11. 256–66). Other 'mortal forms', even ones that were fair, wise and true, fail him (11. 267–71).

In his disillusionment he encounters a quite different figure:

> One stood on my path who seemed
> As like the glorious shape which I had dreamed
> As is the Moon . . . .   (11. 277–9)

Like Endymion he is taken up by this woman who is constant but chaste. In a dream he hears Death and Life speak of him—after the fashion of the voices heard by the Ancient Mariner—and say, 'Away, he is not of our crew' (1. 306). The realm of the moon-like spirit is like an artificial sleep, a living limbo, and it too is ultimately a disappointment, but one from which voluntary escape is impossible. The two ladies, each dangerous in her way, are the two Venuses, Pandemian and Uranian, and they contrast with one another as earthly love and spiritual love do. Within the prevailing allegory of the poem it seems appropriate to understand them as worldly involvement, ambition even, and debilitating devotion to an unattainable abstract idea.

At this critical juncture the author was released from his predicament:

> At length, into the obscure Forest came
> The Vision I had sought through grief and shame . . . .
> I knew it was the Vision veiled from me
> So many years—that it was Emily.   (11. 321–2, 343–4)

The identification of the vision with 'Emily' takes us back to the very beginning of the poem. The title identifies her: *Epipsychidion: Verses Addressed to the Noble and Unfortunate Lady, Emilia V----, Now Imprisoned in the Convent of ----.*[28] Here a connection is implied between the imprisoned (and unreachable) lady and the 'epipsychidion' or 'complementary soul'.[29] Her convent situation may have had overtones for English readers of the disagreeable and frightening predicaments of the Radcliffian heroines, but the Italian epigraph, from 'her own words' is an emphatic denial of the customary despair: 'The loving soul projects itself outside of the created world, and creates its own world for itself in the infinite, how different from this dark and poor abyss'. Emilia V----'s situation—confined within walls until death and yet contentedly projecting her thoughts beyond that confinement—is not merely that of a lady in distress, it is an admirable metaphor for the ancient concept of the human soul imprisoned in the body. The distinction of Emily is that in her case the soul continually aspires and does not repine.

The poem opens with a series of apostrophes to Emily. She is addressed as 'Sweet Spirit', 'Poor captive bird', 'High, spirit-wingèd Heart', 'Seraph of Heaven' and 'Sweet Lamp'. The comparison of her to the nightingale refers to her ability to 'sing' beautifully in the midst of sorrow, and the wings with which she is imagined beating against the bars of her cage are the 'bright plumes of thought' (1. 15). Beautiful though she may be, her physical appearance is unequal to the spiritual reality it masks:

> Seraph of Heaven! too gentle to be human,
> Veiling beneath that radiant form of Woman
> All that is insupportable in thee
> Of light, and love, and immortality!
> Sweet Benediction in the eternal Curse!
> Veiled Glory of this lampless Universe!

> Thou Moon beyond the clouds! Thou living Form
> Among the Dead! Thou Star above the Storm! (11. 21–8)

In order to convey the inexpressible loveliness of the idea for which Emily is being made to stand, Shelley glowingly describes the human loveliness which is only less than the idea it conceals. He begins with his characteristic series of speculative similes (11. 53–71) and then, startlingly in an age that was in the grip of bowdlerization, adopts the suggestive but morally unassailable convention of the Song of Solomon.

The evocative sensuality of these lines will seem extravagant only if they are confined to their literal meaning. From this fate the Song of Solomon itself had long been rescued by the allegorizing ingenuity of the Church Fathers, as Shelley knew perfectly well. Where Shelley is faced with a problem is the point at which his own and his readers' feelings, which he does wish to enlist, cease to be figurative and convey a homelier sincerity.

Lines 41–52 are a good example of the difficulties he has to cope with. They have been taken by some readers for a barefaced repudiation of his wife whereas in fact they constitute a delicate and charming conjugal compliment:

> I never thought before my death to see
> Youth's vision thus made perfect. Emily,
> I love thee; though the world by no thin name
> Will hide that love from its unvalued shame.
> Would we two had been twins of the same mother!
> Or, that the name my heart lent to another
> Could be a sister's bond for her and thee,
> Blending two beams of one eternity!
> Yet were one lawful and the other true,
> These names, though dear, could paint not, as is due,
> How beyond refuge I am thine. Ah me!
> I am not thine: I am a part of *thee*. (11. 41–52)

The desire for union is for union with the complementary soul that Emily represents. It too has its counterpart in the Song of Songs: 'Thou hast ravished my heart, my sister, my spouse . . .' (4.9) and 'O that thou wert as my brother . . .' (8.1). Love of this ideal is comparable to married love only if one's notion of married love is sufficiently exalted. The wish that his relationship to Emily could be like that to a twin sister (1. 45), or that it could be like that to his wife, 'the name my heart lent to another' (1. 46), and that that other could be united in sisterhood (1. 47), 'Blending two beams of one eternity' (1. 48), suggests a blending of marital identities and a well-developed instinct for the good as common to them both. But the metaphor is continued in the author's complaint:

> Spouse! Sister! Angel! Pilot of the Fate
> Whose course has been so starless! O too late

214

Belovèd! O too soon adored, by me!
For in the fields of Immortality
My spirit should at first have worshipped thine,
A divine presence in a place divine;
Or should have moved beside it on this earth,
A shadow of that substance, from its birth . . . .   (11. 130–7)

Awareness of the ideal, like Wordsworth's intimations of immortality, makes
ordinary human experience, which one becomes used to, seem drab and
comfortless by comparison. And yet our adjustment to life need not be limited if we
do not accept the worldly conventions that limit it—and here Shelley daringly
chooses marriage as his example:

I never was attached to that great sect,
Whose doctrine is, that each one should select
Out of the crowd a mistress or a friend,
And all the rest, though fair and wise, commend
To cold oblivion, though it is in the code
Of modern morals, and the beaten road
Which those poor slaves with weary footsteps tread,
Who travel to their home among the dead
By the broad highway of the world, and so
With one chained friend, perhaps a jealous foe,
The dreariest and the longest journey go.   (11. 149–59)

The example is a good one for lifelong devotion to a single religious belief or a point
of view, and the implication is not so much promiscuity as tolerance, receptiveness,
and the ability to doubt. The simile is made explicit by being extended:

Love is like understanding, that grows bright,
Gazing on many truths; 'tis like thy light,
Imagination! which from earth and sky,
And from the depths of human fantasy,
As from a thousand prisms and mirrors, fills
The Universe with glorious beams, and kills
Error, the worm, with many a sun-like arrow
Of its reverberated lightning. Narrow
The heart that loves, the brain that contemplates,
The life that wears, the spirit that creates
One object, and one form . . . .   (11. 162–72)

Having found his Emily, the author wishes to withdraw with her to an idyllic
solitude to experience a union that is spiritual rather than physical:

To whatsoe'er of dull mortality
Is mine, remain a vestal sister still;

215

> To the intense, the deep, the imperishable,
> Not mine, but me, henceforth be thou united
> Even as a bride, delighting and delighted.   (11. 389–93)

His plan to sail with her to a paradisal island in the Ionian Sea (11. 407 ff.) has been anticipated in the 'Advertisement' where the writer is said to have died,

> as he was preparing for a voyage to one of the wildest of the Sporades, which he had bought, and where he had fitted up the ruins of an old building, and where it was his hope to have realized a scheme of life, suited perhaps to that happier and better world of which he is now an inhabitant, but hardly practicable in this.

The notion of an escape to an ideal existence in the Romantic period is more commonly associated with the emptiness of the new world or the exotic primitiveness of the South Seas.[30] The choice of one of the Sporades, a beautiful but deserted relic of the ancient world, is a decided contrast. Even the choice of the ruins of an old building implies a sympathy for the thwarted enterprises of the past. Leibniz's tolerant theory that elements of truth are scattered through many different and imperfect creeds had been popularized effectively by works as diverse as Swift's *Tale of a Tub* and Lessing's *Nathan der Weise*, and it is fitting for the iconoclastic author of lines 147–73 to exhibit a respect for the past to make amends for the freedom he is taking with the present.

The description of the paradisal island is more dependent on previous models than the rest of the poem. The Eden of *Paradise Lost* has been drawn upon and there are less obvious resemblances to Coleridge's 'Kubla Khan' and Keats's *Endymion*. The virtual quotation of a passage from the Countess of Winchelsea's *The Spleen* in lines 450–2, is less to be expected.[31] To note Shelley's dependence here is not to detract from his skill at deploying his materials, but rather to suggest that he is aiming at a stylized essence of paradise. Personal idiosyncrasy is avoided.

The ruined tower and its surroundings are described in terms that are frequently amorous. Earth and ocean 'seem/To sleep in one another's arms' (11. 509–10), the ring-dove 'Keeps up her love-lament' (1. 530), the 'blue heavens bend . . . to touch their paramour . . .' (11. 544–5), the shore 'Trembles and sparkles' under 'the quick, faint kisses of the sea' (11. 547–8), and so on. But the love of the author and his lady is differently described. They are to share books and music, 'Those instruments with which high Spirits call/The future from its cradle, and the past/Out of its grave . . .' (11. 520–2). 'We two will rise, and sit, and walk together . . .' (1. 541). They will strive to be united, but in a way that is difficult if not impossible, and which makes sense only if it is understood in ideal terms:

> we will talk, until thought's melody
> Become too sweet for utterance, and it die
> In words, to live again in looks, which dart
> With thrilling tone into the voiceless heart,

Harmonizing silence without a sound.
Our breath shall intermix, our bosoms bound,
And our veins beat together; and our lips
With other eloquence than words, eclipse
The soul that burns between them, and the wells
Which boil under our being's inmost cells,
The fountains of our deepest life, shall be
Confused in Passion's golden purity,
As mountain-springs under the morning sun.   (11. 560–72)

The rhapsody continues unabated beyond the physical metaphor with which it has begun:

We shall become the same, we shall be one
Spirit within two frames, oh! wherefore two?
One passion in twin-hearts, which grows and grew,
Till like two meteors of expanding flame,
Those spheres instinct with it become the same,
Touch, mingle, are transfigured; ever still
Burning, yet ever inconsumable:
In one another's substance finding food,
Like flames too pure and light and unimbued
To nourish their bright lives with baser prey,
Which point to Heaven and cannot pass away:
One hope within two wills, one will beneath
Two overshadowing minds, one life, one death,
One Heaven, one Hell, one immortality,
And one annihilation.   (11. 573–87)

The ambition to unite is in the end incompatible with life itself. Only by dying can the author and Emily become one.

The original of this concept of love may be found in Plato's *Symposium*, and Shelley is arguably the most thoroughgoing Platonist among English poets. The great challenge to a Platonist poet is to make more down-to-earth readers experience and understand the beauty and importance of ideas. Shelley once commented on *Epipsychidion*:

It is an idealized history of my life and feelings. I think one is always in love with something or other; the error, and I confess it is not easy for spirits cased in flesh and blood to avoid it, consists in seeking in a mortal image the likeness of what is perhaps eternal.[32]

The statement may be true of life, but in poetry the 'eternal' can only be communicated by means of such mortal images.

217

9 Allegorical alternatives

Allegory was not given up altogether in the late eighteenth century, but it came to be thought of condescendingly as a trivial mode that was only suitable for playful occasions. Belinda's struggle with the spleen in *The Rape of the Lock* is the model for Serena's in William Hayley's *The Triumphs of Temper* (1781), but the wit and elegance of the original have been replaced by a kindly charm aimed mainly at Hayley's 'fair Readers' and, one gathers, young ones at that. Mary Tighe excused the wooden allegorizing of her *Psyche; or, the Legend of Love* (1805) by claiming *The Faerie Queene* as her precedent, but she too was writing a cautionary tale for young ladies. Erasmus Darwin introduced the allegorical personifications of *The Botanic Garden* (1791) with the joke that he had reversed Ovid's transformation of people and gods into trees and flowers, but his excuse was that he wished 'to inlist Imagination under the banner of Science . . .' (p. v). Ralph Palin's *Iphotelle; or the Longing-Fit* (1810) was an attempt to comfort expectant mothers. The educational allegories and allegories for the young that appeared from time to time throughout the period were sufficiently rare to require prefatorial apologies.[1]

The revival of interest in Spenserian romance[2] paid more attention to its exotic narrative than to the allegory it might convey, but other allegorical traditions were available to poets. Wordsworth singled them out with characteristic penetration in his 'Preface of 1815':

> The grand storehouses of enthusiastic and meditative Imagination, of poetical, as contradistinguished from human and dramatic Imagination, are the prophetic and lyrical parts of the Holy Scriptures, and the works of Milton; to which I cannot forbear to add those of Spenser.[3]

In terms of form and structure Milton's influence on Wordsworth's contemporaries was to be decisive; the literary influence of the Bible was less obvious and direct, but in the long run it may have been as essential. Wordsworth's apology for including Spenser deferred to current taste; he went on to particularize an aspect that was generally ignored, Spenser's ability 'to give the universality and permanence of abstractions to his human beings, by means of

218

attributes and emblems that belong to the highest moral truths and purest sensations . . .'.[4]

The influence of Milton's *Paradise Lost, Paradise Regained* and *Samson Agonistes* followed two main lines of development. One was a proliferation of devotional verse in which pious imitators supplied the faithful with blank verse renditions of biblical events. Some of these authors aspired to be epic poets in their own right—Richard Cumberland in his *Calvary; or the Death of Christ* (1792) for example—, but most—like the Montgomeries,[5] James with his *The World Before the Flood* (1813) and Robert with his *Satan* (1830) and *Messiah* (1832)—were content to serve the faith in a humbler capacity. The other line of development exploited Milton's mighty characters in a spirit sufficiently out of keeping with the originals to allow scope for vigorous invention. It is difficult to find anyone of heroic stature in a poem of the Romantic period who has not a trace of Milton's Satan. It is almost as difficult to find a landscape that has not been anticipated to some degree by Milton's Heaven, Hell, or Paradise. Two other Miltonic features became commonplaces: the guided tour of the universe given to a mortal by a spirit, and, related to it, the survey of civilization past, present and to come.[6] These may be used in a conventionally devout way, as they are in James Montgomery's *Pelican Island* (1828), or to reinforce the Gothic supernatural, as in Landor's *Gebir* (1798) and James Hogg's *Pilgrims of the Sun* (1815).

The question of biblical allegory provoked theological controversy until well into the eighteenth century, but it was a matter that the Church of England was willing to let rest. In Dissenting circles it persisted as a source of inspiration for popular works like Bunyan's *Pilgrim's Progress* and among the more studious as a possible key to mysteries that orthodoxy rashly and sometimes repressively passed by. At the same time the renewed institutional interest in the study of Hebrew that followed the defence of the Protestant Bible against the criticisms of the Counter-reformation led in turn to an appreciation of the Bible as a work of literature. When the first English translation of Robert Lowth's *The Sacred Poesy of the Hebrews* appeared in 1787,[7] it described the purpose of Old Testament allegory as follows: 'to withdraw the truth for a moment from our sight, in order to conceal whatever it may contain ungraceful or disgusting, and to enable it secretly to insinuate itself, and obtain an ascendancy as it were by stealth'.[8] It was this indirect and seditious power that interested the serious Romantic allegorists, and they conveyed it in terms of the convention they had learned from Milton.

As we have seen in Chapters 6 and 7, reforming zeal places a special burden on the poet. At a time when the free expression of opinion on political and religious matters is being hindered, the burden becomes unbearable. During the conflict with France, and indeed, almost immediately after the French Revolution in 1789, authors and publishers in England were subjected to legal harassment and even threatened with death;[9] this repressive atmosphere continued into the nineteenth century and there was a renewed outbreak of suppression of the press in England following the defeat of Napoleon. These periods of interference with the freedom of the press coincide tellingly with the revivals of serious allegory. In 1792 Thomas Paine, the author of *The Rights of Man* (1791), was imprisoned on a trumped-up

219

charge; in 1794, Horne Tooke, Hardy and Thelwall were tried for high treason and acquitted. In 1803, Blake himself was accused by a drunken soldier of seditious utterances and tried for high treason; he too was acquitted. In 1793 Blake issued his allegorical account of the American Revolution, *America*, and, in 1794, *Europe*, the sequel to it.[10] Thereafter he wrote mainly in allegorical form. In 1794 Southey wrote and then suppressed his play about the Peasants' Revolt, *Wat Tyler*, and he delayed publication of the mildly allegorical *Joan of Arc* until 1796. In 1811, Shelley was sent down from Oxford for refusing to disavow a pamphlet entitled *The Necessity of Atheism*; in 1817 he was deprived of the custody of his children on the grounds of immoral conduct and irreligious views. In 1813, Leigh Hunt was imprisoned for publishing a libel against the Prince Regent. In 1813 Shelley published his allegory *Queen Mab*; in 1816 Hunt published another, *The Descent of Liberty*; Shelley's *The Revolt of Islam* appeared in 1817 and *Prometheus Unbound* in 1819. Harassed and threatened by those in power, radical poets resorted to the indirect expression of their views.

I   *Jerusalem*

Blake spent much of his life trying to transform the biblical myths best known to English readers into a new myth in which the events and personages resemble their predecessors but are identified in ways that introduce a startling change of perspective. He made use of contemporary advances in comparative mythology, and his receptiveness to various and even rival traditions sometimes makes him bewilderingly eclectic, but he was convinced that truth was imperfectly revealed by each and believed that in the end—to use the title of one of his early prose tracts—'All Religions Are One'. Blake's new myth is of interest to us because in his longer poems he assumes that we are familiar with it, rather as Milton asumes in *Paradise Lost* that we are familiar with certain parts of the Bible. But, of course, Blake's myth, unlike the Bible, is not common ground; furthermore, however complete it may have been in his own mind, it now has to be pieced together from the fragmentary but overlapping parts of it that appear in the poems themselves. We must be content to understand his poems imperfectly, but the reader who, as a consequence, fastidiously passes them by, misses one of the most exhilarating experiences the Romantic imagination affords.[11] Blake's challenging definition of 'the Most Sublime Poetry' was 'Allegory address'd to the Intellectual powers, while it is altogether hidden from the Corporeal Understanding . . .'.[12] For him allegory is a higher form as well as a necessary disguise.

His most ambitious finished work, *Jerusalem: The Emanation of the Giant Albion* (c. 1804–7),[13] epitomizes his strengths and weaknesses as a poet and it exhibits in a way that is unusually accessible to analysis most of the elements that make the allegorical writing of the Romantic period compelling to read. It is made up of a hundred engraved plates in which the text and the accompanying pictures and designs are woven into a co-ordinated whole that is part literature and part fine art. It is written in a free verse distinguishable from colourful prose by its repetitive rhythms and by being divided into lines of approximately equal numbers of stressed syllables. Blake explains that at one time he considered 'a monotonous cadence like that used by Milton & Shakespeare & all writers of English blank verse, derived from the modern bondage of rhyming, to be a necessary and indispensable part of verse' (pl. 3, 36–9). But 'Poetry fettered', he maintains, 'fetters the human race' (pl. 3, 46–7). Like Milton, he accepts blank verse as a rebellion against heroic couplets; his own measure, as befits his theme, carries the rebellion a step farther: 'the terrific numbers are reserved for the terrific parts, the mild & gentle for the mild & gentle parts, and the prosaic for inferior parts . . .' (pl. 3, 44–6). The poem is divided into four roughly equal chapters which open with prose addresses to, respectively, the Public, the Jews, the Deists[14] and the Christians. These addresses and the other preliminary matter related to them provide a didactic context for the poem and some guidance as to the way to interpret it.

The action of *Jerusalem* revolves around the condition of the fallen giant, Albion. To the conventional personification of England as Albion, Blake adds a larger dimension by adopting the theory that the Jews of the Old Testament were descended from the Druids of ancient Britain. This notion had a respectable following among English antiquaries of the period[15] and by using it Blake was able to have the fate of Albion comprehend the fate of mankind as well as of England in particular. As he put it, 'All things begin & end in Albion's ancient druid rocky shore' (pl. 27, 9). The personification of England as a giant was traditional. The famous title page of Hobbes's *Leviathan* (1651), for example, bears a picture of a gigantic king whose body is made up of many smaller men. This graphic representation of the 'body politic' was a commonplace in the Renaissance; the human body was used as a metaphor for the universe as well as for the state, partly because of the need to think of the unfamiliar or ideal in terms of ordinary experience, and partly from a belief that in God's creation the organization of the human form, said to be made in His image, must be pervasively analogous to the organization of all other forms.[16] By the Romantic period the detailed application of this analogy had dropped out of fashion in literature, but it was still a part of the stock-in-trade of the artistic circles in which Blake moved.[17] Blake's sympathies were particularly involved with the painters of the Renaissance and he was influenced deeply by the mystical writings of Jakob Boehme and Emmanuel Swedenborg, both of whom dwell upon the metaphor of the human body. It was natural, therefore, for him to people *Jerusalem* with personifications of the various parts of the giant Albion.

At the outset Albion has already fallen. We are introduced to the consequences first, but the nature of his fall is gradually revealed to us by a series of flashbacks as the poem proceeds. Albion, it appears, was one of a group of beings called the Eternals, and he consists of four elements—Blake terms them 'Zoas', using the Greek word for the four beasts seen by St John in The Book of Revelation—the body, the reason, the emotions, and the imagination. Albion's fall takes place when the four Zoas become disordered, the emotions supplanting reason, reason reacting repressively and excessively. Whereas Albion had previously been united

221

with Britannia, she now appears to him to have divided into two female identities. One of these is the innocently sexual Jerusalem, whom he exiles as a seductive harlot, and the other is Vala, a prudish and hypocritical moralizer, whom he allows to have control over him. This version of the fall of man differs from Milton's account in significant ways. In the first place the fall is not prompted by an external agent such as Satan, nor is it foreseen as inevitable by God. The responsibility is Albion's alone and it is not lessened by being shared between gullible Eve and uxorious Adam. The consciousness of sex, reflected in the rejection of Jerusalem, is linked to the cause of the fall and is not merely a result of it as it was in the Garden of Eden. The advantage of Blake's version for the advocate of universal reform is that by making the fallen state of man a symptom of the internal disorder of an individual, regaining paradise by effecting a change in the individual is made conceivable.

The effects of Albion's fall are considered from three points of view. The first is the effect on Albion's own state of mind. He is miserable, suspicious, vengeful and self-pitying. Unable to bear the world that he perceives, he finds fault with it instead of with his imperfect perception of it, tries clumsily and ineffectually to alter it for the better, and finally withdraws into a state of suspended animation or sleep in which he can ignore it. The second point of view is the effect upon the people of Albion. These are personified as his twelve sons and twelve daughters. Their outlook reflects Albion's. His reaction to the appeal of Jesus that he should awaken and embrace love (pl. 4, 3–21) had been to narrow the meaning of love and reject the appeal as a wicked temptation. They divide the world into the contraries of 'good' and 'evil' and oppose the aspect of their mother that is Jerusalem.

> Phantom of the overheated brain, shadow of immortality,
> Seeking to keep my soul a victim to thy love, which binds
> Man the enemy of man into deceitful friendships.
> Jerusalem is not; her daughters are indefinite.
> By demonstration man alone can live, and not by faith.
> My mountains are my own,[18] and I will keep them to myself:
> The Malvern and the Cheviot, the Wolds, Plinlimmon & Snowdon
> Are mine! Here will I build my laws of moral virtue.
> Humanity shall be no more, but war & princedom & victory.
>
> (pl. 4, 23–31)

Like their parent they exhibit an inordinate reliance on their rational powers—and in the Napoleonic period the association of over-optimistic rationalism and war provided a home thrust at England and France. Like him they are separated into masculine and feminine forms, and like him they categorize everything as either 'good' or 'evil'. They deny the physical realities of life and adopt the ideal of chastity for women. In terms of ancient Britain, the sons and daughters of Albion degenerate into the delirium of superstition (plate 65, 5, to

69, 44); in terms of modern Britain this condition is perpetuated in miseries that are unnecessary:

> in the forests
> The oak frowns terrible, the beech & ash & elm enroot
> Among the spiritual fires; loud the cornfields thunder along
> The soldier's fife; the harlot's shriek; the virgin's dismal groan;
> The parent's fear; the brother's jealousy: the sister's curse . . . .
>
> (pl. 16, 3–7)

The consequences of Albion's fall, in short, are the sorrows of human experience.

These two points of view on the effects of the fall are augmented by a third that provides the grain of hope for the revival of Albion's true self. When Albion withdraws into death-like sleep, one by one the Zoas, his body, his emotions and his reason, are laid to rest. Only one remains irrepressible, his imagination, personified in its fallen state as the heroic blacksmith, Los.

Los is the central figure in *Jerusalem*. He is obliged to labour at the forge, tending his furnace and giving an imaginable reality to Albion's ideas, 'Giving a body to falsehood that it may be cast off for ever . . .' (pl. 12, 13). Like the sons of Albion he is handicapped in outlook by the fall, but unlike them he is unwilling to accept it. When his spectre—Blake adopts the term used by the Epicureans for the corporeal understanding—remonstrates with him, he cannot counter its arguments but he resists them with unshakeable loyalty:

> Los answered: 'Although I know not this, I know far worse than this.
> I know that Albion hath divided me and that thou, O my spectre,
> Hast just cause to be irritated. But look steadfastly upon me,
> Comfort thyself in my strength; the time will arrive
> When all Albion's injuries shall cease, & when we shall
> Embrace him tenfold bright, rising from his tomb in immortality.'
>
> (pl. 7, 51–6)

What Los creates in his furnace is necessarily imperfect, as he is well aware; the fall has deprived him of his inspiration. And yet at times he is able to avert the worst consequences of Albion's conceptions—diverting the application of moral laws, for instance, from individuals to states on the ground that 'they are death/To every energy of man, and forbid the springs of life . . .' (pl. 31, 11–12). He labours at alternatives to the existence he observes around him, justifying himself with the blunt assertion, 'I must create a system, or be enslaved by another man's' (pl. 10, 20). In the midst of London he labours at creation of the symmetrically imagined city of Golgonooza (plates 10, 17, to 14, 34), and disguises the myth of the sons of Albion as the story of the twelve tribes of Israel.

Los's conduct is heroic because he is opposed by fearful odds and is quite alone in his resistance to them. His obstinacy displays the courage that the Romantics admired in Milton's Satan without sharing any of Satan's pride or wish to be avenged. But Los is not merely a Satanic revolutionary opposing false laws, false customs and corrupt societies; as the expression of imagination he may be understood as the voice of the poet or artist in a hostile society. His work at the forge has affinities with the metal-work done by Blake in his engraving, and some commentators have argued for evidence of autobiography on this score. Whatever may be the truth of the relationship of Blake's life to Los's—and there does not seem to be evidence on which to base an opinion[19]—the more general role of artist or of the artistic in man opposing the inadequacies of the social organism is inescapable. We are led to sympathize with Los as an underdog who never gives up. He is not a spotless hero. He grows angry; he has moments of despair; he is susceptible to the wiles of the daughters of Albion and is therefore obliged to force himself to avoid them. In his dealings with his spectre he can be as paternally testy as Prospero is with Caliban in *The Tempest*; at times he can sink to the level of domestic wrangling, as he does with his estranged wife, Enitharmon (pl. 86–8). Most of the characters in *Jerusalem* remain as abstract as the heroes of Macpherson's Ossianic poems. They are larger than life, reflecting eighteenth-century notions of the sublimity of the primitive epic, but, as befits personifications of ideas, they lack realistic detail.[20] The cost of their abstractness is that we do not care very much about them unless we already care a great deal about the things they stand for. Los is the exception; one can admire him, feel for him, and be inspired by him. The redeemer in *Jerusalem* succeeds by becoming a man.

The resolution of *Jerusalem*, the redemption of Albion, presents Blake with a complex problem. Having avoided the use of a *deus ex machina* to precipitate Albion's fall, he must preserve the moral advantage he has gained by effecting Albion's re-awaking without the help of an external agent. Because he is looking into the future, furthermore, he carries a heavy responsibility as a moralist to be plausible. Los, as we have seen, is a part of Albion that cannot fall asleep. It is only when Los desperately begins to create in violent opposition to Albion's intentions and contrary to the inhibitions of his own reason or spectre that Albion's condition can be improved. Los himself is terrified by the immediate results, but as the false conventions are shattered one after another, England awakens to a realization of the horrors that have passed.

> Time was finished! The Breath Divine breathed over Albion
> Beneath the furnaces & starry wheels and in the immortal tomb;
> And England, who is Britannia, awoke from death on Albion's bosom.
> She awoke pale & cold; she fainted seven times on the body of Albion:
> 'Oh, piteous sleep! Oh, piteous dream! O God, O God, awake: I have slain!
> In dreams of chastity & moral law I have murdered Albion! Ah!
> In Stonehenge & on London Stone & in the oak groves of Maldon
> I have slain him in my sleep with the knife of the druid!
>   O England!
> O all ye nations of the earth, behold ye the jealous wife!
> The eagle & the wolf & monkey & owl & the king & priest were there!'
> Her voice pierced Albion's clay-cold ear; he moved upon the rock.
>
> (plates 94, 18 to 95, 1)

What follows is the re-establishment of harmony in universal terms; the four Zoas resume their appropriate stations and the false covenants of the past civilizations are overthrown.

The resolution provides for the needed transition from the fallen world to the regained paradise, and it turns upon Los's action. Blake very wisely does not define the nature of the action. Instead he allows us to observe the spirit in which it is undertaken, the circumstances that lead up to it, and the glorious consequences to which it gives rise.

In comparing the conduct of *Jerusalem* with the conduct of *Paradise Lost* we have noticed the absence of divine intervention in Blake's poem and the corresponding emphasis on the state of mind of individual man. There are, however, higher beings who observe the fall of Albion and react to it. The Eternals, of whom Albion is one, are surprised, then amused, and finally appalled by what they see and they eventually turn from the spectacle and appoint the 'Seven Eyes of God' to keep a watching brief on events. They disapprove of the disorder in Albion, but it cannot touch them. One has the feeling that disorder in this world being the exception in an ordered universe, it cannot help being righted and made consistent with its surroundings in the end.

This account of *Jerusalem* is no more than an introductory sketch. The poem is too full of detail, much of it still obscure, for a comprehensive discussion to be either possible or appropriate here. It should be said, however, that a reader who is embarking on it for the first time will be well advised not to pause over things he does not at first understand. *Jerusalem* is not constructed in such a way as to present us with events in the order in which they happen. Rather, being a thoroughgoing allegory, it is constructed so as to present a logical sequence of steps in the mental state of Albion—the 'narrative' used to convey these stages exists only in so far as a consistent metaphor is required. Hence the sense one has of fragmentariness and of lack of sympathy for most of the characters. For Blake what matters is that we should experience his ideas; by exposing ourselves to them without the inhibitions of conventional reading we can.

II   *Prometheus Unbound*

The mythical history to which the action of Shelley's *Prometheus Unbound* belongs is summarized in a retrospective narration halfway through the poem. The lady Asia has followed mysterious voices that bring her to the cave of an enigmatic oracle named Demogorgon. Like Adam in *Paradise Lost*, she asks questions at the oracle's invitation about the creation and order of the world. When Demogorgon replies evasively to one of her questions, she presses for an unambiguous answer and outlines the limits of her knowledge of the past in order to make the purpose of her question clearer. There was, it seems, a contented period in Heaven and Earth. Then Saturn came to power, suspending the effects of the passage of time and allowing to 'earth's primal spirits' 'the calm joy of flowers and living leaves' but denying them

> The birthright of their being, knowledge, power,
> The skill which wields the elements, the thought
> Which pierces this dim universe like light,
> Self-empire, and the majesty of love;
> For thirst of which they fainted.   (II, iv, 39–43)

This contented but vegetable existence was brought to an end by Prometheus the Titan, who personifies the spirit of mankind. By giving 'wisdom, which is strength', to Jupiter, Prometheus enabled him to replace Saturn on the condition that he should 'Let man be free' (II, iv, 43–5).

The immediate effect on mankind of this access of knowledge untamed by experience, and of the unaccustomed consciousness of mutability, was a destructive equivalent of the fall of Man in the Old Testament:

>   for on the race of man
> First famine, and then toil, and then disease,
> Strife, wounds, and ghastly death unseen before,
> Fell; and the unseasonable seasons drove
> With alternating shafts of frost and fire,
> Their shelterless, pale tribes to mountain caves:
> And in their desert hearts fierce wants he sent,
> And mad disquietudes, and shadows idle
> Of unreal good, which levied mutual war,
> So ruining the lair wherein they raged.   (II, iv, 49–58)

Prometheus, however, rose to the challenge, awakening dreams 'That they might hide with thin and rainbow wings/The shape of Death' (II, iv, 59–63), sending Love 'to bind/The disunited tendrils of that vine/Which bears the wine of life, the human heart' (63–5), taming fire so that man had power over minerals, and creating human speech from which in turn followed human thought. From these beginnings science and art eventually developed. Music released listeners from 'mortal care', sculpture drew attention to the beauties of the human form and then outdid them, medicine regulated disease and made death less painful. Astronomy made safe navigation possible and permitted contact between different races. Cities were built. In return for Prometheus's labours, Jupiter, violating the condition by which he had gained power, afflicted mankind with evil and chained Prometheus to a rock to undergo unending torment:

>   the immedicable plague, which, while
> Man looks on his creation like a God
> And sees that it is glorious, drives him on,
> The wreck of his own will, the scorn of earth,
> The outcast, the abandoned, the alone.   (II, iv, 101–5)

226

It is at this point in human history, the present, that the action of *Prometheus Unbound* begins. Under the rule of 'wisdom', or rational knowledge, mankind wilfully misuses its capacities and is made miserable as a consequence.

The first scene opens with Prometheus chained to an icy rock in the Indian Caucasus[21] reflecting upon the three thousand years of torment he has undergone and the eternity of pain that lies ahead of him. He knows the secret of Jupiter's inevitable overthrow and is tortured by Jupiter because he refuses to reveal it, but he does not know when Jupiter will be overthrown. He describes the sufferings he himself has undergone and expresses the anguish and near despair he feels: 'Ah me! alas, pain, pain ever, for ever!/No change, no pause, no hope!' (I, i, 23–4). Dreadful though his sufferings are, Prometheus spares a thought for the ultimate sufferings of Jupiter. Previously the prospect gave him a sense of satisfaction, but now he finds, unexpectedly, that pity has taken the place of resentment in his heart:

> Disdain! Ah no! I pity thee. What ruin
> Will hunt thee undefended through wide Heaven!
> How will thy soul, cloven to its depth with terror,
> Gape like a hell within! I speak in grief,
> Not exultation, for I hate no more,
> As then ere misery made me wise. The curse
> Once breathed on thee I would recall. (I, i, 53–9)

This change in Prometheus's feelings, in which revenge is replaced by sympathy that is a symptom of universal love, is the turning point of Shelley's version of the myth, and it differs subtly from the conventional version that Aeschylus is believed to have used.[22]

Prometheus is attended in his sufferings by spirits that are loyal to him. They are powerless to act on his behalf and they dare not defy Jupiter, but they comfort and encourage the victim. When Prometheus wishes to be reminded of the terms of the curse that he laid upon Jupiter when Jupiter broke faith with him, Earth advises him to summon the unpunishable phantasm[23] of Jupiter to repeat it. The curse turns out to have been a defiance of the tyrant that anticipates the most exquisite tortures—'All that thou canst inflict I bid thee do . . .' (I, i, 263)—and a terrible prediction of infinite punishment—'thine Omnipotence a crown of pain,/To cling like burning gold round thy dissolving brain' (I, i, 290–1).[24] But when Prometheus rejects the curse, Earth, adhering to the commonplace attitude that the height of heroic resolution is to try to resist irresistible despotism, assumes that the three thousand years of torment have broken his spirit and that he is giving in at last. Earth's disappointment is intended by Shelley to anticipate the habitual outlook of his readers. *Prometheus Unbound* is contrived to persuade us that there is a nobler and yet practicable virtue.

The repetition of the curse brings immediate retribution. Jupiter's emissary, Mercury, comes to make a final attempt to persuade Prometheus to give up his secret, and the Furies who delight in torturing the Titan hover around threateningly and can scarcely be restrained. Prometheus is asked to choose either to endure sufferings beyond any he has yet experienced or to dwell 'among the Gods the while/Lapped in voluptuous joy' (I, i, 425–6). His reply is immediate: 'I would not quit/This bleak ravine, these unrepentant pains' (I, i, 426–7). Far from being broken as Earth had feared, Prometheus's heroic resistance persists unsustained by the pettiness of personal rancour. It remains for us to witness the testing of his resolve. The unleashing of the Furies proves to be an unprecedented trial because, avoiding their hitherto unprofitable reliance on physical torture, they concentrate upon the infliction of moral pain. Since Prometheus's new self has risen to heights of sympathy he is to be hurt by being forced to contemplate the sufferings of others, of individual men, that have followed upon his initial refusal to give in to Jupiter. The first to be exhibited is Christ. Three aspects of his fate are revealed—the genuineness of his worth, the agony of his crucifixion, and the perversion of his teaching in subsequent ages. Prometheus suffers in sympathy, indeed suffers almost beyond endurance:

> Remit the anguish of that lighted stare;
> Close those wan lips; let that thorn-wounded brow
> Stream not with blood; it mingles with thy tears!
> Fix, fix those tortured orbs in peace and death,
> So thy sick throes shake not that crucifix,
> So those pale fingers play not with thy gore.
> O, horrible! Thy name I will not speak,
> It hath become a curse. I see, I see
> The wise, the mild, the lofty, and the just,
> Whom thy slaves hate for being like to thee,
> Some hunted by foul lies from their heart's home, . . .
> Some linked to corpses in unwholesome cells:
> Some—Hear I not the multitude laugh loud?—
> Impaled in lingering fire . . . .   (I, i, 597–612)

Prometheus's horror indicts the corrupted course of Christianity with its inquisitions and its involvement in the political repression of national establishments—extensions of Jupiter's perverted rule as they are seen to be—and yet his ability to find room to pity the perpetrators of even these terrible deeds frustrates the Furies. For hate he has learned to return love. The second exhibition is of the failure of the French revolution, and it is more briefly and abstractly rendered. Prometheus reluctantly reports to the accompanying spirits what he has been forced to behold:

> Names are there, Nature's sacred watchwords, they
> Were borne aloft in bright emblazonry;
> The nations thronged around, and cried aloud,
> As with one voice, Truth, liberty, and love!
> Suddenly fierce confusion fell from heaven

Among them: there was strife, deceit, and fear:
Tyrants rushed in, and did divide the spoil.
This was the shadow of the truth I saw.   (I, i, 648–55)

This failure of the ideals of revolutionary France at the reactionary hands of the European monarchies provides Shelley with the political counterpart in recent times of the long-standing perversion of Christianity achieved by organized religion.

The conversion of Prometheus may be thought of as taking place now or whenever the spirit of mankind is ready for it. It appears to be a spontaneous event, and Prometheus is as unaware of its special significance as the sympathetic spirits who attend upon him are. They try to comfort him with rare instances of man's humanity to man and of human inspiration,[25] and symptoms of a more widespread change begin to be reported. Prometheus is appreciative, but after having reflected upon the failures of religious and political revolution he is willing to rely only on the love he feels within himself.

The character of Prometheus combines elements of both Albion and Los in Blake's *Jerusalem*.[26] His bound condition resembles the stony slumber of Albion and we gradually realize that, like Albion, he has had a part, through his hatred of Jupiter, in binding himself. At the same time, since Jupiter is ostensibly responsible for his agonies, it is possible for Prometheus to resist Jupiter's tyranny as Los resists Albion's. His achievement of love for the oppressor takes him three thousand years, whereas Los, though frustrated and angry, never forgets that his endeavours are on Albion's behalf. The fact that the situation is transformed in *Prometheus Unbound* by a change of heart in the sufferer provides a paradigm of conduct for the reader that is both simple and challenging. We are to love those whom we have cause to hate: the responsibility of faithful resistance to moral or political despotism that *Jerusalem* holds out to us is thinkable because it is less immediate; in *Prometheus Unbound* it is harder for the reader to escape the feeling that he may be living in complicity with the forces of evil unawares.

Prometheus's ability to endure pain is far beyond what might be expected of ordinary human beings; whatever our individual sufferings may be, they will be markedly less severe. His change of heart, however, seems to be within human capacities, and, the injuries we resent being less, the effort of forgiving those who injure us should be less too. Prometheus's act is an extreme illustration of Christ's rejection of the old law of the Old Testament; it embodies a precept that is familiar to us all. But by placing it in the unexpected context of conventional poetic justice, and of Greek tragedy in particular, Shelley endows it with the interest of novelty and makes us feel the discrepancy between the teaching of Christianity and the customary habits of mind of readers who usually think of themselves as Christians.

The moral lesson is concluded by the end of Act I; true Christian forgiveness has been presented as the greatest heroism. The rest of *Prometheus Unbound* is devoted to the consequences that flow from such heroism, and Shelley tries to present these in such a way as to make us stir ourselves from moral lethargy in order to bring them about. In *Paradise Lost*[27] and, as we have seen, in *Jerusalem*, the fallen world is the dominant setting, while paradise is observed briefly by way of contrast as a place where the evils of the fallen state are absent. Imagining paradise in positive terms is a severe challenge to a poet, but one that Shelley with his systematic reflections on the ideal world and his extraordinary gift for realistic detail was uniquely fitted to meet.[28]

Prometheus gains by his love what he has been deprived of during his hate. The missing essence that he recovers is personified as a female counterpart, who is the 'light of life,/Shadow of beauty unbeheld . . .'(III, iii, 6–7).[29] The transformation that occurs in her is indicative of the transformation that is to be expected in Nature once the spirit of Mankind has been reunited with it through love. Asia is first seen in solitude, welcoming the signs of spring in a beautiful valley. Panthea comes to her with news of the change in Prometheus, and voices are heard calling upon them to 'follow'. They travel along the valley, through a forest, and arrive at a sublime mountain landscape. The surpassing loveliness of their surroundings is described glowingly, but Asia, in responding to it, reminds us of a loveliness that must be supposed to exceed even it:

> How glorious art thou, Earth! And if thou be
> The shadow of some spirit lovelier still,
> Though evil stain its work, and it should be
> Like its creation, weak yet beautiful,
> I could fall down and worship that and thee.
> Even now my heart adoreth: Wonderful!   (II, iii, 12–17)

Shelley defines the inexpressibly beautiful unknown by describing the most beautiful known and asserting that the unknown is more beautiful still. When Asia descends to the cave of Demogorgon her questions draw our attention to yet another reality beyond the reality we are familiar with. To her questions as to who created the world, who created 'thought, passion, reason, will,/Imagination' (II, iv, 10–11), and who created feelings of sympathy (II, iv, 12–18), Demogorgon answers consistently that God did. When she asks who created evil she is told, evasively, 'He reigns' (II, iv, 28, 31). A distinction is to be made, then, between God and Jupiter; in Shelley as in Blake, Mankind is represented as worshipping and dreading a false substitute for God. With the overthrow of Jupiter, evil itself will be overthrown.

The first physical indication of the imminence of that overthrow is the change that takes place in Asia herself. She has been described to Panthea by Prometheus as 'her whose footsteps pave the world/With loveliness . . .' (II, i, 68–9); now Panthea is struck by the revelation of her true beauty which transcends physical perception, and concludes that it is a portent of a general transformation:

> How thou art changed! I dare not look on thee;
> I feel but see thee not. I scarce endure
> The radiance of thy beauty. Some good change
> Is working in the elements, which suffer
> Thy presence thus unveiled.   (II, v, 16–20)

Asia herself acknowledges the change, answering a voice in the air with a gently ecstatic song of a voyage that takes her beyond the mutable imperfections of the world:

> We have passed Age's icy caves,
>   And Manhood's dark and tossing waves,
> And Youth's smooth ocean, smiling to betray:
>   Beyond the glassy gulfs we flee
>   Of shadow-peopled Infancy,
> Through Death and Birth, to a diviner day . . . .   (II, v, 98–103)

Asia's Act II does not advance the action of the poem, although it yields the reader some necessary information. Rather it reflects the action of Act I and makes us aware of the implications of such an action in the physical world. When the action is resumed in Act III and completed with Jupiter's fall, the social consequences are brought before us. Jupiter's fall comes at the moment at which he mistakenly expects to triumph at last over the rebellious spirit of man. His complacent celebration of human misery costs him whatever sympathy we might have had for him in his fall and it is a reminder of the importance of human resistance:

> Ye congregated powers of heaven, who share
> The glory and the strength of him ye serve,
> Rejoice! henceforth I am omnipotent.
> All else had been subdued to me; alone
> The soul of man, like unextinguished fire,
> Yet burns towards heaven with fierce reproach, and
>   doubt,
> And lamentation, and reluctant prayer,
> Hurling up insurrection, which might make
> Our antique empire insecure, though built
> On eldest faith, and hell's coeval, fear;
> And though my curses through the pendulous air,
> Like snow on herbless peaks, fall flake by flake,
> And cling to it; though under my wrath's night
> It climbs the crags of life, step after step,
> Which wound it, as ice wounds unsandalled feet,
> It yet remains supreme o'er misery,
> Aspiring, unrepressed, yet soon to fall . . . .   (III, i, 1–17)

When Eternity in the form of Demogorgon arrives to carry him down into the abyss, Jupiter is denied the dignity of resolute resistance that was allowed to Milton's Satan and sinks pleading and lamenting like a cowardly bully. Apollo and Ocean mark his fall and Hercules unbinds Prometheus. While Prometheus contemplates an idyllic retirement, reports begin to arrive at his request of the social and political consequences of the reunion of Prometheus with Asia, of the

231

soul of mankind with the 'Shadow of beauty unbeheld'. These are preceded by Earth's testimony to the banishing of age. She explains of death, which remains, that it 'is the veil which those who live call life :/They sleep, and it is lifted . . .' (III, iii, 113–14). The first report is delivered by the Spirit of the Earth. It recalls the customary social behaviour of mankind:

> Thou knowest that toads, and snakes, and loathly worms,
> And venomous and malicious beasts, and boughs
> That bore ill berries in the woods, were ever
> An hindrance to my walks o'er the green world:
> And that, among the haunts of humankind,
> Hard-featured men, or with proud, angry looks,
> Or cold, staid gait, or false and hollow smiles,
> Or the dull sneer of self-loved ignorance,
> Or other such foul masks, with which ill thoughts
> Hide that fair being whom we spirits call man;
> And women too, ugliest of all things evil . . . .   (III, iv, 36–46)

And it records how on a recent night 'Those ugly human shapes and visages' (65) disappeared:

>   and those
> From whom they passed seemed mild and lovely forms
> After some foul disguise had fallen, and all
> Were somewhat changed, and after brief surprise
> And greetings of delighted wonder, all
> Went to their sleep again: and when the dawn
> Came, wouldst thou think that toads, and snakes, and efts,
> Could e'er be beautiful? yet so they were,
> And that with little change of shape or hue:
> All things had put their evil nature off . . . .   (III, iv, 68–77)

The report of the Spirit of the Hour, which follows, is more circumstantial, and, as befits its political subject matter, it mixes institutions such as tyranny, which it is conventional to abuse, with institutions such as the church, which it is conventional to praise. Such barbs are the rightful profits of visionary allegorists and Shelley is no more able to resist indulging in them than Milton was. The Spirit of the Hour describes what has happened to a bad old world that has been changed inwardly rather than outwardly:

> Thrones, altars, judgement-seats, and prisons; wherein,
> And beside which, by wretched men were borne
> Sceptres, tiaras, swords, and chains, and tomes
> Of reasoned wrong, glozed on by ignorance,
> Were like those monstrous and barbaric shapes,

232

The ghosts of a no-more-remembered fame,
Which, from their unworn obelisks, look forth
In triumph o'er the palaces and tombs
Of those who were their conquerors: mouldering round,
These imaged to the pride of kings and priests
A dark yet mighty faith, a power as wide
As is the world it wasted, and are now
But an astonishment; even so the tools
And emblems of its last captivity,
Amid the dwellings of the peopled earth,
Stand, not o'erthrown, but unregarded now.   (III, iv, 164–79)

From among these discarded relics of political organization, people have emerged
who are masters of their own destinies:

The loathsome mask has fallen, the man remains
Sceptreless, free, uncircumscribed, but man
Equal, unclassed, tribeless, and nationless,
Exempt from awe, worship, degree, the king
Over himself; just, gentle, wise: but man
Passionless?—no, yet free from guilt or pain,
Which were, for his will made or suffered them,
Nor yet exempt, though ruling them like slaves,
From chance, and death, and mutability,
The clogs of that which else might oversoar
The loftiest star of unascended heaven,
Pinnacled dim in the intense inane.   (III, iv, 193–204)

This image of man is not so remote from us as to seem unreal or impossible, and it is
defined in terms that make it hard to reject even for readers who do not find
Shelley's political assumptions attractive. By tracing the ultimate success of
revolution to a change of heart in the individual, Shelley effectively sidesteps his
opposition.

Had *Prometheus Unbound* ended with Act III as Shelley originally intended that it
should,[30] the poem would have been symmetrical in structure and morally
complete. The addition of Act IV clarifies some aspects of the preceding acts, but
its main effect is to reflect upon the action of the drama as a whole by presenting us
with abstract analogies to it, rather as illustrations augment Blake's text. Up to this
point Shelley's models have been works like Aeschylus's *Prometheus Bound* and
Milton's *Samson Agonistes*; in Act IV he turns to the outmoded form of the masque.
His songs with their irregular short-rhymed lines suggest that he was aware of
Shakespearean precedents, especially in *The Tempest* and *Cymbeline*, and of
Milton's *Comus*, but his immediate model was probably Hunt's *The Descent of
Liberty* (1815). The pattern of having thinly disguised allegorical figures pass
before us as if in a processional pageant while spectators comment on what they see

233

is preserved, but in all other respects Shelley has escaped into a variant that he has made peculiarly his own and that suits the rarefied conceptions he wishes to edge his readers towards understanding and sharing. The chief figures in this masque are the Earth and the Moon, and the whole action is a cosmic counterpart of the joyful transformation that has taken place in the world as a result of Prometheus's liberation.

The masque is observed and described for us by Panthea and Ione, sisters of Asia who have observed most of the previous action. Ione asks questions about the meaning of what they see and Panthea tries to answer them. At the close Demogorgon appears and makes the meaning explicit. Interpreting a masque is rather like solving a riddle. Demogorgon's explanation is delayed so as to permit us to apply our own ingenuities to the meaning and to encourage our interest and involvement. The explanation is provided at last to confirm or complete our answers. The masque begins with the dawn of the day that is to last for ever. The shadows of past Hours are seen hurrying away before the rising light, carrying 'Time to his tomb in eternity' (IV, i, 14). They are succeeded by semi-choruses of Hours and Spirits who by means of choric dialogue contrast the limitations of their past experience with the sense of freedom and possibility they now feel. They dance and sing together, preparing to 'build/In the void's loose field/A world for the Spirit of Wisdom to wield . . .' (IV, i, 153–5). After their departure 'Two visions of strange radiance' (IV, i, 202) enter upon an idyllic forest scene—a winged infant seated in a crescent-shaped chariot and a child sleeping within a crystal sphere the depths of which reveal the ruins of past history; these are the Spirit of the Moon and the Spirit of the Earth. The Spirit of Earth exults:

> The joy, the triumph, the delight, the madness!
> The boundless, overflowing, bursting gladness,
> The vaporous exultation not to be confined!
> Ha! ha! the animation of delight
> Which wraps me, like an atmosphere of light,
> And bears me as a cloud is borne by its own wind.　　(IV, i, 319–24)

And the Spirit of the Moon acknowledges that she is moved by the warmth that emanates from her brother. Both seem to be awakening from a death-like sleep into a state of conscious mutual attraction. The Moon identifies the force that is causing the change, ''Tis love, all love!' (IV, i, 369). Earth describes the effect of it on Man, released at last from hate and fear and pain:

> His will, with all mean passions, bad delights,
> And selfish cares, its trembling satellites,
> A spirit ill to guide, but mighty to obey,
> 　Is as a tempest-wingèd ship, whose helm
> 　Love rules, through waves which dare not overwhelm,
> Forcing life's wildest shores to own its sovereign sway.　　(IV, i, 406–11)

234

Earth and Moon depart expressing mutual raptures, and their place is taken by Demogorgon, the presiding genius of the poem who has foreseen all, to address an imagined audience that ranges from Earth and Moon through all the intervening spirit world until he comes to man, and to sum up the significance of what has happened. He confirms that Love must be the initiating force in the change (IV, i, 557–61), that it must be backed by Gentleness, Virtue, Wisdom, and Endurance (IV, i, 562–4), and he concludes by returning to the personification of those qualities in Prometheus:

> To suffer woes which Hope thinks infinite;
> To forgive wrongs darker than death or night;
> To defy Power, which seems omnipotent;
> To love, and bear; to hope till Hope creates
> From its own wreck the thing it contemplates;
> Neither to change, nor falter, nor repent;
> This, like thy glory, Titan, is to be
> Good, great and joyous, beautiful and free;
> This is alone Life, Joy, Empire, and Victory. (IV, i, 570–8)

The resounding and rememberable words share the abstraction of the rest of Act IV, but like the harmony of the spheres they sum up the significance of a revolutionary act that has been previously experienced in human terms.

III *Milton*

Blake's *Milton* (c. 1804),[31] like his *Jerusalem*, is a fragment of the complicated myth that he treated more extensively in his unfinished poem *Vala, or the Four Zoas*. It is written in the same free verse as *Jerusalem*; in place of his remarks about the need to abandon rhyme and even blank verse as too restrictive he provides a related discussion of the need to replace reliance on Classical literature with reliance on the Bible—'The stolen and perverted writings of Homer and Ovid, of Plato and Cicero, which all men ought to contemn, are set up by artifice against the sublime of the Bible' (pl. 1, 1–3). The argument of his poem contends with this state of affairs, and the verse in which it is written closely resembles the verses of the King James version, particularly those of the books of the Old Testament. His epigraphic stanzas—'And did those feet in ancient time', made familiar to millions by their inclusion in *Hymns Ancient and Modern* and inseparable now from the lovely musical setting of Sir Charles Parry—announce boldly that he proposes to rouse his readers to make the world ready for Christ. 'Would to God', he concludes, 'that all the Lord's people were prophets!' (pl. 1, 37).

The authority of a prophet is derived, traditionally, from a more powerful spirit who speaks through the medium of the prophet's voice; conventional appeals to the muses are a relic of this expectation. In prophecies as unconventional as Blake's, however, the question of authority is revived. In *Milton*, Blake, whose utterances elsewhere sometimes verge upon cheeky self-confidence, admits the need for authority and works his claims to be believed into the fabric of the poem in a way that is consistent with the practice of the ancient prophets and yet pleasingly convincing as the testimony of an ordinary modern man. While he was walking in the garden of his rustic cottage at Felpham, Blake tells us—and he provides a simple drawing of the place (pl. 36)—he was visited by a supernatural being. Previously, the spirit of imagination, personified as Los—the heroic resister of *Jerusalem*—had entered into him. He attributes his being in Felpham rather than at home in Lambeth to this benign interference in human affairs:

> For when Los joined with me he took me in his fiery
>   whirlwind.
> My vegetated portion was hurried from Lambeth's shades;
> He set me down in Felpham's vale & prepared a beautiful
> Cottage for me that in three years I might write all
>   these visions
> To display nature's cruel holiness, the deceits of
>   natural religion.
> Walking in my cottage garden sudden I beheld
> The virgin Ololon & addressed her as a daughter of
>   Beulah . . .   (pl. 36, 21–7)

He addresses his unexpected visitor hospitably and humbly, but he links her abstractness to the realities of everyday life by mentioning that his wife is unwell:

> Virgin of Providence, fear not to enter into my cottage.
> What is thy message to thy friend? What am I now to do?
> Is it again to plunge into deeper affliction? Behold me
> Ready to obey, but pity thou my shadow of delight.
> Enter my cottage, comfort her, for she is sick with
>   fatigue.   (pl. 36, 28–32)

After the visitation is over and the vision that accompanied it is completed, Blake comes to his senses and finds that his wife is anxiously attending upon him:

> My bones trembled. I fell outstretched upon the
>   path
> A moment, & my soul returned into its mortal state,
> To resurrection & judgement in the vegetable body.
> And my sweet shadow of delight stood trembling by my
>   side.   (pl. 42, 25–8)

The physical effect of the experience suggests how uncommon and overpowering it was for the Blakes; the first-person account and its briefly sketched domesticity lend it a touch of verisimilitude that reminds one of the settings we have observed in the meditations of sympathy.

The influence of Milton on Romantic verse has already been remarked upon, and *Paradise Lost* was a criterion by which most poets of the period aspired to be judged.[32] Blake's relationship to Milton, however, was unique in its complexity and it involved engagement with Milton's matter as much as with his manner and form. In *Milton*—the full title was *Milton: A Poem in 2 Books To Justify the Ways of God to Men*— Blake makes the poet the protagonist in a work whose argument is to be a sympathetic correction of *Paradise Lost* and truer to what he conceived was Milton's real purpose. Blake's comment in *The Marriage of Heaven and Hell* (c. 1790) that Milton 'was a true poet, and of the Devil's party without knowing it' (pl. 5, 54–5) is often quoted as an extreme example of Romantic misreading of *Paradise Lost*; it is also a succinct anticipation of the spirit of Blake's devout and yet critical rehandling of Milton's themes. He cared more about God than about literary history. Blake believed that in depicting the repressive God the Father of *Paradise Lost* who stressed self-discipline, allowed knowledge to make sex seem sinful, and complacently foresaw the fall of the rebel angels and the fall of man, Milton 'wrote in fetters', constrained by the perversion of the truth that prevailed in Christian churches.[33] In warming to Satan's courage and constancy, he felt, Milton had revealed a power that was to be preferred to God the Father's, but he had also attributed to the fallen angel meaner qualities—self-centredness, guile, unfeeling rationality, and an unwitting acceptance of God the Father's values even while he opposes them.

The challenge of not only following in Milton's footsteps but of improving upon *Paradise Lost* must be understood primarily as one of improving the truths *Paradise Lost* conveys. For that, as we have seen, Blake falls back upon supernatural aid as his authority. The more purely literary problem of finding a mode of expression that was an adequate successor either to the precedent of Milton or to his subject remained to be faced. Blake refers to the difficulty in Methodistical language that emphasizes again that he is a mere instrument of a higher power:

> O how can I, with my gross tongue that cleaveth to the
> dust,
> Tell of the fourfold Man, in starry numbers fitly ordered?
> Or how can I with my cold hand of clay? But thou, O Lord,
> Do with me as thou wilt; for I am nothing, and vanity.
> If thou choose to elect a worm, it shall remove the
> mountains.   (pl. 20, 15–19)

And he provides an analogy for his relationship to Milton, in which he recalls the great poet's plaintively harmonious nightingale, and represents himself as a country lark humbly inspired by the nightingale's song and able to waken other singing birds until the nightingale shall resume his exquisite music once more:

> Thou hearest the nightingale begin the song of spring;
> The lark sitting upon his earthy bed, just as the morn

237

> Appears, listens silent; then springing from the waving
>   cornfield loud
> He leads the choir of day—trill, trill, trill, trill,
> Mounting upon the wings of light into the great expanse,
> Re-echoing against the lovely blue & shining heavenly
>   shell.
> His little throat labours with inspiration; every feather
> On throat & breast & wings vibrates with the effluence
>   divine.
> All nature listens silent to him, & the awful sun
> Stands still upon the mountain looking at this little bird
> With eyes of soft humility & wonder, love & awe.
> Then loud from their green covert all the birds begin
>   their song:
> The thrush, the linnet & the goldfinch, robin & the wren
> Awake the sun from his sweet reverie upon the mountain;
> The nightingale again assays his song, & through the day
> And through the night warbles luxuriant, every bird of song
> Attending his loud harmony with admiration & love.   (pl. 31, 28–44)

The cause is all important; Blake's role in serving it is one that does not make claims for special wisdom or special eloquence.

The action of *Milton*, like that of *Jerusalem*, does not proceed in a straightforward chronological sequence. The myth overlaps with the myth of *Jerusalem*, concentrating on the moments surrounding the awakening of Albion and explaining, in terms of human behaviour that approaches the behaviour of Shelley's Prometheus in its practicability, how the change is effected. We are to understand that Milton, having written *Paradise Lost* to 'justifie the wayes of God to men', finds himself 'Unhappy though in heaven . . .' (pl. 2, 18). After a hundred years, he hears a bard's song in which the fall of Satan is recounted in a way that is inconsistent with the version of the story he has used his eloquence to convey, and, knowing that his message has in any case been ineffectual, he decides to abandon his identity by leaving Heaven and returning to earth:

> And Milton said, 'I go to eternal death! The nations
>   still
> Follow after the detestable gods of Priam, in pomp
> Of warlike selfhood, contradicting and blaspheming.
> When will the Resurrection come to deliver the sleeping
>   body
> From corruptibility? O when, Lord Jesus, wilt thou come?'
>
>   (pl. 14, 14–18)

The note of despair and the longing for Christ's intercession reflect his sense of the magnitude of the task that lies ahead of him and the need for divine support in it.

In heaven Milton has been divided from his spectre, or reasoning faculty, which is named Satan, and from his emanation, or imaginative faculty, which is named Ololon. He proposes to reunite his imperfect self with these two imperfect beings to create a whole being that will differ from all three of them. The reuniting of Milton will correspond to the awakening of Albion and the rebalancing of the four Zoas in their appointed relationships to one another.

Satan and Palamabron are sons of the indefatigable Los who labours in fallen Albion in the city of Golgonooza to create forms through imagination. According to the bard's song that Milton hears, Satan usurped the function of Palamabron, exchanging his mills—the sphere of common sense and routine—for Palamabron's fiery horses—the sphere of imagination.[34] Neither is suited to the other's role and after the disastrous day's exchange is over and mutual recriminations ensue, Satan is judged to be in the wrong. Like Albion he resists this judgment and tries to impose his own one-sided morality on everyone else:

> He created seven deadly sins, drawing out his infernal scroll
> Of moral laws and cruel punishments upon the clouds of
> Jehovah,
> To prevent the Divine Voice in its entrance to the earth
> With thunder of war & trumpets' sound, with armies of
> disease,
> Punishments & deaths mustered & numbered; saying, 'I am
> God alone,
> There is no other! Let all obey my principles of moral
> individuality.' (pl. 9, 21–6)

Having misrepresented himself and God in this way he is changed—'his bosom grew/Opaque against the Divine Vision' (pl. 9, 30–1)—and he sinks from Heaven into an abyss called Ulro.

Although Satan is a son of Los, he is also the spectre of Milton. Los's sons, products of the imagination, may be created by poets. In the past Milton has allowed his spectre or rational faculty to control his utterance, and he has neglected Ololon, his emanation or imaginative and sympathetic faculty. On returning to earth he proposes to right the balance. When he reaches earth, we learn, 'Albion's sleeping humanity began to turn upon his couch' (pl. 20, 25), and Milton is compelled to confront the slumbering Zoas. Even Los, who should be sympathetic, forgets for the moment the fallen state of imaginative creation that he represents and considers resistance against the interloper, until he remembers 'an old prophecy' 'That Milton of the land of Albion should up ascend/Forwards from Ulro from the Vale of Felpham and set free/Orc from his Chain of Jealousy' (pl. 20, 59–61). Orc is a revolutionary spirit, and Los, like imaginative human beings even when they are dissatisfied with the status quo, shrinks from unleashing the overthrow of things as they are. But when he recollects himself, he joins forces with Milton's enterprise. Milton, in order to set right what he has previously done wrong, requires a human form, and his spirit enters accordingly into William

239

Blake's foot.[35] Blake is at first unaware of the cause of the new perceptive power he has acquired:

> But I knew not that it was Milton, for man cannot know
> What passes in his members till periods of space & time
> Reveal the secrets of Eternity; for more extensive
> Than any other earthly things are man's earthly
>   lineaments. (pl. 21, 8–11)

Los, in turn, the imaginative power, comes to Blake in a more overwhelming manner and takes possession of him:

> Los descended to me;
> And Los behind me stood, a terrible flaming sun, just close
> Behind my back, I turned round in terror, & behold!
> Los stood in that fierce glowing fire . . . .
>   Trembling I stood
> Exceedingly, with fear & terror, standing in the vale
> Of Lambeth, but he kissed me and wished me health
> And I became one man with him, arising in my strength;
> 'Twas too late now to recede. Los had entered into my
>   soul;
> His terrors now possessed me whole. I arose in fury
>   & strength. (pl. 22, 5–14)

It is to this transformed Blake, imbued with the spirit of Milton and inspired by the imaginative energy of Los, that the vision of Ololon appears outside the cottage at Felpham; and it is at this point that the moral crux of the poem may be said to lie.

Ololon, as Milton's emanation, has come to seek him; wishing to be reunited with him, but wishing to be reunited with him on her own terms. The relationship of Milton to his emanation resembles the relationship of Albion to Vala, in *Jerusalem*; by casting off the sensual aspect of the feminine, Milton has come under the domination of the life-denying prudish aspect and has ended by casting off both and existing independent of them. One of the songs heard as Ololon descends to earth in her quest explains the sequence of such a falling off as if it were a polygamous Old Testament marriage that had turned sour:

> When I first married you, I gave you all my soul;
> I thought that you would love my loves, & joy in my delights,
> Seeking for pleasures in my pleasures, O daughter of
>   Babylon.
> Then thou wast lovely, mild & gentle; now thou art terrible
> In jealousy, & unlovely in my sight, because thou hast
>   cruelly

Cut off my loves in fury, till I have no love left for thee.
Thy love depends on him thou lovest, & on his dear loves
Depend thy pleasures, which thou hast cut off by jealousy.
Therefore I show my jealousy, & set before you death.
Behold Milton descended to redeem the female shade
From death eternal; such your lot, to be continually
  redeemed
By death & misery of those you love, & by annihilation.
When the sixfold female[36] perceives that Milton annihilates
Himself—that, seeing all his loves by her cut off, he
  leaves
Her also, entirely abstracting himself from female loves,
She shall relent in fear of death; she shall begin to give
Her maidens to her husband, delighting in his delight.
And then, & then alone, begins the happy female joy . . . . (pl. 33, 2–19)

The analogy of marriage expresses in familiar terms the relationship of the masculine and feminine aspects that Blake believes together make up a whole person. Like Shelley, and like the Song of Songs that provides both of them with a precedent and a traditional vocabulary, Blake slips into the language of love without feeling obliged to remind us that he is not to be interpreted literally.

Ololon is at the point where she is about to perceive 'that Milton annihilates/Himself . . .'. The Milton whom she encounters is the shadow of Milton, Milton's earthly self as he was before he died, bound by false conventional beliefs; into Blake's garden 'clothed in black; severe & silent he descended' (pl. 38, 8). At the same time, Milton's spectre, Satan, rages resentfully over the sea near Felpham. For the separation of spectre, shadow and emanation to be reunited in the spirit of Milton, it is necessary that the spectre be subdued and that the emanation's will should submit to Milton's. The spectre resists, however. Milton explains to him the difference between his own self-sacrificing intentions in ending a series of conquests and the oppositious intentions that are all Satan is capable of ascribing to an opponent:

Satan, my spectre, I know my power thee to annihilate
And be a greater in thy place, & be thy tabernacle,
A covering for thee to do thy will—till one greater comes
And smites me as I smote thee, & becomes my covering.
Such are the laws of thy false heavens, but laws of Eternity
Are not such. Know thou, I come to self-annihilation.
Such are the laws of Eternity, that each shall mutually
Annihilate himself for other's good, as I for thee.
Thy purpose & the purpose of thy priests & of thy churches
Is to impress on men the fear of death; to teach
Trembling & fear, terror, constriction, abject selfishness.
Mine is to teach men to despise death, & to go on

241

In fearless majesty annihilating self, laughing to scorn
Thy laws & terrors . . . .   (pl. 38, 29–42)

In repudiating Satan's outlook, Milton is repudiating the point of view out of which he formerly created the Satan he now confronts. Predictably, Satan, whose only claim to existence as a spectre is opposition to the shadow from which he is divided, threatens Milton with the false laws that Milton had attributed to God the Father in *Paradise Lost*, and as he does so he pretends that he himself is God as he had at the time of his fall, according to the revised version of the bard's song that Milton heard in Heaven:

> Satan heard, coming in a cloud, with trumpets & flaming
>   fire,
> Saying: 'I am God, the judge of all, the living & the dead.
> Fall therefore down & worship me; submit thy supreme
> Dictate to my eternal will, & to my dictate bow.
> I hold the balances of right & just, & mine the sword.
> Seven angels bear my name & in those seven I appear;
> But I alone am God, & I alone in heaven & earth
> Of all that live dare utter this. Others tremble & bow
> Till all things become one great Satan, in holiness
> Opposed to mercy; and the divine delusion, Jesus, be
>   no more'.   (plates 38, 50 to 39, 2)

This false assumption of divinity, coupled with despotic conduct and an inability to understand any other way of thinking, resembles Jupiter's state of mind at the moment of his fall in *Prometheus Unbound*; and a further similarity is observable between the selflessness of Milton's sacrifice which results in reunion with his feminine emanation Ololon and the selflessness of Prometheus's sympathy which reunites him with Asia. Blake and Shelley, writing quite independently of one another, have invented legends that are partly the same because the ideas for reform that they wished to convey in allegory were partly the same. Satan's threats are as hollow as Jupiter's, because he is only a part of the man he threatens, and he is reduced to 'Howling in his spectre round his [Milton's] body, hungering to devour,/But fearing for the pain; for if he touches a vital,/His torment is unendurable' (pl. 39, 18–20).

The confrontation with Ololon is less terrible; it too involves the conflict of mutually contradictory points of view, but Ololon, instead of blustering threateningly like Satan, tries to achieve her ends by appealing to Milton's gentler side; she is concerned by the prospect of annihilation, but instead of pleading on her own behalf she weeps 'for the little ones, the children of Jerusalem,/Lest they be annihilated in thy annihilation' (pl. 40, 15–16). Milton now perceives the limitations of such charitable appeals to pathos, and in a spirit that recalls the paradox of 'Holy Thursday' in 'Songs of Experience'—'Babes reduced to misery,/Fed with cold and usurous hand' (11. 3–4)—insists upon the absolute charity of annihilation and the importance of spiritual rather than physical existence:

> turning toward Ololon in terrible majesty, Milton
> Replied: 'Obey thou the words of the inspired man!
> All that can be annihilated must be annihilated,
> That the children of Jerusalem may be saved from slavery.
> There is a negation, & there is a contrary:
> The negation must be destroyed to redeem the contraries.
> The negation is the spectre, the reasoning power in man.
> This is a false body, an incrustation over my immortal
> Spirit, a selfhood which must be put off & annihilated
>   alway.'   (pl. 40, 28–36)

Milton reads her a magnificent lecture, on the effect of reliance on the physical appearances of things rather than on their spiritual realities, in which he reels off a series of examples in which, in order to awaken our critical faculties, things we usually despise are mingled with things we usually admire:

> I come in self-annihilation & the grandeur of inspiration
> To cast off rational demonstration by faith in the Saviour;
> To cast off the rotten rags of memory by inspiration;
> To cast off Bacon, Locke & Newton from Albion's covering;
> To take off his filthy garments, & clothe him with
>   imagination;
> To cast aside from poetry all that is not inspiration,
> That it no longer shall dare to mock with the aspersion
>   of madness
> Cast on the inspired, by the tame high finisher of paltry
>   blots
> Indefinite, or paltry rhymes, or paltry harmonies;
> Who creeps into state government like a caterpillar to
>   destroy;
> To cast off the idiot questioner who is always questioning
> But never capable of answering, who sits with a sly grin
> Silent plotting when to question, like a thief in a cave;
> Who publishes doubt & calls it knowledge; whose science
>   is despair,
> Whose pretence to knowledge is envy, whose whole science is
> To destroy the wisdom of ages to gratify ravenous envy,
> That rages round him like a wolf day & night without rest.
> He smiles with condescension; he talks of benevolence &
>   virtue;
> And those who act with benevolence & virtue, they
>   murder time on time.

> These are the destroyers of Jerusalem, these are the
> murderers
> Of Jesus, who deny faith & mock at eternal life . . . .   (pl. 41, 2–22)

Overwhelmed by this tirade, Ololon despairingly parts from her separate identity and flees 'into the depths/Of Milton's shadow . . .' (pl. 42, 5–6) and the self-annihilation of Milton is complete.

Milton's struggle with his spectre and his emanation, like Los's similar struggle in *Jerusalem*, is one which personifies the potential struggle within every man to maintain a balance between his various faculties. It has a political counterpart as well in which the concluding events of *Jerusalem* are seen from a slightly different point of view. In *Jerusalem* the recovery from the fall is not achieved by any single identifiable act; it seems to be inevitable and therefore does not invite us to contribute to bringing it about. In *Milton* a doctrine of selflessness is offered as the means by which the recovery may be achieved. Blake typically does not pay punctilious attention to dates or the passage of time, but he had a fondness for significant numbers. Milton's 'One hundred years' in eternity (pl. 2, 17) may be regarded as a round figure for the number of years that have elapsed since his death in 1674. Blake does not tell us the date of his death, but the coincidence of Milton's centennial with the outbreak of the American revolution in 1774 seems to have been in his mind. When Los reacts fearfully to the coming of Milton, he worries lest Milton should 'set free/Orc from his Chain of Jealousy . . .' (pl. 20, 60–1). In his poem *America* (1793), Blake made Los's son Orc the personification of the revolutionary spirit among the thirteen colonies. The changes that take place in Milton himself, then, are paralleled in changes that take place in the mythical world that surrounds them, and these in turn are indirect references to the actual train of events that took place in Blake's lifetime. Events like the American revolution and later the French revolution were already things of the past by the time Blake wrote *Milton*, but he carries on into the present of the war between France and the rest of Europe and prophesies the imminent end of the world as we know it if the forces released by Milton's coming are able to prevail.

With the advent of Milton, as we have observed, even Los is at first inclined to resist fearfully—he is, after all, only the imagination in its fallen state. Once he remembers the promise of millennium he tries to convince the other inhabitants of his city of Golgonooza that they too should really be on Milton's side. The inability of many of them to be so is not a sign of irredeemable wickedness in them but evidence that the change of allegiance is terribly difficult to achieve. Between the death of Milton and his second coming, various true prophets have tried to prepare the way and have been opposed by false prophets. The true are seized upon by Los's children and their prophecies are distorted as a means of defence. The teachings of Voltaire and Rousseau are adopted as alternatives to the teachings of Christ (pl. 22, 40–4); Swedenborg's visions are opposed by a church imbued with the values of the Graeco-Roman world (pl. 22, 45–54); the Methodist reformers Whitefield and Wesley are mocked as madmen. Nevertheless, with the release of Orc in America, the sleeping Albion begins to stir. Los tries to avoid the internecine war that unnecessarily marred the Reformation (plates 23, 38 to 24, 43), but his sons are not convinced. War follows, expressed as the vintage of the grapes of wrath in a winepress; it is not the winepress of God but the winepress of 'War on earth' (pl. 25, 8). This war is a cause of joy to all the noxious things of the earth, but it is a cause of bitter and pointless agony to men (pl. 25, 11–41). The winepress is located 'on the Rhine' (pl. 26, 3), aptly, in view of its great vineyards, and emblematic of the border between France and the European nations that oppose her, but its effects are felt in every capital:

> The winepress on the Rhine groans aloud, but all its
>   central beams
> Act more terrific in the central cities of the nations,
> Where human thought is crushed beneath the iron hand of
>   power.   (pl. 26, 3–5)

In this war there will be no victory. Time is coming to an end and the vintage will be completed by the Day of Judgment:

> And Los stood & cried to the labourers of the vintage
>   in voice of awe:
> 'Fellow labourers! The great vintage & harvest is now
>   upon earth.
> The whole extent of the globe is explored; every scattered
>   atom
> Of human intellect now is flocking to the sound of the
>   trumpet.
> All the wisdom which was hidden in caves & dens, from ancient
> Time, is now sought out from animal & vegetable &
>   mineral.
> The Awakener is come, outstretched over Europe. The
>   vision of God is fulfilled . . .'.   (pl. 26, 16–22)

From the time of Milton's decision to return to earth, reminders have been given of the seven guardian angels who have kept watch over sleeping Albion. In *Jerusalem* they were named—Lucifer, Molech, Elohim, Shaddai, Pahad, Jehovah and Jesus— and an eighth was mentioned—'he came not, he hid in Albion's forests' (pl. 55, 31–3). The unnamed eighth was Milton. At Milton's descent 'The seven Angels of the Presence wept over Milton's shadow' (pl. 14, 42), and they accompany him to earth and strengthen him. When Milton achieves reunion with his emanation and escapes from the domination of his spectre, he becomes worthy of his place with the other angels. 'With one accord the starry eight became/One man Jesus the Saviour, wonderful!' (pl. 42, 10–11). This is the moment that Los has announced, and it is the moment at which Blake records that his vision ended: 'Immediately the lark mounted with a loud trill from Felpham's vale,/And the wild thyme from Wimbledon's green & empurpled hills'. The apocalyptic ending of the world has been glimpsed.

IV *The Revolt of Islam*

Shelley's *The Revolt of Islam* (1818) was first published under the title *Laon and Cythna* in 1817. It was suppressed by his publishers, and republished in altered form a few months later. Shelley's revisions suggest that the publishers feared that they would be attacked for sedition, blasphemy and obscenity; their fears reflect the anxious condition of liberal intellectual life at the time, and Shelley's own choice of allegory as a means of expressing his radical views exhibits a similar, if inadequate, sense of caution. The poem consists of twelve cantos and is written in the Spenserian stanzas now freed by Byron for general use. But Shelley is truer to the Spenserian spirit than Byron had been, devoting all but the introductory first canto to a narrative that has genuine similarities to *The Faerie Queene* and to Ariosto's *Orlando Furioso* and that like these great predecessors conceals a higher meaning in the intricacies of its plot. It is a tale of lovers who repeatedly risk their lives for one another and yet are prepared to subordinate their love to the higher ideal of love of mankind in general. Its most immediate model is William Sotheby's 1798 translation of Wieland's *Oberon*.

The story of Laon and Cythna is related in the first person by Laon and it includes Cythna's own first-hand account of experiences she had when they were separated. Laon grows up in a dictatorship. When he realizes that there are alternatives to tyranny, he resolves to dedicate his life to the cause of liberty, truth and justice, and begins to preach sedition. He finds a willing pupil in his young foster-sister, Cythna, but their plans are abruptly interrupted when Cythna is abducted and Laon, who tries to save her, is imprisoned. The occasion and the circumstances of his confinement unhinge Laon's mind, and although he is rescued after a few days by a learned hermit, it takes seven years to restore his sanity. In the meantime, Cythna goes mad while being sacrificed to the lust of the tyrant, Othman, and so frightens him that he has her marooned in a remote grotto. There in her delirium she gives birth to Othman's child, a daughter, which is taken from her immediately. Her mind slowly clears, she is released from the grotto by an earthquake, and is picked up by a passing slave ship. On board she lectures the mariners on the iniquity of their trade and persuades them to set the slaves free. The ship sails to Othman's capital, the Golden City, and Cythna, or Laone as she now styles herself in memory of the lost Laon, succeeds in bringing about a pacifist revolution there by arousing the sympathies of the oppressors for the plight of the oppressed. Laon's recovery coincides with Laone's success and the hermit sends him to join forces with the 'patriots'. Laon reaches the camp of the pacifist besiegers just before it is treacherously attacked by the tyrant's forces and he manages to restrain the pacifists from taking an instinctive revenge and to convert the attackers to the revolutionary cause. Together they enter the city and Laon finds Othman sitting by himself on a throne attended only by a little girl. As priestess of the people, Laone celebrates the victory.

The celebrations are cut short by the arrival of a foreign army in the tyrant's pay; the revolutionaries are routed and remorselessly slaughtered. Laon is rescued at the last moment by Cythna who appears suddenly in the battlefield riding a gigantic black horse. They retire together to a safe retreat and consummate their spiritual agreement in a physical union.[37] Laon searches the battle-torn and horribly plague-ridden countryside for food, and when he learns that the tyrant's forces are closing in he goes, incognito, to barter his life for Cythna's freedom. The tyrant agrees, but when Laon's identity is revealed the promise is broken and he is condemned to be burnt to death. Cythna gives herself up to die with him, and as the flames rise they find themselves conveyed to paradisal surroundings.

Reduced to the bare bones of its complicated plot, *The Revolt of Islam* sounds like a number of other works of the period. The prolonged persecution of innocent people is featured in Southey's *Curse of Kehama* and Thomas Moore's 'The Fire Worshippers' (1817); the single-minded pursuit of a political ideal had been central to Southey's *Madoc*; the unexpected and arbitrary turns of fortune had a precedent in an Arabian setting in Southey's *Thalaba*; and the hideously macabre and grotesque incidents that were characteristic of Southey's poems had found a place in such disparate recent works as Moore's 'The Veiled Prophet of Khorassan' (1817) and John Wilson's *The City of the Plague* (1816). Shelley's characters have no more individuality than the heroes of Byron's oriental tales and yet we have to keep company with them much longer; significantly, they are less interesting than the views they expound. His story is less gripping than Southey's stories generally are. Nevertheless, derivative though it is in many respects and inferior in some, *The Revolt of Islam* is, on its own terms, a poem of absorbing interest. Its apparent adoption of popular forms is a disguise designed to capture the attention of readers who would otherwise have passed it by.

The lives of Laon and Cythna have a moral dimension that makes comparison with lives in *The Prelude* and *The Excursion* seem appropriate. The circumstances of Laon's infancy, for example, are as benign as Wordsworth could have wished, although Shelley's choice of images is strikingly different:

> The starlight smile of children, the sweet looks
>   Of women, the fair breast from which I fed,
> The murmur of the unreposing brooks,
>   And the green light which, shifting overhead,
>   Some tangled bower of vines around me shed,
> The shells on the sea-sand, and the wild flowers,
>   The lamplight through the rafters cheerly spread,
>   And on the twining flax—in life's young hours
> These sights and sounds did nurse my spirit's folded powers.

(II, i, 667)

As ever, nature and the physical relation of mother to child afford happiness. The organization of the state and of the family—Shelley was objecting to the legal bondage of wives to husbands—frustrates these promising beginnings:

> The land in which I lived, by a fell bane
>   Was withered up. Tyrants dwelt side by side,

> And stabled in our homes,—until the chain
>   Stifled the captive's cry, and to abide
>   That blasting curse men had no shame—all vied
> In evil, slave and despot . . . .   (II, iv, 694–9)

But although Laon frees himself from the morally crippling assumptions of his time, when his mettle is first tried by the abduction of Cythna his reaction is instinctive and violent:

>   I drew
>   My knife, and with one impulse, suddenly
>   All unaware three of their number slew,
>   And grasped a fourth by the throat, and with loud cry
> My countrymen invoked to death or liberty!   (III, x, 1193–7)

Laon's resistance, as unpremeditated as the ancient mariner's killing of the albatross, of which subsequent events remind us, is ineffectual and inconsistent with his own values.

When he emerges from the years of madness that follow, his first action is in a sense a reformed response to a similar situation. He has learned from the hermit that violence in support of good is a contradiction in terms—'If blood be shed, 'tis but a change and choice/Of bonds . . .' (IV, xxviii, 1657–8). When the patriotic and pacifist besiegers of the Golden City find that ten thousand of their number have been 'Stabbed in their sleep, trampled in treacherous war . . .' (V, vi, 1772), and are so overcome with conventional resentment as to forsake their pacifism, Laon intervenes to remind them of it:

>   and then revenge and fear
>   Made the high virtue of the patriots fail:
>   One pointed on his foe the mortal spear—
> I rushéd before its point, and cried, 'Forbear, forbear!'
>   (V, viii, 1788–91)

With his arm pierced by the spear, Laon exhibits the pacifist approach to an aggressor and tries to break the futile sequence of injuries answered by injuries by showing that, because of the brotherhood of man, to injure others is to injure oneself. He addresses the enemy:

>   Soldiers, our brethren and our friends are slain.
>   Ye murdered them, I think, as they did sleep!
> Alas, what have ye done? the slightest pain
>   Which ye might suffer, there were eyes to weep,
>   But ye have quenched them—there were smiles to steep
> Your hearts in balm, but they are lost in woe;
>   And those whom love did set his watch to keep

248

> Around your tents, truth's freedom to bestow,
> Ye stabbed as they did sleep—but they forgive ye now.   (V, x, 1801–9)

His speech recalls the patriots to their senses and converts the enemy. At the moment when it most matters, Laon is able to live up to the principle that had once been beyond him. His moral development is complete.

The moral development of Cythna is simpler because it does not involve overcoming the instinct for revenge; from the first hers is 'a spirit strong and mild' (II, xxxii, 951). She remains passive when she is abducted, willing to submit to a slavery which she knows is shared by many; she is unaware of the eloquence available to a victim. The madness she experiences upon Othman's violation of her confers that eloquence upon her:

> Her madness was a beam of light, a power
> Which dawned through the rent soul; and words it gave,
> Gestures, and looks, such as in whirlwinds bore
> Which might not be withstood—whence none could save—
> All who approached their sphere,—like some calm wave
> Vexed into whirlpools by the chasms beneath;
> And sympathy made each attendant slave
> Fearless and free . . . .   (VII, vii, 2884–91)

But for a long time she is unconscious of this capacity. When her reason is restored to her in her lonely cave by the sea, an incident occurs that makes her aware of this power to enlist sympathy for the oppressed:

> one even,
> A Nautilus upon the fountain played,
> Spreading his azure sail where breath of Heaven
> Descended not, among the waves and whirlpools driven.
>
> And, when the Eagle came, that lovely thing,
> Oaring with rosy feet its silver boat,
> Fled near me as for shelter; on slow wing,
> The Eagle, hovering o'er his prey did float;
> But when he saw that I with fear did note
> His purpose, proffering my own food to him,
> The eager plumes subsided on his throat—
> He came where that bright child of sea did swim,
> And o'er it cast in peace his shadow broad and dim.
>   (VII, xxvi–xxvii, 3060–72)

Thereafter Cythna uses this power in the cause of social revolution.

The moral stances of Laon and Cythna are achieved without deliberate intent and at a great cost in the experience of personal suffering; they are complementary

249

rather than identical. Laon's persuasiveness addresses itself to the reason—to the sort of thinking that lay behind Bentham's concern for the greatest good for the greatest number—while Cythna's addresses itself to the feelings. Cythna's adoption of the name Laone, a feminine version of Laon, suggests that they represent different aspects of an outlook that when united can reform the world. The lesson is clear enough, but it affects us less deeply than the more elaborate lesson of *The Prelude* because Laon and Cythna themselves are so lacking in individuality that we scarcely extend our sympathies to them.

The presence of a complicated plot and of an original if abstract attention to the moral development of the chief characters are means to an end, however, and not ends in themselves. *The Revolt of Islam* incorporates these elements in the service of an allegory that is worthy of comparison with Blake's. A hostile contemporary reviewer of the poem challenged Shelley to explain 'how his case applies to *us*? or what *we* learn from it to the prejudice of our own institutions?'[38] The implication that the case should apply to us is derived from Canto I, the part of the poem that precedes the story of Laon and Cythna.

In Canto I, the author describes an experience that he had in the midst of the political disillusionment that followed the overthrow of revolutionary France:

> When the last hope of trampled France had failed
>   Like a brief dream of unremaining glory,
> From visions of despair I rose, and scaled
>   The peak of an aëreal promontory,
>   Whose caverned base with the vexed surge was hoary;
> And saw the golden dawn break forth, and waken
>   Each cloud, and every wave:—but transitory
> The calm: for sudden, the firm earth was shaken,
> As if by the last wreck its frame were overtaken.   (I, i, 127–35)

From his vantage point, with its curious similarity to the as yet unpublished Mount Snowdon setting in *The Prelude*, the author observes a warlike storm in the heavens, followed by a moonlit calm, from which emerge an eagle and a serpent twined in the agonies of mutual combat. The struggle is fierce and prolonged, but in the end the serpent falls exhausted into the sea and the eagle flies wearily away. The serpent seeks refuge in the arms of a beautiful woman who is waiting for it on the shore, and the author, who is concerned for her safety, accompanies them in a magical boat and has the meaning of what he has seen explained to him. The struggle of the eagle and the serpent, it transpires, is the struggle between evil and good. In a manner reminiscent of Blake, however, Shelley has reversed the conventional symbols.[39] Evil having gained the upper hand at the beginning, the vanquished good has been transformed by victorious evil into something detested by mankind:

> Thus evil triumphed, and the Spirit of evil,
>   One Power of many shapes which none may know,

> One Shape of many names; the Fiend did revel
>> In victory, reigning o'er a world of woe,
>> For the new race of man went to and fro,
> Famished and homeless, loathed and loathing, wild,
>> And hating good—for his immortal foe,
> He changed from starry shape, beauteous and mild,
> To a dire Snake, with man and beast unreconciled.   (I, xxvii, 361–9)

The author's instinctive dread of the serpent—'Thou fearest not then the Serpent on thy heart?' (I, xlvii, 541)—anticipates the reader's; in what follows we are to be re-educated together.

The woman summarizes the history of civilization since the initial victory of evil, identifying the characteristics of the conqueror as she does so (I, xxviii–xxxii, 370–414): they are death, decay, earthquake, blight, want, madness, fear, hatred, tyranny, and—Shelley cannot resist the opportunity—faith. Though tyranny has prevailed there have been recurrent outbreaks of resistance to it. The author has witnessed one of these:

> Such is this conflict—when mankind doth strive
>> With its oppressors in a strife of blood,
> Or when free thoughts, like lightnings, are alive,
>> And in each bosom of the multitude
>> Justice and truth with Custom's hydra brood
> Wage silent war; when Priests and Kings dissemble
>> In smiles or frowns their fierce disquietude,
>> When round pure hearts a host of hopes assemble,
> The Snake and Eagle meet—the world's foundations tremble!
>> (I, xxxiii, 415–23)

This analysis may be accepted as a general evaluation of resistance to oppression; it may be understood as a guide to the meaning of the story of Laon and Cythna; and although Shelley avoids applying it with explicit sedition to the fall of France, we are expected to remember that the vision followed immediately after 'the last hope of trampled France had failed/Like a brief dream of unremaining glory . . .' (I, i, 127–8).

The revolution to which the title, *The Revolt of Islam*, refers is sufficiently remote and obscure to require such a preface. If Shelley wishes to take the part of the serpent he is wise to preserve some distance between it and the France with which his own country has been at war, on and off, for a quarter of a century. The tyrant against whom Laon and Cythna struggle is Othman; the land in which they live is Greece. The original Othman I, who reigned from A.D. 644 to 655, was a Moslem whose rule was marked by successful foreign conquests and domestic anarchy. He was deposed by a popular uprising and executed.[40] Shelley's readers would not have known much more about him than the average reader does today, but they had some awareness of the nature of Turkish despotism in their own

251

time—through the oriental tales of Byron and others, if not through the newspapers—and it is on this awareness that Shelley's anachronistic story depends. The stirrings of Greek independence had been publicized in *Childe Harold's Pilgrimage*. Given the conditions of the Ottoman Empire, particularly the Moslem faith of its rulers and the Christian origin of its slaves, it was reasonable to hope for a patient reading for revolutionary activity that in a European setting would have seemed incendiary.

The characteristics of Turkish rule were generally accepted as being arbitrary use of power, shameless cruelty, and the complete subjection of women. The combination of political despotism and domestic despotism is especially suitable for Shelley's purposes because the common experience of any family provides a counterpart either to the iniquity of bondage of wife to husband, or to the blessedness of mutual co-operation, or, more realistically, to a mixture of both. Nowadays favourers of women's rights appeal to the law; in Shelley's time it seemed more persuasive to argue for political rights by appeal to the experience of the individual. Shelley's affectionate dedication of the poem to his wife, Mary, links the two themes in a way that the public could recognize by reference to her mother—Mary Wollstonecraft, author of *The Vindication of the Rights of Women*—and to her father, William Godwin, author of *Concerning Political Justice*:

> They say that thou wert lovely from thy birth,
>> Of glorious parents, thou aspiring Child.
> I wonder not—for One then left this earth
>> Whose life was like a setting planet mild,
>> Which clothed thee in the radiance undefiled
> Of its departing glory; still her fame
>> Shines on thee, through the tempests dark and wild
> Which shake these latter days; and thou canst claim
> The shelter, from thy Sire, of an immortal name.   (xii, 100–8)

Shelley's decision to change his title to *The Revolt of Islam* deprives the reader of a useful preliminary hint.[41] The more exotic original—*Laon and Cythna or the Revolution of the Golden City. A Vision of the Nineteenth Century*—has the advantage of making us wonder what the Golden City may be and who Laon and Cythna are. The Golden City might be expected to remind us of the new Jerusalem of the Book of Revelation—'the city was pure gold, clear as glass' (21. 18)—with its implications of the second coming—but the names Laon and Cythna have associations only for those with a smattering of Greek. Laon's name is derived from the Greek word for the people—as distinguished from the nation on the one hand and the mob on the other; Cythna's is derived from the word for seed or germ, and it will be recalled that when she matures morally and politically she adopts the feminine form of Laon's name, Laone. If we attempt to read the adventures of Laon and Cythna in the light of these observations, an allegory begins to emerge from the complex narrative that justifies the shortcomings of plot and characterization. It would run somewhat as follows.

The people (Laon) emerge from the happiness of instinctive infancy to the misery of living in a state of slavery. From their awareness of the alternatives of previous generations, men learn that the political status quo has no absolute claims, and dream of reforming the world in accordance with their ideals. This dream is shared with their female counterparts in whom it flowers in a purer form. The rebuff experienced when the dream is challenged by the prevailing forces of tyranny causes the people to lose sight of their dream temporarily and oppose their tormentors in kind, but the effect of this loss may be regarded as a temporary madness. In *The Revolt of Islam*, after Laon kills some of Cythna's abductors, he is chained on the top of a tall column and left there to suffer from exposure to the sun's heat. His delirium during this trial leads him to imagine that he is eating a corpse that hangs in the air beside him, and as he does so he realizes that it is Cythna's—'and that the flesh was warm/Within my teeth!' (III, xxvi, 1339–40). The revolting image conveyed by this passage reflects the need to find some physical analogy for a superstitious belief that defies reason rather than an enthusiasm for the macabre. The people (Laon) relapse into the madness of religious faith from which it requires the prolonged ministrations of a solitary vegetarian sage to allow them to emerge.[42] When one of the besiegers of the Golden City puts the attackers to flight with the cry 'Laon!' he is evoking the name of the people as well as the memory of the man (V, vii, 1779). When it is decided by the tyrant and his priests that Laon must be sacrificed if tyranny is to remain secure, they are condemning Laon, but also the people. The effect of opposing the uprising of Laon or the people is slaughter, famine and plague. The point of Laon's request that Laone be permitted to withdraw to America (XI, xxiv, 4438–9) is not a wish that she should enjoy unspoilt surroundings like Gertrude of Wyoming, but that in America the people may be free—'Yes, in the desert there is built a home/For Freedom' (XI, xxiv, 4432–3). The final conflagration of Laon and Laone does not bring their existences to an end.[43] The spirit of the people lives on and will reassert itself.

Shelley's attempt to make *The Revolt of Islam* viable at three levels of meaning may be deemed a failure, but if so it is a failure that helps to define the difficulties that faced the original allegorist in the Romantic period. His effort to present a genre that was familiar enough to gain the reader's attention led his poem to be treated as an unskilful example of the genre. His attempt to develop his characters in moral terms failed because it could not explain the distinctiveness of their mature beliefs without making them and their circumstances seem unre-presentative. His allegory went largely unobserved.

The nature of his dilemma is most vividly revealed in the trouble he was caused by the family relationship of Laon and Cythna. In the original edition Cythna was simply identified: 'I had a little sister whose fair eyes/Were lodestars of delight . . .' (II, xxi, 847–8). In *The Revolt of Islam*, a more formal phrasing is substituted: 'An orphan with my parents lived, whose eyes/Were lodestars of delight . . .'. The alteration seems to have been made in order to avoid seeming to countenance incest. After their escape from the tyrant's forces in Canto VI, Laon and Cythna commune with one another, in danger but alone together for the first time since Cythna's abduction. Their feelings are delicately explored in the original version:

> There we unheeding sate, in the communion
>   Of interchangèd vows, which, with a rite
> Of faith most sweet and sacred, stamped our union. —
>   Few were the living hearts which could unite
>   Like ours, or celebrate a bridal-night
> With such close sympathies, for to each other
>   Had high and solemn hopes, the gentle might
> Of earliest love, and all the thoughts which smother
> Cold Evil's power, now linked a sister and a brother.
>
> (VI, xxxix, 2677–85)

Shelley's emphasis is not on the naturalness of incest—an emphasis that might well have made his publishers quail—but on the way in which affection and shared partnership in a common and virtuous cause leads to a degree of happiness that is independent of circumstances. Here, as he would later in *Epipsychidion*, he chooses the traditional image of the physical expression of love as the highest form of happiness and ascribes to Laon and Cythna something beyond even it:

> I know not. What are kisses whose fire clasps
>   The failing heart in languishment, or limb
> Twined within limb? or the quick dying gasps
>   Of the life meeting, when the faint eyes swim
>   Through tears of a wide mist boundless and dim,
> In one caress? What is the strong control
>   Which leads the heart that dizzy steep to climb,
> Where far over the world those vapours roll,
> Which blend two restless frames in one reposing soul?
>
> (VI, xxxvi, 2650–8)

Read literally the behaviour of Laon and Cythna sounds evocatively physical as well as spiritual, and even though, as Shelley says a few stanzas earlier, 'To the pure all things are pure!', it seemed wise to make the relationship one of foster-brother and foster-sister. Hence the intrusive orphan of line 847. Read allegorically, however, as it is meant to be, the union is of representative man and representative woman, who are capable of the highest individual happiness when they live according to their ideals and are able to escape from the falsehoods of the social organization in which they are trapped. Shelley's failure here is related to one of his great strengths; the physical embodiment of his ideas is so arresting that it does not remind us of the idea it conveys. His problem is the opposite of Blake's.

V *Cain*

The major allegories of Blake and Shelley show considerable tact in revising or even reversing conventional theology rather than attacking it point-blank. In Blake's case the tact seems to have been unconscious; as far as one can tell, he believed in the modified religion he expounded. The relationship between Shelley's beliefs and his allegories is harder to define because he was aware of the danger of censorship and indeed, as we have noticed, had personally experienced legal prosecution for his unorthodox ideas. He did in fact try his hand early on at a blunt attack on Christianity in his anonymous and privately circulated *Queen Mab* (1813). There his spokesman is the Wandering Jew, Ahasuerus, who reports God's explanation to the murderer, Moses, of His wicked purpose in creating man:

> I placed him in a Paradise, and there
> Planted the tree of evil, so that he
> Might eat and perish, and My soul procure
> Wherewith to sate its malice, and to turn,
> Even like a heartless conqueror of the earth,
> All misery to My fame. (VII, 109–14)

When Moses pleads on man's behalf, God adds a further refinement in proposing to offer the supposed ransom of Christ's crucifixion:

> so that the few
> On whom My grace descends, those who are marked
> As vessels to the honour of their God,
> May credit this strange sacrifice, and save
> Their souls alive: millions shall live and die,
> Who ne'er shall call upon their Saviour's name,
> But, unredeemed, go to the gaping grave.
> Thousands shall deem it an old woman's tale,
> Such as the nurses frighten babes withal:
> These in a gulf of anguish and of flame
> Shall curse their reprobation endlessly . . . . (VII, 139–49)

At this recital 'Even the murderer's cheek/was blanched with horror . . .' (VII, 157–8). Such sentiments were calculated to offend orthodoxy not to convert it. Later, in the 1820s, they became popular in radical circles.[44] The only effective direct attack upon God issued from the pen of Lord Byron.

Byron's *Cain* (1821) first appeared as part of a volume entitled *Sardanapalus, A Tragedy. The Two Foscari, A Tragedy. Cain, A Mystery.* In terming it a 'mystery' Byron associated it vaguely with the late medieval cycle plays that brought biblical stories to life on the stage, and by contrasting it with the tragedies it accompanied he invited his readers to characterize for themselves the events that surrounded the death of Abel.[45] It is tempting to regard the poem as being of the same kind as *Manfred*, the character of the protagonist seeming by comparison to be lacking in personality and presence, but in *Cain* Byron was working more austerely in the allegorical mode we have encountered in Blake and Shelley. His argument is not so much about Cain's predicament as about the relationship of mankind to God and he has muted the character of his protagonist accordingly.

The first murder was a popular topic in the eighteenth century. The isolation involved in Cain's punishment and the defiant quality of his deed interested the sentimental; moralists were fascinated by the problem of distinguishing between original sin and individual guilt and found Cain to be a test case of the current theory that because man's behaviour was predetermined by his experience he was therefore not a free agent.[46] Solomon Gessner's *The Death of Abel* was translated into English in 1761. It was received by the devout as a popular sequel to *Paradise Lost* and passed through more than twenty editions by 1800. A new translation went through a dozen more between 1807 and 1821.[47] Byron capitalized upon the familiarity of his subject by taking strategic liberties with it that he could be sure would be noticed and he used them to undermine the assumptions of Miltonian orthodoxy.

Byron depicts Adam and his family—Eve, Abel, Adah and Zillah[48]—as being filled with a sense of their own unworthiness and unstinting in their grateful worship of God. Their outlook is epitomized by Zillah who sums up the hymn of adoration with which the poem begins:

> Oh, God! who loving, making, blessing all,
> Yet didst permit the Serpent to creep in,
> And drive my father forth from Paradise,
> Keep us from further evil:—Hail! All Hail! (I, i, 18–21)

Cain is more critical of the situation in which he finds himself and is unable to join them in prayer. His first soliloquy formulates the common objections to the consequences of the fall of man concisely:

> And this is
> Life?—Toil! and wherefore should I toil?—because
> My father could not keep his place in Eden?
> What had *I* done in this?—I was unborn:
> I sought not to be born; nor love the state
> To which that birth has brought me. Why did he
> Yield to the Serpent and the woman? or
> Yielding—why suffer? What was there in this?
> The tree was planted, and why not for him?
> If not, why place him near it, where it grew
> The fairest in the centre? They have but
> One answer to all questions, ''Twas *his* will,
> And *he* is good.' How know I that? Because
> He is all-powerful, must all-good, too, follow?
> I judge but by the fruits—and they are bitter . . . . (I, i, 64–78)

The members of Adam's family are first presented to us uttering these opposing sentiments before we have any clue to their individual characters; they are little more than puppets who express the conflict of conventional piety and conventional doubt. It is only after their positions in the argument have been defined that traces of personality begin to accrue to them. Cain, for example, is no pert atheist who takes pleasure in triumphing over the naiveté of the faithful. When the others remonstrate with him he is full of consideration for them:

> I fain would be alone a little while.
> Abel, I'm sick at heart; but it will pass;
> Precede me, brother—I will follow shortly.
> And you, too, sisters, tarry not behind;
> Your gentleness must not be harshly met . . . .   (I, i, 57–61)

At this early stage it is easy to accept him as an embodiment of the sceptical side of honest doubt—unwilling to pretend the doubt is not there and yet uneasy at not finding it generally shared.

Once he is alone Cain is visited by Lucifer who confirms his doubts with an alternative theology that is more consistent with his experience. The dialogue with Lucifer occupies most of the first two acts and it develops Cain's scepticism in ways that go well beond the scepticism of the average person and yet would have been familiar to any controversialist of the period. Lucifer maintains that the God who rules the universe is evil and that this God and he are eternally contending with one another. There is a parallel here to the struggle of the eagle and the serpent in *The Revolt of Islam*, but God in *Cain* seems to be impervious to resistance and no prospect of deliverance is offered. The only comfort allowed us is to sympathize with one another in our misery:

> Let him crowd orb on orb: he is alone
> Indefinite, Indissoluble Tyrant;
> Could he but crush himself, 'twere the best boon
> He ever granted: but let him reign on!
> And multiply himself in misery!
> Spirits and Men, at least we sympathise—
> And, suffering in concert, make our pangs
> Innumerable, more endurable,
> By the unbounded sympathy of all
> With all!   (I, i, 152–61)

People, it is implied, may sustain one another by recognizing their common plight and not pretending, hypocritically, to be happy. But Lucifer adds to the argument for sympathy an argument for a pride in standing up to the evil God and maintains that a kind of immortality is granted to the independent mind. To Cain's question as to how we may avoid death Lucifer replies:

> By being
> Yourselves, in your resistance. Nothing can
> Quench the mind, if the mind will be itself

257

> And centre of surrounding things— 'tis made
> To sway. (I, i, 212–16)

This is a more dangerous doctrine, and although it resembles the resolution of Manfred the adoption of it by Cain has different consequences for him that are deeply disturbing.

Lucifer's re-education of Cain is accomplished partly by the exposition of an inverted theology and partly by the offering of a different perspective on human affairs. He divests Cain of the few delusions of happiness he has left by increasing his knowledge. Human misery in the first generation after the fall of man is nothing to what it will become. Cain assumes that man is important. By being allowed to compare man's little earth with the immense and beautiful universe during a flight with Lucifer through space, Cain is given a lesson in relativity (II, i); seeing in the world of death phantoms of the mightier creatures who inhabited the earth before man,[49] the ultimate meaning of mutability to the human race is brought home to him (II, ii). Man is not only miserable but insignificant. To Lucifer's challenge, 'Didst thou not require/Knowledge? And have I not, in what I showed,/Taught thee to know thyself?', Cain can only reply, 'Alas! I seem/Nothing' (II, ii, 418–21).

The true action of the poem may be said to begin in the third and final act when the re-educated Cain returns to his family. He has been moved from uncomplicated doubt to a scepticism that is informed by systematic abstract thought and confirmed by the sights he has seen. His reaction is not selfish; he repines rather for the fate that awaits those he loves. When Adah tries to interest him in their sleeping child Enoch, Cain is so obsessed with the ghastly future of mankind as to think of thwarting it by killing the child:

> Little deems our young blooming sleeper, there,
> The germs of an eternal misery
> To myriads is within him! better 'twere
> I snatched him in his sleep, and dashed him 'gainst
> The rocks, than let him live to— .... (III, i, 122–6)

When Abel appears and with a fervour that seems smugly officious presses his brother to join him in worship, Cain strives to master his revulsion and to spare Abel's feelings. But when his own reluctant vegetable sacrifice is scattered by a whirlwind and Abel's pyre of bleeding lambs is received into heaven by a column of fire, his indignation at the evil preference of God's 'immortal pleasure' overcomes him and he tries to cast Abel's altar down:

> *His pleasure!* what was his high pleasure in
> The fumes of scorching flesh and smoking blood,
> To the pain of the bleating mothers, which
> Still yearn for their dead offspring? or the pangs
> Of the sad ignorant victims underneath

Thy pious knife? Give way! this bloody record
Shall not stand in the sun, to shame creation!　　　　(III, i, 298–304)

Uttering these pacific sentiments and enraged by Abel's resistance he strikes him down, killing him without meaning to. The irony of the situation is complete. Adam and Eve and Zillah combine in their reproaches, the Angel of the Lord arrives to mark Cain's brow, and Adah alone stands by Cain loyally but uncomprehendingly as he departs for the wilderness.

There has been disagreement over the correct interpretation of Cain's state of mind at the close.[50] Some have seen him as chastened into an acceptance of God, and as having recovered from the impiety into which he has been led by his own doubts and by Lucifer's temptation. Others have felt that he is unregenerate to the end in his attitude towards God, but regretful about having killed Abel. Personal sympathies still affect our interpretations of the poem, but readers are baffled by what seems to be an unresolved mixture of genres in the poem. Cain's dialogue with Lucifer is clear and rational, Cain's behaviour before and after his meeting with Lucifer is not. The exquisite confusion into which Cain is thrown at the end is not intended to reveal his views on God or man but his feelings on having committed the worst of sins while imbued with an overpowering resentment against God, the author of all sin. For the moment the theological issue is swallowed up for Cain by his horror at what he has done; doctrine has yielded to empathy and we are permitted to appreciate the feelings of the first criminal even if we abhor his crime. There is, furthermore, no direct connection made between the killing of Abel and Cain's belief that God is evil; what emerges, rather, is the paradox that by acting unconventionally in what we conceive to be the best interests of our fellow creatures we may unwittingly do them the worst wrongs. A sincere atheist would find himself in such a dilemma if he convinced someone of the non-existence of God and the after-life only to have his convert commit suicide in despair.[51] Less extreme analogies are easily imagined. Cain's anguish does not seem to be related narrowly or specifically to his views about God, it is rather the quintessential illustration of the misery of inheriting original sin.

The publication of *Cain* caused something of a flutter in the literary world, and the Lord Chancellor declined to protect the poem from piracy on the ground that it was 'of a nature to preclude his interference in protecting the plaintiff's property'.[52] Quite the most interesting reaction, however, came from no less a person than William Blake. In a short poem in dramatic form, *The Ghost of Abel* (1822), he added to Byron's version of the myth a scene that opposed Byron's pessimism and yet remained consistent with the events that had led to it. As might be expected from the author of *Jerusalem* and *Milton*, Blake was wholly sympathetic to the kinds of objections made in *Cain* to the moral shortcomings of God and to the hypocritical cant and superficial piety of organized religion. But as we have seen, while he rejected the immoral God and perverted church as degenerate substitutes, he argued for devotion to the true God and true church. What Byron communicates in *Cain* might be true within the limits of physical experience, but it made too little allowance for the higher reality of the mind which

259

had made his outburst possible in the first place. In a prefatory exhortation, Blake addressed his contemporary as a true prophet temporarily bewildered and called upon him to trust the poet within himself:

> To Lord Byron in the wilderness:
> What doest thou here, Elijah?
> Can a poet doubt the visions of Jehovah? Nature has
> no outline; but Imagination has. Nature has no
> time; but Imagination has! Nature has no supernatural
> and dissolves: Imagination is Eternity.   (pl. 1)

In the scene that follows, Adam and Eve are found lamenting over the body of Abel, Abel's ghost appears to them calling to be avenged in kind, and Satan and Jehovah debate the question. Cain does not appear.

In Byron's poem, Cain is at odds with his family from the outset. The death of Abel occasions extravagant expressions of a lack of mutual sympathy that was already fixed. By omitting Cain and concentrating on the painful feelings of Adam and Eve, Blake is able to bridge the gulf that Byron had assumed existed between conventional believers and honest doubters. Blake attacks particularly Byron's adoption of the Old Testament notion of justice as 'an eye for an eye, a tooth for a tooth'. Adam and Eve show no such tendency. The fact of death and not its cause is what strikes them. They are beside themselves with grief at their first experience of it and they cannot for the moment bring themselves to attend to the voice of Jehovah, but when the Ghost of Abel appears calling for blood they come to their senses again. Adam is at first inclined to ignore both the ghost and Jehovah as being equally dubious:

> It is all a vain delusion of the all-creative imagination.
> Eve, come away and let us not believe these vain delusions:
> Abel is dead and Cain slew him. We shall also die a death
> And then—what then? Be as poor Abel, a thought, or as
> This! Oh what shall I call thee, form divine, Father
>   of Mercies
> That appearest to my spiritual vision?   (pl. 1, 17–22)

But Eve persuades him to hear the debate. When Jehovah proposes to the ghost of Abel the sacrifice of a lamb rather than of Cain, Satan appears reinforcing the demand for vengeful justice:

> I will have human blood and not the blood of bulls or goats,
> And no atonement, O Jehovah! The Elohim[53] live on sacrifice
> Of men: hence I am God of men: thou human, O Jehovah.
> By the rock and oak of the druid, creeping mistletoe and
>   thorn,

Cain's city built with human blood, not blood of bulls
　　and goats,
Thou shalt thyself be sacrificed to me thy God, on Calvary!

(pl. 2, 13–18)

This false God is the God against whom Byron has made Lucifer inveigh in *Cain*. The criticism of social values in Blake's poem is written in the same spirit, but he insists on looking beyond the viciousness of human life to a time when the 'covenant of the forgiveness of sins' shall bring about 'peace, brotherhood and love' (plates 2, 24, and 26). Byron, by concentrating on what is, rather than on what might be, was able to vex his contemporaries into an awareness of their weakness. Of all the allegorists of the period he came closest to getting an interested hearing.

10   Afterword

If satirical verse has only been touched on incidentally up to this point, it is not for any dearth of material. Byron's *Don Juan* and *Beppo*, Crabbe's *The Borough*, and the double-edged social comments of Cowper, Burns, Blake and Southey, have already been considered in other contexts. No history of literary taste from 1780 to 1800 would be complete, however, without some mention of the sly sarcasms of William Mason, the anonymous scurrilities of William Combe, the occasionally hilarious lampoons of Peter Pindar, the literary invective of William Gifford and T. J. Mathias, and the literary parodies of George Canning and J. H. Frere. After the turn of the century the writing of satirical verse continued unabated, with George Huddesford's anti-French tirades, with unflattering imitations of contemporary poets in James and Horace Smith's *Rejected Addresses* (1812) and James Hogg's *Poetic Mirror* (1816), and with the droll political squibs of Thomas Moore. It is easier to record the names of these witty, ingenious and accomplished men than it is to think of a single satirical poem by any of them that is still read for pleasure. Nevertheless, in their own day their works were popular in much the same way as the caricatures of Rowlandson, Gillray and Cruikshank were.

If we turn to the poets who still have a following, we find that several of them wrote some satirical verse. But poems like Coleridge's 'Fire, Famine and Slaughter' (1798) and Shelley's 'Mask of Anarchy' (1832)[1] depend for much of their effect upon our knowing and respecting William Pitt and Lord Castlereagh. Lord Byron's *English Bards, and Scotch Reviewers* (1809) seems to be read now mainly because it is Lord Byron's, and in spite of the fact that the accuracy or inaccuracy of most of his characterizations of contemporary writers can no longer be appreciated. It is with satire as it is with portrait painting: if we know the sitter we insist upon a likeness; if we do not, the likeness or lack of it is irrelevant to our appreciation of the picture. In the romantic period, verse satire aimed at likeness and contemporary effect; its subsequent obscurity is often a measure of its original success.[2]

One poem at least survives intact. In modern estimation, Byron's 'The Vision of Judgment' (1822) stands head and shoulders above every other satire of the period. Its survival is due in part to a series of accidents. Southey's *A Vision of Judgement* (1821) was the occasion and cause of Byron's poem. It fell to Southey's lot, as poet laureate, to write the official elegy on George III. He seldom did anything by halves, and rose to this challenge with a long experiment in dactylic hexameters. In *A Vision*, the poet hears a bell tolling to announce the death of the king and, thinking of the event as a merciful release, he falls into a trance. Guided by an unseen voice he finds himself in the royal burial vault and witnesses the apotheosis of the king's spirit. The king, whose mental powers are restored, learns for the first time that the war with France is over and that Napoleon has been defeated, and he expresses his satisfaction; he is borne upward to the Celestial City to be judged:

> Beaming afar it shone; its towers and cupolas rising
> High in the air serene, with the brightness of gold in
>   the furnace,
> Where on their breadth the splendour lay intense and
>   quiescent:
> Part with a fierier glow, and a short quick tremulous
>   motion,
> Like the burning pyropus; and turrets and pinnacles
>   sparkled,
> Playing in jets of light, with a diamond-like glory
>   coruscant.   (Vol. 10, p. 221)

Two witnesses against the king are summoned by the Fiend, 'the Spirit by which his righteous reign had been troubled' (p. 223). The first is recognizable as John Wilkes—'Him by the cast of his eye oblique, I knew as the firebrand/Whom the unthinking populace held for their idol and hero,/Lord of Misrule in his day' (p. 224); the second—'Nameless the libeller lived' (p. 225)—seems to be the anonymous pamphleteer Junius. Both are so conscious of their guilt that they cannot utter a word. George Washington meets the king and is reconciled to him—'Thou too didst act with upright heart' (p. 228)—and the king is received into Heaven and rejuvenated. There he meets the great sovereigns of the past—among them, Charles I— and the great writers, thinkers and statesmen of recent as well as distant times, and he is reunited with the previously deceased members of his own family. Wishing to join this happy scene, the poet awakens from his trance to find that the bell is still tolling.

Southey's poem is a dignified and diplomatic performance, but he disfigured it with a preface that was inflammatory in the extreme. Students of Byron generally single out Southey's attack on 'the Satanic school'—'those monstrous combinations of horrors and mockery, lewdness and impiety, with which English poetry has, in our days, first been polluted' (Vol. 10, p. 203)—as having stung Byron into action. Byron's own preface does concentrate upon this charge, but his poem is directed at a less personal but more serious offence. Southey was obliged by his brief to praise George III as a king and as a man. The king's madness had been a fact of public life for years and it was appropriate in reviewing the achievements of his reign to look back to his more vigorous days, to his opposition to the revolutionary politics of John Wilkes in the 1760s and 1770s, for example, and to the troubled era of the American revolution. Southey chose to represent the king's reign as one of steady resistance to the forces of anarchy, and to regard the recent defeat of Napoleon as a decisive blow to a spirit of unrest that had been disturbing the world for half a century. The dedication to King George IV is a fair example of his tone:

> We owe much to the House of Brunswick; but to none of that illustrious House more than to Your Majesty, under whose government the military renown of Great Britain has been carried to the highest point of glory. From that pure glory there has been nothing to detract. . . . The same perfect integrity has been manifested in the whole administration of public affairs . . . the Metropolis is rivalling in beauty those cities which it has long surpassed in greatness: sciences, arts, and letters are flourishing beyond all former example . . . (Vol. 10, pp. 191–2).

A certain amount of self-congratulatory patriotism may be allowed to a poet laureate, but these sentiments in the wake of the Peterloo Massacre, to say nothing of the scandalous private conduct of George IV in his days as Prince Regent, would have caused any liberal to raise a quizzical eyebrow. To Byron, convinced, as we have seen he was, of the futility of Waterloo and of the prevalence of political hypocrisy and social humbug, they must have seemed unbelievably offensive. In 'The Vision of Judgment', however, he shows no sign of ill humour. He avoids casting personal aspersions on the royal family; he remains aloof in his satire, 'laughing like Rabelais in his easy chair', and one looks in vain for any hint of malice. The effect is devastating, not to the king or even to the real Southey, but to the political assumptions and public posturings of *A Vision of Judgement*.

Byron replaces Southey's quaintly imagined Heaven with Milton's.[3] Instead of making Heaven dominant as Southey had done, Byron has the old rivalry with Hell still at an impasse. His Satan is respected as a force to reckon with. The Archangel Michael greets him:

> He turned as to an equal, not too low,
> > But kindly; Satan met his ancient friend
> With more hauteur, as might an old Castilian
> Poor Noble meet a mushroom rich civilian. (xxxvi)

St Peter, keeping the gates of Heaven, is depicted as a choleric and sleepy old fellow, showing a consciousness of class distinctions even in Heaven with his gibe at St Paul 'the parvenù!' (xx). When Satan is asked to present witnesses against the king, instead of the unsatisfactory two found with difficulty in Southey's poem, a 'cloud' of them appears:

> But such a cloud! No land ere saw a crowd
> > Of locusts numerous as the heavens saw these;

> They shadowed with their myriads Space; their loud
>   And varied cries were like those of wild geese,
> (If nations may be likened to a goose),
> And realised the phrase of 'Hell broke loose'.   (lviii)

Satan concedes the king's domestic virtues. His claim on him is that he has presided over public crimes:

> The New World shook him off; the Old yet groans
>   Beneath what he and his prepared, if not
> Completed . . . .   (xlvii)

Michael reminds Satan that 'two honest, clean,/True testimonies are enough . . .' (lxiii), and two, the same two, Wilkes and Junius, are accordingly called upon.

Byron's Wilkes is talkative without being vindictive. At first, not realizing where he is, but ever the irrepressible politician, he tries to solicit votes, beginning with St Peter's. He refuses to accuse the king whose conduct he explains 'was but natural in a prince' (lxx) and blames instead the king's ministers, who, it turns out, are already in Hell. He gives the impression of being a good-humoured and clubbable man, but his casual remarks confirm the charge of bad government. The pseudonymous Junius is described variously, in keeping with Byron's suggestion, 'that what Junius we are wont to call,/Was *really—truly*—nobody at all' (lxxx). He refers Michael to his writings and affirms gloomily, 'I loved my country, and I hated him' (lxxxiii). These exchanges are amusing even if we know nothing about Wilkes and Junius. The two men are given space enough to establish characters for themselves in our minds, and their complete indifference to the expectations of either Satan or Michael keeps the pretensions of Heaven and Hell in their place.

The arrival of Southey on the scene, flown up by a devil who has caught him writing his blasphemous poem, interrupts the flow of witnesses before Washington, Horne Tooke and Franklin can be called to give evidence. Southey himself takes the stand, but before he can begin to recite his 'spavined dactyls', Heaven is in an uproar of consternation: 'The tumult grew; an universal cough/Convulsed the skies . . .' (xciii). When he is asked to plead 'his own bad cause', he explains that 'He meant no harm in scribbling; 'twas his way/Upon all topics; 'twas, besides, his bread,/Of which he buttered both sides . . .' (xcvi). When he concludes a long recitation of the titles of the various works of contrary tendency to one another that he has written by beginning to read his latest, his 'Vision', St Peter knocks him back to earth with a blow from his keys. The character given here of Southey has been enjoyed ever since by readers who have never read a line of him. Like Pope's 'piddling Theobald' and Dryden's Shadwell who 'never deviates into sense', Southey has been immortalized as a conceited, humourless, unprincipled mangler of verse. Byron's characterization is as funny as it is unfair.

With the facts at his finger-tips, Byron was as willing to create a wounding likeness as anyone else.[4] But when he wrote 'The Vision of Judgment' he had not been in England for almost six years. He knew perfectly well that he was out of touch with its personalities and politics. He could not have written topically even if he had wanted to. The model he worked with was not topical either, because it was not a satire, and because the early date of the king's madness made it necessary to concentrate on events that had become placidly historical. Thrown on his own resources Byron communicates directly with the modern reader and releases satire for a moment from the bondage of current events.

Appendix: Chronological Table

This annotated list of significant or typical verse published each year from 1780 to 1835 may be supplemented usefully by reference to J. C. Ghosh, *Annals of English Literature 1475–1950*, 2nd edn (Oxford, 1961), and to the chronological tables in W. L. Renwick, *English Literature 1789–1815* (Oxford, 1963), and Ian Jack, *English Literature 1815–1832* (Oxford, 1963). Names of poets who published anonymously are given in square brackets; page numbers are provided as a rough guide to the size of volumes. Unless there is a comment to the contrary, poems are dated by their first appearance in book form. Blake's engraved works are dated according to the dates on their title pages. Works that are discussed at any length in the text are preceded here by an asterisk * and recorded briefly; the Index should be consulted for cross-references. Other events of literary interest are included after the verse entries.

1780

[Christopher Anstey]. *Speculation; or, a Defence of Mankind.* . . . (pp. 52)   A light-hearted but casually written satire in Hudibrastic couplets on various kinds of financial speculation—investment, lending (at the outrageous rate of 7 per cent), gambling, etc.

[James Bland Burges]. *Heroic Epistle from Serjeant Bradshaw, in the Shades, to John Dunning, Esq.* (pp. 14)   Bradshaw, the judge who arraigned Charles I, praises a modern successor.

[William Combe]. *The Fast-Day: a Lambeth Eclogue* . . . . (pp. xiii + 32)   The daily routine of Piscopella, the fashionable wife of the Archbishop of Canterbury, modelled on Pope's Belinda in *The Rape of the Lock*.

Hannah Cowley. *The Maid of Aragon; a Tale*, Part I. (pp. iv + 49)   A blank-verse Gothic romance set in crusading times about the Christian princess Osmida's attempts to escape the unwanted love of the fierce Moor, Zorador. Part II was not forthcoming.

George Crabbe. *The Candidate; a Poetical Epistle to the Authors of the Monthly Review.* (pp. 34)   A fledgling author who fears the reviewers is advised by a sage to publish cautiously. Lively and amusing.

William Hayley. *An Essay on History; in Three Epistles to Edward Gibbon, Esq* ....
(pp. 159)   An informative and judicious survey in heroic couplets, maintaining that history and poetry are allies, surveying historians from the middle ages
to the present, and summarizing the sources of weakness in history. Half the
volume consists of prose notes.

William Hayley. *Ode, Inscribed to John Howard . . . Author of 'The State of English and
Foreign Prisons'.* (pp. 19)   Praise of Howard and an account of the good effects
of some of his prison reforms.

Anna Seward. *Elegy on Captain Cook* .... (pp. 23)   Cook's fate in Otaheite
compared to the fate of Orpheus in monotonous, if irregular, heroic couplets.

Samuel Johnson's edition of *The Works of the English Poets* (1779–81) in progress.

1781

[William Cowper]. *Anti-Thelyphthora* .... (pp. 15)   A good-natured allegorical satire, in heroic couplets; one of a number of rejoinders to Martin
Madan's claim, in *Thelyphthora* (1780), that Christian men should be polygamous.

[George Crabbe]. *The Library* .... (pp. 34)   An account, in heroic couplets, of
the various kinds of books, with some critical comments.

Philip Freneau. *The British Prison-Ship.* (pp. 23) A spirited American diatribe
against the detested British tyrants.

William Hayley. *The Triumphs of Temper; a Poem. In Six Cantos.*
(pp. xii + 164)   Young Serena avoids losing her temper in spite of the three
grave frustrations of being forbidden at the last minute to go to a fancy-dress
ball, reading an unfounded scandal about herself in the newspaper, and being
insulted at another ball by Lord Filigree. She is rewarded with the hand of
Young Falkland who has attended the ball dressed as Edwin from Beattie's *The
Minstrel* (1771–4). *The Triumphs of Temper* passed through ten editions by 1800.

William Mason. *The English Garden . . . Book the Fourth.* (pp. 54)   The final
instalment of a blank-verse poem that began to appear in 1772. Attacks artificial
ornaments and prefers British taste to Classical precedents. Alcander's
picturesque garden is improved by the advice of an American lady whom he
saves from a shipwreck; on her death he devotes himself to charity.

Thomas James Mathias. *Runic Odes. Imitated from the Norse Tongue in the Manner of
Mr. Gray.* (pp. 33)

William Julius Mickle. *Almada Hill: an Epistle from Lisbon.* (pp. vii + 35)   A
celebration of Iberian history by the translator of Camoëns' *Lusiad.*

[Lady Anne Miller, ed.]. *Poetical Amusements at a Villa near Bath,* vol. 4.
(pp. xi + 219)   The last in a series of volumes sold to support charities in Bath.
It offered contributions by Edward Jerningham, Christopher Anstey, Anna
Seward, Richard Graves, William Hayley, Samuel Jackson Pratt and others.

Thomas Penrose. *Poems.* (pp. viii + 120)   This posthumous collection included a
reprinting of 'Flights of Fancy' (1775), with its supernatural enthusiasms, 'The
Helmets', 'The Carousal of Odin' and 'Madness'. Penrose follows the pre-

cedents of Gray and Thomas Warton, but was himself influential as a metrical innovator.

Anna Seward. *Monody on Major André* .... (pp. iv + 47) Having mourned Captain Cook in an elegy the year before, Miss Seward felt obliged to mourn the associate of Benedict Arnold, whom she actually knew, when he was executed as a spy by the Americans. She looks forward to the imminent fall of George Washington.

The third volume of Thomas Warton's *History of English Poetry* (1774, 1778); the surrender of General Cornwallis at Yorktown; two translations of Homer's *Hymn to Ceres*; the first volume of Robert Potter's translation of Euripides' tragedies; and an anonymous satire to interest the orthographer, entitled *Xsmwhdribunwlxy*.

1782

[William Cowper]. *'The Entertaining and Facetious History of John Gilpin .... To the Tune of—Chevy Chace', in *The Public Advertiser*, 14 November. For the enormous and immediate popularity of this work, see Norma Russell, *A Bibliography of William Cowper to 1837* (Oxford, 1963).

William Cowper. *Poems*. (pp. ii + 368) Includes 'Table Talk', 'The Progress of Error', 'Truth', 'Expostulation', 'Hope', 'Charity', 'Conversation', 'Retirement', 'Verses, Supposed to Have Been Written by Alexander Selkirk' ('I am monarch of all I survey') and 'The Poet, the Oyster, and Sensitive Plant'. The most impressive volume of verse since *The Deserted Village* in 1770.

William Hayley. *An Essay on Epic Poetry; in Five Epistles to the Rev. Mr. Mason*. (pp. 298) An informative survey in heroic couplets, expressing the hope that a modern epic may be forthcoming and stressing the importance of being able to sympathize with the characters in it.

[William Mason]. *An Archaeological Epistle to the Reverend and Worshipful Jeremiah Milles, D. D. Dean of Exeter* .... (pp. 18) An amusing spoof in which Mason translates modern English, including the beginning of *Paradise Lost* and Hamlet's 'To be or not to be' soliloquy, into the 'Archaeological style' of Chatterton by using the glossary from Milles's 1782 edition of Chatterton's Rowley poems.

[William Julius Mickle]. *The Prophecy of Queen Emma; an Ancient Ballad Lately Discovered* .... (pp. 40) More mockery of Ossian and Chatterton's Rowley with some deliberately anachronistic parallels to the recent alliance of America and France.

[John Pinkerton]. *Two Dithyrambic Odes. I. On Enthusiasm. II. To Laughter.* (pp. 12)

Anna Seward. *Poem to the Memory of Lady Miller* .... (pp. ii + 20)

[Thomas Warton]. *Verses on Sir Joshua Reynolds' Painted Window at New College, Oxford.* (pp. 8) A fine expression, in heroic couplets, of contemporary aesthetic issues, with Reynolds's 'chaste design' being praised for winning the author back from his enthusiasm for the Gothic to a more Classical taste.

[Helen Maria Williams]. *Edwin and Eltruda. A Legendary Tale.* (pp. iii + 31)

1783

W[illiam] B[lake]. *Poetical Sketches.* (pp. ii + 70)   No contemporary reference to Blake's first publication is known and he is believed to have distributed the book privately. It contains his fragment of a play in blank verse, 'King Edward the Third', the macabre ballad *'Fair Elenor', and other derivative short pieces that reveal his acquaintance with the Bible, especially the Book of Psalms, and with Milton and Shakespeare, Macpherson's *Ossian*, Gray's odes, Chatterton's Rowley poems and Spenser.

Harriet Chilcot (later Meziere). *Elmar and Ethlinda; a Legendary Tale: and Adalba and Ahmora, an Indian Tale* . . . . (pp. xxii + 90)   A typical conjunction of medieval, oriental and Peruvian tales about unfortunate lovers.

T. Coombe. *The Peasant of Auburn; or, the Emigrant.* . . . (pp. 18)   Edwin, forced into exile from Goldsmith's 'deserted village', finds unhappiness on the banks of the Ohio. The American dream turns out to be an illusion.

George Crabbe. * *The Village* . . . . (pp. 38)   An anti-pastoral 'real picture' of the rural poor with a private elegy on the younger brother of Crabbe's patron awkwardly spliced into it.

Thomas Holcroft. *Human Happiness; or the Sceptic* . . . . (pp. 76)   An improving dialogue in Hudibrastic couplets between the pessimistic Sir Thomas and his more sanguine cousin William.

[Samuel Hoole]. *Aurelia; or, the Contest* . . . . (pp. viii + 77)   A young lady stoops to use cosmetics in order to triumph over a rival, is exposed when she forgetfully agrees to dance and begins to perspire; after an admonitory dream she resolves not to disguise the passage of time.

Henry James Pye. *The Progress of Refinement* . . . . (pp. 104)   A smooth didactic survey in heroic couplets.

1784

Hugh Downman. *Editha. A Tragedy.* (pp. 87)   A complicated version of a legendary tale in which aged father and chaste daughter are pawns in a see-saw battle between the forces of good and evil and escape unharmed. The setting is a Danish invasion of England after the pattern of Chatterton's *Aella* (1777).

Edward Jerningham. *The Rise and Progress of the Scandinavian Poetry* . . . . (pp. 31)   An example of contemporary interest in the Edda.

Anna Seward. *Louisa, a Poetical Novel, in Four Epistles.* (pp. vi + 95)   A sentimental romance in which Louisa's Eugenio allows her to think him false when he marries Elmira in order to save his father from ruin. His father's debts are repaid, Elmira's death follows conveniently upon her abrupt moral decline, and the frustrated lovers marry.

Charlotte Smith. *Elegiac Sonnets, and Other Essays.* (pp. viii + 26)   Written to beguile the novelist's 'melancholy moments'. With the exception of 'The Origin of Flattery', a gloomy collection.

[Thomas Warwick]. *Edwy. A Dramatic Poem.* (pp. ii + 76)   A legendary tale disguised as an Elizabethan play and focusing on the conflicts of church with state, Rome with England, and tyranny with democracy, in what purports implausibly to be the tenth century.

Helen Maria Williams. *Peru, A Poem* . . . . (pp. viii + 95)   The Spaniards in Edenic Peru: exotic setting, primitivism, cruel imperialists, superstitious bigotry, battle, imprisonment, torture, death through despair, suicide, children separated from parents, lovers and loyal friends parted—in short the epic pathetic.

Death of Samuel Johnson.

1785

[William Combe]. *The Royal Dream; or the P----- in a Panic* . . . . (pp. xii + 24)   Florello—the future George IV—is visited in a dream by his ancestors. They advise him to drink, eat, whore and gamble before the responsibilities of the crown force him to reform; the notes inform us that he has anticipated their advice.

William Cowper. *Poems*, vol. 2.   (pp. viii + 360)   Includes * *The Task*; 'Tirocinium: or, a Review of Schools'—Cowper's criticism of the moral weaknesses of the education of the wealthy at public schools (he argues for their reform rather than for abolition)—and a reprinting of 'The Diverting History of John Gilpin'. (Subsequent London editions of the *Poems* appeared in 1786, 1787, 1788, 1793, 1794–5, 1798, 1799, 1800–1.)

George Crabbe. *The News-paper: a Poem.* (pp. viii + 29)   An amusing and comprehensive sketch of contemporary newspapers, in heroic couplets, and a pleasing companion piece to Cowper's description in Book IV of *The Task*.

[Samuel Jackson Pratt]. *Landscapes in Verse. Taken in Spring* . . . . (pp. viii + 63)   Theodorus imagines a walk taken with his absent Cleone; a mawkish tale of true rustic love interrupted by drowning and madness is included.

John Sargent. *The Mine: a Dramatic Poem.* (pp. xvi + 63)   When Count Maurice is condemned unjustly to hard labour in a mine, his wife, Juliana, follows him incognito and looks after him without being recognized. The underground setting is replete with geological imagery—Sargent cites John Aikin's *Essay on the Poetical Use of Natural History* as support—and with gnomes borrowed from the Cave of Spleen in *The Rape of the Lock*. Eventually, after trials and adventures, both are released and reunited.

[John Wolcot] Peter Pindar. *The Lousiad: an Heroi-Comic Poem*, Canto I. (pp. 39)   On the commotion caused when a louse falls on King George's plate, with various amusing scandalous and politically partisan asides and a lively frontispiece by Wigstead.

Ann Yearsley. *Poems, on Several Occasions. By . . . a Milkwoman of Bristol.* (pp. xxx + 127)   Derivative verses by an 'illiterate' protégée of Hannah More:

'You will find her, like all unlettered Poets, abounding in imagery, metaphor, and personification . . .' (p. vii). A mildly feminist example of the vogue for 'woodnotes wild'.

1786

Roberts Burns. *Poems, Chiefly in the Scottish Dialect.* (pp. xvii + 240)   Includes most of the poems for which Burns is now known: 'The Holy Faire', 'Address to the Deil', *'The Cotter's Saturday Night', 'To a Mouse', 'Man was made to mourn', 'To a Mountain-Daisy', 'To a Louse', 'Epistle to J[ohn] L[aprai]k'. A brief glossary is included at the end, following the precedent of Chatterton's Rowley poems.

[Hannah More]. *Florio: a Tale, for Fine Gentlemen and Fine Ladies* . . . . (pp. v + 89)   A fashionable but not vicious young man chooses provincial virtue and renounces city vice. The volume also contains 'The Bas Bleu: or, Conversation', in praise of Mrs Vesey's blue-stocking salon.

T. C. Rickman. *The Fallen Cottage* . . . . (pp. xviii + 26)   Reflections on the advantages of rural life and worries about its decay—in the wake of *The Deserted Village* with hints from Thomson, Beattie and Cowper.

Helen Maria Williams. *Poems. In Two Volumes.* (pp. 116 and 202)   A miscellany, most of which is devoted to rehearsing sentimental feelings.

[John Williams]. *The Children of Thespis* . . . . (pp. 67)   Doggerel dialogue between Covent Garden and Drury Lane on the shortcomings of their respective performers.

[John Wolcot] Peter Pindar. *Bozzy and Piozzi, or the British Biographers* . . . . (pp. 54)   Sir John Hawkins is imagined presiding over the rival anecdotes about Dr. Johnson offered by Boswell and Mrs Piozzi (formerly Mrs Thrale). Johnson visits Hawkins in a dream to instruct Hawkins to silence them. Hawkins tries to and then hurries off to write his own biography of Johnson.

1787

L[uke] Booker. *The Highlanders* . . . . (pp. x + 31)   An attempt to arouse sympathy for people living in abject circumstances in the Highlands.

Robert Burns. *Poems, Chiefly in the Scottish Dialect.* 2nd edn (pp. lvii + 368)   Adds 'The Brigs of Ayr', 'To a Haggis', 'Address to the Unco Guid'.

Robert Burns. First songs contributed to James Johnson's *Scots Musical Museum.*

Samuel Hoole. *Edward; or, the Curate* . . . . (pp. 49)   A lugubrious moral tale in Spenserian stanzas; in the school of *The Minstrel.*

Robert Merry. *Paulina; or, the Russian Daughter* . . . . (pp. iv + 55)   A departure from Merry's usual Della Cruscan prettinesses into a surreptitious amour, accidental death, brutal lust and vengeful murder.

[John Ogilvie]. *The Fane of the Druids* . . . . (pp. viii + 50)   A compilation of all that was known about the Druids—citing source materials—with the love story of Edgar and Florella and, unexpectedly, a rejection of modern life in favour of the worthier primitivism of the South Seas.

Theophilus Swift. *The Temple of Folly* . . . . (pp. xvi + 96)   The poet dreams allegorically of contemporary social vices and fashionable amusements.

Ann Yearsley. *Poems on Various Subjects, by . . . a Milkwoman of Bristol* . . . . (pp. xl + 168)

1788

[Christopher Anstey]. *Liberality; or, the Decayed Macaroni. A Sentimental Piece.* (pp. 12)   A spendthrift claims merely to have been good-natured.

Robert Burns. 'The Birks of Aberfeldy', 'O'er the water to Charlie', and other songs in the *Scots Musical Museum*, vol. 2.

William Collins. 'An Ode on the Popular Superstitions of the Highlands of Scotland'. Published posthumously with notes and missing stanzas supplied by Henry Mackenzie in *Transactions of the Royal Society of Edinburgh*.

[William Crowe]. *Lewesdon Hill* . . . . (pp. iv + 29)

[James Hurdis]. *The Village Curate* . . . . (pp. 144)   Rural life arranged by season with reflections of a pious sort modelled on *The Task*.

Hugh Mulligan. *Poems Chiefly on Slavery and Oppression* . . . . (pp. iii + 90)   A series of 'eclogues'—Asiatic, European and American—in which the lives of oppressed people and races are a reproach to the oppressors.

[Samuel Jackson Pratt]. *Humanity, or the Rights of Nature* . . . . (pp. iv + 114)   The progress of British liberty chronicled in the hope of having it extended to slaves.

Thomas Sedgwick Whalley. *Mont Blanc: an Irregular Lyric Poem* . . . . (pp. 57)

[John Wolcot] Peter Pindar. *Sir Joseph Banks and the Emperor of Morocco* . . . . (pp. 27)   Elaborate mockery of the president of the Royal Society as foolish virtuoso.

William Blake. *All Religions are One*, prose pamphlet, and *There is No Natural Religion*, an emblem book, both dated conjecturally 1788–94.

1789

William Blake. **The Book of Thel.* (plates 8)

William Blake. *Songs of Innocence.* (plates 31)   Includes *'The Echoing Green', *'The Little Black Boy', 'The Little Boy Lost', 'The Blossom', 'The Nurse's Song', 'Laughing Song', 'Divine Image', *'The Chimney Sweeper', *'Holy Thursday', 'The Little Boy Found', *'The Lamb', and 'Infant Joy'.

W[illiam] L[isle] Bowles. *Sonnets, Written Chiefly on Picturesque Spots* . . . . (pp. 31)   Elegiac verse related to landscapes.

W[illiam] L[isle] Bowles. *Verses to John Howard* . . . . (pp. ii + 17)   Praise of Howard's efforts towards the reform of prisons.

[Erasmus Darwin]. *The Botanic Garden, Part II. Containing the Loves of the Plants.* (pp. xx + 184)   Part I was published in 1791. The Linnaean botany is introduced systematically, in heroic couplets, with male and female plants being personified and endowed with appropriate characters. A popular didactic work abounding in moral and scientific digressions.

Richard Hole. *Arthur; or, the Northern Enchantment* . . .   (pp. xvi + 253)   Romantic narrative in heroic couplets, based on a literal interpretation of Spenser and Ariosto, with debts to Ossian, the Arabian Nights and Scandinavian mythology.

[Hector MacNeill], *The Harp. A Legendary Tale* . . . . (pp. 24)   A feeble explanation of the Hebridean saying 'I'll never burn my harp for a woman'.

Joseph Sterling. *Poems* . . . . (pp. xii + 232)   A briefer edition appeared in Dublin in 1787. Includes a re-telling and completion of Chaucer's and Spenser's tales of Cambuscan, and 'Odes from the Icelandic' after Gray.

[John Wolcot] Peter Pindar. *Subjects for Painters.* (pp. ii + 105)   A miscellany of moral tales mocking fashionable life.

Revolution in France.

1790

W[illiam] L[isle] Bowles. *The Grave of Howard* . . . . (pp. 11)   An elegy for the great prison reformer.

Robert Burns. 'Whistle o'er the lave o't', 'My heart's in the Highlands', 'John Anderson my Jo', 'Awa whigs awa', and other songs in the *Scots Musical Museum*, vol. 3.

[James Hurdis]. *Adriano; or, the First of June* . . . . (pp. 105)   A sentimental legendary tale in a modern setting, with impressive scenes of storm and sea.

Robert Merry. *The Laurel of Liberty* . . . . (pp. vi + 32)   A celebration of the democratic possibilities of revolutionary France with a reminder of the bad effects—in England, Florence and America—of social inequality.

Frank Sayers. *Dramatic Sketches of the Ancient Northern Mythology.* (pp. iv + 112).

[John Williams] Anthony Pasquin. *A Postscript to the New Bath Guide* . . . . (pp. 152)   Comic and satirical epistolary anecdotes from Bath in Christopher Anstey's vein.

[John Wolcot] Peter Pindar. *Advice to the Future Laureat: an Ode* . . . . (pp. 18)   Speculations about Thomas Warton's successor and suggestions for topics that will make him popular at court—animal husbandry, etc.

[John Wolcot] Peter Pindar. *A Benevolent Epistle to Sylvanus Urban* . . . . (pp. ii + 34)   An ironical attack on the editor of *The Gentleman's Magazine*, to which is added an amusing account of the attempt of the President of the Royal Society to prove that lobsters were related to fleas—'Sir Joseph Banks and the Boiled Fleas'.

1791

John Aikin. *Poems.* (pp. x + 136)   A miscellany containing some of the earliest English imitations of Bürger's Gothic ballads—'Duncan's Warning', 'Susanna's Vigil' and 'Arthur and Matilda'.

William Blake. *The French Revolution* . . . . (pp. 16)   Only one copy of the page proofs of Book I exists. A dramatization of the confrontation between the National Assembly and the crown.

William Lisle Bowles. **Monody, Written at Matlock, October 1791.* (pp. 20)

Robert Burns. *'Tam o'Shanter. A Tale', in *The Edinburgh Magazine, The Edinburgh Herald* and in Francis Grose's *The Antiquities of Scotland.*

[Erasmus Darwin]. *The Botanic Garden; A Poem, in Two Parts. Part I. Containing the Economy of Vegetation. Part II. The Loves of the Plants* . . . . (pp. xii + 214 + 126) Part II had been published separately in 1789. This handsome quarto, containing illustrations by Fuseli—one of them engraved by William Blake—attempted, with some success, to make natural science attractive. Its poetic model is *The Rape of the Lock.*

[William Gifford]. *The Baviad, a Periphrastic Imitation of the First Satire of Persius.* (pp. 51)   Personal satire in the tradition of *The Dunciad,* mocking the sentimentality of the Della Cruscans and their periodical, *The World,* satirizing the intellectual pretensions of the blue-stockings and others, and wishing for the unadorned simplicity of earlier writers.

[George Huddesford]. *Salmagundi* . . . . (pp. iv + 151)   A miscellany containing some high-spirited and occasionally indelicate doggerel. The 'Monody on the Death of Dick, an Academical Cat' will be appreciated by those who enjoy Christopher Smart's verses on Jeoffry.

Mary Robinson. *Poems,* vol. I. (pp. xxiv + 223)   Fashionable verse.

James Boswell, *Life of Johnson;* William Cowper, trans., *The Iliad* and *The Odyssey;* George Ellis, ed., *Specimens of the Early English Poets;* Edmond Malone, ed., *The Plays and Poems of William Shakespeare,* 10 vols; Thomas Paine, *The Rights of Man,* Part I; Joseph Ritson, *Ancient Popular Poetry; The Rolliad* (collected from newspapers from 1784 on, satire in verse and prose).

1792

William Blake. 'A Song of Liberty'. (plates 3—usually appended to *The Marriage of Heaven and Hell* (1793). It is believed to have been occasioned by the failure of anti-revolutionary armies to invade France in 1792.

Robert Burns. 'The Banks o' Doon', 'Afton Water', 'The Deil's awa wi' the Exciseman', and other songs, in the *Scots Musical Museum,* vol. 4.

Richard Cumberland. *Calvary; or the Death of Christ* . . . . (pp. 291)   A sequel to *Paradise Regained,* now interesting mainly for its harrowing of Hell scene in Book VII which anticipates similar scenes in Landor and Southey.

George Dyer. *Poems.* (pp. viii + 55)   Anticipations of Coleridge and Wordsworth by Lamb's eccentric Cambridge friend.

[Sarah] Farrell. *Charlotte, or, A Sequel to the Sorrows of Werter* . . . .
(pp. x + 80)   Charlotte dies of grief on Werter's grave—polite Gothicism; with
other poems of the same kidney.

[Susannah] Gunning (formerly Minifie). *Virginius and Virginia* . . . .
(pp. x + 65)   Livy's story of Appius and Virginia is treated in sentimental
terms.

Edward Jerningham. *Abelard to Eloisa* . . . . (pp. vii + 15)   A weak re-run of
Jerningham's *Arabert, Monk of La Trappe* (1771); comparison with Pope's *Eloisa
to Abelard* makes Jerningham seem thin indeed.

George Richards. *Songs of the Aboriginal Bards of Britain.* (pp. iv + 28)   In the
tradition of Gray's odes and William Mason's play *Caractacus* (1759).

[Samuel Rogers]. *The Pleasures of Memory* . . . . (pp. vi + 71)   This popular
poem, which went through four editions in its first year and was in its fifteenth in
1806, established a fame which Rogers continued to enjoy until his death in
1855.

[John Wolcot] Peter Pindar. *The Tears of St. Margaret* . . . . (pp. vi + 47) Amusing
collection of satires on current events.

John Hoole, trans., Tasso's *Rinaldo*; Mary Wollstonecraft, *Vindication of the Rights of
Women.*

1793

William Blake. *America a Prophecy.* (plates 18)   An allegorical rendering of the
American revolution in which the activities of Washington and King George
claim a place beside the awakening of red Orc, the personification of revolution,
and the uneasy stirring of the repressive Urizen. An early example of Blake's
private myth.

William Blake. *For Children: the Gates of Paradise.* (plates 18)   An emblem book.

William Blake. *Visions of the Daughters of Albion.* (plates 11)   The adulterous love
of Oothoon for Bromion is presented in terms of the conflict between instinctive
desires and repressive restraints. Analogies are drawn with America and slavery.

Robert Burns. *Poems, Chiefly in the Scottish Dialect.* 2nd edn enlarged, 2 vols.   Adds
'On seeing a Wounded Hare' and 'The Whistle'.

Robert Burns. 'Here awa, there awa' and other songs, in *A Select Collection of
Original Scotish Airs*, vol. 1.

[George Huddesford]. *Topsy Turvy* . . . . (pp. iv + 56)   A satire on revolutionary
ideals in which the viciousness of French politics is documented and mocked.

George Richards. *Modern France* . . . . (pp. 19)   A companion piece for *The
Aboriginal Britons* (1791), lamenting the fall of France into anarchy.

Charlotte Smith. *The Emigrants* . . . . (pp. xii + 68)   The plight of the French
émigrés is used as a reminder of the need for reforms in England.

William Wordsworth. *Descriptive Sketches. In Verse. Taken During a Pedestrian Tour in
the Italian, Grison, Swiss, and Savoyard Alps.* (pp. iv + 55)   A slim, gentleman's
quarto in heroic couplets. Descriptions of landscape are combined with
sympathetic reflections on the lives of the ordinary people who live in the midst

of it. Democratic sentiment is muted but apparent even in the decision to make the Grand Tour on foot.

William Wordsworth. *An Evening Walk* . . . . (pp. iv + 27)   Another quarto in heroic couplets. The combination of landscape setting and the occupations of the poor is observed in the Lake District. This poem and *Descriptive Sketches* were later drawn upon as materials for *The Prelude* (1850).

[William Blake]. *The Marriage of Heaven and Hell* (dated conjecturally 1790–93)   This prose work is often used as a central resource in the interpretation of Blake's poetry. William Godwin, *An Enquiry Concerning the Principles of Political Justice* . . ., 2 vols; Joseph Ritson, ed., *The English Anthology*.

1794

William Blake. *Europe a Prophecy.* (plates 18)   An allegory of the confrontation of Britain and revolutionary France, in which Albion's angel opposes fiery Orc, and the repressive Enitharmon rejoices over the perversion of revolutionary freedoms.

William Blake. *Songs of Innocence and of Experience* . . . . (plates 54)—see also 1789   The previously published *Songs of Innocence* are juxtaposed with the 'Songs of Experience', *'The Lamb' with *'The Tyger', one *'Holy Thursday' with another, one *'The Chimney Sweeper' with another, and so on. *'The Nurse's Song', 'London', 'The Clod and the Pebble' and 'The Sick Rose', also appear for the first time. The various copies of this book vary in contents, arrangement and colouring.

William Blake. *The First Book of Urizen.* (plates 28)   A retelling of the myth of *Genesis*, with Urizen, as a God gone wrong, creating the material world in a spirit of misery and Los as Adam suffering but resisting.

Samuel Taylor Coleridge [and Robert Southey]. *The Fall of Robespierre. An Historic Drama.* (pp. 37)   The first act of this blank-verse tragedy was by Coleridge; acts II and III were Southey's. Coleridge's part concentrates on the domestic feelings and consciences of the revolutionary leaders; Southey brings a touch of the Ossianic sublime to their public appearances.

Samuel Taylor Coleridge. 'Monody on the Death of Chatterton', in *Poems by Thomas Rowley*, ed. Lancelot Sharpe.

Robert Jephson. *Roman Portraits, A Poem, in Heroick Verse* . . . . (pp. xxxvi + 277)   A didactic survey of Roman history with a sceptical view of Roman politics and comparisons with that modern republic, France.

Edward Jerningham. *The Siege of Berwick, a Tragedy* . . . . (pp. viii + 68)   A play about two sons in which father, mother, and the brothers themselves, are each in turn called on to decide which son shall die. Our heart strings having been exercised, the two miraculously survive.

Richard Payne Knight. *The Landscape, A Didactic Poem* . . . . (pp. 77)   Opposes the picturesque meddling of Humphrey Repton, Capability Brown and Sir William Chambers; prefers the native trees and shrubs to foreign imports, the mellowing of time to the rudeness of innovation. An argument, in landscape

277

terms, for the vernacular rather than the Classical, the empirical rather than the
ideal, and for the British constitution rather than the French Revolution.

[Thomas James Mathias]. *The Pursuits of Literature, or What You Will: a Satirical
Poem in Dialogue.* Part the First. (pp. iv + 40) Mockery of Hayley, Darwin,
Percy, Chatterton and Shakespearean scholarship—the polite and antiquarian
sectors—and praise for Pope, Gray, Mason and, unexpectedly, Thomas
Penrose. Elaborate and amusing prose notes.

Edward Williams. *Poems, Lyric and Pastoral,* 2 vols. (pp. xxxix + 216 and
viii + 256) A competent miscellany of poems by a 'self-tutored Journeyman
Mason' from Wales.

Robert Anderson, ed., *The Works of the British Poets,* 13 vols.

1795

William Blake. *The Book of Ahania.* (plates 5) Blake's retelling of *Exodus.* Fuzon
rebels against the repressive Urizen, dividing him from Ahania, his soul, but is
himself destroyed and his body is nailed to the 'Tree of Mystery'. Ahania
laments being separated from Urizen.

William Blake. *The Book of Los.* (plates 5) Los breaks free from his bondage and
falls 'thro' the void' and gradually assumes a physical state. He starts to work as
a blacksmith at a forge and begins to bind Urizen.

William Blake. *The Song of Los.* (plates 8) A lament for the fall of man and the rise
of science and philosophy. The revolutionary Orc escapes from his bondage.

[William Gifford]. *The Maeviad.* (pp. 62) General mockery of the Della Cruscan
poets continued from *The Baviad* (1791). Pope's spirit is invoked and hopes are
expressed for the compositions of John Burgoyne and William Mason.

Walter Savage Landor. *Poems.* (pp. vii + 217) A miscellany marked by democratic sentiments and containing the 'Birth of Poesy' with its unusual echoes
of Ovid, Catullus and Dryden and anticipations of Moore, Hunt and Keats.

Robert Lovell and Robert Southey. *Poems* . . . . (pp. viii + 131) Most notable for
Southey's charming but insufficiently polished poem 'The Retrospect', and a
mixture of Scandinavian sublimities after Gray and Ossian.

[Thomas James Mathias]. *The Imperial Epistle from Kien Long, Emperor of China, to
George the Third* . . . .(pp. x + 37) Ironical praise for recent repressive measures
from one tyrant to another. In heroic couplets.

John Thelwall. *Poems Written in Close Confinement in the Tower and Newgate, Under a
Charge of High Treason.* (pp. iv + 32) Uninspired verse of political protest by a
man whose life influenced better poets.

1796

Gottfried Augustus Bürger. Translations of his Gothic ballads *'Lenore', 'The
Chase' and *'The Fair Lass of Wone', by various enthusiasts; among them
Walter Scott, W. R. Spencer, William Taylor and Henry Pye.

Robert Burns. 'Comin thro the rye', 'Blue Bonnets', 'Bannocks o' bear meal' and other songs, in the *Scots Musical Museum*, vol. 5.

Samuel Taylor Coleridge. *Ode on the Departing Year.* (pp. 16)   A libertarian attack on Britain's international misconduct.

Samuel Taylor Coleridge. *Poems on Various Subjects.* (pp. xvi + 188)   A considerable range of styles with a predominantly sentimental cast. 'Religious Musings' and 'The Eolian Harp' are the most substantial poems, apart from the 'Monody on the Death of Chatterton', which is reprinted.

Samuel Taylor Coleridge. 'Reflections on Having Left a Place of Retirement', in *The Monthly Magazine.*

William Gilbert. *The Hurricane: a Theosophical and Western Eclogue* . . . . (pp. 105)   A Swedenborgian analysis of the relation of America to Europe. Each country is represented as having a distinct personal character. Deliberate violations of the metrical regularity of the blank verse are presented in a Blakean spirit. This eccentric and sometimes ludicrous poem with its assertive missionary notes was well known in Bristol during the residence of Southey and Coleridge there.

Richard Payne Knight. *The Progress of Civil Society. A Didactic Poem* . . . . (pp. xxiv + 155)   A sensible but dull survey in heroic couplets.

M. G. Lewis. *'Alonzo the Brave and Fair Imogene' and 'The Water-King', both Gothic ballads, in his novel *The Monk: A Romance.*

[Thomas James Mathias]. *The Pursuits of Literature*, parts 2 and 3. (For part 1, see 1794.)

Robert Merry. *The Pains of Memory* . . . . (pp. 36)   A companion piece for Rogers's *Pleasures* of 1792; competent but gloomy reflective verse.

[Richard Polwhele]. *The Influence of Local Attachment With Respect to Home* . . . . (pp. ii + 68)   Interesting for its early use of association theory.

Anna Seward. *Llangollen Vale, with Other Poems.* (pp. ii + 48)   The romantic and superstitious past of this lovely spot and the enlightened life of two of its present inhabitants, that 'peerless twain', Lady Eleanor and Miss Ponsonby.

Robert Southey. *Joan of Arc, an Epic Poem.* (pp. xi + 409)   A celebration of the just defeat of England by France that is topical without being tendentious. Joan's vision, 450 lines of Book II, was contributed by Coleridge.

Alexander Thomson. *The Paradise of Taste.* (pp. xv + 124)   An allegory in varying measures in which groups of authors are visited in landscapes suited to their muse. Goethe is found with Sterne and Richardson in the Vale of Pity. Homer and Milton are to be found on the summit of the Mountain of Sublimity, and Pindar, Dryden and Gray farther down. Shakespeare occupies a rock on the Island of Fancy.

Death of Burns.

1797

William Blake. *The Four Zoas* . . . . (pp. 139)   Also known as *Vala*. The manuscript of this unfinished and unpublished poem is written on proof-sheets of

Blake's engravings for an edition of Young's *Night Thoughts*. Blake is believed to have worked on it from 1797 to 1800, making revisions until 1803 and a few changes thereafter. The poem overlaps in subject matter with *Jerusalem* (1804) and *Milton* (1804) and is an indispensable resource for the student of Blake's mythical figures.

Samuel Taylor Coleridge. *Poems, Second Edition. To Which are Now Added Poems by Charles Lamb, and Charles Lloyd.* (pp. xx + 278) 'To Charles Lloyd, on His Proposing to Domesticate with the Author', and 'On the Christening of a Friend's Child' are included; 'Reflections on Having Left a Place of Retirement' is reprinted.

George Colman the Younger. *My Night-Gown and Slippers; or Tales in Verse.* (pp. 33) Humorous verse with a rustic spoof of the Gothic ballads, 'The Maid of the Moor, or the Water-Fiends'.

[Thomas James Mathias]. *The Pursuits of Literature . . . Part the Fourth and Last.* (pp. 104) Satire of contemporary writing continued. (For previous parts, see 1794 and 1796.)

[Richard Polwhele]. *The Old English Gentleman . . . .* (pp. vii + 146) A vanishing and valuable social institution is glimpsed in Cornwall—a country squire after the fashion of Goldsmith's Hardcastle in *She Stoops to Conquer*.

Robert Southey. *Poems.* (pp. viii + 220) A miscellany of social protest—'Poems on the Slave Trade', 'Botany Bay Eclogues', etc.—Gothic ballads—'Donica', 'Rudiger', 'Mary'—and occasional verses.

The Anti-Jacobin commenced publication; *Icelandic Poetry, or the Edda of Saemund*, trans. A. S. Cottle; *The Satires of Persius*, trans. William Drummond; Gilbert Wakefield's edition of Lucretius, *De Rerum Natura*, completed in 3 vols.

1798

Samuel Taylor Coleridge. **Fears in Solitude . . . To Which are Added, France, an Ode; and *Frost at Midnight.* (pp. iv + 23)

Joseph Cottle. *Malvern Hills: a Poem.* (pp. 71) Blank-verse reflections in a landscape.

[Walter Savage Landor]. *Gebir; a Poem in Seven Books.* (pp. ii + 74) Pronounced 'jébber'. Striking treatment of a story by Clara Reeve, set in Egypt and replete with nymph, sorceress, shepherd, king and princess, as well as a journey into the underworld and a flight through the sky.

Charles Lloyd and Charles Lamb. *Blank Verse.* (pp. 95) Includes Lamb's 'The Old Familiar Faces' and 'Composed at Midnight'.

Henry James Pye. *Naucratia; or Naval Dominion . . . .* (pp. 76) A historical survey in heroic couplets of ships from the time of the Deluge to the present with the British navy keeping France at bay.

[Samuel Rogers]. *An Epistle to a Friend, with Other Poems.* (pp. 47) Describes retired life at his country retreat, to illustrate 'the virtue of True Taste'.

[William Wordsworth and Samuel Taylor Coleridge]. *Lyrical Ballads, with a Few Other Poems*. (pp. x + 210)   Includes *'The Rime of the Ancyent Marinere', 'The Foster-Mother's Tale', 'The Convict', 'The Nightingale' (in some copies 'Lewti') by Coleridge, and by Wordsworth, 'Lines Left upon a Seat in a Yew-Tree', 'The Female Vagrant', 'Goody Blake and Harry Gill', 'Simon Lee', 'Anecdote for Fathers', *'We are Seven', *'The Thorn', *'The Idiot Boy', 'Expostulation and Reply', 'The Tables Turned', 'The Complaint of the Forsaken Indian Woman', and *'Lines Written a Few Miles above Tintern Abbey'.

Malthus, *Principles of Population*; Wieland, *Oberon* (1780) was translated into Spenserian stanzas by William Sotheby. For the remarkable and immediate influence of this poem on English verse, see Werner W. Beyer, *The Enchanted Forest* (Oxford, 1963). See also Beyer's *Keats and the Demon King* (New York, 1947)

1799

The Annual Anthology, vol. I. (pp. vi + 300)   By various hands and edited by Southey. Includes Southey's 'You are old, Father William', and his Gothic 'Bishop Bruno'.

Luke Booker. *The Hop Garden, a Didactic Poem*. (pp. vi + 118)   A blank-verse successor to John Philips's *Cyder* of 1708; its short narrative vignettes would have suited *The Annual Anthology*.

Thomas Campbell. *The Pleasures of Hope; with Other Poems*. (pp. viii + 135)   After *The Pleasures of Memory*. Includes 'Gilderoy' and 'The Harper'.

[George Huddesford]. *Bubble and Squeak, a Galli-Maufry of British Beef with the Chopp'd Cabbage of Gallic Philosophy and Radical Reform*. (pp. 55)   Lively anti-Jacobin doggerel.

[George Huddesford]. *Crambe Repetita, A Second Course of Bubble and Squeak . . . .* (pp. ii + 83)   Attacks Charles James Fox and the Pro-French Whigs.

[Thomas Maurice]. *Grove-Hill, a Descriptive Poem . . . .* (pp. vi + 76)   A country estate surveyed from a series of picturesque vantage points, with reflections intermixed.

Poetry of the Anti-Jacobin. (pp. iv + 240)   Includes parody of Southey's sapphics in 'The Friend of Humanity and the Knife-Grinder', his dactylics in 'The Soldier's Friend', of Darwin in 'The Loves of the Triangles' and of Kotzebue's sentimental German tragedies—seven of which were performed in London in 1799—in 'The Rovers or the Double Arrangement'.

Anna Seward. *Original Sonnets on Various Subjects . . . .* (pp. x + 179)   A respectable attempt to revive the form.

Robert Southey. *Poems. The Second Volume*. (pp. 232)   The same mixture as in vol. 1. *'English Eclogues', Gothic ballads—'Jaspar', 'Lord William', 'The Old Woman of Berkeley' and the parody of it, 'The Surgeon's Warning'—and social protest—'The Complaints of the Poor', 'The Sailor's Mother', 'The Sailor Who Had Served in the Slave Trade', *'The Ruined Cottage'.

[Robert Southey and Samuel Taylor Coleridge]. 'The Devil's Thoughts' in *The Morning Post*.

1800

The Annual Anthology. Volume II. (pp. iv + 299)   Edited by Robert Southey. Includes Coleridge's 'This Lime-Tree Bower', 'Lines Written in the Album at Elbingerode', 'The British Stripling's War Song', 'Something Childish but Very Natural'; 'Lewti' and 'Fire, Famine and Slaughter' are reprinted from *The Morning Post* of 1798; Southey's monodrama 'Lucretia', his 'God's Judgment on a Bishop', and 'The Show, an English Eclogue'—printed sideways on the page to accommodate its dactylic hexameters; and Mary Robinson's Gothic-sentimental 'Jasper'.

Anon. *Tales of Terror.* (pp. ii + 149)   A collection of Gothic ballads, mostly but not entirely parodic. M. G. Lewis is sometimes credited with these, incorrectly. The title page is misleadingly dated 1801.

Robert Bloomfield. *The Farmer's Boy; a Rural Poem.* (pp. xvi + 102)   The life of Giles, an orphan farm labourer, described season by season in heroic couplets. Bloomfield writes from experience, but his point of view is truer to the city shoemaker he was than to a genuine farmer's, and like most self-taught poets he leans heavily on previous writers.

[Robert Burns]. Contributions to *Merry Muses of Caledonia*, a collection of bawdy songs for a drinking club.

Samuel Taylor Coleridge, trans. Friedrich Schiller's *The Piccolomini . . .* (pp. viii + 216) and *The Death of Wallenstein . . . .* (pp. viii + 157)   A beautiful, if very occasionally inaccurate, blank-verse translation that brings out Schiller's affinities to Shakespeare's history plays.

James Hurdis. *The Favorite Village.* (pp. iv + 210)   Another sentimental account of country life arranged season by season with pious digressions.

Thomas Moore, trans. *Odes of Anacreon.* (pp. xx + 255)   This handsome quarto gained entrance to respectable homes where the delicate and occasionally erotic hedonism of the verses achieved a mildly scandalous reputation. The annotations, in Greek, Latin, French and German, lend balance to the frivolity. The author was known henceforth as 'Anacreon' Moore.

Mary Robinson. *Lyrical Tales.* (pp. ii + 218)   A miscellany of sentimental and Gothic verse issued by the publisher of *Lyrical Ballads* and *The Annual Anthology*. It includes *'All Alone' and 'The Deserted Cottage'. Mrs Robinson has a good ear.

William Wordsworth. *Lyrical Ballads, with Other Poems*, 2 vols. (pp. xlvi + 215 and iv + 227)   Wordsworth acknowledges his authorship, adds his now famous 'Preface' and includes the following new poems: 'Hart-leap Well', 'There was a Boy', 'The Brothers', 'Strange Fits of Passion I have Known', 'A Slumber Did My Spirit Seal', 'Lucy Gray', 'The Idle Shepherd-Boys', 'Two April Mornings', 'Nutting', 'The Old Cumberland Beggar', 'Poems on the Naming of Places',

*'Michael, a Pastoral', and Coleridge's 'Love'. (Subsequent editions in 1802 and 1805.)

Death of Cowper.

1801

Thomas Campbell. 'Ye Mariners of England', in *The Morning Chronicle.*

[Hannah] Cowley. *The Siege of Acre. An Epic Poem* . . . . (pp. 156)   A celebration in heroic couplets of the successful defence of Acre against the French.

Leigh Hunt. *Juvenilia; or, a Collection of Poems. Written Between the Ages of Twelve and Sixteen.* (pp. xxiv + 209)   A miscellany, including 'The Palace of Pleasure; an Allegorical Poem . . . Written in Imitation of Spenser', which seems to owe as much to Thomson's *Castle of Indolence* as to Spenser.

W. H. Ireland. *Ballads in Imitation of the Ancient.* (pp. 201)   The unthinking reliance on form that marked Ireland's Shakespearean forgeries is exhibited once more.

M. G. Lewis, ed. * *Tales of Wonder*, 2 vols. (pp. ii + 236 and ii + 245)   Gothic ballads, including Walter Scott's 'Glenfinlas', and *The Eve of St. John'; translations from Goethe, and Bürger; and, in the second volume, examples of older ballads from Mallet to Burns.

[Thomas Moore]. *The Poetical Works of the Late Thomas Little, Esq.* (pp. xx + 175)   Love songs, drinking songs, Gothic ballads—among them, 'The Ring'.

[Mary] Robinson. *Memoirs of the Late Mrs. Robinson*, 4 vols.   Contains some verse, including Coleridge's 'A Stranger Minstrel' and 'Mrs. Robinson to the Poet Coleridge'.

Robert Southey. *Thalaba the Destroyer*, 2 vols. (pp. xiv + 314 and 327)   An Arabian romance in irregular metres that are derived from Frank Sayers, *Dramatic Sketches of the Ancient Northern Mythology* (1790). Thalaba thwarts the attempts of the evil magicians of Domdaniel to exterminate the race of which he is the last survivor. A magic ring helps him to survive various ingenious attacks, but when he is taunted for his reliance on magic he throws the ring away and relies instead on the talisman of faith. After various harrowing experiences, including a period of madness, Thalaba overthrows the Domdaniel and is received into heaven. This remarkable if finally unsatisfying poem brings the worlds of Beckford's *Vathek* (1786) and Landor's *Gebir* within the fold of conventional verse. The effects may be traced through Shelley.

1802

Joanna Baillie. *A Series of Plays: In Which It is Attempted To Delineate the Stronger Passions of the Mind* . . ., vol. 2. (pp. xii + 478)   Contains the blank-verse tragedy 'Ethwald' in which the passion is ambition.

[Anne Bannerman]. *Tales of Superstition and Chivalry.* (pp. iv + 144)   Gothic ballads.

Robert Bloomfield. *Rural Tales, Ballads, and Songs.* (pp. xiv + 105)   Stories of rustic life, Gothic ballads, patriotic and sentimental songs.

Samuel Taylor Coleridge. *'Dejection: an Ode' and *'Hymn before Sun-Rise . . .', in *The Morning Post.*

George Colman, the Younger. *Broad Grins* . . . . (pp. viii + 125)   A new edition of *My Night-Gown and Slippers* adding his ribald poem 'The Knight and the Friar'.

[John Finlay]. *Wallace; or, the Vale of Ellerslie* . . . . (pp. 127)   The boyhood of a patriotic revolutionary, in Spenserian stanzas, modelled on Beattie's *The Minstrel.*

William Holloway. *The Peasant's Fate: A Rural Poem. With Miscellaneous Poems.* (pp. xii + 128)   Humble country life. Issued by Bloomfield's publishers.

Charles Lamb. *John Woodvil A Tragedy.* (pp. 128) A pseudo-Shakespearean piece set in the Restoration.

[Walter Savage Landor]. *Poetry by the Author of Gebir.* (pp. ii + 64)   Blank-verse renditions of classical legends.

[Amelia] Opie. *Poems.* (pp. iv + 192)   Mostly about objects of pity—prisoners, slaves, unwed mothers, soldiers' orphans, widows, etc.

William Cowper, trans., *The Iliad and Odyssey of Homer*, revised, 4 vols; *The Edinburgh Review* founded; William Gifford, trans., *The Satires of . . . Juvenalis;* Joseph Ritson, ed., *Ancient engleish Metrical Romanceës,* 3 vols; Walter Scott, ed., *The Minstrelsy of the Scottish Border*, vols 1 and 2.

1803

[Alexander Boswell]. *Epistle to the Edinburgh Reviewers.* (pp. 7)   Condescending advice to the new review (founded in 1802): 'A critic must be *just,* as well as clever'.

W. Lisle Bowles. *The Picture; Verses . . . Suggested by a Magnificent Landscape of Rubens, in Possession of Sir George Beaumont.* (pp. 20)   A predecessor for Wordsworth's 'Elegiac Stanzas on a Picture of Peele Castle', but more interesting when seen as an example of the way in which landscapes were interpreted.

[E. W. Brayley and W. Herbert]. *Syr Reginalde, or the Black Tower; a Romance of the Twelfth Century, with Tales, and Other Poems.* (pp. vi + 168)   Gothic romance, serious tales of terror and parodic ones, social satires, love songs, elegies and pastorals.

Thomas Campbell. *The Pleasures of Hope*, 7th edn. Includes 'Lochiel's Warning' and 'Hohenlinden'.

Samuel Taylor Coleridge. *Poems*, 3rd edn. (pp. xii + 202).

William Cowper. 'The Cast-Away', 'To Mary', and other poems in William Hayley, *The Life and Posthumous Writings . . .* (1803–6), 3 vols.

Erasmus Darwin. *The Temple of Nature; or, the Origin of Society* . . . .
(pp. iv + 174 + 124)   Remarkable blending of myth, philosophy and scientific
theory, devoting a book to each of the 'Production of Life', 'Reproduction of
Life', 'Progress of the Mind' and 'Good and Evil'. One of the best of the didactic
surveys. In heroic couplets.

Isaac D'Israeli. *Narrative Poems.* (pp. ii + 55)   Mediocre love stories in which the
women make all the sacrifices.

[George Huddesford]. *Bonaparte; An Heroic Ballad* . . . . (pp. 48)   Lively abuse
directed at Napoleon's treacherous conduct of his Egyptian campaign.

W. H. Ireland. *Rhapsodies.* (pp. 200)   Mostly imitations, of which the best is 'The
Little Red Woman', a Gothic tale.

The Poetical Register, and Repository for Fugitive Poetry, for 1802. (pp. xvi
+ 456) Society verse for the most part, but it contains Thomas Campbell's
'Hohenlinden', Coleridge's *'Chamouny. The Hour Before Sunrise' and 'The
Picture, or, the Lover's Resolution', and Cowper's *'The Negro's Complaint'.

Thomas Chatterton, *The Works*, ed. Robert Southey and Joseph Cottle; William
Hayley, ed., *The Life and Posthumous Writings of William Cowper, Esq.*, 3 vols;
William Godwin, *Life of Chaucer*; William Rhodes, trans., *The Satires of Juvenal*;
Walter Scott, *Minstrelsy of the Scottish Border*, vol. 3. Much patriotic verse inspired
by the resumption of war with France.

1804

William Blake. **Jerusalem: The Emanation of the Giant Albion.* (plates 100) The
earliest known copy cannot have been printed before 1818.

William Blake. **Milton: A Poem in 2 Books* . . . . (plates 50)   Composition is
believed to have continued from 1803 to 1808.

William Blake. The 'Pickering Manuscript' (dated approximately). It includes
'The Mental Traveller' and 'Auguries of Innocence'.

Robert Bloomfield. *Good tidings; or, News from the Farm* . . . . (pp. 37)   One of a
number of poems publicizing the importance of being vaccinated for smallpox
and describing various affecting cases.

William Lisle Bowles. *The Spirit of Discovery; or, The Conquest of Ocean* . . . .
(pp. xxii + 254)   A blank-verse survey from Noah's ark to the British navy.

[James Grahame]. *The Sabbath.* (pp. 96)

George Huddesford, ed. *The Wiccamical Chaplet, A Selection of Original Poetry* . . . .
(pp. xvi + 223)   Mostly humorous verse, the best being of a burlesque kind, by
'gentlemen educated at Winchester'. On the model of *The Oxford Sausage* (1764).

George Richards. *Poems*, 2 vols. (pp. 219 and 194)   Includes 'Odin', a blank-
verse tragedy in imitation of Aeschylus in which Scandinavian mythology is
linked with the Classical world. The beleaguered Odin retreats from the
Romans to the hard primitive conditions of the north.

Richard Wharton. **Fables: Consisting of Select Parts from Dante, Berni, Chaucer, and
Ariosto. Imitated in English Heroic Verse.* (pp. 142)   Mostly macabre choices.

1805

Robert Anderson. *Ballads in the Cumberland Dialect* . . . . (pp. x + 174)   A miscellaneous collection of poems about rustics, revealing the conventional literary stereotypes of them that authors like Bloomfield catered to. Wordsworth seems positively ethereal by comparison.

Luke Booker. *Tobias: a Poem.* (pp. x + 87)   Uplifting narrative stressing faith; based on the apocryphal *Tobit.*

William Hayley. *Ballads . . . Founded on Anecdotes Relating to Animals* . . . . (pp. ii + 212)   Stories about the instinctive virtues of animals and birds. Illustrations by William Blake.

J. Hoppner, trans. *Oriental Tales.* (pp. xxiv + 123)   From several sources. Most are like *Arabian Nights* tales, but with a moral tendency more akin to Aesop's or La Fontaine's.

[George Huddesford]. *Les Champignons du Diable; or, Imperial Mushrooms: a Mock Heroic Poem* . . . . (pp. ii + 204)   Satan is imagined taking an interest in French affairs, particularly in the proclamation of Napoleon as emperor. Satan persuades the Pope to canonize him as well.

Walter Scott. * *The Lay of the Last Minstrel* . . . . (pp. iv + 319)

Robert Southey. *Madoc.* (pp. xvi + 557)   A twelfth-century epic in blank verse. Part I begins with Madoc's return to Wales from the new world. He tells of his voyage westward—material here from Camoëns' *Lusiad*—and of finding a conquered nation in America in which he has helped to overthrow its Aztec conquerors. Madoc has returned for more settlers, but his plans are largely frustrated by civil dissension. In Part II Madoc returns to America where the Aztecs are reasserting themselves. Kidnapping, human sacrifices, single combats, and full-scale battles follow. The Aztecs are eventually overwhelmed by a volcano.

[Mary Tighe]. *Psyche; or, the Legend of Love.* (pp. viii + 214)   Crude Spenserian allegory in which the legend of Cupid and Psyche is expanded into a romance with a medieval setting. Like Hayley's *The Triumphs of Temper*, moral advice for young women, but utterly humourless.

William Wordsworth. * 'The Prelude', first version, completed in manuscript. The poem was first published in 1850, in a revised form.

Death of Nelson; William Gifford, ed., *The Works of Massinger.*

1806

[Robert Bland and J. H. Merivale]. *Translations Chiefly from the Greek Anthology* . . . . (pp. lx + 233)   The authors chosen include Meleager, Sappho, Anacreon, Bion and Moschus. Some original tales follow: 'Paris and Oenone', an anticipation of the lush Classical world of Keats's *Endymion*; 'The Abbot of Dol', a Gothic ballad related to Bürger's 'Der wilde Jäger'; and 'The Wraith', another Gothic piece.

Robert Bloomfield. *Wild Flowers; or, Pastoral and Local Poetry.* (pp. xii + 132)   More rustic tales.

Lord Byron. *Fugitive Pieces.* (pp. iv + 66)   Privately printed, suppressed and reissued in 1807 as *Poems on Various Occasions* without the amorous 'To Mary' which had offended some readers.

John Evans. *The Bees . . .*, Book I. (Books II and III published in 1808 and 1813 respectively; pp. 79 in all.)   A didactic extension of Virgil's *Georgics* with digressive reflections throughout.

James Grahame. *The Birds of Scotland, with Other Poems.* (pp. xii + 248)   To 'delineate the *manners and characters* of Birds', and based on personal observation. Like *The Bees*, didactic with reflective digressions, attacking press gangs, kidnapping, 'improvers' of the countryside, slavery, etc.

Thomas Holcroft. *Tales in Verse; Critical, Satirical, and Humorous*, 2 vols. (pp. x + 179 and 142)   Moral and feebly amusing anecdotes of an egalitarian tendency.

James Montgomery. *The Wanderer of Switzerland, and Other Poems.* (pp. 175)   A sentimental tale about Swiss exiles going to America after the Battle of Unterwalden; some Gothic ballads, a good translation of Papageno's song from *The Magic Flute*, and other short poems.

Thomas Moore. **Epistles, Odes, and Other Poems.* (pp. xvi + 341)   Written during his visit to North America: descriptive and reflective epistles in which the politically alert traveller finds matter to confute democrats and revolutionaries; Gothic ballads; the 'Canadian Boat-Song'; mildly suggestive amatory verse. A volume of some distinction.

Thomas Love Peacock. *Palmyra, and Other Poems.* (pp. viii + 141)   A miscellaneous and merely competent collection.

Numerous patriotic elegies on the death of Nelson.

1807

Lord Byron. *Hours of Idleness, A Series of Poems, Original and Translated.* (pp. xiv + 187)   Includes 'Oscar of Alva', a Gothic ballad.

Lord Byron. *Poems on Various Occasions.* (pp xii + 144)   Privately printed. The prevailing themes friendship, fame, gallantry, death and leave-takings.

George Crabbe. *Poems.* (pp. xxvi + 256)   Reprints 'The Library', *'The Village' and 'The Newspaper'. Adds *'The Parish Register'—a social anatomization of a small country town, claiming to be realistic, and mixing satire and humour but lacking a cumulative moral; 'The Birth of Flattery'—an allegory; 'Sir Eustace Grey'; 'The Hall of Justice', and other poems.

[Richard Cumberland and Sir James Bland Burges]. *The Exodiad, a Poem.* (pp. vi + 224)   Blank-verse epic on the journey to Israel after the destruction of Pharaoh's army. First four books only. (Completed in 1808.)

James Hogg. *The Mountain Bard; Consisting of Ballads and Songs, founded on Facts and Legendary Tales.* (pp. xxiii + 202)   Gothic ballads, including 'Sir David Graeme', and rustic pieces, some of them humorous.

Charles Kirkpatrick Sharpe. *Metrical Legends, and Other Poems.* (pp. ii + 107)
Gothic ballads and Boccaccio's tale of *Lorenzo and Isabella.

Henry Kirk White. *The Remains of . . .,* ed. Robert Southey, 2 vols. (pp. viii + 322
and viii + 300) A miscellaneous collection by a young poet who died while he
was being rescued from obscurity.

William Wordsworth. *Poems, in Two Volumes.* (pp. viii + 158 and
viii + 170) Volume 1 includes 'To the Daisy', 'She was a Phantom of Delight',
'Character of the Happy Warrior'—Wordsworth's wise and stately tribute to
Nelson—'Ode to Duty', 'To a Sky-lark', 'Alice Fell', *'Resolution and
Independence'; sonnets, including 'Nuns fret not', 'Westminster Bridge', 'The
world is too much with us', 'It is a beauteous evening', 'I griev'd for
Buonaparte', 'Two Voices are there', 'Milton! thou shouldst be living', 'Great
Men have been among us', and 'It is not to be thought of'. Volume 2 includes
'The Solitary Reaper', 'My heart leaps up', 'I wandered lonely as a cloud', 'To
the Cuckoo', 'Elegiac Stanzas . . . Peele Castle', and *'Ode: Intimations of
Immortality'. These volumes, perhaps the finest of the decade, were harshly
treated by the reviews. The decision to place the poems most like *Lyrical Ballads*
in style first in each volume was dearly bought.

Francis Hodgson, trans., *The Satires of Juvenal.*

1808

Anon. *The Crusaders, or the Minstrels of Acre . . . .* (pp. ii + 152) An imitation of
Scott set in the time of Richard I. After the crusaders take Acre, a feast is
held at which minstrels compete. Two of them have grown up in the Lake
District.

Robert Bland. *Edwy and Elgiva, and Sir Everard; Two Tales.* (pp. viii + 187)
Gloomy romances about the early middle ages in England.

Felicia Dorothea Browne (later Hemans). *Poems.* (pp. xxviii + 111) Derivative
but polished verse from a girl of fifteen.

Lord Byron. *Poems Original and Translated.* (pp. x + 174) Overlaps considerably
with his two 1807 volumes.

[W. H. Ireland] H. C. Esq. *The Fisher-Boy . . . .* (pp. viii + 116)

Thomas Moore. *Irish Melodies,* vols 1 and 2. (Vol. 10 appeared in 1834.) Issued
with music by Sir John Stevenson and later Sir Henry Bishop.

Walter Scott. *Marmion; a Tale of Flodden Field.* (pp. 317 + cxxvi)

William Tighe. *The Plants, A Poem. Cantos the First and Second . . . .*
(pp. viii + 159) · Accounts of the rose and the oak, combining botany, legend
and history.

Henry Francis Cary, trans., *The Inferno of Dante Alighieri*; S. T. Coleridge's lectures
on poetry; William Cowper, trans. (posthumous), *Latin and Italian Poems* of
Milton; R. H. Cromek, ed., *Reliques of Robert Burns*; James Deare, trans., Virgil's
Georgics; Leigh Hunt's journal, *The Examiner*, founded; Charles Lamb, *Specimens of
English Dramatic Poets*; Walter Scott, ed., *Works of John Dryden* in 18 vols.

1809

Robert Bland. *The Four Slaves of Cythera, A Romance, in Ten Cantos.* (pp. 276)   Crusaders returning home are captured by Moslems, fall in love with Moslem ladies and after a series of improbable adventures escape with them. The poem is punctuated by self-mocking remarks, and the mixture of humour and sentimental adventures anticipates Byron's manner in *Don Juan* to some extent.

[Lord Byron]. ** English Bards, and Scotch Reviewers. A Satire.* (pp. iv + 54)   Characterizes his contemporaries fairly accurately, but often chooses works that are now considered minor. Mocks Southey, Scott, Wordsworth and Coleridge; praises James Montgomery, Thomas Campbell, Samuel Rogers, William Gifford.

Thomas Campbell. *Gertrude of Wyoming; a Pennsylvanian Tale. And Other Poems.* (pp. ii + 134)   Pronounced Wyoming. A legendary tale about the love of Waldegrave for Gertrude in an Edenic new world. Gertrude and her father are massacred by Indians. Includes Gothic ballads—'Glenara' and 'Lord Ullin's Daughter'—and 'The Battle of the Baltic'.

James Grahame. *British Georgics.* (pp. viii + 342)   A Scottish farmer's calendar, divided into months. A combination of practical advice, records of local customs, and political and religious reflections.

[Thomas Hill] Peter Pry. *Marmion Travestied; a Tale of Modern Times.* (pp. xx + 277)   Translates the action of *Marmion* to regency London, with the prince as Marmion. Amusing and ingenious but so topical as to require considerable reading in the newspapers of the time.

Francis Hodgson. *Lady Jane Grey . . . with Miscellaneous Poems . . . .* (pp. xvi + 352)   Lady Jane, in spite of her preference for rustic obscurity, is imprisoned by Queen Mary as a rival and executed. The volume also includes 'A Gentle Alternative Prepared for the reviewers', in which the *Edinburgh Review* is criticized for its attacks on Byron and on Southey's *Thalaba* and *Madoc*.

[Margaret Holford]. *Wallace; or, the Fight of Falkirk; a Metrical Romance.* (pp. viii + 248)   Imitates Scott's scenery and events, but lacks his interesting plots and characters.

[W. H. Ireland] H. C. Esq. *The Sailor-Boy . . . Illustrative of the Navy of Great Britain.* (pp. vi + 208)   Dick rises to the rank of captain and participates in the victory at Trafalgar.

Walter Rodwell Wright. *Horae Ionicae: A Poem, Descriptive of the Ionian Islands, and Part of the Adjacent Coast of Greece.* (pp. viii + 67)   Based on first-hand experience. Contrasts the present with the Classical past.

William Blake, *Descriptive Catalogue of Pictures*; Samuel Taylor Coleridge's journal, *The Friend*, begun; *Quarterly Review* founded.

1810

Joanna Baillie. *The Family Legend: A Tragedy.* (pp. xiv + 152)   A weak-willed Chief of the Macleans is persuaded by feuding clansmen to have his innocent wife put to death because she is a Campbell. Chance and the presence of mind of a noble admirer save her and the guilty are brought to book.

George Crabbe. *The Borough: a Poem, in Twenty-four Letters.* (pp. xlii + 344)

John Dudley. *The Metamorphosis of Sona; a Hindu Tale . . . Descriptive of the Mythology of the Sastras.* (pp. xvi + 144) A legendary tale with Indian lore superimposed.

Charles A. Elton. *Tales of Romance, with Other Poems, including Selections from Propertius.* (pp. viii + 136) Moral anecdotes from the *Gesta Romanorum* and rural meditations.

Francis Hodgson. *Sir Edgar; a Tale . . . with Serious Translations from the Ancients; and Merry Imitations of a Modern.* (pp. vi + 318) Moral comparison of a lady's true and false love. The mildly amusing imitations are of George Colman the Younger.

Ralph Palin. *Iphotelle; or The Longing-Fit.* (pp. ii + 71) An allegory on the model of *The Triumphs of Temper* to persuade pregnant women that longing-fits and 'maternal impressions' are imaginary.

Samuel Jackson Pratt. *The Lower World . . . .* (pp. xii + 148) In favour of being kind to animals.

Walter Scott. *The Lady of the Lake . . . .* (pp. vi + 419) The conflict of the passionate and gloomy but honourable Highland rebel, Roderick Dhu, with King James of Scotland frames the love story of young Ellen and Malcolm. Scott's most popular poem.

[Percy Bysshe Shelley and Elizabeth Shelley]. *Original Poetry by Victor and Cazire.* (pp. xxvii + 66) A miscellany of pleasantly affectionate epistles in doggerel, gloomy and sentimental songs, and heavy-handed Gothic extravagances.

William Sotheby. *Constance de Castile. A Poem, in Ten Cantos.* (pp. ii + 191) Romance of love and honour in a Spain besieged by the Moors. The character of the guilty Pedro, Constance's father, anticipates Southey's hero in *Roderick, Last of the Goths* to some extent.

Robert Southey. *The Curse of Kehama.* (pp. xvi + 376) The wicked career of the priestly Hindu magician, Kehama, inflicts suffering on an innocent maiden and her elderly father. The love of the maiden for an angel, or 'Glendoveer', is made possible by her death. Scenes worthy of Cecil B. De Mille and a compelling guiding principle, but flawed by an excess of Indian lore, arbitrary incidents, and characters who are too good, or bad, to be true.

Alexander Chalmers, ed., *Works of the English Poets*, 21 vols.

1811

Peregrine Bingham. *The Pains of Memory . . . .* (pp. 103) A gloomy answer to Rogers's *Pleasures of Memory* by the son-in-law of William Lisle Bowles.

Robert Bloomfield. *The Banks of the Wye . . . .* (pp. viii + 134) Digressive reflections inspired by a tour of the area.

Richard Cumberland. *Retrospection, A Poem in Familiar Verse.* (pp. 71) The calm but melancholy recollections in blank verse of a member of the older generation of poets, in which friendship is seen to be more valuable than fame.

Leigh Hunt. 'The Feast of the Poets' in *The Reflector*. (See 1814.)

Mary Russell Mitford. *Christina, the Maid of the South Seas* . . . . (pp. xii + 332) A young American encounters Fletcher Christian, the 'Bounty' mutineer, on a Pacific island, and falls in love with his daughter, Christina. Modelled on *Gertrude of Wyoming*.

Anna Maria Porter. *Ballad Romances, and Other Poems*. (pp. viii + 196) Includes some respectable tales of terror, 'Eugene', 'Lord Malcolm', 'The Maid of Erin'.

Walter Scott. *The Vision of Don Roderick* . . . . (pp. xii + 122) Roderick's prophetic glimpse of the Moorish conquest of Spain is extended to Wellington's victory over Napoleon.

William Robert Spencer. *Poems*. (pp. viii + 240) Miscellaneous society verse, reprinting his 'Year of Sorrow' (1804) and his translation of 'Lenore' (1796) with the original on facing pages.

William Tighe. *The Plants . . . Cantos the Third and Fourth* . . . . (pp. viii + 239) Concludes the poem with 'The Vine' and 'The Palm'.

1812

[Bernard Barton]. *Metrical Effusions* . . . . (pp. viii + 223) Includes a 'Pains of Memory', and the sad tale of 'Jane Ashford', both in Spenserian stanzas.

Lord Byron. **Childe Harold's Pilgrimage. A Romaunt*. (pp. viii + 226) Cantos I and II and some short poems, 'Maid of Athens' and 'To Thyrza' among them.

George Colman the Younger. *Poetical Vagaries* . . . . (pp. 144) Parodies, satires, and good-natured nonsense.

George Crabbe. *Tales*. (pp. xxiv + 398) Studies of human frailty in which plot matters more than it did in *The Borough*.

John Galt. *The Tragedies of Maddalen, Agamemnon, Lady Macbeth* . . . . (pp. vi + 262) The destruction of innocent people in untoward circumstances, foreshadowing Shelley's *The Cenci*.

Reginald Heber. *Poems and Translations*. (pp. viii + 180) Biblical history, European politics, translations of Pindar.

[Walter Savage Landor]. *Count Julian: a Tragedy*. (pp. viii + 128) Cf. Southey's *Roderick* (1814). The same events from Julian's point of view.

Alicia Lefanu. *Rosara's Chain: or, the Choice of Life* . . . . (pp. ii + 108) Experience prepares Amantor and Rosara to appreciate and accept one another. An allegory.

Thomas Love Peacock. *The Philosophy of Melancholy* . . . . (pp. viii + 125) Further variations on the 'Pains of Memory' theme, and the short 'Spirit of Fire' on Zoroastrian resistance to the Moslems.

[James and Horace Smith]. *Rejected Addresses: or the New Theatrum Poetarum*. (pp. xvi + 126) Parodies of contemporary poets who are pretended to have submitted these verses for the opening of the rebuilt Theatre Royal, Drury

Lane. Wordsworth, Southey, Coleridge, Lewis, Scott and Byron are hit off recognizably.

John Wilson. *The Isle of Palms, and Other Poems.* (pp. x + 415) Unmarried lovers are shipwrecked and find their way to an idyllic uninhabited island. Years later they are rescued and return to Wales. Adds 'The Angler's Tent', an account of a fishing expedition in the Lake District in which Wordsworth took part.

William Combe, *The Tour of Dr. Syntax in Search of the Picturesque*—written to accompany Rowlandson's comic plates; sequels in 1820 and 1821.

1813

[William Lisle Bowles]. *The Missionary* . . . . (pp. viii + 136) Bowles keeps pace with literary fashion by setting true lovers and a hermit (the missionary) in Chile during the Spanish invasion.

Lord Byron. *The Bride of Abydos. A Turkish Tale.* (pp. iv + 72) The attempt of the young pirate to carry off his cousin Zuleika, the beautiful daughter of the despotic Giaffir, fails and both die.

Lord Byron. *The Giaour, A Fragment of a Turkish Tale.* (pp. vi + 41) The word is pronounced 'jowr'.

Samuel Taylor Coleridge. *Remorse. A Tragedy* . . . . (pp. xii + 72) Alvar attempts to make the brother who tried to have him murdered repent and he tests the constancy of Teresa, to whom he was betrothed before his disappearance. Performed with some success at Drury Lane.

James Hogg. *The Queen's Wake: a Legendary Poem.* (pp. vi + 353) For three nights minstrels compete before Mary Queen of Scots. Their songs vary in character from the comic Gothicism of 'The Witch of Fife' to the beautiful fairy-tale of 'Kilmeny'.

James Montgomery. *The World Before the Flood* . . . . (pp. xxiv + 304) The virtuous inhabitants of Eden overcome the invading descendants of Cain by passive resistance and God's help. The love of Javan for Zillah provides a focus for sympathy.

[Thomas Moore] Thomas Brown the younger. *Intercepted Letters; or the Twopenny Post-Bag.* (pp. xvi + 109)

[John Hamilton Reynolds]. *Leaves of Laurel* . . . . edited by Q. Q. and W. W. (pp. 25) A contest of contemporary poets for the vacant post of laureate.

[Walter Scott]. *The Bridal of Triermain* . . . . (pp. xviii + 233)

Walter Scott. *Rokeby* . . . . (pp. vi + 330 + cxvi) Treachery, love, and honour after the Battle of Marston Moor. The dangerous and unprincipled Bertram sacrifices himself in the end for a just cause.

Percy Bysshe Shelley. *Queen Mab; a Philosophical Poem* . . . . (pp. ii + 240) The soul of the sleeping Ianthe is permitted by Queen Mab to see how 'to accomplish the great end/For which it hath its being'. Together they observe the universe and the passage of civilizations past, present and to come, unhampered by matter, space and time. Ahasuerus reveals God's wickedness, and the morals to be drawn throughout are subversive of religious and political institutions. The prose notes that follow are even more outspoken. The volume was suppressed.

1814

Lord Byron. *The Corsair, a Tale.* (pp. xii + 100).

[Lord Byron and Samuel Rogers]. *Lara, a Tale. Jacqueline, a Tale.* (pp. viii + 128) Byron's gloomy hero carries the volume; Jacqueline runs away from home rather than marry the man her father forces on her, is rescued by her lover and both are reconciled with her father. Rogers's domestic sentimentality seems largely speculative.

[George Daniel]. *The Modern Dunciad* . . . . (pp. ii + 106) Praise for Crabbe, Campbell, Rogers, Montgomery; reservations about Southey, Scott and Byron; omission of Wordsworth and Coleridge. Claims to prefer Pope and Churchill to the moderns.

William Haygarth. *Greece, a Poem* . . . . (pp. xii + 304) Interesting for the coincidence of its scenery with Byron's *Childe Harold's Pilgrimage*—Athens, Albania, etc.

[Leigh Hunt]. *The Feast of the Poets* . . . . (pp. xiv + 157) Apollo tests the quality of contemporary verse; Moore is congratulated for his *Irish Melodies*, Wordsworth is advised not to misapply his genuine talents. An earlier version appeared in *The Reflector* in 1811.

J. H. Reynolds. *The Eden of Imagination* . . . . (pp. 41) Old-fashioned reflections in a landscape based on Wordsworth, Coleridge and Rogers particularly.

J. H. Reynolds. *Safie. An Eastern Tale.* (pp. ii + 91) Disappointed lover is a weak substitute for the misanthropist required by a Byronic tale.

Robert Southey. *Roderick, the Last of the Goths.* (pp. xii + 340 + cxxxvii)

William Wordsworth. *The Excursion, Being a Portion of the Recluse* . . . . (pp. xxii + 447)

Henry Francis Cary, trans., *The Vision; or, Hell, Purgatory, and Paradise of Dante*, 3 vols; Thomas James Mathias, ed., *The Works of Thomas Gray*, 2 vols.

1815

Lord Byron. *Hebrew Melodies.* (pp. viii + 53) Includes 'She walks in beauty', 'Vision of Belshazzar' and 'The Destruction of Sennacherib'. Written 'on the sacred model' to fit traditional Hebrew airs arranged by Isaac Nathan.

Sir Joseph Cheakill. *The Cross-Bath Guide* . . . . (pp. 91) An epistolary satire on social climbing, modelled on Anstey's *New Bath Guide* (1766).

[William Combe]. *The English Dance of Death, From the Designs of Thomas Rowlandson* . . . , vol. 1. (pp. xiv + 295) Vol. 2 in 1816; originally published in parts in 1814. A satirical survey of English society in Hudibrastic couplets to match Rowlandson's plates.

James Hogg. *The Pilgrims of the Sun* . . . . (pp. viii + 148)   Mary Lee, noted for her beauty, learning and piety, is given a moral tour of the universe by a supernatural guide. When she returns she finds that she has been supposed dead but she fails to convince her family of the truth of her vision. She marries a mortal who resembles her guide, has five sons, and when she dies her husband vanishes. A mixture of Shelley's *Queen Mab* and Hogg's own 'Kilmeny', but devoid of Shelley's abrasively unconventional points of view.

Leigh Hunt. *The Descent of Liberty, a Mask*. (pp. lix + 82)   Political allegory of the fall of Napoleon with reminders of lingering deficiencies in English freedom.

[W. H. Ireland]. Anser Pen-drag-on, Esq., ed. *Scribbleomania; or, the Printer's Devil's Polichronicon. A Sublime Poem*. (pp. viii + 341)   Doggerel but representative summation of opinion about contemporary authors.

Henry Hart Milman. *Fazio. A Tragedy*. (pp. iv + 103)   A young alchemist comes into a fortune by taking advantage of another man's crime, courts a proud lady who had previously jilted him, and is betrayed to the authorities by his doting but jealous wife. The play had some success on stage.

[Richard Polwhele]. *The Fair Isabel of Cotehele, a Cornish Romance* . . . . (pp. ii + 371)   A cross between a Gothic novel and Scott's narrative verse, set in the time of Mary I.

Walter Scott. *The Field of Waterloo; a Poem*. (pp. 54)   Dignified occasional verse to raise money for needy survivors.

Walter Scott. *The Lord of the Isles* . . . . (pp. iv + 275 + clxv)   The return of Robert the Bruce and his defeat of the English at Bannockburn is interwoven with a love triangle and with descriptions of the west coast of Scotland.

William Wordsworth. *The White Doe of Rylstone; or the Fate of the Nortons* . . . . (pp. xii + 162)   Includes the Gothic ballad 'The Force of Prayer; or the Founding of Bolton Priory . . .'.

William Wordsworth. *Poems* . . ., 2 vols, a collected edition. Among the poems appearing for the first time are 'Laodamia' and 'To the Daisy'. Includes the famous preface.

1816

Lord Byron. *Childe Harold's Pilgrimage. Canto the Third*. (pp. iv + 79).

Lord Byron. *The Prisoner of Chillon, and Other Poems*. (pp. iv + 60)   The fable examines the reluctance to leave confinement that follows prolonged imprisonment. It may be read as an allegory of what happens to those who are given political liberty or of the need to preserve those one loves if liberty is to be relished. Some of the other poems in this uncharacteristic but fascinating volume—'Darkness', 'Dream'—invite allegorical interpretation as well.

Lord Byron. *The Siege of Corinth. A Poem. Parisina. A Poem*. (pp. iv + 91)   A misanthropical outcast with a soft spot for a lady learns that she died before his last meeting with her. The assault on Corinth provides hideous battle-scenes. Parisina's incestuous passion for her step-son is discovered; he is executed and she is never seen or heard again. Exercises in sinister awareness.

Samuel Taylor Coleridge. *Christabel: Kubla Khan, a Vision; the Pains of Sleep.* (pp. viii + 64)

James Hogg. *Mador of the Moor* . . . . (pp. vi + 140) Narrative that owes much to *The Lady of the Lake* without achieving its suspense or effective characterization and yet has a convincing trace of folklore running through it.

[James Hogg]. *The Poetic Mirror, or the Living Bards of Britain.* (pp. vi + 275) Parodies of Byron, Scott, Wordsworth, Coleridge, Southey, John Wilson, and, by way of disguise, of Hogg himself. Unfortunately he had the good taste to mock poems that have been forgotten.

Leigh Hunt. * *The Story of Rimini* . . . . (pp. xx + 111)   The unhappy love of Paolo and Francesca told with luxuriant descriptive detail. Now mainly of interest for its influence on Keats.

John Keats. 'On First Looking into Chapman's Homer', in *The Examiner.*

Charles Robert Maturin. *Bertram; or, the Castle of St. Aldobrand* . . . . (pp. iv + 94) A fallen aristocrat turned pirate is shipwrecked near the castle of the man responsible for his fall. The woman he loved and who loves him still has been forced to marry his enemy. He murders the husband, the wife goes mad, and he commits suicide. Now chiefly remembered for Coleridge's hostile criticism in *Biographia Literaria.*

Percy Bysshe Shelley. *Alastor; or, the Spirit of Solitude: and Other Poems.* (pp. viii + 101) An allegory of a poet irretrievably committed to a search for an unfindable ideal. In his loneliness he contemplates the prospect of death and ventures into a boat that carries him ultimately to death but by way of the experience of life. The volume also contains 'The Daemon of the World'.

Robert Southey. *The Poet's Pilgrimage to Waterloo.* (pp. vi + 232) The journey of the poet laureate described in homely terms and distinguished by two allegorical visions of the future, one pessimistic and the other optimistic.

John Wilson. *The City of the Plague, and Other Poems.* (pp. ii + 299) A naval officer returns to look for his mother in plague-stricken London. The moral decay of the survivors is observed. The officer, who finds that his mother and younger brother have already died, dies too and is followed by the woman who loved him. Sentimental but consistent development of an interesting situation.

William Wordsworth. *Thanksgiving Ode . . . With Other Short Pieces, Chiefly Referring to Recent Public Events.* (pp. xii + 52)

1817

Lord Byron. *The Lament of Tasso.* (pp. 19) An examination of the troubled mind of the imprisoned poet, sustained by the love for which he has been condemned and by the capacity of his imagination to free Jerusalem itself in writing his *Jerusalem Delivered.*

Lord Byron. * *Manfred, a Dramatic Poem.* (pp. 80).

Samuel Taylor Coleridge. *Sibylline Leaves: a Collection of Poems.* (pp. xii + 303) Retrospective edition. The first appearance of the gloss to the

*'Rime of the Ancient Mariner', and the first appearance in book form of
*'Dejection: an Ode' (1802).

S. T. Coleridge. *Zapolya: a Christmas Tale* .... (pp. viii + 128)   A usurper is
dethroned twenty years later by the rightful heir who has come of age. Intended
for performance but rejected by the theatre. Contains the song 'A sunny shaft
did I behold'.

[George Croly]. *Paris in 1815* .... (pp. xvi + 75)   Detailed reflections on the
occupied city. Croly's sympathy seems cold, his contempt real; as a consequence
his account does not survive the scenes it describes.

[John Hookham Frere]. William and Robert Whistlecraft. *Prospectus and Specimen
of an Intended National Work* ..., Cantos I and II. (pp. viii + 55)   Burlesque of
Arthurian romance.

John Keats. *Poems.* (pp. viii + 121)   Includes 'I stood tip-toe', epistles,
sonnets—among them 'Great spirits now on earth'—and 'Sleep and Poetry'.

Thomas Moore. *Lalla Rookh, an Oriental Romance.* (pp. ii + 405)   The journey of
Lalla Rookh to marry the young king of Bucharia is enlivened by the presence of
the minstrel Feramorz who tells four tales: *'The Veiled Prophet of Khorassan'
plumbs the depths of wickedness; 'Paradise and the Peri' reveals 'the Gift that is
most dear to Heaven'—the tears of a hardened criminal who sees an innocent
child at prayer; 'The Fire Worshippers'—a Byronic tale much like *The Bride of
Abydos* but with horrors all its own; and 'The Light of the Haram' in which
Nourmahal wins back the affections of her estranged but equally unhappy
husband. The tales are linked by prose in which the Chamberlain of the Haram,
Fadladeen, offers amusingly contemptuous critiques of each tale in turn.
Feramorz turns out to be the young king in disguise.

[Walter Scott]. *Harold the Dauntless* .... (pp. 200)   Romance set at the time of the
Danish occupation of England. Harold undergoes trials to gain land and the
hand of the maiden Metelill; he gains instead the hand of Eivir who has served
him faithfully disguised as a page.

Percy Bysshe Shelley. *Laon and Cythna* .... (pp. xxxiv + 270)   Incorrectly dated
1818 and withdrawn after publication. Reissued in 1818 as *The Revolt of Islam*.

Robert Southey. *Wat Tyler: a Dramatic Poem.* (pp. 70)   Written in 1794 and
published to embarrass the author turned Tory.

Blackwood's Magazine founded; William Hazlitt, *The Characters of Shakespear's
Plays*.

1818

William Blake. 'The Everlasting Gospel'. In manuscript and dated conjecturally.

[Lord Byron]. *Beppo, a Venetian Story.* (pp. iv + 49)   An Italian husband returns
after being given up for dead and comes to an amicable arrangement with his
wife and her 'cavalier servente'.

Lord Byron. *Childe Harold's Pilgrimage. Canto the Fourth.* (pp. xvi + 257)

[John Hookham Frere] William and Robert Whistlecraft. *Prospectus and Specimen . . .*, Cantos III and IV. (pp. 61)

Leigh Hunt. *Foliage; or Poems Original and Translated.* (pp. 40 + cxxxvi + 111) An attractive miscellany without a single poem of real distinction.

John Keats. *Endymion: a Poetic Romance.* (pp. xii + 208) Endymion explains to his sister Peona that his abstractedness during the rites of Pan is a consequence of his dream of courting Cynthia, the moon. To Peona's reproaches he speaks of the value of an 'ardent listlessness'. He descends into the depths of the earth in search of Cynthia and dreams once more of meeting her. Beneath the sea he frees the enchanted Glaucus and all join in the worship of Neptune. Endymion encounters Phoebe and giving up his ideal falls in love with her reality. She turns out to be Cynthia and vanishes with Endymion. Exquisite physical detail obscures the meaning of the poem, but it bears comparison with *Alastor*.

Henry Hart Milman. *Samor, Lord of the Bright City. An Heroic Poem.* (pp. viii + 368) Samor swears vengeance against the Saxon invaders of Britain in the time of Vortigern. As the Avenger he terrorizes the countryside. He resists the blandishments of Rowena but is temporarily distracted. Merlin revives his spirits. He joins forces with Uther Pendragon and the Saxons are defeated. A mixture of Scott and Southey that does not quite come up to either.

[Thomas Moore]. *The Fudge Family in Paris.* Edited by Thomas Brown the Younger. (pp. viii + 168) Epistolary satire of the *nouveaux riches* and their servants on tour. Derived from Anstey's *New Bath Guide* and equal to it.

[Thomas Love Peacock]. *Rhododaphne: or the Thessalian Spell . . . .* (pp. xii + 181) Young Anthemion tries to resist Rhododaphne's dangerous enchantment and remain true to his beloved Calliroë. For a while, believing Calliroë to be dead, he luxuriates in a magical palace with Rhododaphne, but Apollo intervenes and frees him. Anticipations of 'Lamia'.

Percy Bysshe Shelley. *The Revolt of Islam* (see *Laon and Cythna*, 1817).

William Hazlitt, *Lectures on the English Poets.*

1819

[Lord Byron]. *Don Juan*, Cantos I and II. (pp. iv + 227)

Lord Byron. *Mazeppa . . . .* (pp. iv + 71)

George Crabbe. *Tales of the Hall*, 2 vols. (pp. xxiv + 326 and viii + 353) Two brothers of opposite tempers and fortunes are reunited in friendship in their sixties. They exchange stories of their contrasting experiences of life and together reflect upon the lives of various neighbours and old acquaintances. The emphasis, because of retrospection, is on elderly people, and the fortunes of marriage provide a recurrent theme.

Leigh Hunt. *Hero and Leander, and Bacchus and Ariadne.* (pp. iv + 56) Published as a part of vol. 2 of *The Poetical Works*. Notable for their influence on Keats.

John Keats. 'The Fall of Hyperion' written. Published in 1856.

[John Keats]. *'Ode to a Nightingale' and *'Ode on a Grecian Urn' in *Annals of the Fine Arts*.

Thomas Babington Macaulay. *Pompeii* . . . . (pp. 15)   A Cambridge prize poem about the eruption. The section on the burial of the living has some Gothic vigour to it.

[John Hamilton Reynolds]. *Peter Bell. A Lyrical Ballad.* (pp. viii + 29)   General parody of the style of *Lyrical Ballads*, published in advance of Wordsworth's *Peter Bell*.

Samuel Rogers. *Human Life* . . . . (pp. 94)   Traces the social development of an individual; the emphasis is on the later years.

Percy Bysshe Shelley. *Rosalind and Helen, a Modern Eclogue; with Other Poems.* (pp. viii + 92)   Rosalind and Helen, social exiles living in Italy, exchange the stories of their lives in which social conventions, and particularly the convention of marriage, have opposed their natural and virtuous feelings and rendered them miserable. The volume includes *'Lines written among the Euganean Hills', *'Hymn to Intellectual Beauty' and 'Ozymandias'.

William Wordsworth. *Peter Bell, a Tale in Verse.* (pp. viii + 88)   The conscience of a hard-hearted man is awakened by a series of accidents that he mistakenly imagines are supernatural. The story is naively and even garrulously told. Sonnets are included in the volume.

William Wordsworth. *The Waggoner, a Poem* . . . . (pp. iv + 68)   Benjamin picks up a sailor's indigent family on his route and unwisely stops at an inn where he drinks too much. His master, who has warned him before, dismisses him. Sonnets are included in the volume.

Thomas Campbell, ed., *Specimens of the British Poets*, 7 vols; Leigh Hunt's journal, *The Indicator*, founded.

1820

Elizabeth Barrett (later Browning). *The Battle of Marathon* . . . . (pp. xvi + 72)   Epic verse in heroic couplets, modelled on Glover's *Leonidas* and Pope's *Homer*. Miss Barrett was eleven years old at the time of composition.

John Clare. *Poems Descriptive of Rural Life and Scenery.* (pp. xxxii + 222)   Clare is described as a Northamptonshire peasant. Includes the Goldsmithian 'Helpstone', the Burnsian 'Address to a Lark', the amusingly unsentimental but affectionate 'My Mary', 'The Harvest Morning' and 'Dolly's Mistake', and the more sinister 'Crazy Nell'.

Felicia Hemans. *The Sceptic; a Poem.* (pp. 38)   Arguments for faith.

John Abraham Heraud. *The Legend of St. Loy; with Other Poems.* (pp. xvi + 223)   Elaborate 'legendary tale' influenced by Scott's romances.

[John Keats] Caviare. 'La Belle Dame sans Merci', in *The Indicator*.

John Keats. *Lamia, *Isabella, *The Eve of St. Agnes, and Other Poems.* (pp. viii + 200)   Includes *'Ode to a Nightingale', *'Ode on a Grecian Urn' (both reprinted), 'Ode to Psyche', 'To Autumn', 'Ode on Melancholy' and the unfinished 'Hyperion'.

James Sheridan Knowles. *Virginius: a Tragedy.* (pp. 87)   A relatively successful acting tragedy tailored for Macready at Covent Garden.

Henry Hart Milman. **The Fall of Jerusalem . . . .* (pp. viii + 167)

[Bryan Waller Procter] Barry Cornwall. *Marcian Colonna . . .and Other Poems.* (pp. viii + 190)   A tale of love and madness in which the return of a supposedly dead husband has tragic consequences. Includes as well a dramatic rendition of the death scene of 'Julian the Apostate' based on Gibbon.

Percy Bysshe Shelley. **The Cenci. A Tragedy . . . .* (pp. xiv + 104)   Printed in Italy and dated 1819.

Percy Bysshe Shelley. **Prometheus Unbound . . . with Other Poems.* (pp. 222)   Includes 'The Sensitive Plant', 'Ode to the West Wind', 'The Cloud' and 'To a Skylark'.

William Wordsworth. *The River Duddon, a Series of Sonnets . . . and Other Poems.* (pp. viii + 321)   Reflections on the topography of the river and intermittent analogies between its course and human life. The volume includes 'Vaudracour and Julia' and 'Ode, Composed Upon an Evening of Extraordinary Splendour and Beauty'.

Thomas Bowdler, ed., *The Family Shakespeare*; John Bowring, *Specimens of the Russian Poets*; William Hazlitt, *Lectures on the Dramatic Literature of the Age of Elizabeth*; Thomas Love Peacock, 'The Four Ages of Poetry'.

1821

Joanna Baillie. *Metrical Legends of Exalted Characters.* (pp. xxxvi + 373)   Stories of William Wallace, Christopher Columbus, and the redoubtable Lady Griseld Baillie, and some competent Gothic ballads.

Thomas Lovell Beddoes. *The Improvisatore . . . with Other Poems.* (pp. 128)   Disgusting but lively experiments with the macabre.

[Lord Byron]. **Don Juan. Cantos III, IV, and V.* (pp. iv + 218)

Lord Byron, **Marino Faliero, Doge of Venice . . . .* (pp. xxii + 261)   Includes 'The Prophecy of Dante'.

Lord Byron, **Sardanapalus, a Tragedy. * The Two Foscari, a Tragedy. *Cain, a Mystery.* (pp. viii + 439)   Taken as a group these poems constitute a powerful reply to critics of Byron's personal conduct.

John Clare. *The Village Minstrel, and Other Poems*, 2 vols. (pp. xxviii + 216 and iv + 211)   Includes some remarkable descriptions of rainfall and its aftermath in 'Recollections after a Ramble'; more close observation of nature in 'The Woodman', and humorous rusticity in 'Rural Morning' and 'Rural Evening'.

Percy Bysshe Shelley. **Adonais; an Elegy . . . .* (pp. 25)

Percy Bysshe Shelley, **Epipsychidion . . . .* (pp. 31)

Robert Southey. **A Vision of Judgement.* (pp. xxxii + 79)

Lord Byron, *A Letter on W. L. Bowles' Strictures on Pope*; William Gifford, trans., *The*

Satires of Persius; death of Keats; Percy Bysshe Shelley, 'A Defence of Poetry' written (published in 1840).

1822

Bernard Barton. *Napoleon, and Other Poems.* (pp. xvi + 256)   The reflections of a Quaker on the career of the late emperor; opposition to war is tempered by respect for his talents.

Thomas Lovell Beddoes. *The Bride's Tragedy.* (pp. viii + 130)   Hesperus, forced to marry to obtain his father's release from debtor's prison, murders the woman to whom he is already secretly married and goes mad. The situation is elaborately contrived to provide occasions for emotional conflict and harks back to Otway and Rowe if not to Jacobean drama.

William Blake. * *The Ghost of Abel.* (plates 2)

[Leigh Hunt], ed. *The Liberal. Verse and Prose from the South. Volume the First.* (pp. xii + 402)   Includes Byron's anonymous *'The Vision of Judgment' and Shelley's 'May-Day Night' translated from Goethe's *Faust.*

Henry Hart Milman. *The Martyr of Antioch: a Dramatic Poem.* (pp. viii + 168)   A Roman maiden is converted to Christianity and dies in the amphitheatre for her faith. The story is from Gibbon's *Decline and Fall.*

[Samuel Rogers]. *Italy, a Poem. Part the First.* (pp. 164)   Reflections on a tour from Lake Geneva to Florence. Includes the striking Gothic tale of 'Genevra'.

Sir Walter Scott. *Halidon Hill; a Dramatic Sketch, from Scottish History.* (pp. 111)   A reminder of Scott's noble and generous characterizations in a battle-scene that is not an adequate vehicle for them.

Percy Bysshe Shelley. *Hellas a Lyrical Drama.* (pp. xii + 60)   In opposition to the alliance of Britain and Turkey against the Greek bid for liberation and based on Aeschylus's *Persae.* The tyrant Mahmud, disturbed by rebellions in his empire, seeks the prophetic advice of the Jew Ahasuerus. The fall of the empire is predicted, but news of the betrayal of the Greeks by the European nations arrives.

William Wordsworth. *Ecclesiastical Sketches.* (pp. x + 123)   A collection of sonnets on the Church of England inspired in part by the currency of the question of Roman Catholic emancipation. Part I traces Christianity up to the Pope's humbling of Frederick Barbarossa. Part II carries the story to the execution of Charles I and includes fine sonnets on the dissolution of the monasteries, on Cranmer, Hooker and Laud. Part III brings the account to the present and adds the magnificent sonnet 'Mutability'. There are moments here equal to any of Wordsworth's earlier verse, but the arrangement of the collection as a whole seems to cramp his style.

William Wordsworth, *Memorials of a Tour on the Continent, 1820.* (pp. viii + 103)   A miscellaneous collection in which one of the best poems, the sonnet on the Jungfrau, is borrowed from *Ecclesiastical Sketches* and, robbed of its companion poem on 'Troubles of Charles the First', loses its point.

Death of Shelley.

300

1823

Joanna Baillie, ed. *A Collection of Poems . . . for the Benefit of a Friend.* (pp. xliv + 330)   Contributions from Scott, Southey—'The Cataract of Lodore, Described in Rhymes for the Nursery'—Wordsworth, Crabbe and others.

[Lord Byron]. *The Age of Bronze; or, Carmen Seculare et Annus Haud Mirabilis.* (pp. 36)   The wealth of topics for satire forestalls Byron's profitable digressions.

[Lord Byron]. *Don Juan. Cantos VI.-VII.-VIII.* (pp. x + 184)

[Lord Byron]. *Don Juan. Cantos IX.-X.-and XI.* (pp. 148)

[Lord Byron]. *Don Juan. Cantos XII.-XIII.-and XIV.* (pp. 168)

Lord Byron. *The Island, or Christian and His Comrades.* (pp. 94)   The mutiny on HMS Bounty is led by the conscience-stricken Fletcher Christian—''Tis that! 'tis that! I am in Hell! in Hell!'. The mutineers' subsequent idyll on a Pacific island is brought to an end by the arrival of a British ship. Christian is killed, many are captured, one youth is saved by the resourcefulness of a native girl.

Lord Byron. *Werner, a Tragedy.* (pp. viii + 188)   Dedicated to Goethe.

Thomas Campbell. 'The Last Man', in the *New Monthly Magazine.*

[Leigh Hunt], ed. *The Liberal. Verse and Prose from the South,* vol. 2 (pp. viii + 377)   Includes Byron's anonymous 'The Blues, a Literary Eclogue' and 'Heaven and Earth'—on the loves of angels for mortals. Cf. Moore, below.

Leigh Hunt. *Ultra-Crepidarius; a Satire on William Gifford.* (pp. 40)

Thomas Moore. *Fables for the Holy Alliance.* (pp. xvi + 200)   Political and social satire. Includes 'Rhymes on the Road', a facetious grand tour.

Thomas Moore. *The Loves of the Angels . . . .* (pp. x + 148)   Three angels describe how they came to give up their immortality for the love of mortal women.

Percy Bysshe Shelley. *Poetical Pieces.* A reissue with a new title page, of *Prometheus Unbound, Hellas, The Cenci,* and *Rosalind and Helen.*

1824

Edwin Atherstone. *A Midsummer Day's Dream . . . .* (pp. 173)   An angel visits the author in a dream and takes him on a journey through space and time reminiscent of *Queen Mab* but innocent of original point of view. Apocalyptic illustrations by John Martin.

Lord Byron. *The Deformed Transformed.* (pp. 88)   Arnold the hunchback despairingly contemplates suicide but is dissuaded by a stranger who offers him supernatural powers and beauty in return for his soul. Arnold chooses the form of Achilles and the stranger, who calls himself Caesar, adopts Arnold's former shape. They join in the siege of Rome and adventures in love and war begin, with Caesar making ironical remarks on the absurdities of human ambition. The poem is unfinished.

[Lord Byron]. *Don Juan. Cantos XV. and XVI.* (pp. 129)   The fragment of Canto XVII was first published in 1903.

Thomas Campbell. *Theodric; a Domestic Tale; and Other Poems.* (pp. 149)   In 'Theodric', young Julia falls in love with her brother's commanding officer, Theodric, who in turn is engaged to marry. He remains true to his vows, Julia dies of a broken heart and while Theodric is visiting her his wife dies of a serious illness. A study in conflicting loyalties. Some Gothic ballads follow and another tale of conflicting feelings, 'The Ritter Bann'.

[Letitia E. Landon] L.E.L. *The Improvisatrice; and other Poems....* (pp. viii + 327)   The unhappy love of a young woman for a man who is plighted to another. By the time his wife dies she too is dying. A series of brief tales follows, some Gothic, most involving active handsome men and passionate but stoical women.

James Montgomery, ed. *The Chimney-Sweeper's Friend, and Climbing Boy's Album.* (pp. xvi + 428)   A contribution to the campaign against the abuse of children in this work. A mixture of solicited prose and verse. Blake's 'The Chimney Sweeper' is rescued from obscurity by Charles Lamb. Montgomery's *'The Climbing-Boy's Soliloquies', modelled on Blake and Southey, are of some interest.

Percy Bysshe Shelley. *Posthumous Poems.* (pp. xii + 415)   Includes *'Julian and Maddalo'; 'The Witch of Atlas'—a fanciful personification of the spirit of love that draws freely and fascinatingly on a wide range of literary precedents; *'Letter to [Maria Gisborne]'; 'The Triumph of Life'—an unfinished allegory of the conquest of human vision by experience; *'Mont Blanc'; and 'The Fugitives'—an unpolished idealization of a Gothic ballad.

Death of Lord Byron.

1825

Henry Austen Driver. *The Arabs: a Tale, in Four Cantos.* (pp. viii + 99)   An elaborate oriental tale of heroism, young love and resistance to foreign tyranny, in which some effort is made to be true to actual Arab customs.

Felicia Hemans. *The Forest Sanctuary; and Other Poems.* (pp. vi + 205)   In the North American forest, a refugee from the Spanish Inquisition in the sixteenth century looks forward to an idyllic life for his child and recalls with horror the world he has left. (Catholic emancipation was a major political issue in 1825 and the re-establishment of the Inquisition in Spain in 1814 was an ill-timed complication.)

James Hogg. *Queen Hynde....* (pp. ii + 443)   A romance after Scott's manner, but more humorous, set in sixth-century Scotland besieged by the Norsemen. McHouston, a rustic stranger from Ireland, saves the queen by out-fighting and out-playing all comers. The queen accepts his hand in spite of his uncouth ways and it is then revealed that he is the long-lost Scottish prince.

[Thomas Hood and John Hamilton Reynolds]. *Odes and Addresses to Great People.* (pp. viii + 136)   Light satire on such figures as Scott—'the great unknown'—McAdam the roadbuilder, Mrs Fry the prison reformer and Grimaldi the clown.

George Hyde. *Alphonzus; a Tragedy, in Five Acts.* (pp. 92) The virtuous and happy family of King Alphonzus of Spain is sacrificed in a conflict between the treachery of wicked rebels and the king's inflexible honour.

[Letitia E. Landon] L. E. L. *The Troubadour; Catalogue of Pictures, and Historical Sketches.* (pp. vi + 326) In 'The Troubadour', modelled on Scott's romances, true love is frustrated for years by circumstances but eventually wins through. The 'Catalogue' is a description or dramatization of paintings by contemporaries; the 'Sketches' are ballads on famous moments in history.

Mrs Henry Rolls. *Legends of the North, or, the Feudal Christmas . . . .* (pp. xii + 272) Gothic tales told during the twelve days of Christmas in a fifteenth-century manor in Yorkshire. Hogg and soda water.

Robert Southey. *A Tale of Paraguay.* (pp. xx + 199) Innocents cut off from civilization by a smallpox epidemic live happily in the woods until encountered by a missionary who brings them back to society, Christianity and death.

William Hazlitt. *The Spirit of the Age.*

1826

Joanna Baillie. *The Martyr: a Drama . . . .* (pp. xviii + 78) A noble young Roman is converted to Christianity and loses the woman he loves and a fortune and is condemned to death by Nero. A male counterpart to Milman's *Martyr of Antioch.*

[Elizabeth Barrett] (later Browning). *An Essay on Mind, with Other Poems.* (pp. xvi + 152) Didactic reflections on history, science and metaphysics.

Thomas Hood. *Whims and Oddities, in Prose and Verse . . . .* (pp. xii + 147) Droll punning stories anticipating Victorian comic verse. 'Faithless Nelly Gray. A Pathetic Ballad' ('Ben Battle was a soldier bold . . .') is the most successful.

Chandos Leigh. *Epistles to a Friend in Town, Golconda's Fête, and Other Poems.* (pp. xii + 260) The epistles, written by a young lawyer, reflect on the past pleasures of youth, the beauties of country life, the responsibilities of adult life and its advantages. The volume includes 'The View', a brief imitation of *Childe Harold's Pilgrimage.* The school of Byron and Rogers.

Henry Hart Milman. *Anne Boleyn: a Dramatic Poem.* (pp. viii + 171) The villainous Jesuit, Angelo Caraffa, brings about the deaths of the queen and of an innocent young man whom he contrives to have falsely admit adultery with her.

Mary Russell Mitford. *Foscari: a Tragedy.* (pp. iv + 78) Independent of Byron's 'The Two Foscari'; with its larger minor roles, better suited to the stage but lacking in moral complexity.

James Montgomery. **The Pelican Island, and Other Poems.* (pp. xii + 264) The voyage of a spirit through space and time with reflections on the progress of evolution from underwater creatures to man. Man's noble capacities are contrasted with his fallen condition. Finally the spirit meets an aged man who seems truly noble, accompanied by a small child. Together they pray. An elaborate parable.

1827

John Clare. *The Shepherd's Calendar; with Village Stories, and Other Poems.*
(viii + 238)   A detailed and convincing description of rural life month by
month. Little social comment, but people are observed as well as the flora and
fauna.

[George Croly]. *May Fair* . . . . (pp. ii + 194)   Topical satire of fashionable life, of
a mildly Whiggish cast.

Richard H. Dana. *Poems.* (pp. xii + 113)   Includes 'The Buccaneer' in which the
conscience of a criminal is confirmed by supernatural visitations, and 'The
Changes of Home', a man's visit to the place where he grew up.

George Darley. *Sylvia; or, the May Queen. A Lyrical Drama* (pp. viii + 217) Romance
in which fairyland interferes with the course of rustic love; heavily indebted to *A
Midsummer Night's Dream.*

Reginald Heber. *Hymns, Written and Adapted to the Weekly Church Service of the Year.*
(pp. xii + 153)   Includes 'Hark! the herald Angels sing', 'Holy, holy, holy,
Lord God Almighty!', 'Jesus Christ is risen to-day' and other favourites.

Thomas Hood. *The Plea of the Midsummer Fairies, Hero and Leander* . . . . *and Other
Poems.* (pp. viii + 222)   An allegorical account of the usefulness of the fairies in
A Midsummer Night's Dream; an account of Leander's death that seems to be
modelled on Keats's *Endymion*; and other Huntian or Keatsian experiments.

[Edgar Allan Poe] A Bostonian. *Tamerlane and Other Poems.* (pp. 40)

[Alfred and Charles Tennyson]. *Poems, by Two Brothers.* (pp. xii + 228)   Competent imitations suggesting an acquaintance with the lyrics of Moore, Byron,
Campbell and Scott.

[?Chauncey Hare Townshend]. *The Reigning Vice: a Satirical Essay* . . . .
(pp. xvi + 182)   A belated reply to Pope's *Essay on Man* in which self-love is
singled out as the cause of human unhappiness. Books III and IV satirize
contemporary examples.

Death of Blake; William Gifford, ed., *The Dramatic Works of John Ford*, 2 vols;
William Wordsworth, *The Poetical Works*, 5 vols.

1828

The Amulet, or Christian and Literary Remembrancer, ed. S. C. Hall, vol. 4.
(pp. xiv + 394)   A sanctimonious and sentimental collection of prose and
verse, including Coleridge's 'I stood on Brocken's sovran height' and contributions by Clare, Mrs Hemans and Southey.

Edwin Atherstone, *The Fall of Nineveh* . . . *The First Six Books*, vol. 1.
(pp. xvi + 288)   Frontispiece by John Martin. Shifts the emphasis from
Byron's moral characterization of Sardanapalus to epic renderings of battle
after Southey's manner, and sides with the rebels.

The Bijou; or Annual of Literature and the Arts, ed. W. F. (pp. xiv + 320)   Includes
Coleridge's 'Work without Hope', prose fragment 'The Wanderings of Cain',
'Youth and Age', and 'The Two Founts'.

The Gem, a Literary Annual [for 1829], ed. Thomas Hood. (pp. 324)   Includes Hood's 'The Dream of Eugene Aram'.

Mary Russell Mitford. *Rienzi: a Tragedy* . . . . (pp. 66)   The rise and fall in fourteenth-century Rome of an able democrat whose character is marred by pride. The aristocratic opposition is modelled on *Romeo and Juliet*; Rienzi himself has much in common with Marino Faliero; and the play centres on the moment in which Rienzi yields to his daughter's plea for the life of her aristocratic but rebellious husband only to learn, moments later, that he is already dead.

[Thomas Moore]. *Odes upon Cash, Corn, Catholics, and Other Matters.* (pp. vi + 183)   Good-natured satire on such topics as inflation, national debt, corn laws, food shortages, elections, Catholic emancipation, misgovernment of Ireland, the debasement of the peerage and anonymous poetry.

Samuel Rogers. *Italy, a Poem. Part the Second.* (pp. ii + 188)   Reflections on a tour continued.

Samuel Taylor Coleridge, *The Poetical Works*, 3 vols.

1829

[Ebenezer Elliott]. *The Village Patriarch* . . . . (pp. viii + 198)   Rural life summed up in the experience, reminiscences, reflections and expectations of Enoch Wray, an old, blind mason. The poem is modelled on Crabbe, but has a sharp political focus closer to the radical verse of the 1790s; people in authority are directly blamed for the conditions of the poor. The tale of Hanna Wray in Book VIII is particularly powerful.

Thomas Hood. *The Epping Hunt* . . . . (pp. 29)   John Huggins unwisely joins a stag hunt and comes to grief when his hired horse bolts.

[Letitia E. Landon] L. E. L. *The Venetian Bracelet . . . and Other Poems.* (pp. x + 307)   The title poem is a study of female love, jealousy and hatred. The volume is devoted to the unhappy or unfulfilled loves of young aristocratic ladies in olden days. 'The Ancestress', based on Grillparzer's *Die Ahnfrau* (1817), has some Gothic life to it.

C. Redding. *Gabrielle, a Tale of the Swiss Mountains.* (pp. viii + 136)   The story of Gabrielle, a girl who goes mad when she sees her home and family overwhelmed by an avalanche, is followed by other poems in which sentiment, patriotism, and the macabre appear by turns.

Charles Doyne Sillery. *Vallery; or, the Citadel of the Lake* . . ., 2 vols. (pp. xii + 274 and 303)   Chivalric conflict between Spaniards and Moors in the Pyrenees. Scott seems to be the model, the Scott of *The Bridal of Triermain*, but Sillery is unfortunately better at description than at characterization or plot.

Robert Southey. *All for Love; and the Pilgrim to Compostella.* (pp. iv + 221)   In 'All for Love' a young man wins his bride by selling his soul to Lucifer but his happiness is interrupted when she is prompted by a dream to insist that he wash away the red spot on his heart. 'The Pilgrim' is a comic tale of homely miracles and seems to mock Roman Catholic credulity.

Alfred Tennyson. 'Timbuctoo . . .', in *Prolusiones Academicae* . . . . A Cambridge prize poem. The author is granted a vision of the unknown city by a seraph and is advised to 'sway the heart of man : and teach him to attain/By shadowing forth the Unattainable . . .'. Echoes of Byron and Keats.

1830

Edwin Atherstone. *The Fall of Nineveh* . . ., vol. 2. (pp. 308) Battle-scenes and heroics continue. Our sympathies remain with the rebels.

[Ebenezer Elliott]. *Corn Law Rhymes*. (pp. xii + 115) Published in Sheffield. Brisk political satire depicting the miseries of the starving poor and blaming the profiteers from bread tax for their condition. Includes 'The Ranter', *'Child is thy father dead?', 'The Death Feast', 'Burns, from the Dead', 'The Black Hole of Calcutta', 'Death of a Child at Sea'.

Felicia Hemans. *Songs of the Affections, with Other Poems*. (pp. iv + 259) Depictions of unusual states of feeling, mostly virtuous ones. Includes 'A Spirit's return' in which a woman is given comforting information about the hereafter by the ghost of her departed lover, and 'The Lady of Provence', in which a wife, refusing to believe that her husband fled from battle, goes to the battlefield to recover his body and subsequently expires at his funeral.

Charles Lamb. *Album Verses, with a Few Others*. (pp. viii + 150) A retrospective collection of scraps put together for Lamb's young publishing friend, Moxon. Includes translation from Vincent Bourne's Latin of 'The Ballad Singers', a dramatization of a tale from Crabbe, 'The Wife's Trial', and some mildly amusing shorter pieces.

[Charles Lamb]. *Satan in Search of a Wife* . . . . By an Eye Witness. (pp. 36) A parody of Moore's *Loves of the Angels* in which the devil, after 20,000 years of bachelorhood, courts a tailor's daughter while disguised as a Dutchman. To win her he has to reveal his identity.

Robert Montgomery. *Satan* . . . . (pp. 391) Satan surveys the passage of civilizations and the condition of modern Europe; he reflects upon the unavoidable circumstances of life, and turns finally to the promising but often disappointing example of England. Satan's view, which sees the true value of things, is not sufficiently disentangled from the author's, which is merely pious.

Sir Walter Scott. *The Doom of Devorgoil, a Melo-Drama. Auchindrane; or, the Ayrshire Tragedy*. (pp. 337) 'The Doom' is comic Gothicism intended for the stage. It includes the song 'Bonny Dundee' and the female lead, Kathleen, a flirtatious tomboy, almost saves the play. 'Auchindrane' occasionally reminds one of *Rokeby* but fails to make 'pride, vengeance and ambition' interesting.

Alfred Tennyson. *Poems, Chiefly Lyrical*. (pp. ii + 154) Includes 'Mariana', 'Supposed Confessions of a Second-rate Sensitive Mind not in Unity with Itself', 'The Kraken', 'The Ballad of Oriana'. The evocation of mood and atmosphere, displayed at its best in 'Mariana', is the distinctive feature of this volume.

Charles Tennyson (later Turner). *Sonnets and Fugitive Pieces*. (pp. 83)

Thomas Hood, ed., *The Comic Annual* (1830–42); William Maginn, 'Gallery of Illustrious Literary Characters' in *Fraser's Magazine* (1830–38); Frank Sayers, *Poetical Works*, ed. William Taylor.

1831

[James Hogg]. *Songs, by the Ettrick Shepherd* . . . . (pp. viii + 311)   Patriotic songs, sentimental love songs, comic songs, drinking songs, mostly in Scottish dialect. Annotated in the droll, self-conscious manner of the Ettrick Shepherd in 'Noctes Ambrosianae' (*Blackwood's Magazine*, 1822–35).

John Greenleaf Whittier. *Legends of New England*. (pp. 142)   Versifications of local tales, some Gothic, one with an Indian chief, Metacom, modelled on Byron's Conrad (*The Corsair*), and several concerned with the feelings of Indians dispossessed of their land.

1832

Robert Montgomery. *The Messiah.* (pp. xi + 300)

Percy Bysshe Shelley. *The Mask of Anarchy*, ed. Leigh Hunt. (pp. xx + 47)   Incendiary protest against the 'Peterloo Massacre' in Manchester, written in 1819, in which Murder, Fraud and Anarchy are defied by Hope and put to flight by the spirit of Freedom.

Deaths of Crabbe and Scott.

1833

[Robert Browning]. *Pauline.* (pp. 71)   A confession, similar in manner to the monologue of the Maniac in Shelley's 'Julian and Maddalo', in which the conflict of experience with youthful ideals and feelings is reflected upon and shared with a beloved confidante.

Hartley Coleridge. *Poems.* (pp. 157)   Includes 'She is not fair to outward view' and a number of interesting sonnets.

Alfred Tennyson. *Poems.* (pp. vi + 163)   Includes 'The Two Voices', 'OEnone', 'The Lotos-Eaters', 'The Lady of Shalott', 'The Palace of Art' and 'Mariana in the South'.

Elizabeth Barrett (later Browning), trans. Aeschylus, *Prometheus Bound.*

1834

Death of Coleridge.

1835

Robert Browning. *Paracelsus*. (pp. xi + 216)   The man who devotes his life to science learns from a poet that he has fatally neglected sympathy for others. An allegory of the choice of life theme, reminiscent of *Faust*.

John Clare. *The Rural Muse*. (pp. x + 175)   Includes *'The Nightingale's Nest' and other poems on birds' nests and more than eighty sonnets.

George Darley. *Nepenthe*. (pp. 69)   An absorbing but unfinished allegory in which the 'deleterious effects of ultra-natural joy' and 'ultra-natural melancholy' are represented.

Thomas Moore. *The Fudges in England*. (pp. ix + 140)   A sequel to the Paris episode with an older Miss Fudge. Her fortune-hunting suitors are members of the Low Church movement.

William Wordsworth. *Yarrow Revisited, and Other Poems*. (pp. xvii + 349)   The title poem and a series of sonnets commemorate Wordsworth's visit to Scotland in 1831. Miscellaneous poems follow, including 'The Russian Fugitive' and 'The Egyptian Maid', the 'Evening Voluntaries', and the series of 'Sonnets, 1833'.

Death of Hogg.

Notes

Chapter 1   Deliberate simplicities

1 *Lives of the English Poets*, ed. George Birk-beck Hill (Oxford, 1905), vol. 3, p. 251.

2 *The Correspondence of Edmund Burke*, ed. Thomas W. Copeland *et al.* (Cambridge and Chicago, 1958–70), vol. 9, p. 183: to Edward Jerningham, 18 December 1796.

3 *The Correspondence of William Cowper*, ed. Thomas Wright (1904), vol. 2, p. 287; to Joseph Johnson.

4 *The Poetical Works of the Late Mrs. Mary Robinson* (1806), vol. 2, p. 99.

5 Ebenezer Elliott, *The Splendid Village . . . and Other Poems* (1834), vol. 1, pp. 60–1.

6 Lines 109–11; an extravagance at which even the child's father felt obliged to de-mur. See Samuel Taylor Coleridge, *Biographia Literaria*, ed. George Watson (1956), p. 260.

7 William Wordsworth, *The Poetical Works*, ed. E. de Selincourt and Helen Darbishire (Oxford, 1965–8), vol. 2, p. 478; statement to Isabella Fenwick. For an excellent and full discussion of the poem, see Mary Jacobus, 'The Idiot Boy', in *Bicentenary Wordsworth Studies . . .*, ed. Jonathan Words-worth (Ithaca and London, 1970), pp. 238–65.

8 Lines 87–9. Altered in editions subsequent to 1820.

9 J. M. S. Tompkins has noticed a more exotic rendition of the same experience in Ann Radcliffe's novel *The Italian* (1797). See *The Popular Novel in England 1770–1800* (1932; rpt 1969), p. 264.

10 William Gifford, *The Baviad, and Maeviad* (1797), p. 55n. For an account of polite verse during the period, see W. N. Hargreaves-Mawdsley, *The English Della Cruscans and their Time* (The Hague, 1967).

11 He also departs significantly from the supernatural aura conveyed by Bürger's 'The Lass of Fair Wone'—the particular poem upon which 'The Thorn' is based. Bürger's title was 'Des Pfarrers Tochter von Taubenhain'; Wordsworth knew William Taylor's translation in *The Monthly Magazine*, vol. 1 (1796), pp. 223–4. For an excellent account of Wordsworth's use of previous poems, see Mary Jacobus, *Tradition and Experiment in Wordsworth's 'Lyrical Ballads' (1798)* (Oxford, 1976), pp. 240–50.

12 Gossip that dismissively sums up the facts of the case in Bürger's poem.

13 No. II, 27 November; reprinted in *Poetry of the Anti-Jacobin* (1801), 4th edn, p. 9.

14 For a helpful account of the hymn-writing tradition and Blake's place in it, see Martha Winburn England and John Sparrow, *Hymns Unbidden* (New York, 1966), pp. 43–112.

15 Blackness seems to be uniformly regarded as ugly in the period, and a plea is generally made for the beauty of the soul it conceals. Even Phyllis Wheatley, an emancipated American slave, can write in 'On Being brought from Africa to America' (1773):

> Some view our sable race with scornful eye,
> 'Their colour is a diabolic die'.
> Remember, *Christians*, *Negros*, black as *Cain*,
> May be refin'd, and join th'angelic train.

The same argument appears in poems as diverse as Graves's 'The Fair Parthian' (1776), Pratt's *Humanity* (1788), Day's *The*

309

Dying Negro (1773), and Mrs Opie's 'The Negro Boy's Tale' (1802). Cowper's 'The Negro's Complaint' (written in 1788) avoids the solecism.

16 *The Correspondence of William Cowper*, vol. 3, p. 252; to Samuel Rose, 29 March.

17 The detail sounds convincing, but Goldsmith found most of it equally applicable to his 'Description of an Author's Bedchamber'; see Oliver Goldsmith, *Collected Works*, ed. Arthur Friedman (Oxford, 1966), vol. 4, pp. 374–5.

18 The earliest editions showed her in a title-page engraving by Isaac Taylor.

19 Quoted from *The Poems of Thomas Gray . . .*, ed. Roger Lonsdale (1969), p. 117.

20 See *The Prose Works of William Wordsworth*, ed. W. J. B. Owen and Jane Worthington Smyser (Oxford, 1974), vol. 1, p. 124.

21 Page v. Ireland at this time was notorious for his Shakespearean hoaxes—for which see John Mair, *The Fourth Forger* (1938)— and disguised himself discreetly as H. C. Esq.

22 Vernor and Hood, who were Bloomfield's publishers also, had brought out nine editions of *The Farmer's Boy* by 1806; *The Fisher Boy* took sufficiently for them to follow it in 1809 with Ireland's post-Nelsonian *The Sailor Boy. A Poem in Four Cantos Illustrative of the Navy of Great Britain*.

23 Wilkie may be thought of as a successor to artists like the French Jean-Baptiste Greuze and Joseph Wright of Derby; all of them came from the provinces.

24 In the volume of the same name.

25 *Letters of Charles Lamb*, ed. E. V. Lucas (1935), vol. 2, p. 328; 31 August 1822.

26 'On the Cockney School of Poetry', *Blackwood's Magazine* (1817–18), vol. 2, pp. 38–41, 194–201, etc.

27 In 'The Nymphs', lines 217–18, published in *Foliage* (1818).

28 Eric Robinson and Geoffrey Summerfield, eds, *Selected Poems and Prose of John Clare* (1967), p. 73.
Subsequent references to the poem are to this edition.

Chapter 2   From terror to wonder

1 See J. M. S. Tompkins, *The Popular Novel in England 1770–1800* (1932), ch. 7; Patricia Meyer Spacks, *The Insistence of Horror: Aspects of the Supernatural in Eighteenth-Century Poetry* (Cambridge, Mass., 1962); Karl S. Guthke, *Englische Vorromantik und Deutscher Sturm und Drang . . .* (Göttingen, 1958); Montague Summers, *The Gothic Quest* (n.d.).

2 T. J. Mathias, *The Pursuits of Literature . . .*, 5th edn (1798), p. 81n.

3 Coleridge describes the effect of such metres as 'not unlike that of galloping over a paved road in a German stage-waggon without springs'. Samuel Taylor Coleridge, *Biographia Literaria* (1817), ch. xvi.

4 The incident seems to be based on a similar one in C. R. Maturin's novel, *Melmoth the Wanderer* (1820), ch. 3.

5 The particular evils expand a couplet in *The Deserted Village*: 'For him no wretches, born to work and weep,/Explore the mine, or tempt the dangerous deep . . .' (11. 103–4).

6 In James Hogg, *The Mountain Bard; Consisting of Ballads and Songs . . .* (Edinburgh, 1807).

7 *Monthly Review* (1804), vol. 45, p. 413.

8 In *Biographia Literaria*, ch. xiv.

9 For alternative versions of the proposed plot, see Humphry House, *Coleridge* (1953), pp. 126–8.

10 Samuel Taylor Coleridge, *Shakespearean Criticism*, ed. T. M. Raysor (1960), vol. 1, p. 38.

11 Scott records the incident in the Introduction to the 1830 edition of *The Lay of the Last Minstrel*. John Stoddart, later the editor of *The Times*, was the friend.

12 For Johnson's immediate parody of the easy style of *The Hermit*, see Boswell's *Life of Johnson*, ed. George Birkbeck Hill (Oxford, 1905), vol. 2, p. 136. Among the better known examples of the genre are Edmund Cartwright's *Armine and Elvira* (1771), John Langhorne's *Owen of Carron* (1778), and Helen Maria Williams's *Edwin and Eltruda* (1782); the form persists in Harriet Chilcot's *Elmar and Ethlinda* (1783), and D. Deacon's 'Edwin and Clarinda' in his *Poems* (1790), and is then absorbed into the Gothic ballad. There were precedents for Percy, of course, David Mallet's *Amyntor and Theodore, or the Hermit* (1747) and Goldsmith's 'Edwin and Angelina' (1765) being among the more notable. Legendary tales were mixed indiscriminately with older ballads in collections such as Thomas Evans's *Old Ballads* (1784).

13 [Lady Charlotte Bury], *Diary Illustrative of the Times of George the Fourth* (1838), vol. 1, p. 186.

14 Scott borrows the name of Geraldine's father in 'Christabel'.

15 Page xvi.
16 Hunt calls her Genevra.
17 The poem passed through four editions by 1815. It was included in James Montgomery, *The Poetical Works* (1819). The scene is a virtuous version of the nocturnal visit of Partenopex to the fairy, in Canto II of Le Grand's *Partenopex de Blois*. A translation by William Stewart Rose was published in 1807 by Scott's publishers, in a beautiful quarto volume with antiquarian notes and engraved illustrations. Keats would have expected his readers to share his memory of Eve's awakening in *Paradise Lost*, bk V, ll. 8ff.
18 *John Keats, The Poetical Works*, ed. H. W. Garrod (Oxford, 1958), p. 252n. There has, however, been some doubt from the first as to what Porphyro's melting into Madeline's dream implies. Richard Woodhouse reports Keats as saying 'that he should despise a man who would be such an eunuch in sentiment as to leave a (Girl) maid, with that Character about her, in such a situation: & should despise himself to write about it &c &c &c'. Letter to Keats's publisher, John Taylor, in *The Letters of John Keats*, ed. Hyder Edward Rollins (Cambridge, Mass., 1958), vol. 2, p. 163. For modern comment consonant with this side of Keats, see Jack Stillinger, *The Hoodwinking of Madeline and Other Essays . . .* (Urbana, 1971), pp. 67–93. See also Earl R. Wasserman, *The Finer Tone: Keats' Major Poems* (Baltimore, 1953), pp. 97–137,

for a most ingenious philosophical interpretation with which my own reading is regretfully at odds. For a discussion of the poem in the context of Keats's poetical development, see Stuart M. Sperry, *Keats the Poet* (Princeton, 1973), pp. 198–220; for discussion of it in the context of Keats's life, see Walter Jackson Bate, *John Keats* (Cambridge, Mass., 1963), pp. 418–51, and Robert Gittings, *John Keats* (1969), pp. 277–85.
19 For cogent arguments that it has a meaning, nevertheless, see George Watson, *Coleridge the Poet* (1966), pp. 117–30; John Beer, *Coleridge the Visionary* (1959), pp. 199–276; and E. S. Shaffer, '*Kubla Khan*' and '*The Fall of Jerusalem*' . . . (Cambridge, 1975), pp. 62–190.
20 *The Letters of Charles Lamb*, ed. E. V. Lucas (1935), vol. 2, p. 190; dated 26 April 1816.
21 *The Poetical Works of the Late Mrs. Mary Robinson* (1806), 3 vols; vol. 1, p. 229.
22 'The Fatal Sisters. An Ode' (1768), ll. 1–12. Quoted from *The Poems of Thomas Gray . . .*, ed. Roger Lonsdale (1969), pp. 216–17.
23 If only at second hand. William Mason's anonymous spoof, 'An Heroic Epistle to Sir William Chambers' (1773), was to be found in popular anthologies of the time, and in Vicesimus Knox's *Elegant Extracts* (1789, etc.). It was annotated with these and other quotations from Chambers.
24 *The Poetical Works of the Late Mrs. Mary Robinson*, vol. 1, pp. 227–8.

Chapter 3   The ambiguities of guilt

1 For a survey of the genre, see J. M. S. Tompkins, *The Popular Novel in England 1770–1800* (1932), ch. 7. Its relations to poetry are outlined in Peter Thorslev, *The Byronic Hero* (Minneapolis, 1962), pp. 51ff.
2 Jane Austen's Catherine Morland in *Northanger Abbey* (1818, but begun in 1798) provides a good example of amused contemporary awareness of the form.
3 Ambrosio, in Matthew G. Lewis's *The Monk* (1796), is a lively instance of the extravagant results.
4 Lamb called Restoration comedy 'altogether a speculative scene of things, which has no reference whatever to the world that is'. 'The Artificial Comedy of the Last Century', *The Works of Charles and Mary Lamb*, E. V. Lucas (1903), vol. 2, p. 143. Lamb's essay exhibits good taste struggling with the moral squeamishness of the time.

5 The religious conventions that Shelley ascribes to Italian Catholicism in the preface to *The Cenci* (p. 277) resemble those ascribed to Hinduism by Southey in *The Curse of Kehama*. The parallel is probably deliberate.
6 'True, I was happier than I am, while yet/Manhood remained to act the thing I thought;/While lust was sweeter than revenge . . .' (I, i, 96–8).
7 For a full discussion of the play, see Stuart Curran, *Shelley's 'Cenci': Scorpions Ringed With Fire* (Princeton, 1970).
8 The dates of composition are given here. *Osorio* was revised as *Remorse* and staged at Drury Lane in 1813; *The Borderers* was not published until 1842.
9 See Edgar Johnson, *Sir Walter Scott: the Great Unknown* (New York, 1970), vol. 1, pp. 261–2 and 279.

10 Of which 25,000 copies were sold in eight months. See Johnson, vol. 1, p. 335.
11 In a generally adverse assessment, *Edinburgh Review*, vol. 12 (1808), p. 22.
12 In Scott's time the stress fell on the first syllable of 'cement'.
13 Leaving that more prosaic refinement for Edgar Allan Poe's grim tale, 'The Cask of Amontillado'.
14 It is possible that as a member of the legal profession and an antiquary, Scott regarded falsification of documents as being more reprehensible than I have allowed, but the difference would not affect the analysis.
15 Introduction to 'Marmion' in Sir Walter Scott, *The Poetical Works* (1833–4), vol. 7, p. 13.
16 Lord Byron. *English Bards, and Scotch Reviewers. A Satire* (1809), 1. 168.
17 Leslie A. Marchand, *Byron: A Biography* (New York, 1957), vol. 1, p. 433.
18 *Byron's Letters and Journals*, ed. Leslie A. Marchand (Cambridge, Mass., 1973–), vol. 3, p. 214; 22 November 1813.
19 Unfortunately the brief vogue for such poems was already past—not even Scott's *Lord of the Isles* (1815) sold well.
20 *Byron's Letters and Journals*, vol. 4, p. 235; 28 November 1814. This unusual opinion was addressed to his staid fiancée, Annabella Milbanke, and may have been affected by Byron's wish to find a point of sympathy between them.
21 The original of Shelley's madwoman in *The Revolt of Islam*.
22 With reference, presumably, to the Maccabean revolt of the Jews against the attempt of Antiochus IV (175 BC) to Hellenize them by force.
23 The contrast between Byron's characterizations of Ali Pacha and Napoleon, in *Childe Harold's Pilgrimage* Cantos II (1812) and III (1816) respectively, exemplify the change in his approach. For these, see Chapter 6, below.
24 Resembling David in Dryden's *Absalom and Achitophel* (1681).
25 Both plays were staged in London in 1821 in spite of Byron's objections.
26 Lord Byron, *The Works: Poetry*, ed. E. H. Coleridge, vol. 4, p. 339.
27 Byron's mention of Milman's poem may have been prompted by the wish to help along the sales of another of his own publisher's authors, but he does seem to have read *The Fall of Jerusalem*—see *Byron's Letters and Journals*, vol. 7, p. 138; letter to Murray of 22 July 1820.

Chapter 4 The human predicament

1 See Hubert F. Babinski, *The Mazeppa Legend in European Romanticism* (New York, 1974), pp. 65ff.
2 It was reinterpreted many times; by Géricault, Delacroix, Victor Hugo and Liszt, among others. See Babinski, pp. 53–8 and 66–73.
3 *The Letters of Charles Lamb*, ed. E. V. Lucas (1935), vol. 1, p. 240; 30 January 1801, to Wordsworth.
4 Robert Southey, writing anonymously for *The Critical Review*; see *Coleridge: the Critical Heritage*, ed. J. R. de J. Jackson (1970), p. 53.
5 In *The Vicar of Wakefield* (1766).
6 Goethe reviewed the poem in 1820. 'Byron's tragedy', he said, '. . . was to me a wonderful phenomenon, and one that closely touched me. This singular intellectual poet has taken my *Faustus* to himself, and extracted from it the strangest nourishment for his hypochondriac humour'. Translation by Hoppner, in *The Works of Lord Byron: Letters and Journals*, ed. Rowland E. Prothero (1901), vol. 5, p. 506.
7 *The Letters of Robert Burns*, ed. J. De Lanccy Ferguson (Oxford, 1931), vol. 1, p. 156; 5 January 1788.
8 *Byron's Letters and Journals*, ed. Leslie A. Marchand (Cambridge, Mass., 1973–), vol. 5, p. 257.
9 In *Beppo* (1818), xix.
10 Its resemblance in certain respects to Byron's *Lament of Tasso* (1817) is outlined persuasively in Carlos Baker, *Shelley's Major Poetry: The Fabric of a Vision* (Princeton, 1948), pp. 128–38. Maddalo's name, which also appears in Shelley's fragment of a drama entitled 'Tasso', apparently is taken from Tasso's acquaintance, Count Maddalo Fucci (Baker, p. 129). Julian's name seems to be taken from Julian the Apostate (d. 363), who disavowed Christianity for moral reasons and shortly after died of battle-wounds calmly discussing the immortality of the soul.
11 In view of my comment above, p. 84, on the political connotations of the nationalities of Julian and Maddalo, it is worth noting that the lady who is said to have

caused the Maniac's downfall 'came with him from France' (1. 246), and that on her return to Venice it is reported by Maddalo's daughter that 'Her mien had been imperious, but she now/Looked meek—perhaps remorse had brought her

low' (11. 600–1). It seems entirely possible that the experience of the French revolution and its aftermath is being hinted at, limiting the Maniac's idealism to a political sphere.

Chapter 5   Meditations of sympathy

1 For the standard account of such poems as a distinctive genre, see M. H. Abrams, 'Structure and Style in the Greater Romantic Lyric', in Frederick W. Hilles and Harold Bloom, eds, *From Sensibility to Romanticism: Essays Presented to Frederick Pottle* (New York, 1965), pp. 527–60.
2 *Lives of the English Poets*, ed. George Birkbeck Hill (Oxford, 1905), vol. 1, p. 77.
3 Famous hills in foreign countries provided a further resource. For a different and more detailed perspective on the relationship of landscape to poetry, see John Barrell, *The Idea of Landscape and the Sense of Place 1730–1840* (Cambridge, 1972).
4 Joseph Wright's portrait in the Tate Gallery of the reclining Sir Brooke Boothby (1780–1) captures the pose admirably. For a reproduction, see Benedict Nicolson, *Joseph Wright of Derby: Painter of Light* (1968), vol. 2, p. 136. Boothby (1743–1824) was a minor poet and a member of Anna Seward's Lichfield circle.
5 For a thorough recent analysis of Wordsworth's use of convention in *Lyrical Ballads*, see Mary Jacobus, *Tradition and Experiment in Wordsworth's 'Lyrical Ballads' (1798)* (Oxford, 1976), pp. 104–30.
6 Gray's popular ode, 'On a Distant Prospect of Eton College' (1747), in which the happiness of the boys at play is contrasted with the miseries that lie ahead of them when they grow up, is typical of the precedents that Wordsworth is abandoning.
7 See especially Book I, stanzas xix–xxiv, liii–lvi, and II, vi–viii.
8 Cf. Coleridge's own complimentary verses 'On the Christening of a Friend's Child' (1797).
9 The nocturnal meditation had already been established on a grand scale by Edward Young's *The Complaint: or, Night Thoughts* (1744).
10 Thomson's 'Ode on Aeolus's Harp' and Mason's 'Ode to an Aeolus's Harp' were both to be found in Dodsley's popular *Collection of Poems* (1775), vol. 3, pp. 4–5 and vol. 4, pp. 267–8. The description of the harp in Thomson's *The Castle of*

Indolence, Canto I, stanzas xl–xli, was also well known.
11 For discussion of the longer version, see Humphry House, *Coleridge* (1953), pp. 133–41, and George Whalley, *Coleridge and Sara Hutchinson and the Asra Poems* (1955), pp. 127–9, and 155–64. For detailed comment on the purpose of the structure of 'Dejection: An Ode' and 'Frost at Midnight', see Reeve Parker, *Coleridge's Meditative Art* (1975), pp. 181–209 and 127–38.
12 Keats, like Coleridge—see 'The Nightingale' (1798)—departs from the tradition of the melancholy nightingale. His precedent seems to be Dryden's rendering of the pseudo-Chaucerian poem 'The Flower and the Leaf' in *Fables Ancient and Modern* (1700)—see especially lines 114–45.
13 *Night Thoughts*, I, 14 lines from the end. Modern critics often assume that Keats is describing the effects of writing poetry rather than of reading it—see, for example, Walter Jackson Bate, *John Keats* (Cambridge, Mass., 1963), p. 505—allowing their justifiable interest in Keats the poet to replace Keats's wider claim to kinship with his readers as a fellow-reader.
14 The poem was composed in 1820, but published posthumously in 1824. Shelley's playful tone owes much to Leigh Hunt's series of verse epistles, 'Harry Brown's Letters to His Friends' in *The Examiner* in 1816.
15 Coming from an Irishman, Moore's rather facile patriotism sometimes has ironical overtones of which he was aware, but in this poem at least he seems to be sincere.
16 Castlereagh's period as chief secretary for Ireland (1799–1801), and title of Marquis of Londonderry, as well as the active part he played in the political ordering of Europe at the Congress of Vienna in 1814–15, make him an obvious candidate for the role of 'Celtic Anarch'. Shelley was soon to attack him by name in *The Mask of Anarchy* (1819) for his part in the Peterloo Massacre.
17 See, however, Ian Jack's stimulating

313

discussion of it from a contrary point of view in *Keats and the Mirror of Art* (Oxford, 1967), pp. 214–24.

18 Keats would have found a precedent for this enigmatic close in the final lines uttered in the ruined abbey in Wordsworth's *The White Doe of Rylstone* (1815): 'Thou, thou art not a Child of Time,/But Daughter of the Eternal Prime'

(11. 1909–10), as well as for his opening description of the urn as 'foster-child of silence and slow Time'.

19 For accounts of the part played by the meditations of sympathy in the development of various forms of verse, see Abbie Findlay Potts, *The Elegiac Mode* (1967), and Robert Langbaum, *The Poetry of Experience* (1957).

Chapter 6   Testimonies of individual experience

1 Johnson was paying sly tribute to a sermon that he himself had ghost-written for Dodd. See James Boswell, *Life of Johnson*, ed. George Birkbeck Hill (Oxford, 1887), vol. 3, p. 167. The sermon was *The Convict's Address to His Unhappy Brethren* (1777).

2 See Roy Pascal, *Design and Truth in Autobiography* (Cambridge, Mass., 1960) for a general account of the forms available to an author. The first chapter of G. A. Starr, *Defoe and Spiritual Autobiography* (Princeton, 1965) describes the conventions of late seventeenth- and early eighteenth-century lives in a way that holds remarkably well for Romantic practice. See also Paul Delany, *British Autobiography in the Seventeenth Century* (1969), esp. ch. 6, 'The Autobiographers of the Sects'.

3 See *The Letters of Charles Lamb . . .*, ed. E. V. Lucas (1935), vol. 1, p. 73, and *Collected Letters of Samuel Taylor Coleridge*, ed. Earl Leslie Griggs (Oxford, 1956–71), vol. 1, p. 279. The phrase was Coleridge's.

4 *The Correspondence of William Cowper*, ed. Thomas Wright (1904), vol. 3, p. 301; see also vol. 2, pp. 252–3.

5 See 'Preface', in Edward Young, *Night Thoughts*.

6 'Winter', 11. 84–9, in James Thomson, *The Complete Poetical Works*, ed. J. Logie Robertson (1908), p. 188.

7 The thought is developed from Thomson's

The Castle of Indolence (1748), II, iii. (*The Complete Poetical Works*, p. 280)

8 *The Prelude* has long been known popularly in the revised version published posthumously in 1850. Now that the 1805 version is widely available in inexpensive editions it seems permissible and less anachronistic to quote it.

9 The lines were published as an independent poem in *Lyrical Ballads* in 1800.

10 *The Life & Correspondence of the Late Robert Southey*, ed. Charles Cuthbert Southey (1850), vol. 3, p. 214.

11 A more remote precedent for both Wright and Byron is to be found in William Falconer's *The Shipwreck* (1762) which is also set in the eastern Mediterranean and comments in passing on the politically fallen state of modern Greece. Byron knew the poem.

12 See *Byron: the Critical Heritage*, ed. Andrew Rutherford (1970), p. 35.

13 Thomas Moore, *Letters and Journals of Lord Byron* (1830), vol. 1, p. 347.

14 *Essay on Man*, Epistle II, 16–18, in *The Poems of Alexander Pope*, ed. John Butt (1963), p. 516.

15 For the most persuasive biographical interpretation of the poem, see Jerome J. McGann, *Fiery Dust: Byron's Poetic Development* (Chicago and London, 1968), pp. 94–138.

Chapter 7   Reappraisals of society

1 For the changing nature of this public, see Richard D. Altick, *The English Common Reader . . . .* (Chicago, 1957), pp. 81–98.

2 Uncle Oliver in Sheridan's *The School for Scandal* (1777) is something of an exception, but even he is assumed to be made of money and gullible until he appears in person.

3 For contemporary reactions see *Crabbe: the*

Critical Heritage, ed. Arthur Pollard (1972).

4 *The Prose Works of William Wordsworth*, ed. W. J. B. Owen and Jane Worthington Smyser (Oxford, 1974), vol. 1, p. 130.

5 Reviving Addison's attack in *The Spectator*, 16 April 1711.

6 Crabbe's corrective to the excesses of fiction parallels the sentimental sensationalism of Thomas Campbell's *Gertrude of Wyoming*

(1809) in which heroine and paternal sage are wantonly killed off in an Indian massacre. Both writers are departing from convention, but with opposite intentions.

7 In his libretto for Benjamin Britten's opera *Peter Grimes* (1945), Montagu Slater is obliged to replace Crabbe's monster with a man who is 'visionary, ambitious, impetuous and frustrated' and he softens his character with a romantic attachment to a transformed Ellen Orford.

8 Wordsworth is believed to have found this Indian name for the Whip-poor-will in Carver's *Travels in North America* (1772)—see William Wordsworth, *The Poetical Works*, ed. E. de Selincourt and Helen Darbishire (Oxford, 1965–8), vol. 5, p. 423n.

9 Cf. William Cowper's similar complaint to John Newton, *The Correspondence of William Cowper*, ed. Thomas Wright (1904) vol. 3, pp. 40–3. Dorothy Wordsworth was reading Cowper's *Life and Posthumous Writings* in 1805. See *The Letters of William and Dorothy Wordsworth*, ed. Ernest de Selincourt and Chester L. Shaver (Oxford, 1967–), vol. 1, p. 577.

10 See *On Books and Their Writers*, ed. Edith J. Morley (1938), vol. 1, pp. 158–9. For a thoroughgoing condemnation, see Blake's 'Annotations to *The Excursion*', in *The Complete Writings*, ed. Geoffrey Keynes (1966), p. 784.

11 The tale is in fact the only one told by the Pastor about living people.

12 The personal implications for Wordsworth are beyond our scope here and are explored challengingly in Geoffrey H. Hartman, *Wordsworth's Poetry 1787–1814* (New Haven and London, 1964).

13 Cf. Altick, *The English Common Reader*, pp. 67–172.

14 We have already noticed Cowper's assertion of it in *The Task*; and it crops up as an assumption in foreign works such as Schiller's *Kabale und Liebe* (1784), in Milady Milford's democratic sympathies, and in Blondchen's rebuke to Osmin in Mozart's *Die Entführung aus dem Serail* (1782): 'Ich bin eine Engländerin und zur Freiheit geboren!' ('I am an Englishwoman and born free!')

15 Frere was writing in an unfamiliar Italian tradition. Pulci's *Morgante Maggiori*, Berni's parody of Boiardo's *Orlando inamorato* and Casti's *Gli animali parlanti* have been identified as sources, the last having been published in an English translation by William Stewart Rose in 1816. Byron seems to have begun with Frere and then to have acquainted himself with the Italians.

16 *Edinburgh Review*, vol. 29 (1818), p. 302.

17 Byron drew upon published sources for the details of events outside his own experience. As a consequence, his accounts of shipwreck and siege are convincingly realistic.

18 For instance William Blackwood, who wrote of 'the vile, heartless, and cold-blooded way this fiend attempted to degrade every sacred and tender feeling of the human heart'. Quoted in the *Variorum Don Juan*, ed. Truman Guy Steffan and Willis W. Pratt (Austin, 1957), vol. 4, p. 296.

19 *Don Juan*, like *Beppo*, was published anonymously, but its authorship was an open secret. Cantos I and II appeared in 1819; Cantos III–V in 1821. In 1823 Cantos VI–VIII, IX–XI and XII–XIV appeared in three separate volumes over the imprint of John and Leigh Hunt; Cantos XV and XVI were published in 1824. The fragment of Canto XVII was first published with the poem in 1924.

20 The threat of a hundred cantos may seem extravagant to readers of Homer, Virgil, Spenser and Milton; Byron would have expected his readers to think of the long romances of Ariosto too.

21 Anacharsis Cloots (1755–94), fanatical opponent of tyranny during the French revolution, known as 'orator of the human race'.

22 To John Murray, 16 February 1821; *Letters and Journals*, ed. Rowland E. Prothero (1901), vol. 5, p. 242.

23 In Samuel Taylor Coleridge, *Biographia Literaria* (1817), vol. 2, p. 262. The case for Coleridge's influence is plausibly argued in Ernest Hartley Coleridge, ed., *The Works of Lord Byron . . . Poetry* (1924), vol. 6, pp. xvii–xix.

24 English translations of *La Nouvelle Héloïse* (1761) and *Emile* (1762) were available within a year of the first appearance of the books. Byron assumes his readers' familiarity with the former in Canto III of *Childe Harold's Pilgrimage*.

25 *The Faerie Queene*, line 9.

26 For the influence of Wieland's *Oberon* on this scene and on the harem sequence in *The Corsair*, see Werner W. Beyer, *The Enchanted Forest* (Oxford, 1963), pp. 250–3.

27 See, for instance, Carl Woodring, *Politics in English Romantic Poetry* (Cambridge, Mass., 1970), pp. 203 ff.

28 An exception is made of Nelson in stanza iv, in order to point out that he has already been forgotten by the public.

Chapter 8 Unfamiliar ideas

1 See *Lives of the English Poets*, ed. George Birkbeck Hill (Oxford, 1905), vol. 1, pp. 19ff.

2 It ran through a dozen editions between 1748 and 1782.

3 *The Life and Correspondence of the Late Robert Southey*, ed. C. C. Southey (1849–50), vol. 3, p. 126; 8 December 1807.

4 For a full discussion of the increased interest in mountains, see Marjorie Hope Nicolson, *Mountain Gloom and Mountain Glory: The Development of the Aesthetics of the Infinite* (Ithaca, 1959).

5 William Wordsworth *Descriptive Sketches . . .* (1793), ll. 702ff.

6 See Samuel Taylor Coleridge, *The Complete Poetical Works*, ed. Ernest Hartley Coleridge (Oxford, 1912) vol. 1, p. 377n.

7 Ibid.

8 See Plato, *The Republic*, Book VII, section 514.

9 It was first climbed in 1786, but, rather as Everest does today, it still retained its aura of inaccessibility and danger.

10 Shelley continued to write poems in which the admirable characteristics of natural phenomena were set off against the limitations of human experience, however. And his 'Ode to the West Wind' (1820) and 'To a Skylark' (1820), in which the emphasis is on the phenomena rather than on the experience, have achieved considerable popularity.

11 Percy Bysshe Shelley, *The Complete Poetical Works*, ed. Thomas Hutchinson (1960), p. 430.

12 The most plausible explanation that has been given for his alteration of the name to 'Adonais' is that he wished it to carry implications of a semitic rebirth cult. This view is presented with appropriately contemporary evidence by Earl Wasserman in *Shelley: A Critical Reading* (Baltimore and London, 1971), pp. 464–5.

13 Although William Gifford preserves it in *The Baviad* (1794) and *The Maeviad* (1795).

14 These were better known to English readers then than now. Both were set pieces for students of Greek. The most popular recent translation, Richard Polwhele's, went through four editions between 1792 and 1813; Coleridge and Southey used the names Bion and Moschus as pseudonyms in the 1790s. Fragments of translations by Shelley are to be found in *The Complete Poetical Works*, ed. Thomas Hutchinson (1960), pp. 721–2.

15
> There came poison, sweet Bion, to thy mouth, and poison thou didst eat—O how could it approach such lips as those and not turn to sweetness? And what mortal man so barbarous and wild as to mix it for thee or give it thee at thy call?—and Song went cold and still.

Trans. J. M. Edmonds, *The Greek Bucolic Poets* (1912), p. 453. Cf. stanza xxxvi of *Adonais* particularly.

16 It is possible that the nightingale and eagle of stanza xvii refer to Keats's ode and to his 'On Seeing the Elgin Marbles', but the nightingale at least is to be found in Moschus, and the eagle sounds more like a refugee from Milton's *Areopagitica*.

17 Polwhele's translation, ll. 115–18.

18 *Quarterly Review*, vol. 19 (1818), p. 208.

19 *Ibid.*, vol. 18 (1817), p. 335; review of *Foliage*. Cf. Shelley's contemporaneous tribute in the Dedication to *The Cenci* (1820).

20 For a brief summary of the various interpretations that have been offered, see William Blake, *The Book of Thel . . .*, ed. Nancy Bogen (Providence, 1971).

21 William Wordsworth, *The Poetical Works*, ed. Ernest de Selincourt and Helen Darbishire (Oxford, 1965–8), vol. 3, p. 548n.

22 The rapport of animals and hermits was a familiar convention. The frontispiece of some editions of Beattie's *The Minstrel*, for instance, shows a stag laying its head in the hermit's lap.

23 Elsewhere Shelley described the *Vita Nuova* as follows:

> an inexhaustible fountain of purity of sentiment and language: it is the idealized history of that period, and those intervals of his life which were dedicated to love. His apotheosis of Beatrice in Paradise, and the gradations of his own love and her loveliness, by which as by steps he feigns himself to have ascended to the throne of the Supreme Cause, is the most glorious imagination of modern poetry.

Defence of Poetry, Works, ed. M. Buxton Forman (1880), vol. 7, p. 125. Written in the spring of 1821—just after *Epipsychidion*; not published until 1840.

24 He read the proofs of John Taaffe's *Comment on the Divine Comedy* (1822), and recommended the book to his own publishers.

The Letters of Percy Bysshe Shelley, ed.
Frederick L. Jones (Oxford, 1964), vol. 2,
pp. 293, 303–4.

25 See Kenneth Neill Cameron, Shelley: the
Golden Years (Cambridge, Mass., 1974),
pp. 252–310.

26 Letters, vol. 2, p. 363.

27 The problem of distinguishing between the
meaning of Shelley's poems and the events
of his life is generally a difficult one to
solve; in the case of Epipsychidion it is
crucial to the interpretation of the poem.
Readers who prefer a more biographical
bias will find it ably and elaborately set out
in Cameron, Shelley: the Golden Years,
pp. 275–88. Harold Bloom manages to

avoid both biography and platonism, in
Shelley's Mythmaking (New Haven, 1959),
pp. 205–19.

28 In the body of the poem itself her name is
given in its English form.

29 Literally, 'soul upon the soul'.

30 One thinks of Southey's and Coleridge's
pantisocracy scheme, and of poems such as
Thomas Campbell's Gertrude of Wyoming
(1809), Mary Russell Mitford's Christina
(1811), John Wilson's The Isle of Palms
(1812), and Southey's A Tale of Paraguay
(1825).

31 Pope's similar compliment in his Essay on
Man, Epistle 1, line 200, is better known.

32 Letters, vol. 2, p. 434.

Chapter 9   Allegorical alternatives

1 Other competent examples would be
Alexander Thomson's The Paradise of Taste
(1796), Alicia Lefanu's Rosara's Chain; or,
the Choice of Life (1812), and Edwin Atherstone's A Midsummer Day's Dream (1824).

2 For which see Arthur Johnston, Enchanted
Ground: The Study of Medieval Romance in the
Eighteenth Century (1964), particularly
pp. 100–7.

3 The Prose Works of William Wordsworth, ed.
W. J. B. Owen and Jane Worthington
Smyser (Oxford, 1974), vol. 3, p. 34.

4 Ibid., vol. 3, p. 35.

5 They do not seem to have been related to
one another.

6 For general accounts of the use made of
Milton, see Raymond Dexter Havens, The
Influence of Milton on English Poetry
(Cambridge, Mass., 1922), and Leslie
Brisman, Milton's Poetry of Choice and Its
Romantic Heirs (Ithaca, 1973). Joseph
Anthony Wittreich Jr collects opinions
expressed during the Romantic period in
The Romantics on Milton (Cleveland, 1970).

7 It was published in Latin in 1753.

8 Robert Lowth, The Sacred Poesy of the
Hebrews (London, 1787), vol. 1, p. 234.

9 Thomas Hardy, John Horne Tooke and
John Thelwall were all tried and acquitted
in 1794.

10 These poems, like the rest of Blake's 'prophecies', were disposed of privately in a few
copies.

11 The following books provide a helpful
introduction to Blake: W. H. Stevenson
and David V. Erdman, eds, The Poems
of William Blake (1971); David V.
Erdman, ed., The Illuminated Blake
(New York, 1974); S. Foster Damon,

A Blake Dictionary (Providence, 1965);
Northrop Frye, Fearful Symmetry (Princeton,
1947), and David V. Erdman, Blake,
Prophet Against Empire (Princeton, 1954);
Kathleen Raine, Blake and Tradition
(Princeton, 1968), 2 vols; and Désirée
Hirst, Hidden Riches: Traditional Symbolism
from the Renaissance to Blake (1964).

12 Letter to Butts, 6 July 1803; see Geoffrey
Keynes, ed., The Letters of William Blake
(Cambridge, Mass., 1970), p. 69.

13 The title-page is dated 1804; Blake is
believed to have been occupied with the
poem from 1804 to 1807; there is evidence
of work on it as early as 1801–2 and as
late as 1818–20.

14 The name given in the eighteenth century
to people who thought that belief in God
was deducible from the evidence of ordered
Nature and regarded the revelation of the
Bible as being inessential to religious belief.

15 See A. L. Owen, The Famous Druids
(Oxford, 1962), pp. 227ff.

16 See, for instance, Leonard Barkan, Nature's
Work of Art: The Human Body as Image of the
World (New Haven, 1975). See also Anne
Kostelanetz Mellor, Blake's Human Form
Divine (Berkeley and Los Angeles, 1974).

17 Cf. Haydon's protests against the prevailing
indifference to observing human anatomy
for oneself rather than simply reproducing
the stylized forms of the past. See The Diary
of Benjamin Robert Haydon, ed. Willard
Bissell Pope (Cambridge, Mass., 1960–3),
vol. 1, pp. 28ff.

18 Blake seems to use the mountains as a
metaphor for places of thought.

19 For a reliable presentation of all that is
known about Blake's life see G. E. Bentley

Jr, *Blake Records* (Oxford, 1969). For the relationship of the poem to the prophecy of Ezekiel, see Harold Bloom, *The Ringers in the Tower* (1971), pp. 65–79.

20 The illustrations add to our sense of them, but they are stylized so as to convey mental or spiritual attitudes rather than individuality.

21 Thought in Shelley's time to be the highest point on earth.

22 Shelley refers to the difference in his preface. In Aeschylus's lost version, Prometheus is believed to have been reconciled with Jupiter after disclosing the secret and averting Jupiter's fall. For Shelley's use of Cicero's anecdote of Prometheus and the Stoics, see Earl Wasserman, *Shelley: A Critical Reading* (Baltimore and London, 1971), pp. 282–3 and note.

23 Earth explains that each living entity has a phantasm or double in the world of death.

24 The terms of the curse owe something to the vehemence of the curse laid upon Ladurlad in Southey's *The Curse of Kehama* (1810).

25 One of these, the man who, at the expense of his own life, saves an enemy from drowning, suggests that Shelley had in his recollection the sequence of things pleasing to heaven in Thomas Moore's popular tale 'Paradise and the Peri' from *Lalla Rookh* (1817).

26 There is no evidence to suggest that Shelley was familiar with Blake's prophecies. Harold Bloom's concentration on the 'mythopoeic' strain in Romantic poetry has made him especially sensitive to such parallels; see *Blake's Apocalypse* (1963) and *Shelley's Mythmaking* (1959). The similarities should not be taken to imply influence, but they suggest similarity of purpose and common sources of inspiration.

27 *Paradise Regained* moves eventually from the fallen world to Heaven itself, but treats even Heaven in a short compass.

28 Readers who are sceptical of this capacity in Shelley are invited to look again at his 'The Sensitive Plant'.

29 Asia is also identified with Venus, or love. For a discussion of the traditional associations upon which Shelley drew, see Wasserman, *Shelley: A Critical Reading*, pp. 275–8. Just as Albion is deprived of Jerusalem during his long slumber while he is under the domination of Urizen, and Los of Enitharmon, Prometheus is deprived of Asia during his imprisonment by Jupiter. The parallel is not wholly consistent, but the use of a female personification to which the protagonist must be reunited is similar.

30 Mary Shelley makes the statement in her note to *Prometheus Unbound*; see Percy Bysshe Shelley, *The Complete Poetical Works*, ed. Thomas Hutchinson (1960), p. 271.

31 The title-page is dated 1804; Blake is believed to have worked on the poem from 1800 on; the paper of the earliest copies is watermarked 1808.

32 See note 6, above.

33 *The Marriage of Heaven and Hell*, pl. 6, 52.

34 This mistake comes about through the feminine wiles of Leutha or Sin who is not satisfied to be Satan's partner and longs to be Los's.

35 More specifically into the part of his foot called the tarsus. Blake is punning on the name that was St Paul's, Saul of Tarsus, at the time when the spirit of God entered into him.

36 The appositeness of this scheme lies in the historical Milton's having had difficulties with his three wives and three daughters and in his having written his divorce tracts. These facts are of interest to the reader of *Milton* mainly because they explain the repeated references to Ololon as being 'sixfold'.

37 It is at this point that Cythna tells Laon of her own experiences after her abduction.

38 John Taylor Coleridge, *Quarterly Review*, 1819. Reprinted in *Shelley: the Critical Heritage*, ed. James E. Barcus (London and Boston, 1975), p. 129.

39 See, for instance, the disguise of the good in *The Marriage of Heaven and Hell*: 'Now the sneaking serpent walks/In mild humility,/And the just man rages in the wilds/Where lions roam' (pl. 2, 17–20).

40 For the standard knowledge of Othman, see Abraham Rees, *The Cyclopaedia; or, Universal Dictionary of Arts, Sciences, and Literature* (1819–20), vol. 25, entry 'Othman'. The name was also used for Turks in general; cf 'Ottoman'.

41 Shelley's most recent editor, Neville Rogers, restores the original title and gives good reasons for doing so. See *The Complete Poetical Works of Percy Bysshe Shelley* (1972–), vol. 2, pp. 360–1. Quotations given below from the original version are taken from Rogers's edition.

42 For Shelley's views on the iniquity of eating meat, see his notes to *Queen Mab* (1813) and his unpublished prose tract, 'On the Vegetable System of Diet' in *The Complete Works* (New York, 1926–30), ed. Roger Ingpen and Walter E. Peck, vol. 6, pp. 335–44. It is possible that a criticism of the Christian communion as a form of cannibalism is intended.

318

43 Shelley would have found a precedent for the funeral pyre of noble and willing lovers in Wieland's *Oberon*, Canto XII, xxv ff.

44 *Queen Mab* was reprinted in a pirated edition in 1821 and went through fourteen more editions by 1840.

45 Byron's 'Heaven and Earth' in *The Liberal* (1822) is also subtitled 'A Mystery' with, presumably, similar intent.

46 Henry Crabb Robinson, one of Byron's first readers, was surprised that so little was made of this doctrine of necessity in *Cain*. See *On Books and Their Writers*, ed. E. J. Morley (1938), vol. 1, p. 352.

47 W. C. Oulton's blank-verse version—a futile attempt to make it a worthier successor to Milton—appeared in 1811; Coleridge's prose fragment 'The Wanderings of Cain' was not published until 1828.

48 Adah and Zillah are the sister-wives of Cain and Abel. Byron explained in his preface that he chose the earliest female names—apart from Eve—in Genesis.

49 Byron adopts Cuvier's theories about antediluvian life.

50 The interpretations are usefully collected in Truman Guy Steffan, *Lord Byron's Cain* (Austin, 1968), pp. 289 ff.

51 On hearing that one of the readers of *Cain* had shot himself, Byron is reported to have said, 'Had I known such an event was likely to happen, I should never have written the book.' See Ernest J. Lovell Jr, ed., *His Very Self and Voice: Collected Conversations of Lord Byron* (New York, 1954), p. 442.

52 Quoted in Steffan, p. 13. The plaintiff was, of course, Byron's publisher, Murray.

53 The Hebrew word for 'Judges' used to denote the just aspect of God in the Old Testament rather than the merciful.

Chapter 10   Afterword

1 Written in 1819.

2 For an account of satire in the period, see John Wardroper, *Kings, Lords and Wicked Libellers: Satire and Protest 1760–1837* (1973).

3 Or, to be more precise, with the popularizations of Milton in political cartoons of the time. M. Dorothy George, *English Political Caricature . . .* (Oxford, 1959), 2 vols, cites an example as early as 1784 (vol. 1, p. 166) and provides a plate of James Gillray's famous 'Gloria Mundi, or—The Devil addressing the Sun' (pl. 63) of the same year. For continuation of the practice, see her plates 16, 65, and 76b (vol. 2). By comparison with contemporary cartoons, however, Byron is the soul of delicacy.

4 For his subsequent regret over *English Bards and Scotch Reviewers*, however, see Leslie A. Marchand, *Byron: A Biography* (New York, 1957), vol. 1, p. 324.

Index

The dates of persons who lived during or before the Romantic period are given in parentheses after their names. Periodicals, annuals and works of unknown authorship are entered by title. Page numbers from 267 on refer to the Chronological Table or the Notes.